SIMPSONS™

COMICS

COLOSSAL COMPENDIUM

VOLUME ONE

TITAN BOOKS

SIMPSONS COMICS COLOSSAL COMPENDIUM
VOLUME ONE

Materials previously published in
*Radioactive Man #8, Simpsons Comics #150, 156, 161, 182, 184,
Simpsons Super Spectacular #1, 2, The Simpsons Summer Shindig #1, 3*

Published in the UK by Titan Books, a division of Titan Publishing Group Ltd.,
144 Southwark St., London SE1 0UP, under licence from Bongo Entertainment, Inc.

FIRST EDITION: JULY 2013

ISBN 9781781169193

2 4 6 8 10 9 7 5 3

Publisher: Matt Groening
Creative Director: Nathan Kane
Managing Editor: Terry Delegeane
Director of Operations: Robert Zaugh
Art Director: Chia-Hsien Jason Ho
Art Director Special Projects: Serban Cristescu
Assistant Art Director: Mike Rote
Production Manager: Christopher Ungar
Assistant Editor: Karen Bates
Production: Nathan Hamill, Art Villanueva
Administration: Ruth Waytz, Pete Benson
Editorial Assistant: Max Davison
Legal Guardian: Susan A. Grode

Printed in Spain

MATT GROENING
presents

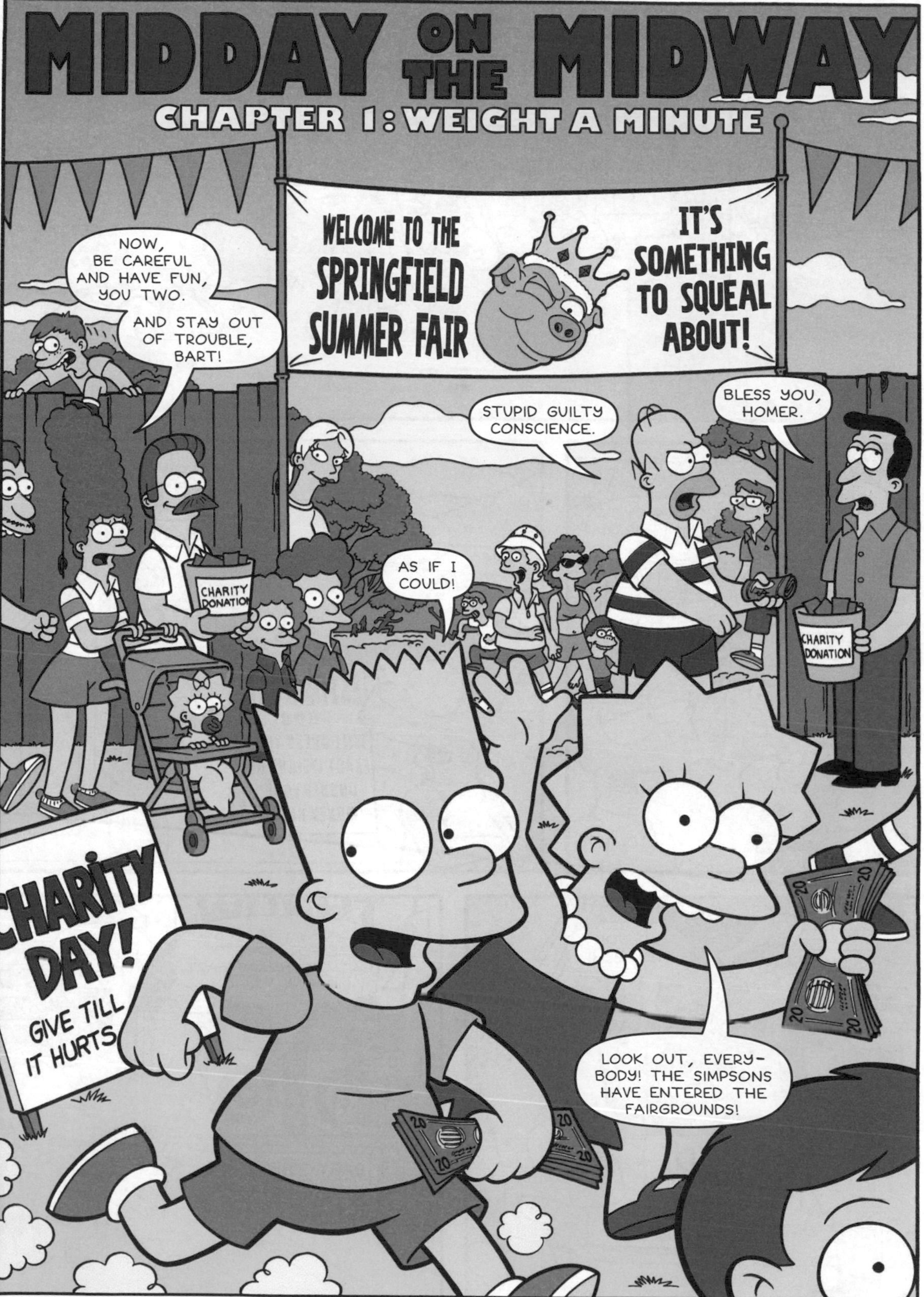

MIDDAY ON THE MIDWAY
CHAPTER 1: WEIGHT A MINUTE
WELCOME TO THE SPRINGFIELD SUMMER FAIR
IT'S SOMETHING TO SQUEAL ABOUT!
NOW, BE CAREFUL AND HAVE FUN, YOU TWO.
AND STAY OUT OF TROUBLE, BART!
STUPID GUILTY CONSCIENCE.
BLESS YOU, HOMER.
CHARITY DONATION
AS IF I COULD!
CHARITY DONATION
CHARITY DAY! GIVE TILL IT HURTS
LOOK OUT, EVERYBODY! THE SIMPSONS HAVE ENTERED THE FAIRGROUNDS!

CHRIS YAMBAR	PHIL ORTIZ	MIKE DECARLO	NATHAN HAMILL & ART VILLANUEVA	KAREN BATES	BILL MORRISON
SCRIPT	PENCILS	INKS	COLORS	LETTERS	EDITOR

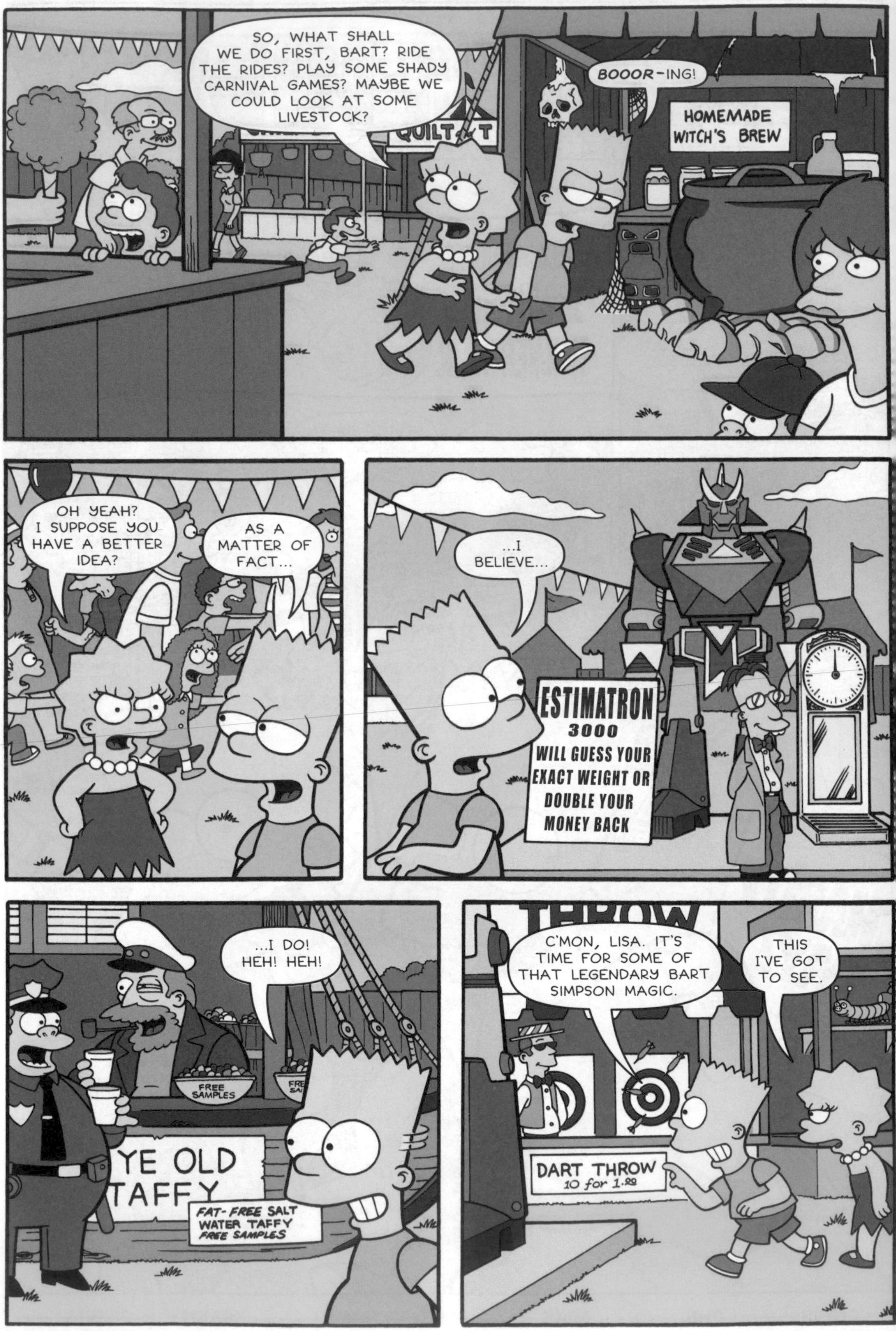
SO, WHAT SHALL WE DO FIRST, BART? RIDE THE RIDES? PLAY SOME SHADY CARNIVAL GAMES? MAYBE WE COULD LOOK AT SOME LIVESTOCK?
BOOOR-ING!
HOMEMADE WITCH'S BREW
OH YEAH? I SUPPOSE YOU HAVE A BETTER IDEA?
AS A MATTER OF FACT...
...I BELIEVE...
ESTIMATRON 3000 WILL GUESS YOUR EXACT WEIGHT OR DOUBLE YOUR MONEY BACK
...I DO! HEH! HEH!
FREE SAMPLES
YE OLD TAFFY
FAT-FREE SALT WATER TAFFY FREE SAMPLES
C'MON, LISA. IT'S TIME FOR SOME OF THAT LEGENDARY BART SIMPSON MAGIC.
THIS I'VE GOT TO SEE.
THROW
DART THROW 10 for 1.00

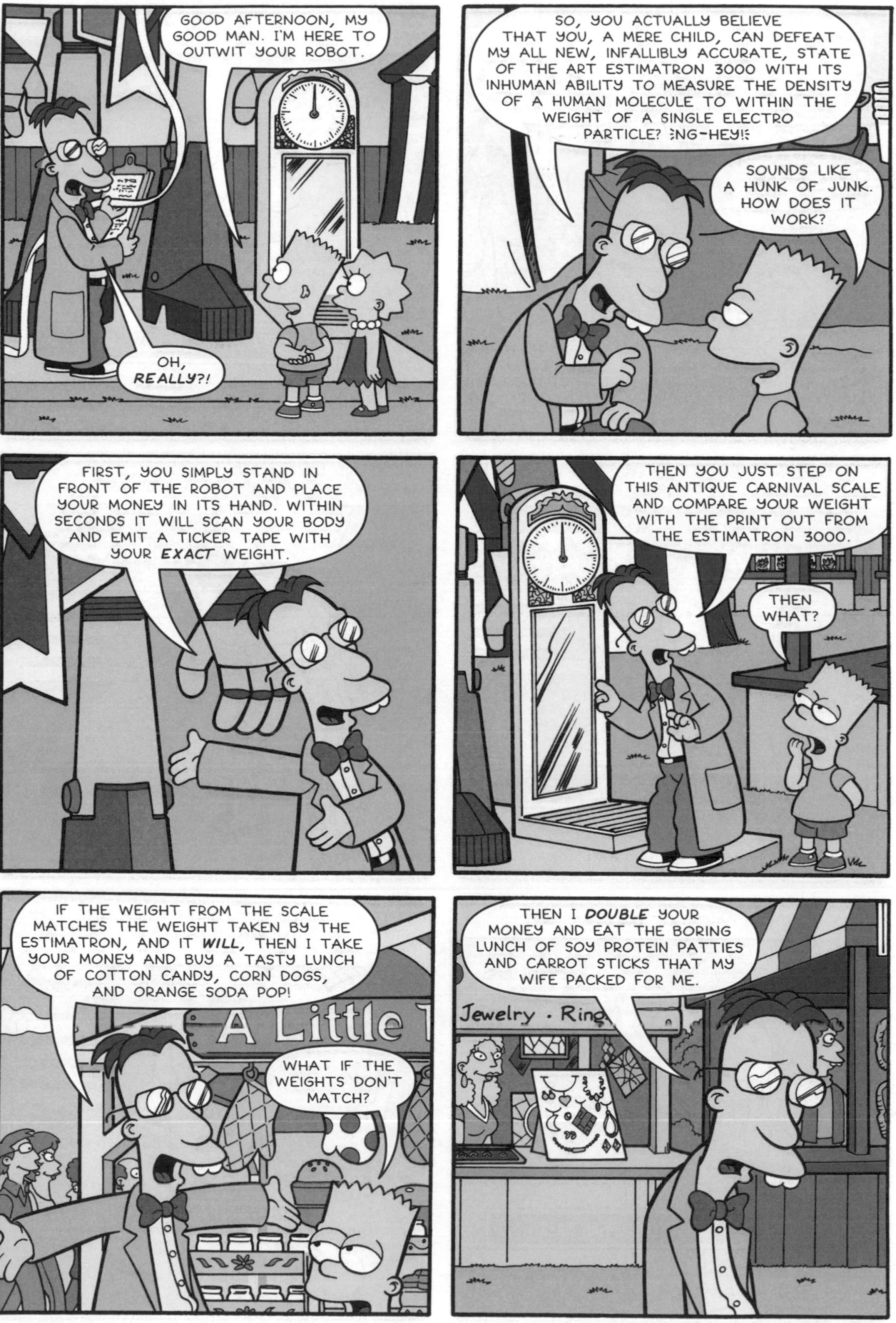
GOOD AFTERNOON, MY GOOD MAN. I'M HERE TO OUTWIT YOUR ROBOT.
OH, REALLY?!
SO, YOU ACTUALLY BELIEVE THAT YOU, A MERE CHILD, CAN DEFEAT MY ALL NEW, INFALLIBLY ACCURATE, STATE OF THE ART ESTIMATRON 3000 WITH ITS INHUMAN ABILITY TO MEASURE THE DENSITY OF A HUMAN MOLECULE TO WITHIN THE WEIGHT OF A SINGLE ELECTRO PARTICLE? NG-HEY!
SOUNDS LIKE A HUNK OF JUNK. HOW DOES IT WORK?
FIRST, YOU SIMPLY STAND IN FRONT OF THE ROBOT AND PLACE YOUR MONEY IN ITS HAND. WITHIN SECONDS IT WILL SCAN YOUR BODY AND EMIT A TICKER TAPE WITH YOUR EXACT WEIGHT.
THEN YOU JUST STEP ON THIS ANTIQUE CARNIVAL SCALE AND COMPARE YOUR WEIGHT WITH THE PRINT OUT FROM THE ESTIMATRON 3000.
THEN WHAT?
IF THE WEIGHT FROM THE SCALE MATCHES THE WEIGHT TAKEN BY THE ESTIMATRON, AND IT WILL, THEN I TAKE YOUR MONEY AND BUY A TASTY LUNCH OF COTTON CANDY, CORN DOGS, AND ORANGE SODA POP!
A Little
WHAT IF THE WEIGHTS DON'T MATCH?
THEN I DOUBLE YOUR MONEY AND EAT THE BORING LUNCH OF SOY PROTEIN PATTIES AND CARROT STICKS THAT MY WIFE PACKED FOR ME.
Jewelry · Ring

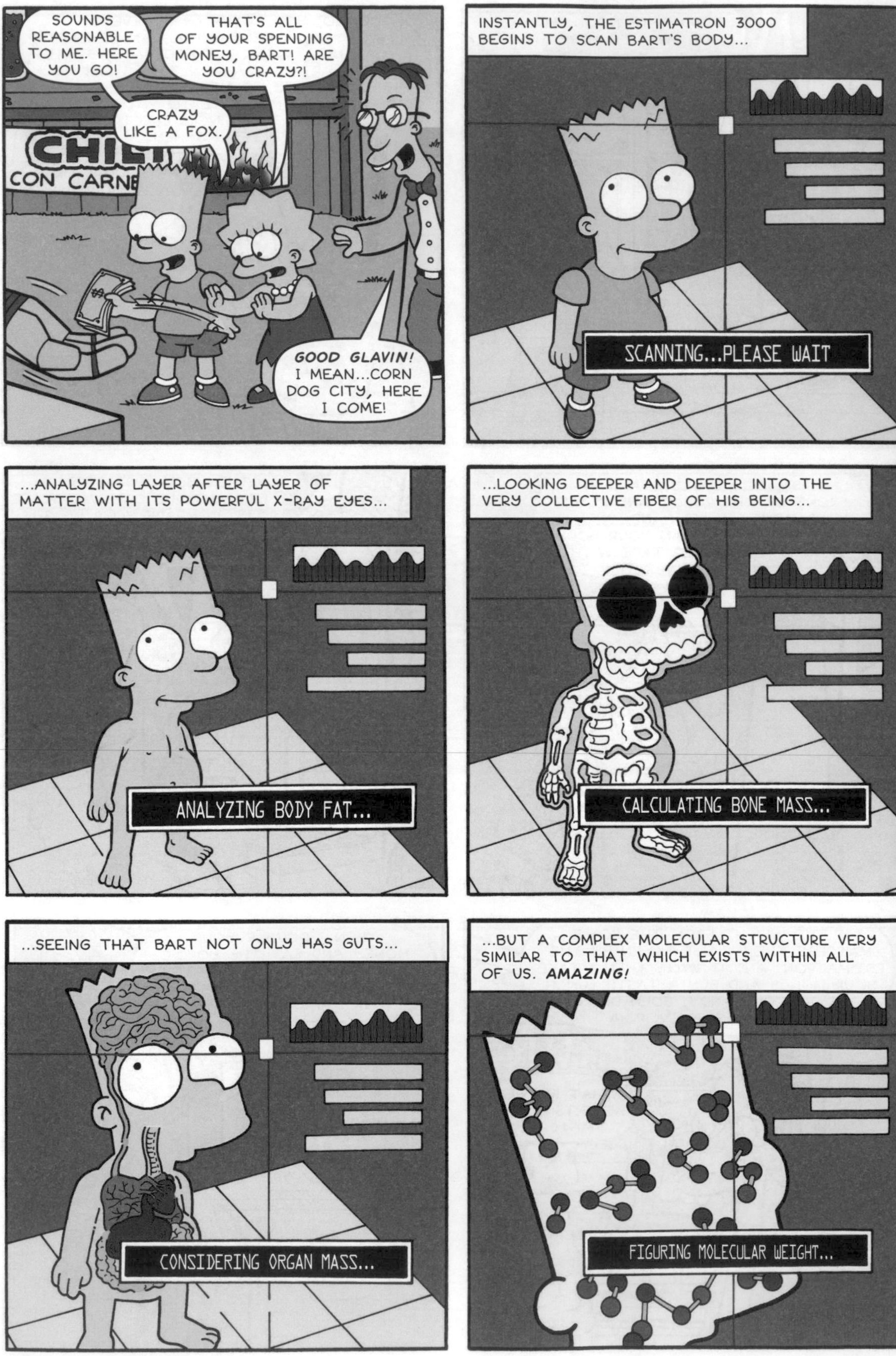

SOUNDS REASONABLE TO ME. HERE YOU GO!
THAT'S ALL OF YOUR SPENDING MONEY, BART! ARE YOU CRAZY?!
CRAZY LIKE A FOX.
CHILI CON CARNE
GOOD GLAVIN! I MEAN...CORN DOG CITY, HERE I COME!
INSTANTLY, THE ESTIMATRON 3000 BEGINS TO SCAN BART'S BODY...
SCANNING...PLEASE WAIT
...ANALYZING LAYER AFTER LAYER OF MATTER WITH ITS POWERFUL X-RAY EYES...
ANALYZING BODY FAT...
...LOOKING DEEPER AND DEEPER INTO THE VERY COLLECTIVE FIBER OF HIS BEING...
CALCULATING BONE MASS...
...SEEING THAT BART NOT ONLY HAS GUTS...
CONSIDERING ORGAN MASS...
...BUT A COMPLEX MOLECULAR STRUCTURE VERY SIMILAR TO THAT WHICH EXISTS WITHIN ALL OF US. AMAZING!
FIGURING MOLECULAR WEIGHT...

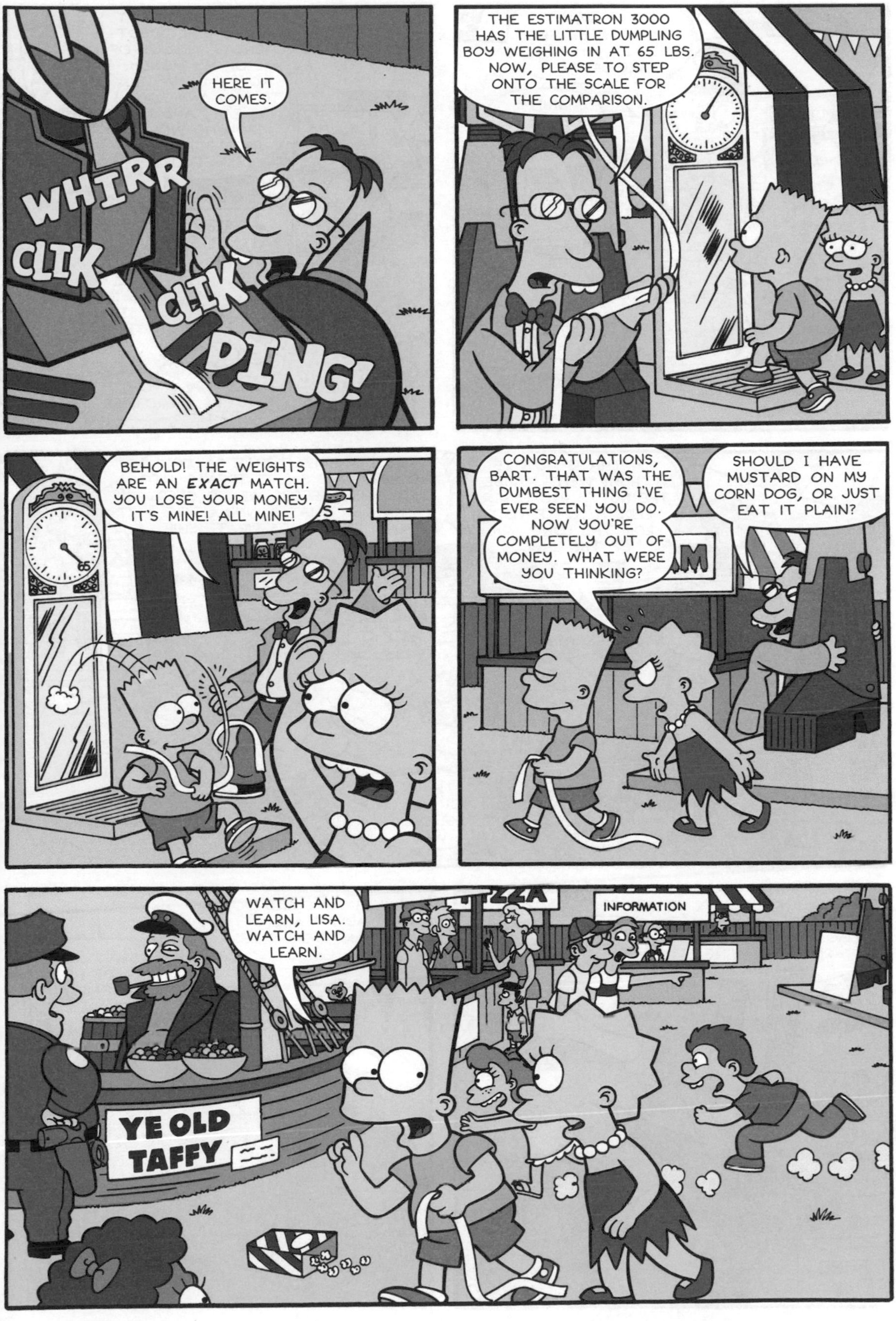
HERE IT COMES.
WHIRR
CLIK
CLIK
DING!
THE ESTIMATRON 3000 HAS THE LITTLE DUMPLING BOY WEIGHING IN AT 65 LBS. NOW, PLEASE TO STEP ONTO THE SCALE FOR THE COMPARISON.
BEHOLD! THE WEIGHTS ARE AN *EXACT* MATCH. YOU LOSE YOUR MONEY. IT'S MINE! ALL MINE!
65
CONGRATULATIONS, BART. THAT WAS THE DUMBEST THING I'VE EVER SEEN YOU DO. NOW YOU'RE COMPLETELY OUT OF MONEY. WHAT WERE YOU THINKING?
SHOULD I HAVE MUSTARD ON MY CORN DOG, OR JUST EAT IT PLAIN?
WATCH AND LEARN, LISA. WATCH AND LEARN.
INFORMATION
YE OLD TAFFY

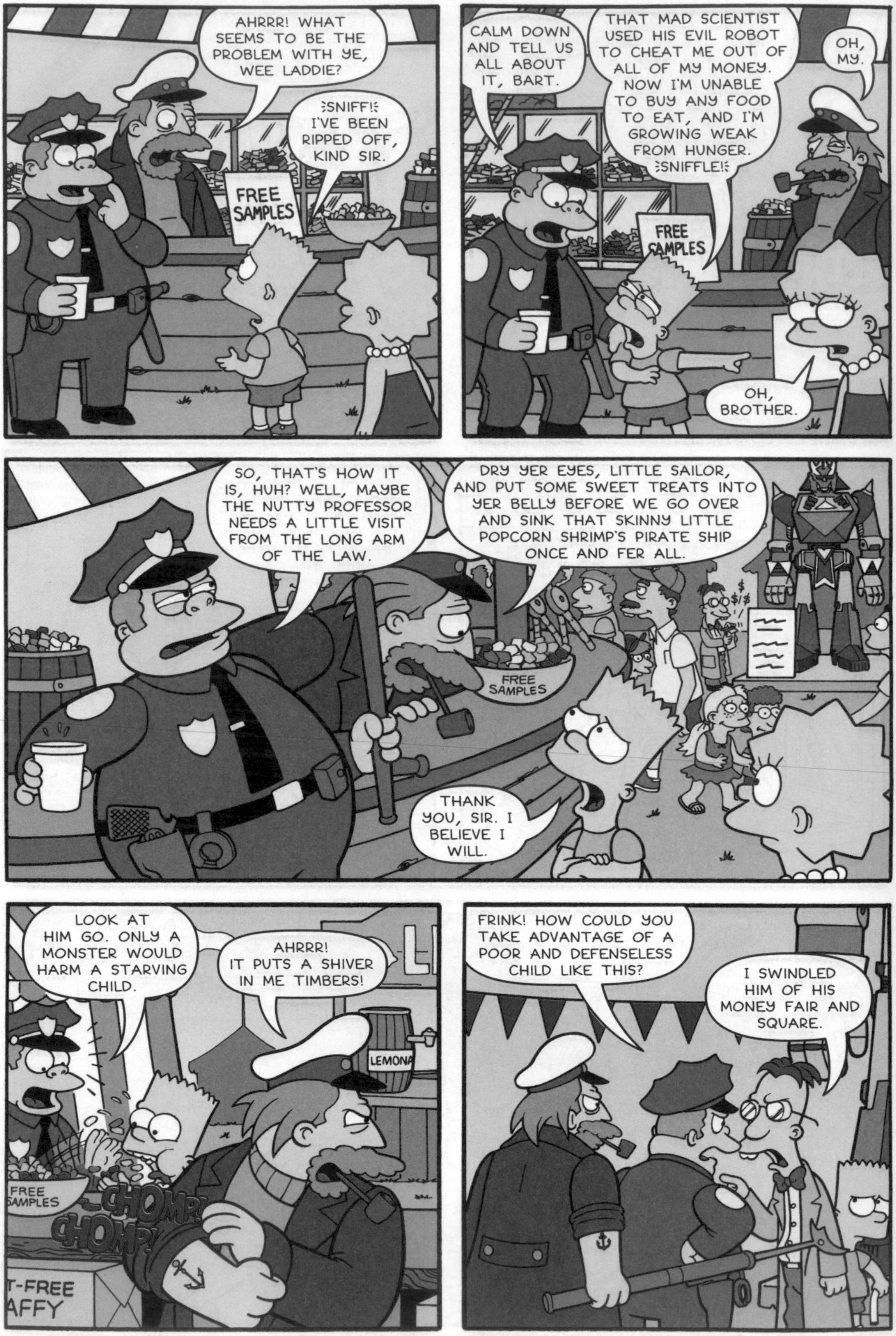
AHRRR! WHAT SEEMS TO BE THE PROBLEM WITH YE, WEE LADDIE?
SNIFF! I'VE BEEN RIPPED OFF, KIND SIR.
FREE SAMPLES
CALM DOWN AND TELL US ALL ABOUT IT, BART.
THAT MAD SCIENTIST USED HIS EVIL ROBOT TO CHEAT ME OUT OF ALL OF MY MONEY. NOW I'M UNABLE TO BUY ANY FOOD TO EAT, AND I'M GROWING WEAK FROM HUNGER. SNIFFLE!
OH, MY.
FREE SAMPLES
OH, BROTHER.
SO, THAT'S HOW IT IS, HUH? WELL, MAYBE THE NUTTY PROFESSOR NEEDS A LITTLE VISIT FROM THE LONG ARM OF THE LAW.
DRY YER EYES, LITTLE SAILOR, AND PUT SOME SWEET TREATS INTO YER BELLY BEFORE WE GO OVER AND SINK THAT SKINNY LITTLE POPCORN SHRIMP'S PIRATE SHIP ONCE AND FER ALL.
FREE SAMPLES
THANK YOU, SIR. I BELIEVE I WILL.
LOOK AT HIM GO. ONLY A MONSTER WOULD HARM A STARVING CHILD.
AHRRR! IT PUTS A SHIVER IN ME TIMBERS!
LEMONA
FREE SAMPLES
CHOMP! CHOMP!
T-FREE AFFY
FRINK! HOW COULD YOU TAKE ADVANTAGE OF A POOR AND DEFENSELESS CHILD LIKE THIS?
I SWINDLED HIM OF HIS MONEY FAIR AND SQUARE.

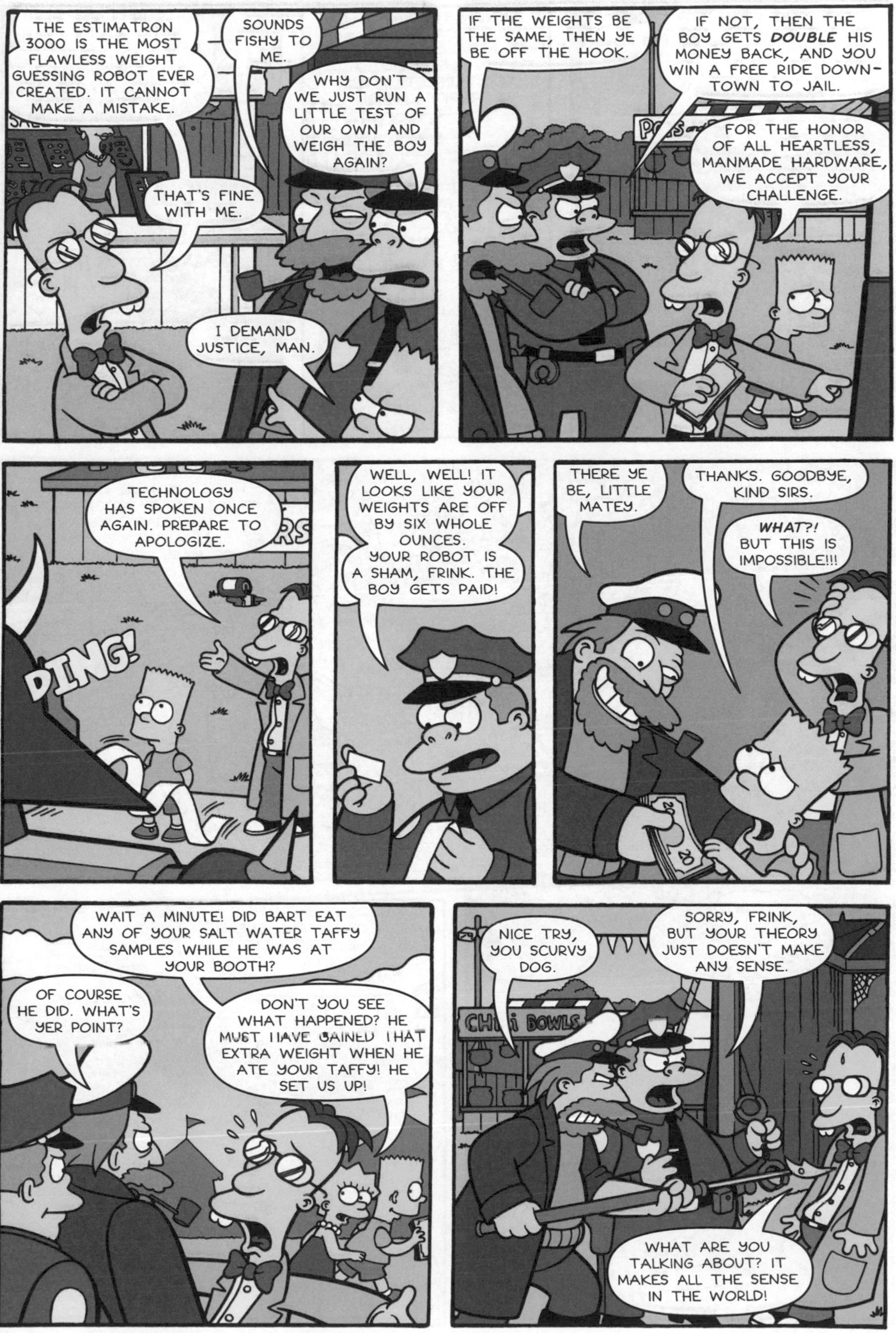
THE ESTIMATRON 3000 IS THE MOST FLAWLESS WEIGHT GUESSING ROBOT EVER CREATED. IT CANNOT MAKE A MISTAKE.
SOUNDS FISHY TO ME.
WHY DON'T WE JUST RUN A LITTLE TEST OF OUR OWN AND WEIGH THE BOY AGAIN?
THAT'S FINE WITH ME.
I DEMAND JUSTICE, MAN.
IF THE WEIGHTS BE THE SAME, THEN YE BE OFF THE HOOK.
IF NOT, THEN THE BOY GETS DOUBLE HIS MONEY BACK, AND YOU WIN A FREE RIDE DOWN-TOWN TO JAIL.
FOR THE HONOR OF ALL HEARTLESS, MANMADE HARDWARE, WE ACCEPT YOUR CHALLENGE.
TECHNOLOGY HAS SPOKEN ONCE AGAIN. PREPARE TO APOLOGIZE.
DING!
WELL, WELL! IT LOOKS LIKE YOUR WEIGHTS ARE OFF BY SIX WHOLE OUNCES. YOUR ROBOT IS A SHAM, FRINK. THE BOY GETS PAID!
THERE YE BE, LITTLE MATEY.
THANKS. GOODBYE, KIND SIRS.
WHAT?! BUT THIS IS IMPOSSIBLE!!!
WAIT A MINUTE! DID BART EAT ANY OF YOUR SALT WATER TAFFY SAMPLES WHILE HE WAS AT YOUR BOOTH?
OF COURSE HE DID. WHAT'S YER POINT?
DON'T YOU SEE WHAT HAPPENED? HE MUST HAVE GAINED THAT EXTRA WEIGHT WHEN HE ATE YOUR TAFFY! HE SET US UP!
NICE TRY, YOU SCURVY DOG.
SORRY, FRINK, BUT YOUR THEORY JUST DOESN'T MAKE ANY SENSE.
WHAT ARE YOU TALKING ABOUT? IT MAKES ALL THE SENSE IN THE WORLD!
CHILI BOWLS

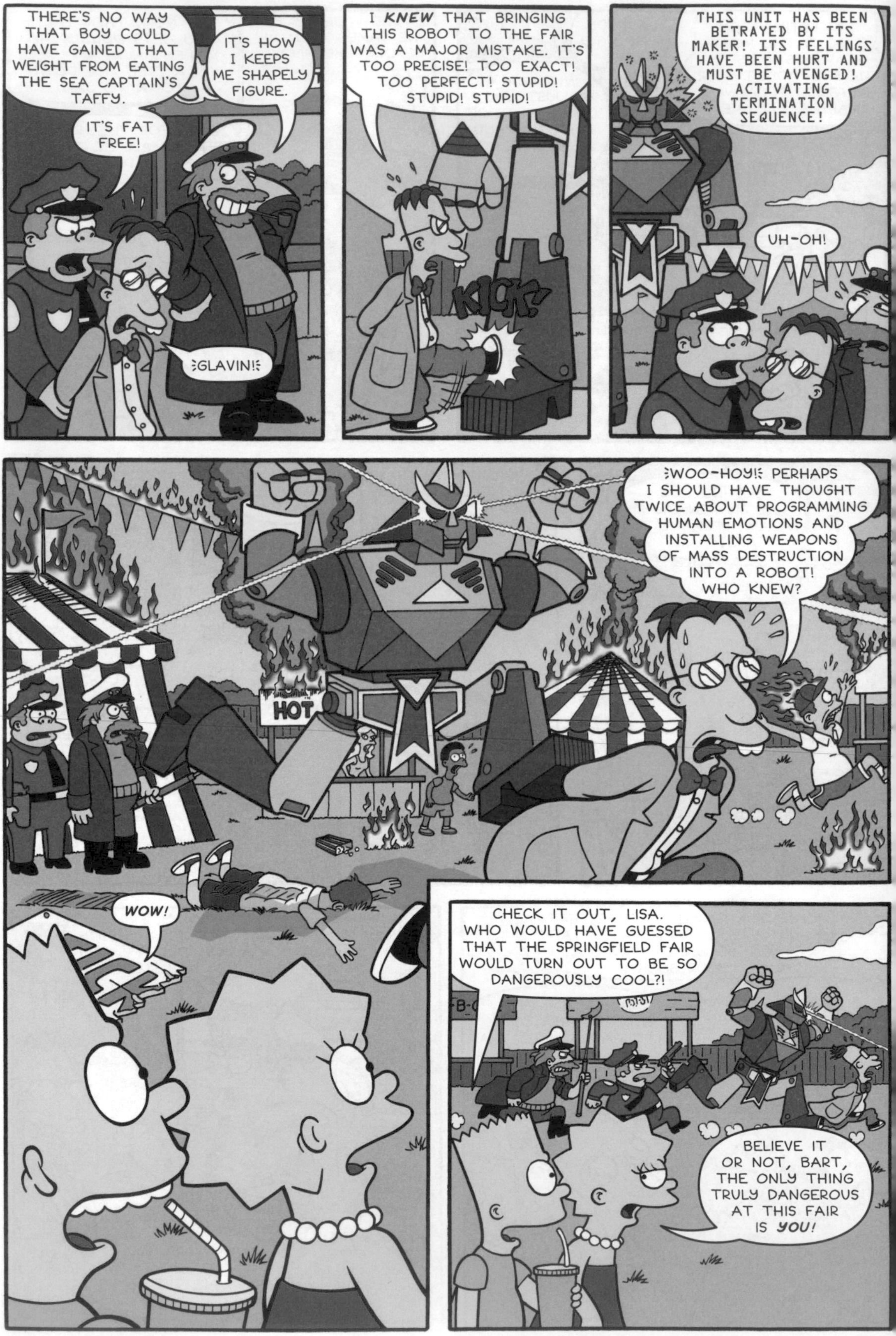
THERE'S NO WAY THAT BOY COULD HAVE GAINED THAT WEIGHT FROM EATING THE SEA CAPTAIN'S TAFFY.
IT'S HOW I KEEPS ME SHAPELY FIGURE.
IT'S FAT FREE!
GLAVIN!
I KNEW THAT BRINGING THIS ROBOT TO THE FAIR WAS A MAJOR MISTAKE. IT'S TOO PRECISE! TOO EXACT! TOO PERFECT! STUPID! STUPID! STUPID!
KICK!
THIS UNIT HAS BEEN BETRAYED BY ITS MAKER! ITS FEELINGS HAVE BEEN HURT AND MUST BE AVENGED! ACTIVATING TERMINATION SEQUENCE!
UH-OH!
WOO-HOY! PERHAPS I SHOULD HAVE THOUGHT TWICE ABOUT PROGRAMMING HUMAN EMOTIONS AND INSTALLING WEAPONS OF MASS DESTRUCTION INTO A ROBOT! WHO KNEW?
HOT
WOW!
CHECK IT OUT, LISA. WHO WOULD HAVE GUESSED THAT THE SPRINGFIELD FAIR WOULD TURN OUT TO BE SO DANGEROUSLY COOL?!
BELIEVE IT OR NOT, BART, THE ONLY THING TRULY DANGEROUS AT THIS FAIR IS YOU!

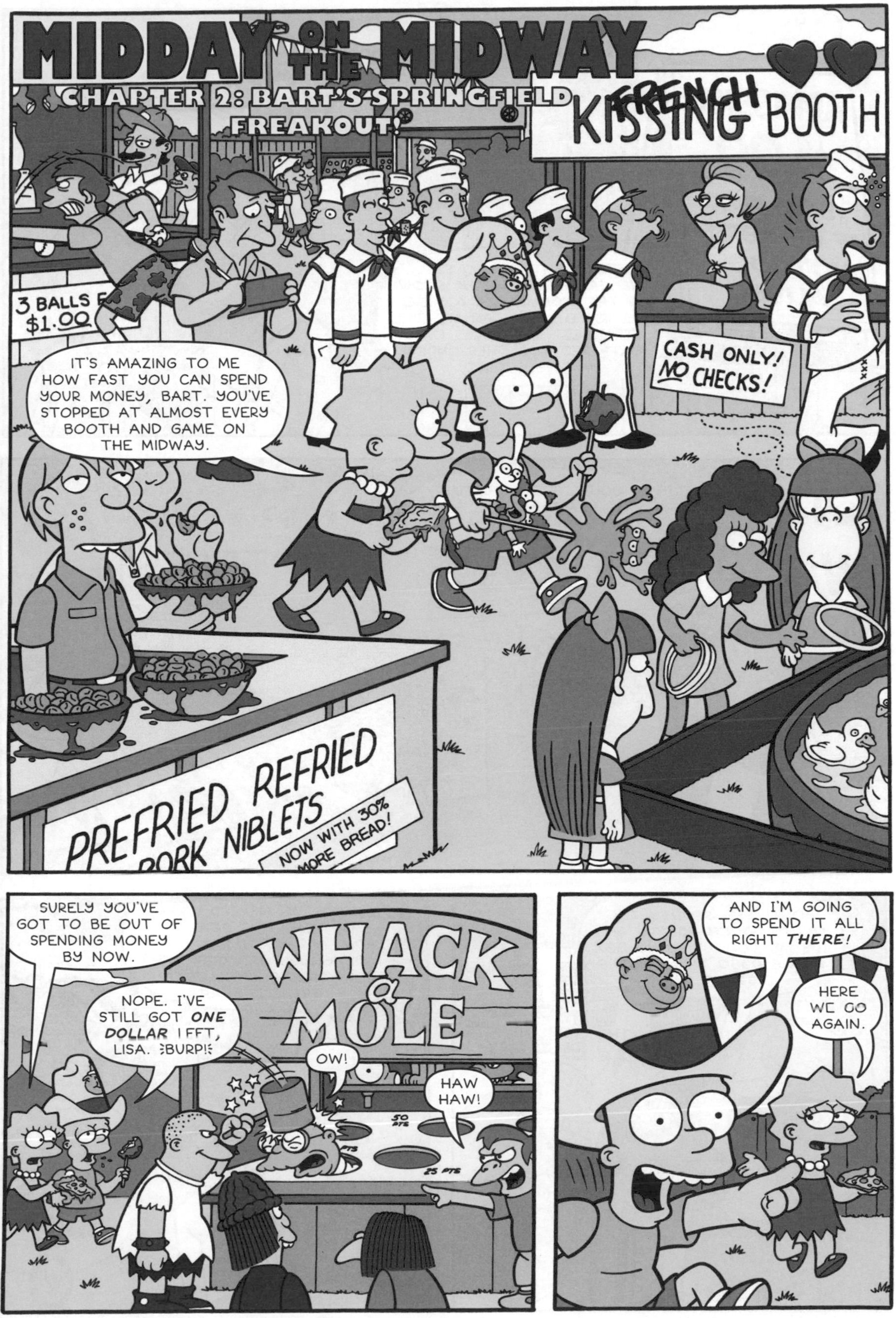
MIDDAY ON THE MIDWAY
CHAPTER 2: BART'S SPRINGFIELD FREAKOUT!
FRENCH KISSING BOOTH
3 BALLS F
$1.00
CASH ONLY! NO CHECKS!
IT'S AMAZING TO ME HOW FAST YOU CAN SPEND YOUR MONEY, BART. YOU'VE STOPPED AT ALMOST EVERY BOOTH AND GAME ON THE MIDWAY.
PREFRIED REFRIED PORK NIBLETS
NOW WITH 30% MORE BREAD!
SURELY YOU'VE GOT TO BE OUT OF SPENDING MONEY BY NOW.
WHACK a MOLE
NOPE. I'VE STILL GOT ONE DOLLAR LEFT, LISA. BURP!
OW!
HAW HAW!
50 PTS
25 PTS
AND I'M GOING TO SPEND IT ALL RIGHT THERE!
HERE WE GO AGAIN.

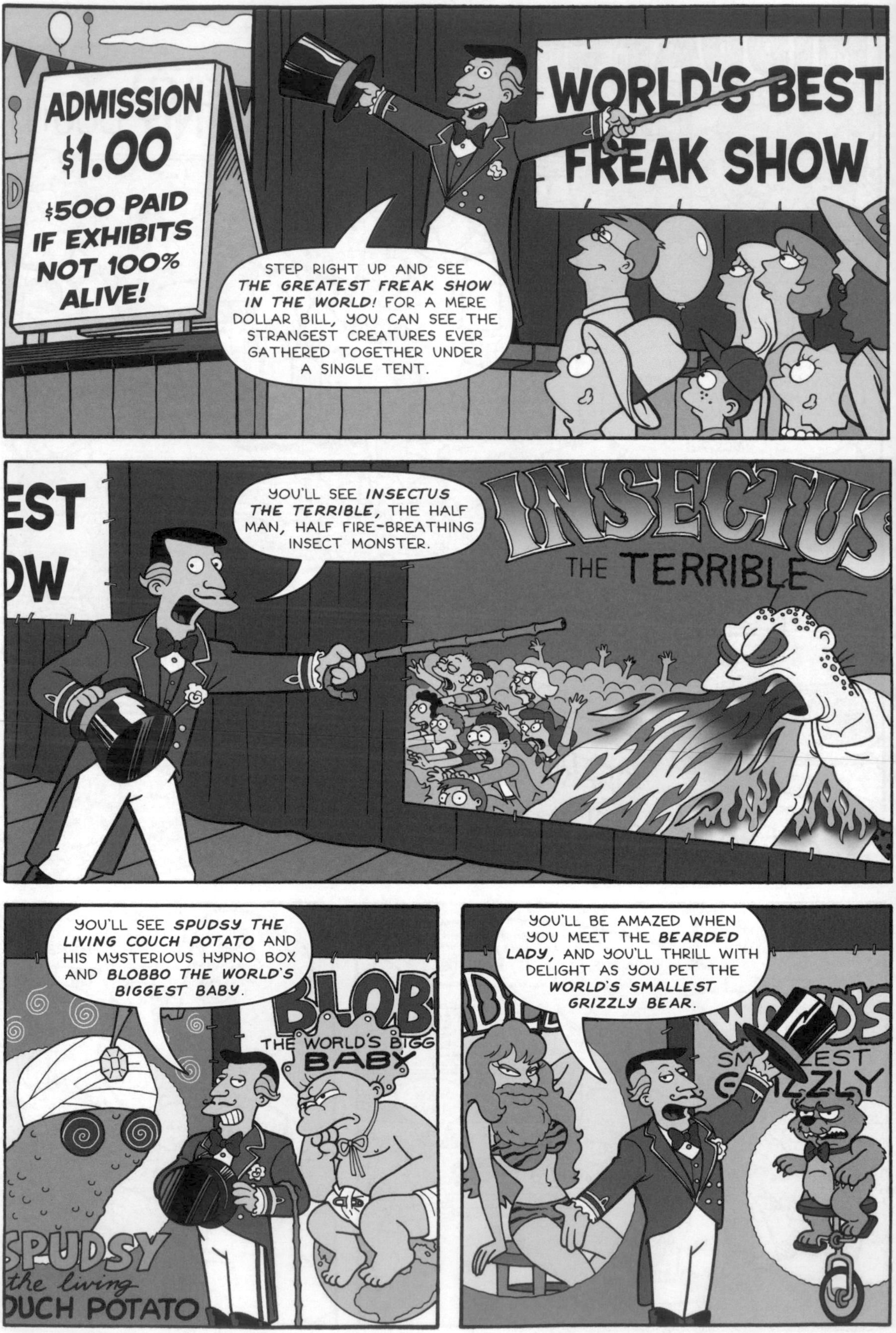
ADMISSION $1.00 $500 PAID IF EXHIBITS NOT 100% ALIVE!
WORLD'S BEST FREAK SHOW
STEP RIGHT UP AND SEE THE GREATEST FREAK SHOW IN THE WORLD! FOR A MERE DOLLAR BILL, YOU CAN SEE THE STRANGEST CREATURES EVER GATHERED TOGETHER UNDER A SINGLE TENT.
YOU'LL SEE INSECTUS THE TERRIBLE, THE HALF MAN, HALF FIRE-BREATHING INSECT MONSTER.
INSECTUS THE TERRIBLE
YOU'LL SEE SPUDSY THE LIVING COUCH POTATO AND HIS MYSTERIOUS HYPNO BOX AND BLOBBO THE WORLD'S BIGGEST BABY.
THE WORLD'S BIGG BABY
SPUDSY the living OUCH POTATO
YOU'LL BE AMAZED WHEN YOU MEET THE BEARDED LADY, AND YOU'LL THRILL WITH DELIGHT AS YOU PET THE WORLD'S SMALLEST GRIZZLY BEAR.
GRIZZLY

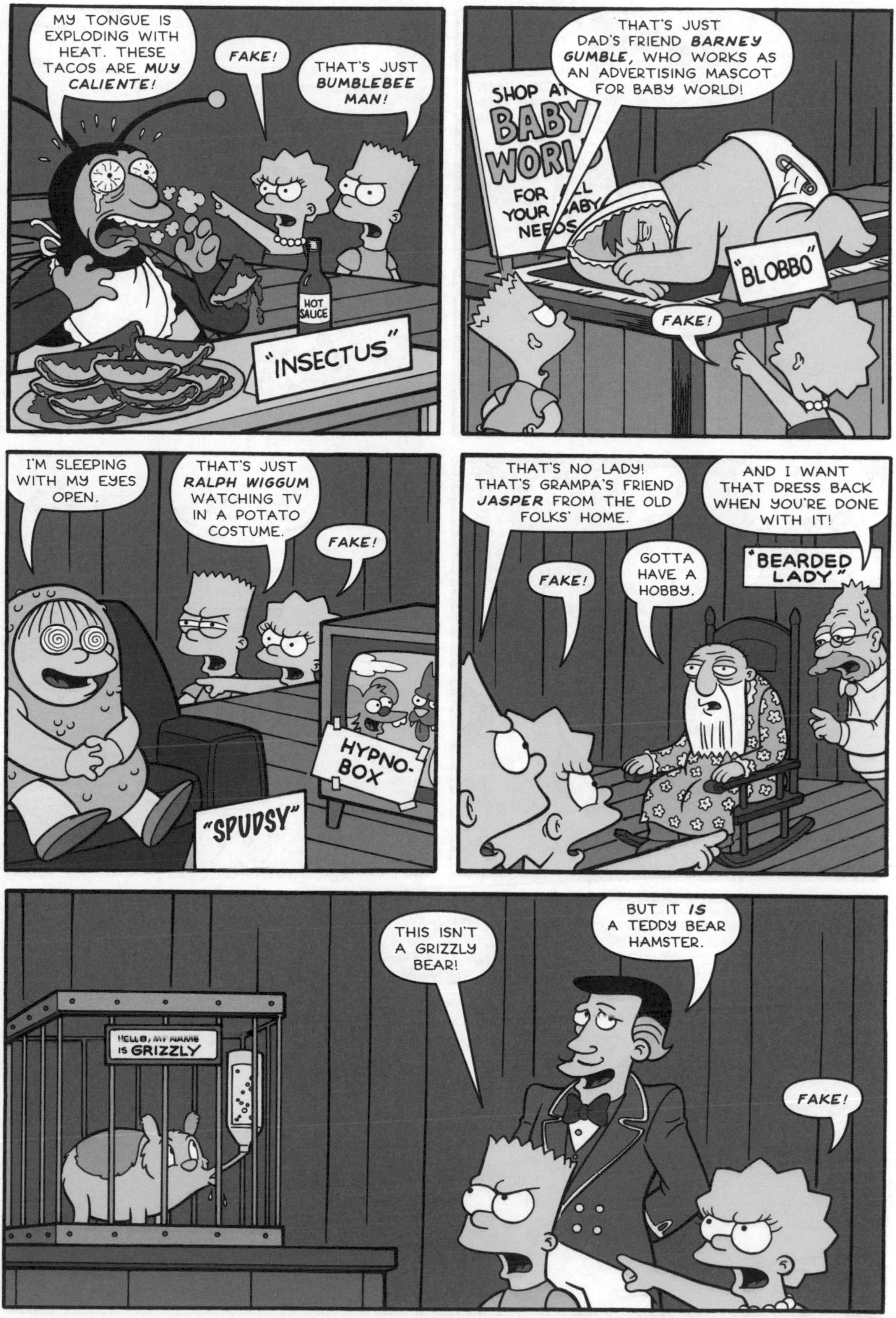
MY TONGUE IS EXPLODING WITH HEAT. THESE TACOS ARE *MUY CALIENTE!*
FAKE!
THAT'S JUST *BUMBLEBEE MAN!*
HOT SAUCE
"INSECTUS"
THAT'S JUST DAD'S FRIEND *BARNEY GUMBLE,* WHO WORKS AS AN ADVERTISING MASCOT FOR BABY WORLD!
SHOP AT BABY WORLD FOR ALL YOUR BABY NEEDS
"BLOBBO"
FAKE!
I'M SLEEPING WITH MY EYES OPEN.
THAT'S JUST *RALPH WIGGUM* WATCHING TV IN A POTATO COSTUME.
FAKE!
HYPNO-BOX
"SPUDSY"
THAT'S NO LADY! THAT'S GRAMPA'S FRIEND *JASPER* FROM THE OLD FOLKS' HOME.
AND I WANT THAT DRESS BACK WHEN YOU'RE DONE WITH IT!
"BEARDED LADY"
FAKE!
GOTTA HAVE A HOBBY.
THIS ISN'T A GRIZZLY BEAR!
BUT IT *IS* A TEDDY BEAR HAMSTER.
HELLO, MY NAME IS GRIZZLY
FAKE!

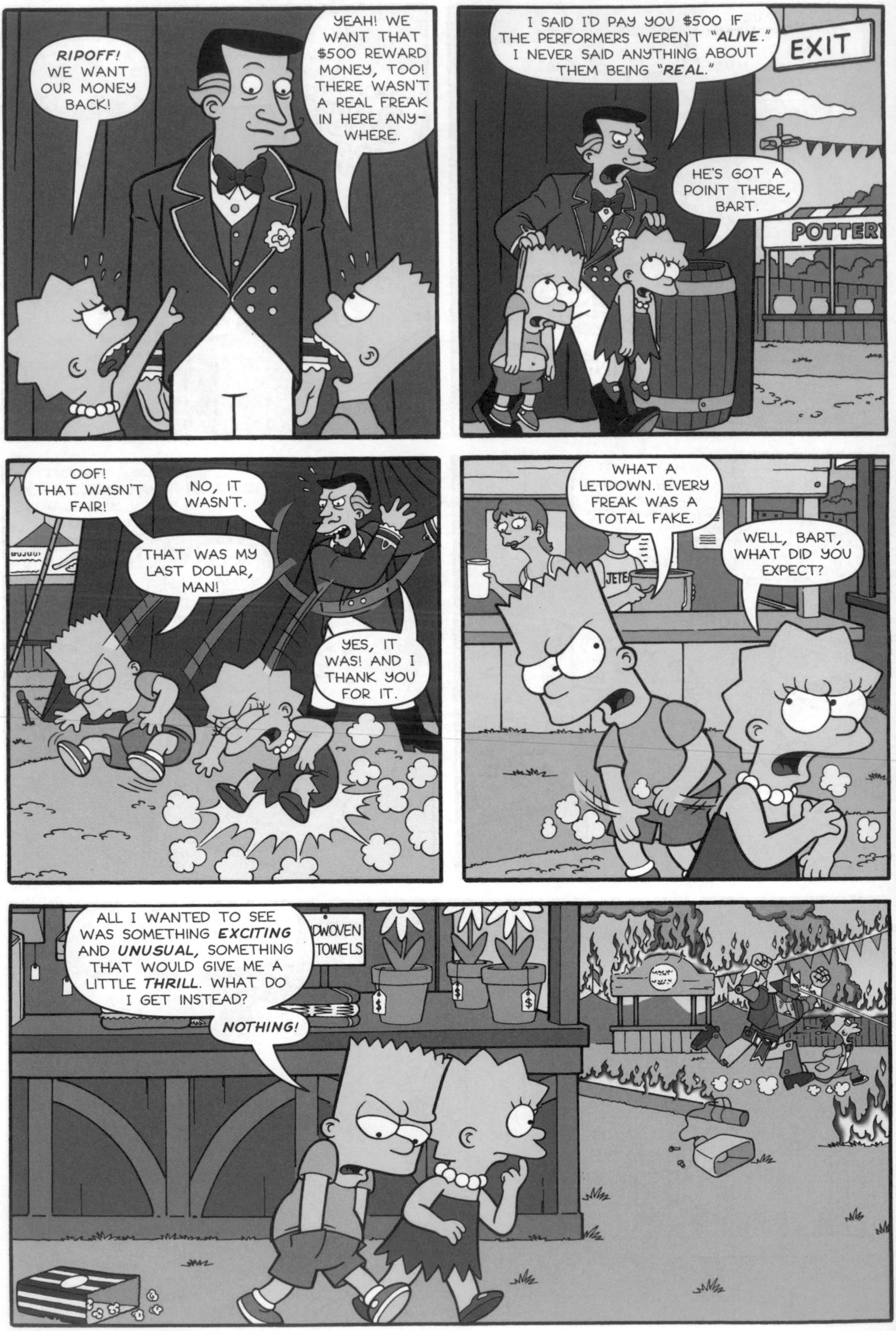

RIPOFF! WE WANT OUR MONEY BACK!
YEAH! WE WANT THAT $500 REWARD MONEY, TOO! THERE WASN'T A REAL FREAK IN HERE ANY-WHERE.
I SAID I'D PAY YOU $500 IF THE PERFORMERS WEREN'T "ALIVE." I NEVER SAID ANYTHING ABOUT THEM BEING "REAL."
EXIT
HE'S GOT A POINT THERE, BART.
POTTERY
OOF! THAT WASN'T FAIR!
NO, IT WASN'T.
THAT WAS MY LAST DOLLAR, MAN!
YES, IT WAS! AND I THANK YOU FOR IT.
WHAT A LETDOWN. EVERY FREAK WAS A TOTAL FAKE.
WELL, BART, WHAT DID YOU EXPECT?
ALL I WANTED TO SEE WAS SOMETHING EXCITING AND UNUSUAL, SOMETHING THAT WOULD GIVE ME A LITTLE THRILL. WHAT DO I GET INSTEAD?
NOTHING!
DWOVEN TOWELS

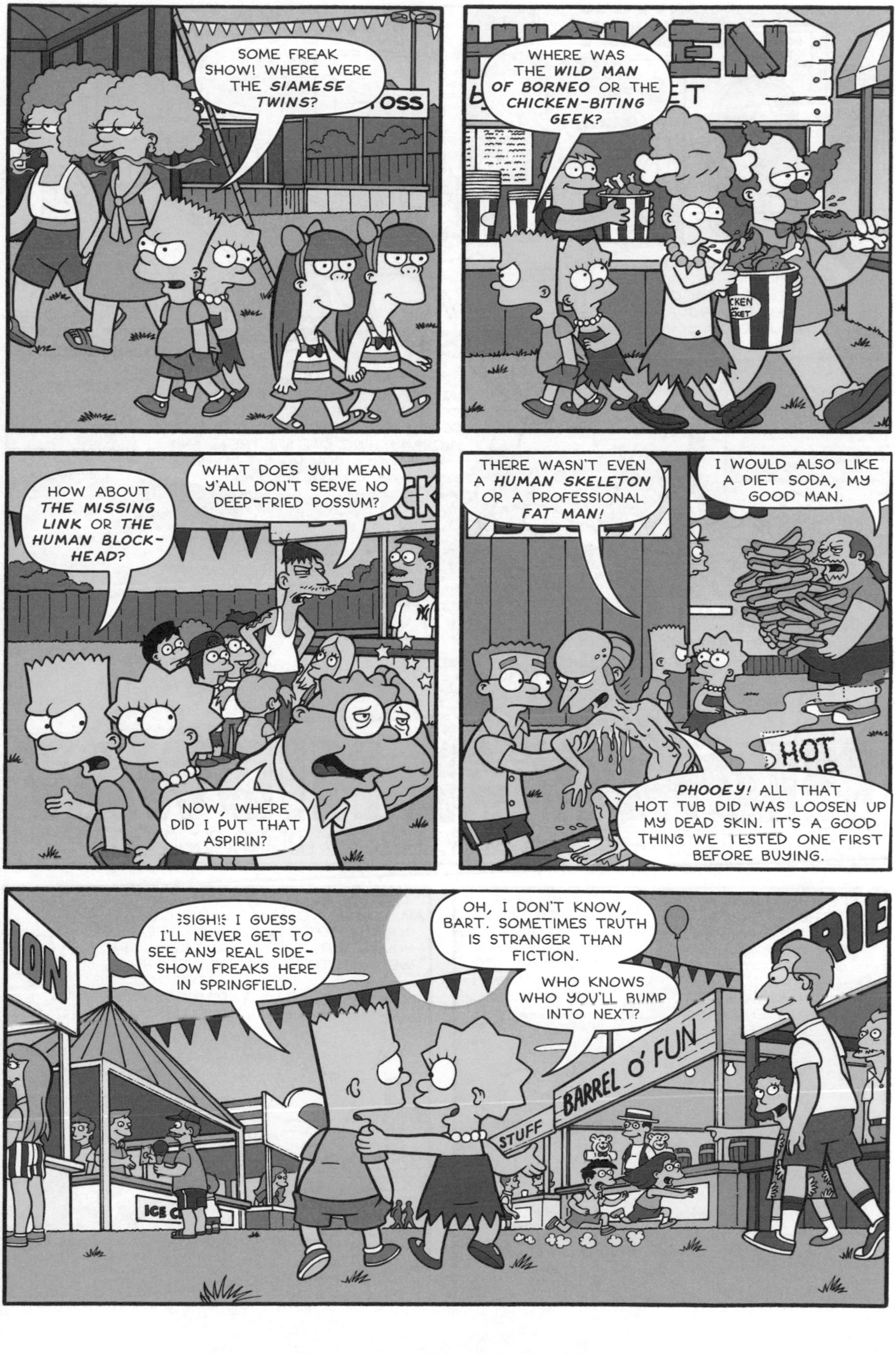
SOME FREAK SHOW! WHERE WERE THE *SIAMESE TWINS*?
TOSS
WHERE WAS THE *WILD MAN OF BORNEO* OR THE *CHICKEN-BITING GEEK*?
HOW ABOUT *THE MISSING LINK* OR *THE HUMAN BLOCK-HEAD*?
WHAT DOES YUH MEAN Y'ALL DON'T SERVE NO DEEP-FRIED POSSUM?
NOW, WHERE DID I PUT THAT ASPIRIN?
THERE WASN'T EVEN A *HUMAN SKELETON* OR A PROFESSIONAL *FAT MAN!*
I WOULD ALSO LIKE A DIET SODA, MY GOOD MAN.
HOT
PHOOEY! ALL THAT HOT TUB DID WAS LOOSEN UP MY DEAD SKIN. IT'S A GOOD THING WE TESTED ONE FIRST BEFORE BUYING.
SIGH! I GUESS I'LL NEVER GET TO SEE ANY REAL SIDE-SHOW FREAKS HERE IN SPRINGFIELD.
OH, I DON'T KNOW, BART. SOMETIMES TRUTH IS STRANGER THAN FICTION.
WHO KNOWS WHO YOU'LL BUMP INTO NEXT?
BARREL O' FUN
STUFF

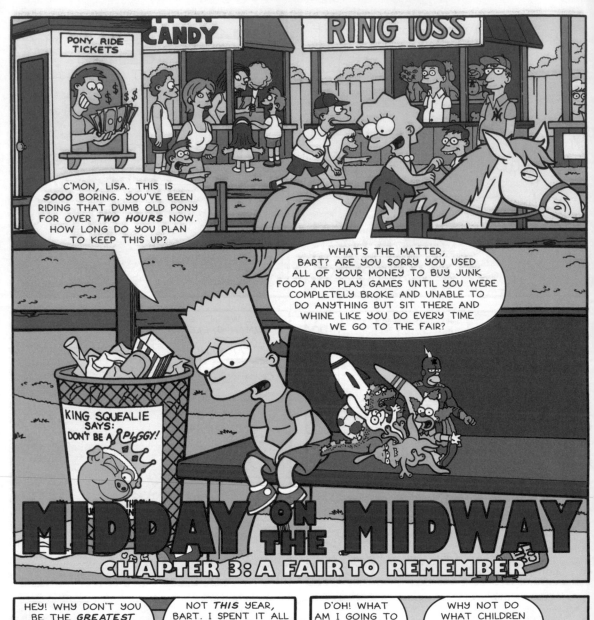

PONY RIDE TICKETS

CANDY

RING TOSS

KING SQUEALIE SAYS: DON'T BE A *PIGGY!*

C'MON, LISA. THIS IS *SOOO* BORING. YOU'VE BEEN RIDING THAT DUMB OLD PONY FOR OVER *TWO HOURS* NOW. HOW LONG DO YOU PLAN TO KEEP THIS UP?

WHAT'S THE MATTER, BART? ARE YOU SORRY YOU USED ALL OF YOUR MONEY TO BUY JUNK FOOD AND PLAY GAMES UNTIL YOU WERE COMPLETELY BROKE AND UNABLE TO DO ANYTHING BUT SIT THERE AND WHINE LIKE YOU DO EVERY TIME WE GO TO THE FAIR?

MIDDAY ON THE MIDWAY
CHAPTER 3: A FAIR TO REMEMBER

HEY! WHY DON'T YOU BE THE *GREATEST SISTER EVER* AND GIVE YOUR BIG BROTHER SOME OF *YOUR* MONEY? YOU ALWAYS HAVE PLENTY LEFT OVER.

NOT *THIS* YEAR, BART. I SPENT IT ALL HERE SO I COULD RIDE CONTINUALLY UNTIL CLOSING TIME. YOU KNOW HOW MUCH I LOVE PONIES!

D'OH! WHAT AM I GOING TO DO? I'VE GOT *HOURS* UNTIL WE HAVE TO GO HOME.

WHY NOT DO WHAT CHILDREN AROUND THE WORLD HAVE DONE SINCE THE BEGINNING OF TIME? GO BEG *DAD* FOR MORE MONEY.

SQUEALIE SAYS: BE A *PIGGY!*

THROW

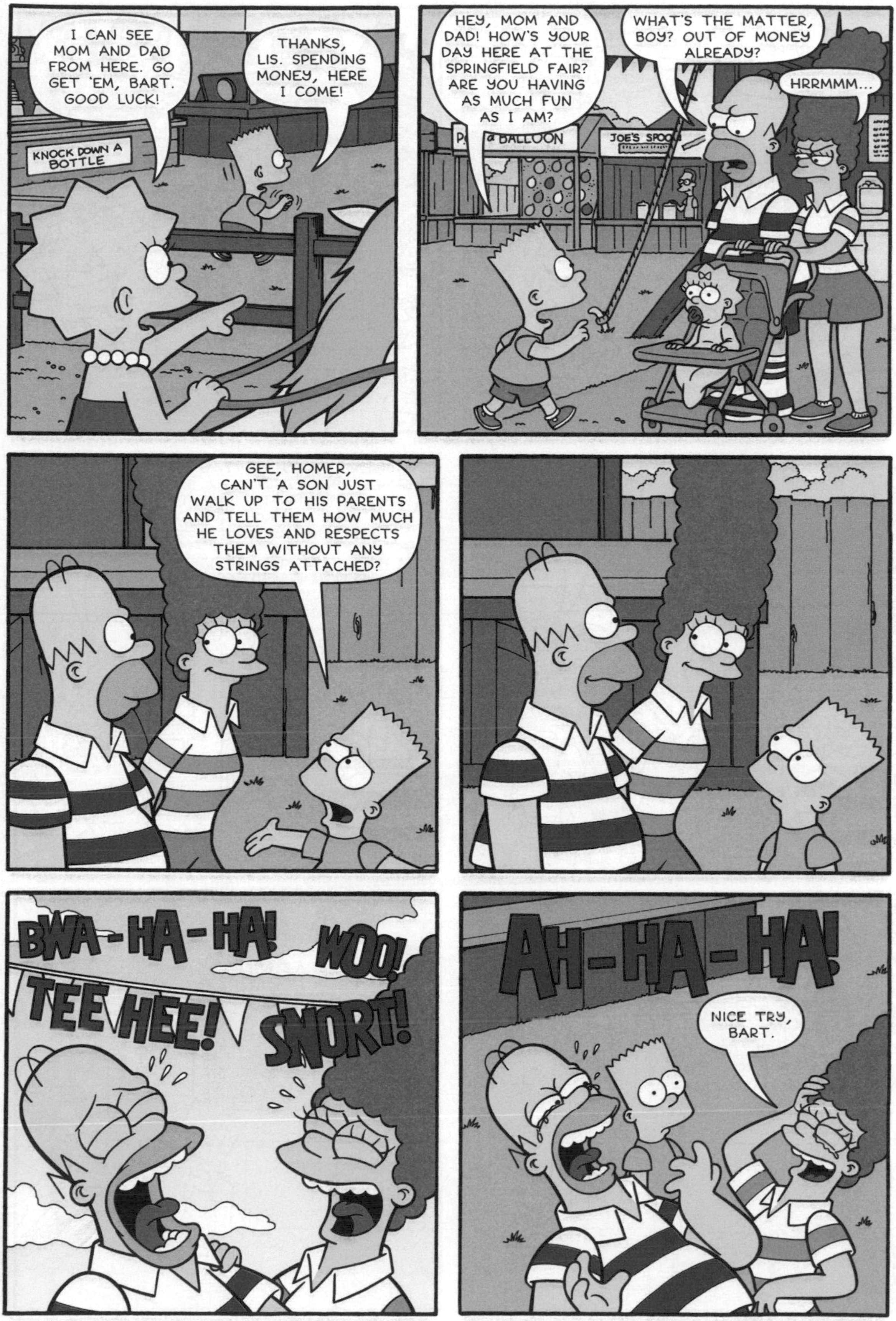
I CAN SEE MOM AND DAD FROM HERE. GO GET 'EM, BART. GOOD LUCK!
THANKS, LIS. SPENDING MONEY, HERE I COME!
KNOCK DOWN A BOTTLE
HEY, MOM AND DAD! HOW'S YOUR DAY HERE AT THE SPRINGFIELD FAIR? ARE YOU HAVING AS MUCH FUN AS I AM?
WHAT'S THE MATTER, BOY? OUT OF MONEY ALREADY?
HRRMMM...
JOE'S SPOO
GEE, HOMER, CAN'T A SON JUST WALK UP TO HIS PARENTS AND TELL THEM HOW MUCH HE LOVES AND RESPECTS THEM WITHOUT ANY STRINGS ATTACHED?
BWA-HA-HA!
WOO!
TEE HEE!
SNORT!
AH-HA-HA!
NICE TRY, BART.

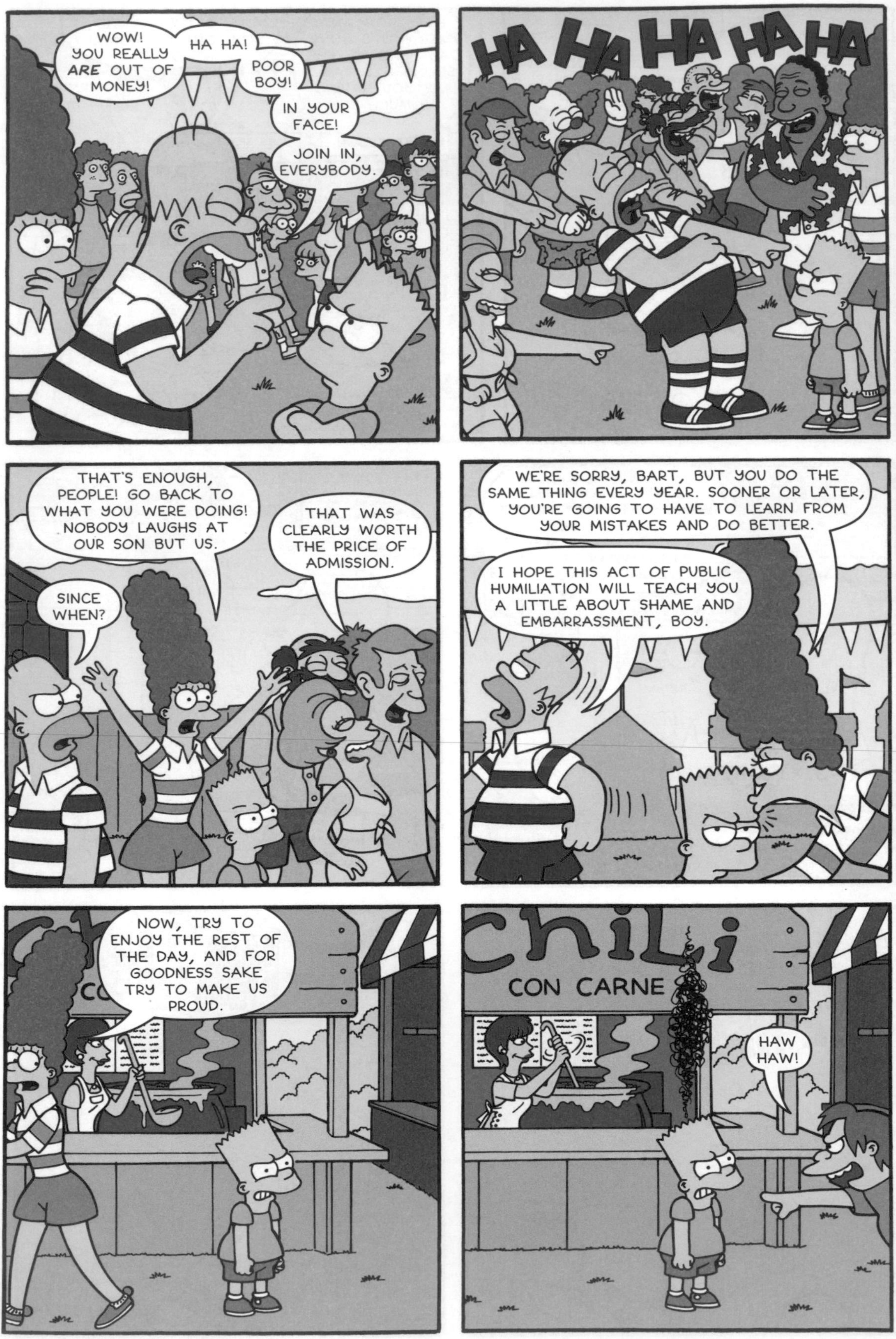

WOW! YOU REALLY ARE OUT OF MONEY!
HA HA!
POOR BOY!
IN YOUR FACE!
JOIN IN, EVERYBODY.
HA HA HA HA HA
THAT'S ENOUGH, PEOPLE! GO BACK TO WHAT YOU WERE DOING! NOBODY LAUGHS AT OUR SON BUT US.
THAT WAS CLEARLY WORTH THE PRICE OF ADMISSION.
SINCE WHEN?
WE'RE SORRY, BART, BUT YOU DO THE SAME THING EVERY YEAR. SOONER OR LATER, YOU'RE GOING TO HAVE TO LEARN FROM YOUR MISTAKES AND DO BETTER.
I HOPE THIS ACT OF PUBLIC HUMILIATION WILL TEACH YOU A LITTLE ABOUT SHAME AND EMBARRASSMENT, BOY.
NOW, TRY TO ENJOY THE REST OF THE DAY, AND FOR GOODNESS SAKE TRY TO MAKE US PROUD.
ChiLi
CON CARNE
HAW HAW!

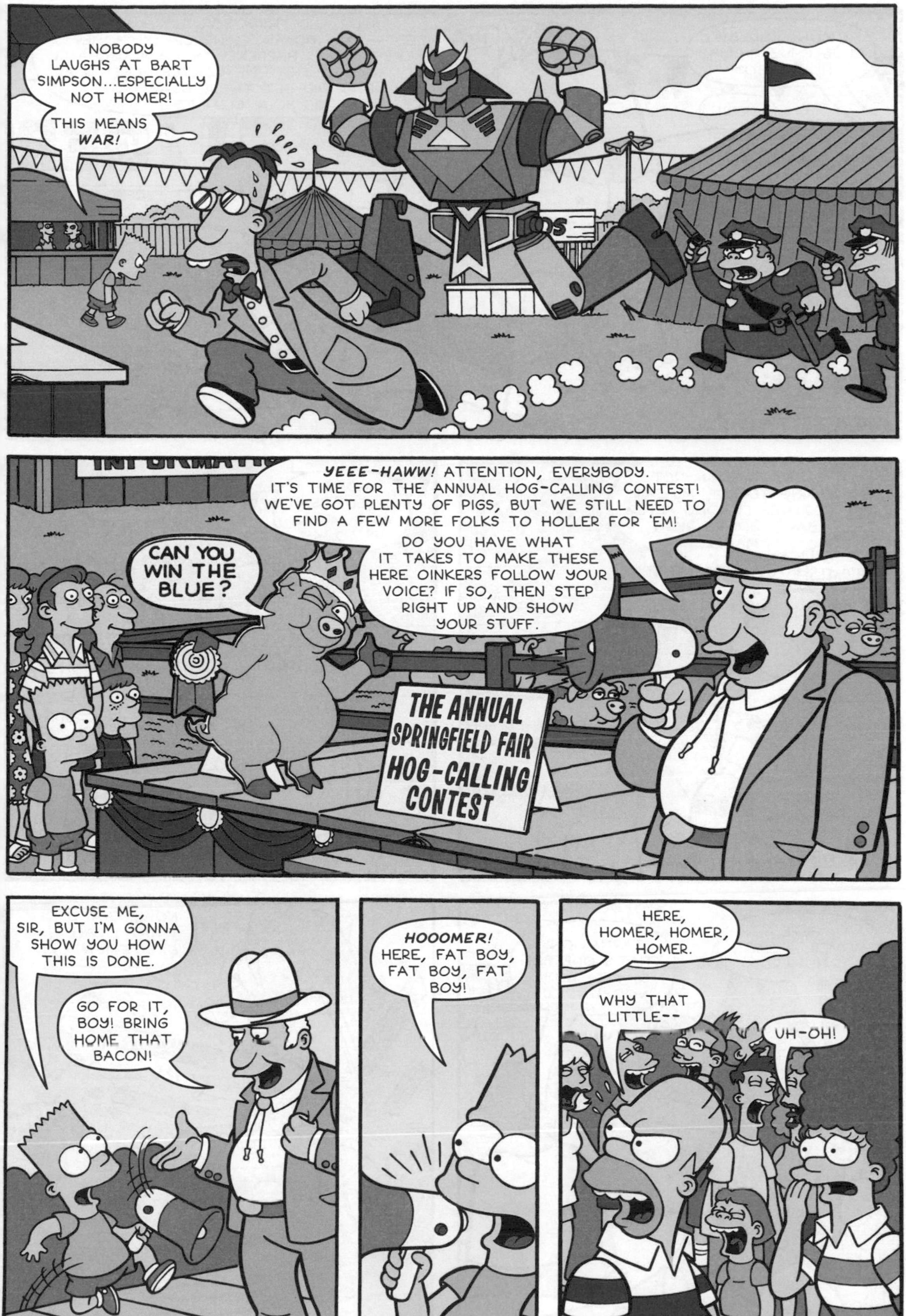
NOBODY LAUGHS AT BART SIMPSON...ESPECIALLY NOT HOMER!
THIS MEANS WAR!
YEEE-HAWW! ATTENTION, EVERYBODY. IT'S TIME FOR THE ANNUAL HOG-CALLING CONTEST! WE'VE GOT PLENTY OF PIGS, BUT WE STILL NEED TO FIND A FEW MORE FOLKS TO HOLLER FOR 'EM!
DO YOU HAVE WHAT IT TAKES TO MAKE THESE HERE OINKERS FOLLOW YOUR VOICE? IF SO, THEN STEP RIGHT UP AND SHOW YOUR STUFF.
CAN YOU WIN THE BLUE?
THE ANNUAL SPRINGFIELD FAIR HOG-CALLING CONTEST
EXCUSE ME, SIR, BUT I'M GONNA SHOW YOU HOW THIS IS DONE.
GO FOR IT, BOY! BRING HOME THAT BACON!
HOOOMER! HERE, FAT BOY, FAT BOY, FAT BOY!
HERE, HOMER, HOMER, HOMER.
WHY THAT LITTLE--
UH-OH!

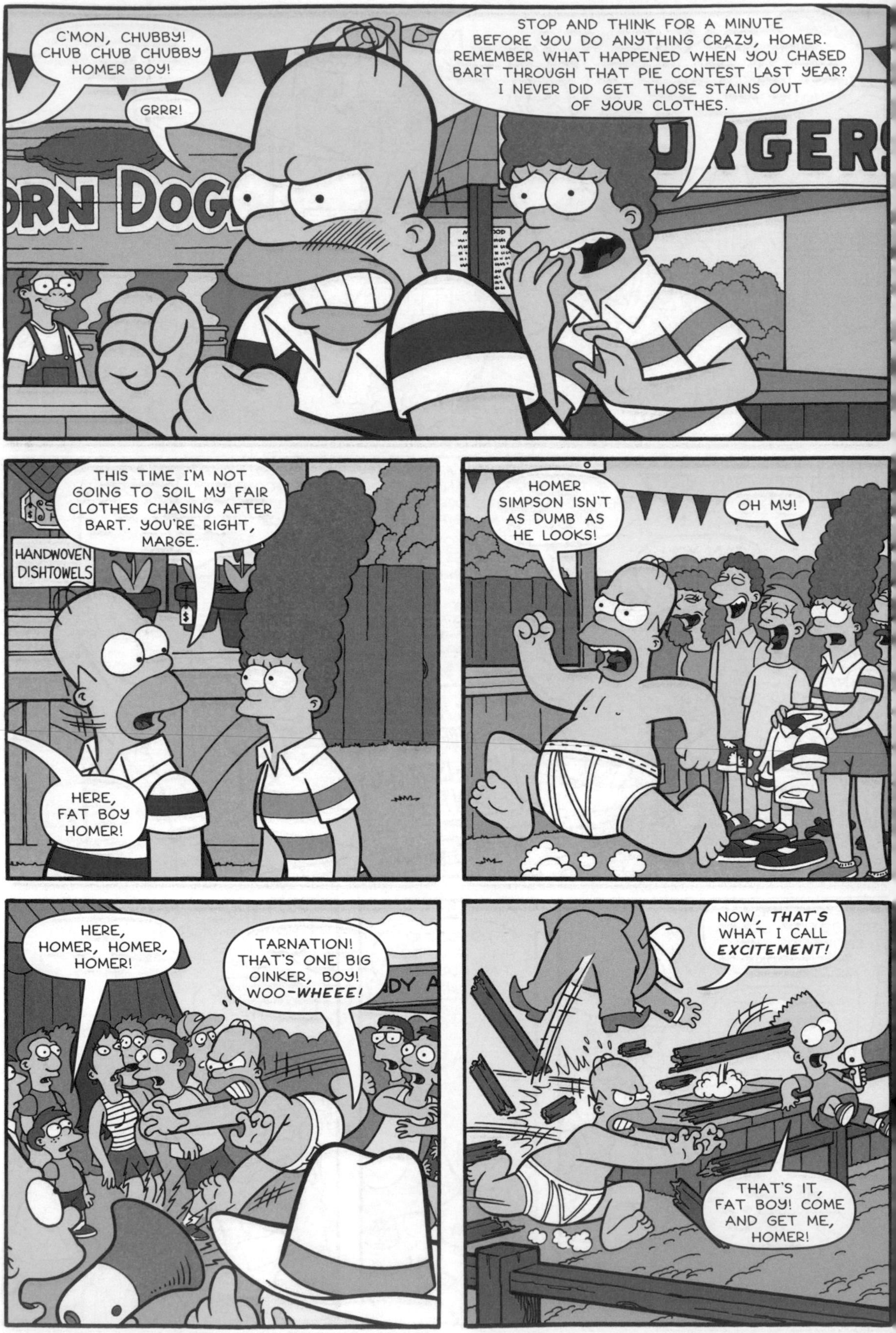
C'MON, CHUBBY! CHUB CHUB CHUBBY HOMER BOY!
GRRR!
STOP AND THINK FOR A MINUTE BEFORE YOU DO ANYTHING CRAZY, HOMER. REMEMBER WHAT HAPPENED WHEN YOU CHASED BART THROUGH THAT PIE CONTEST LAST YEAR? I NEVER DID GET THOSE STAINS OUT OF YOUR CLOTHES.
URGERS
THIS TIME I'M NOT GOING TO SOIL MY FAIR CLOTHES CHASING AFTER BART. YOU'RE RIGHT, MARGE.
HANDWOVEN DISHTOWELS
HERE, FAT BOY HOMER!
HOMER SIMPSON ISN'T AS DUMB AS HE LOOKS!
OH MY!
HERE, HOMER, HOMER, HOMER!
TARNATION! THAT'S ONE BIG OINKER, BOY! WOO-*WHEEE!*
NOW, *THAT'S* WHAT I CALL *EXCITEMENT!*
THAT'S IT, FAT BOY! COME AND GET ME, HOMER!

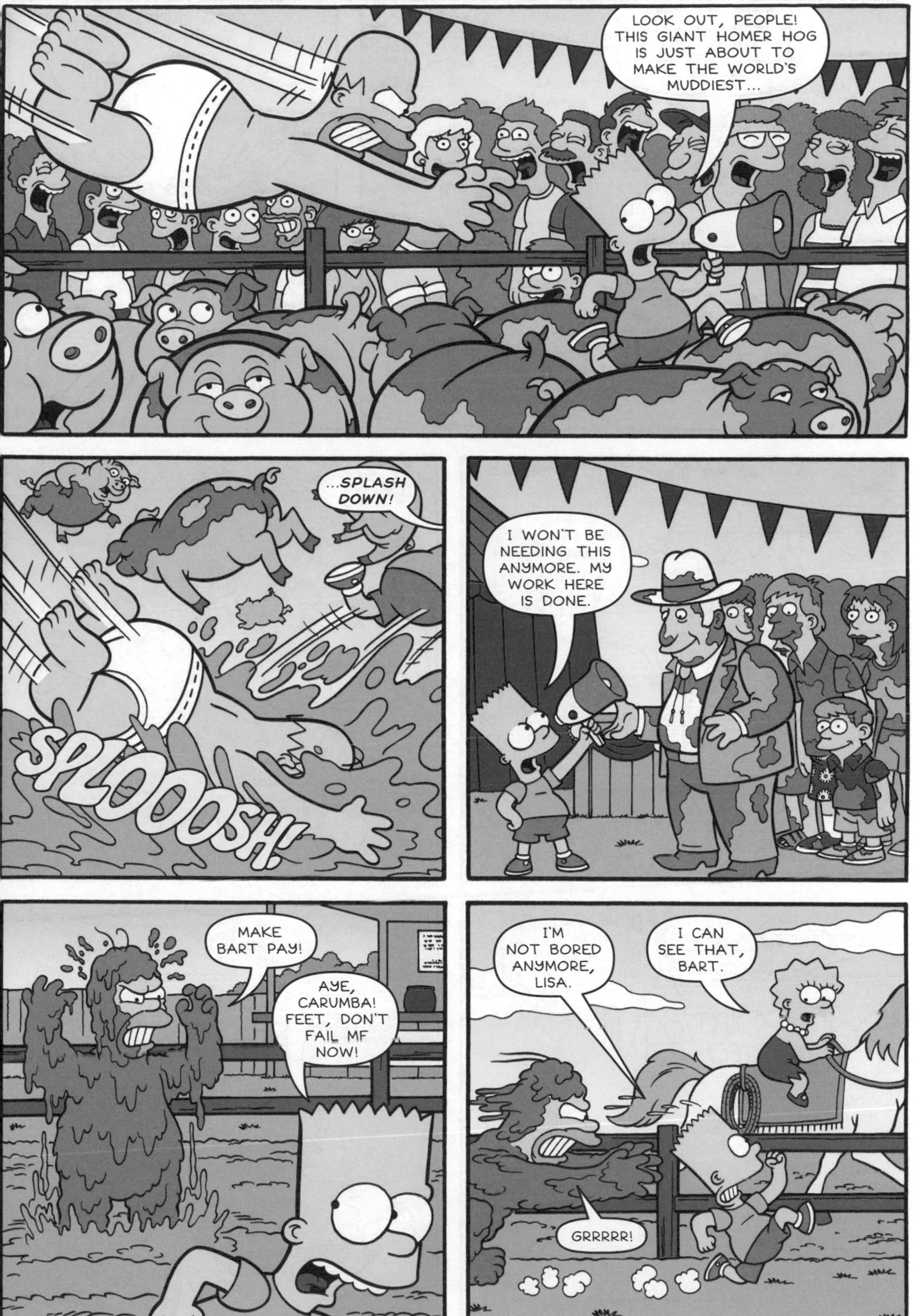

LOOK OUT, PEOPLE! THIS GIANT HOMER HOG IS JUST ABOUT TO MAKE THE WORLD'S MUDDIEST...
...SPLASH DOWN!
SPLOOOSH!
I WON'T BE NEEDING THIS ANYMORE. MY WORK HERE IS DONE.
MAKE BART PAY!
AYE, CARUMBA! FEET, DON'T FAIL ME NOW!
I'M NOT BORED ANYMORE, LISA.
I CAN SEE THAT, BART.
GRRRRR!

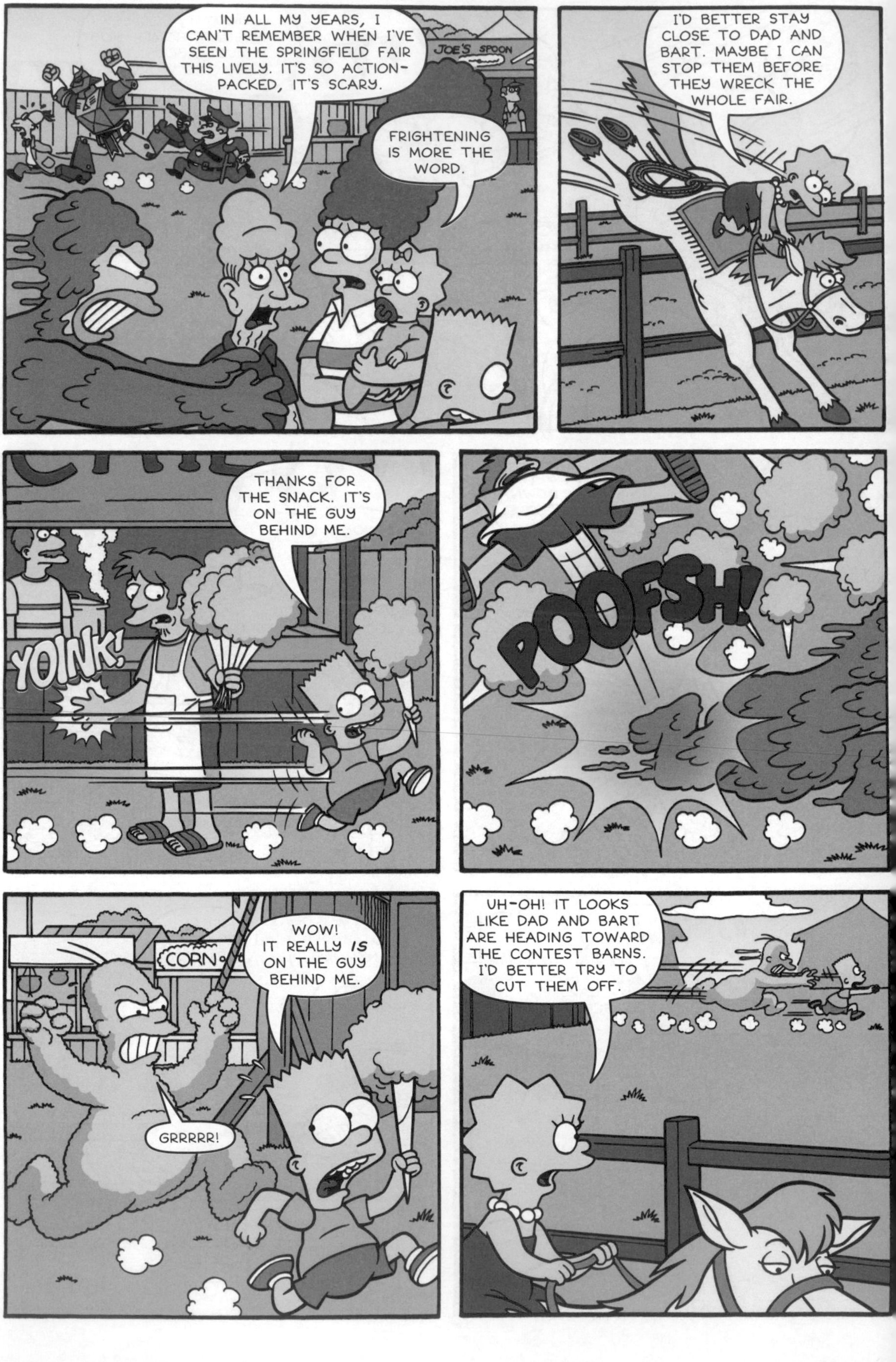

IN ALL MY YEARS, I CAN'T REMEMBER WHEN I'VE SEEN THE SPRINGFIELD FAIR THIS LIVELY. IT'S SO ACTION-PACKED, IT'S SCARY.
JOE'S SPOON
FRIGHTENING IS MORE THE WORD.
I'D BETTER STAY CLOSE TO DAD AND BART. MAYBE I CAN STOP THEM BEFORE THEY WRECK THE WHOLE FAIR.
THANKS FOR THE SNACK. IT'S ON THE GUY BEHIND ME.
YOINK!
POOFSH!
CORN
WOW! IT REALLY *IS* ON THE GUY BEHIND ME.
GRRRRR!
UH-OH! IT LOOKS LIKE DAD AND BART ARE HEADING TOWARD THE CONTEST BARNS. I'D BETTER TRY TO CUT THEM OFF.

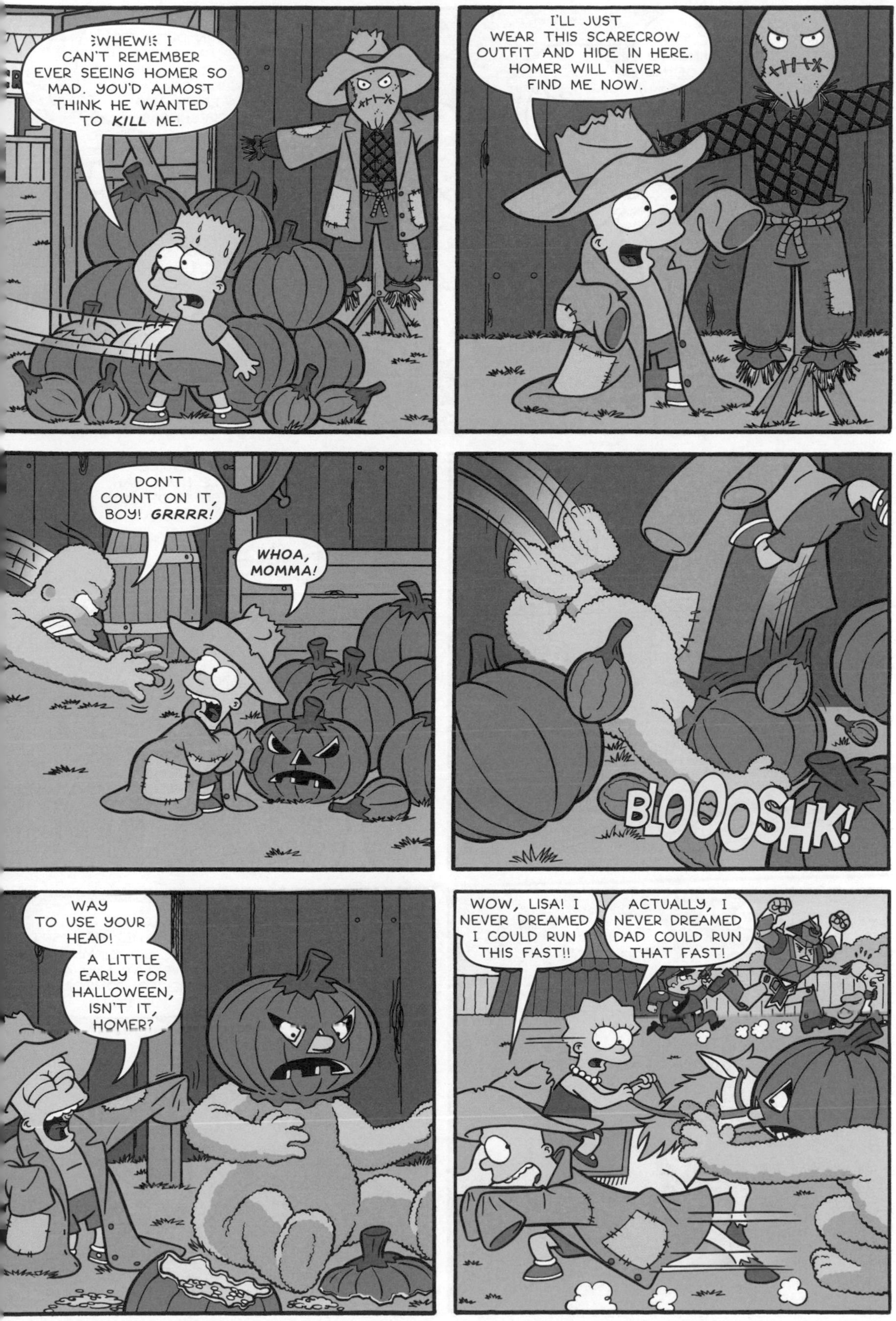
WHEW! I CAN'T REMEMBER EVER SEEING HOMER SO MAD. YOU'D ALMOST THINK HE WANTED TO KILL ME.
I'LL JUST WEAR THIS SCARECROW OUTFIT AND HIDE IN HERE. HOMER WILL NEVER FIND ME NOW.
DON'T COUNT ON IT, BOY! GRRRR!
WHOA, MOMMA!
BLOOOSHK!
WAY TO USE YOUR HEAD!
A LITTLE EARLY FOR HALLOWEEN, ISN'T IT, HOMER?
WOW, LISA! I NEVER DREAMED I COULD RUN THIS FAST!!
ACTUALLY, I NEVER DREAMED DAD COULD RUN THAT FAST!

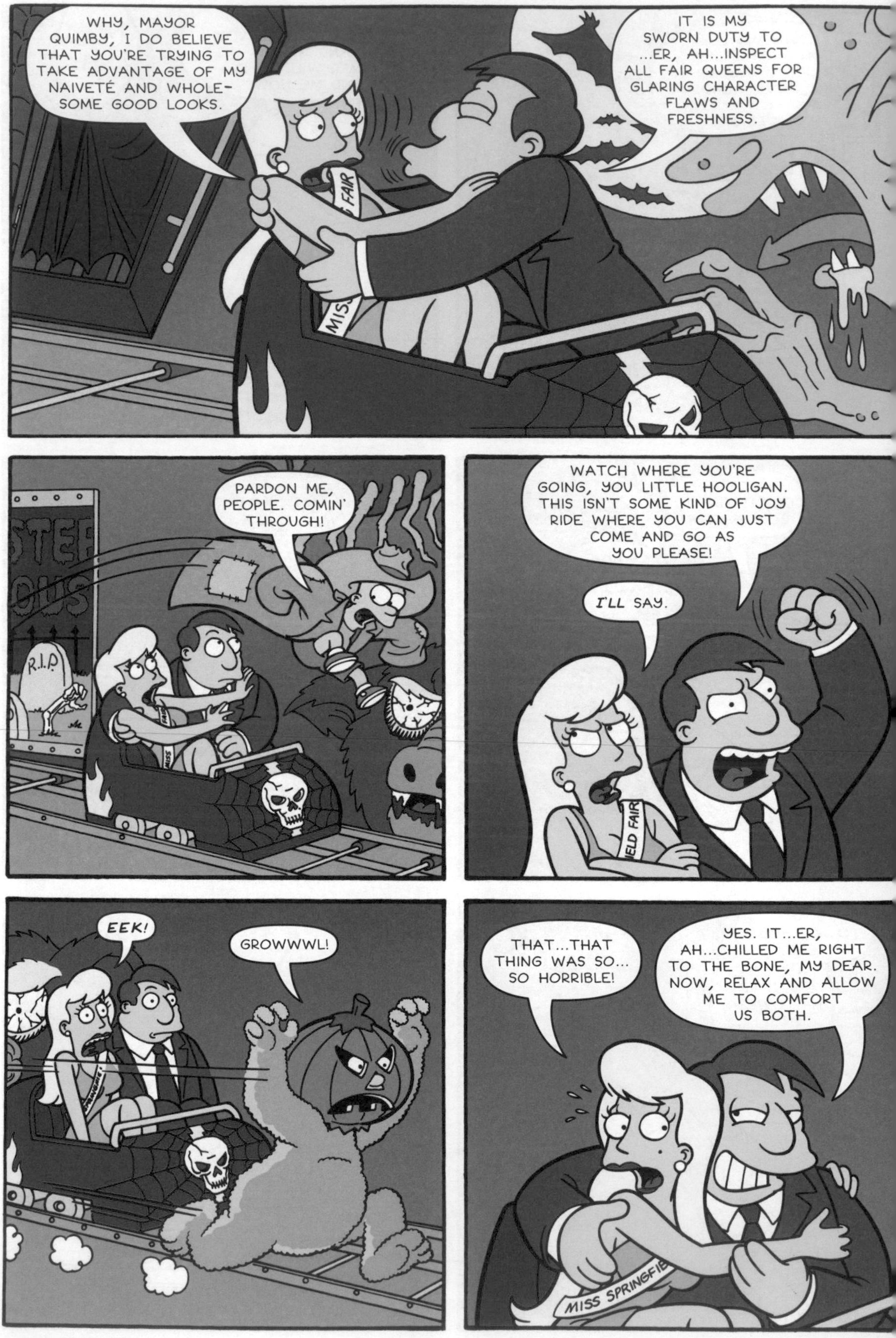
WHY, MAYOR QUIMBY, I DO BELIEVE THAT YOU'RE TRYING TO TAKE ADVANTAGE OF MY NAIVETÉ AND WHOLE-SOME GOOD LOOKS.
IT IS MY SWORN DUTY TO ...ER, AH...INSPECT ALL FAIR QUEENS FOR GLARING CHARACTER FLAWS AND FRESHNESS.
MISS FAIR
PARDON ME, PEOPLE. COMIN' THROUGH!
R.I.P.
WATCH WHERE YOU'RE GOING, YOU LITTLE HOOLIGAN. THIS ISN'T SOME KIND OF JOY RIDE WHERE YOU CAN JUST COME AND GO AS YOU PLEASE!
I'LL SAY.
EEK!
GROWWWL!
THAT...THAT THING WAS SO... SO HORRIBLE!
YES. IT...ER, AH...CHILLED ME RIGHT TO THE BONE, MY DEAR. NOW, RELAX AND ALLOW ME TO COMFORT US BOTH.
MISS SPRINGFIE

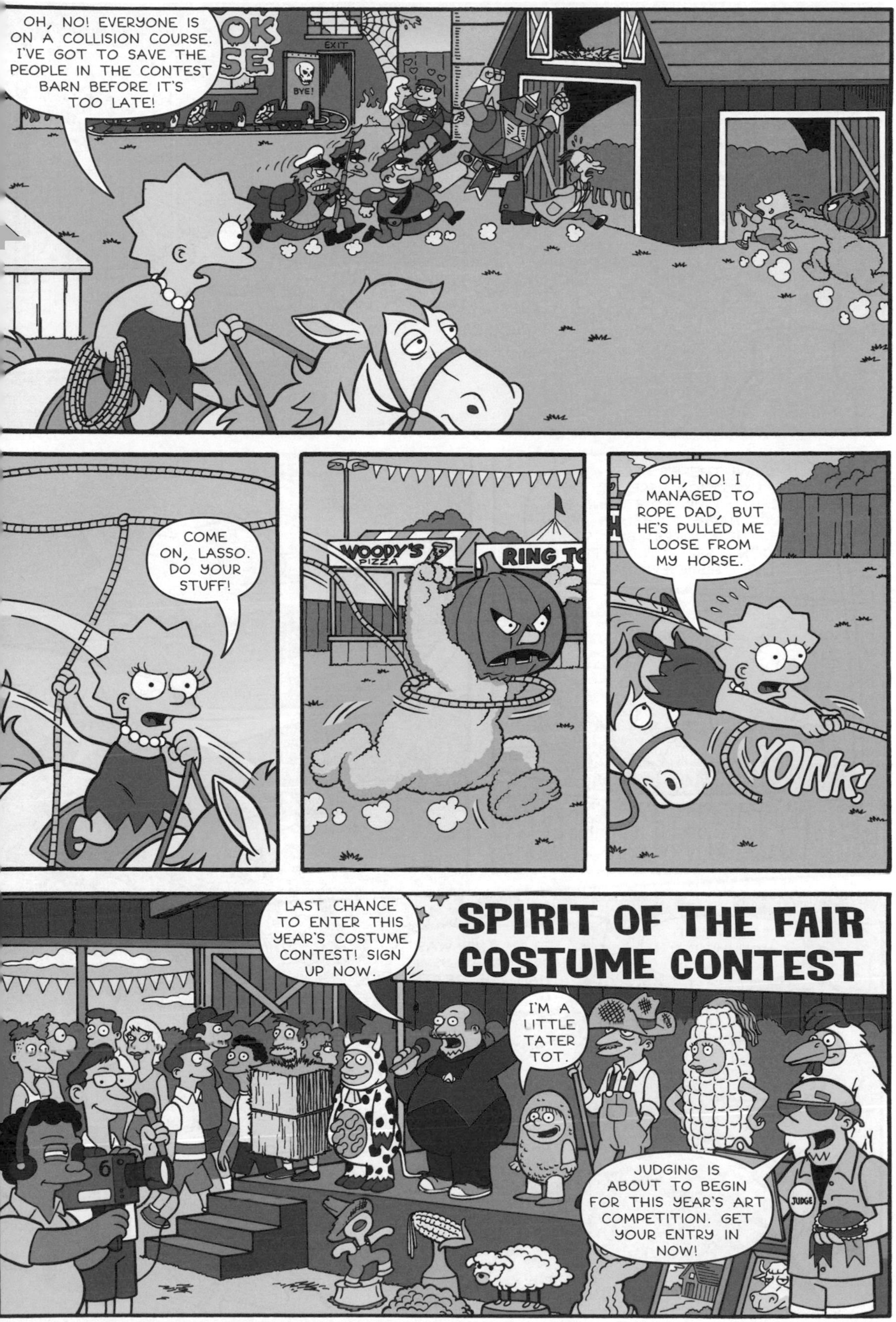
OH, NO! EVERYONE IS ON A COLLISION COURSE. I'VE GOT TO SAVE THE PEOPLE IN THE CONTEST BARN BEFORE IT'S TOO LATE!
EXIT
BYE!
COME ON, LASSO. DO YOUR STUFF!
WOODY'S PIZZA
RING TO
OH, NO! I MANAGED TO ROPE DAD, BUT HE'S PULLED ME LOOSE FROM MY HORSE.
YOINK!
SPIRIT OF THE FAIR COSTUME CONTEST
LAST CHANCE TO ENTER THIS YEAR'S COSTUME CONTEST! SIGN UP NOW.
I'M A LITTLE TATER TOT.
JUDGING IS ABOUT TO BEGIN FOR THIS YEAR'S ART COMPETITION. GET YOUR ENTRY IN NOW!
JUDGE

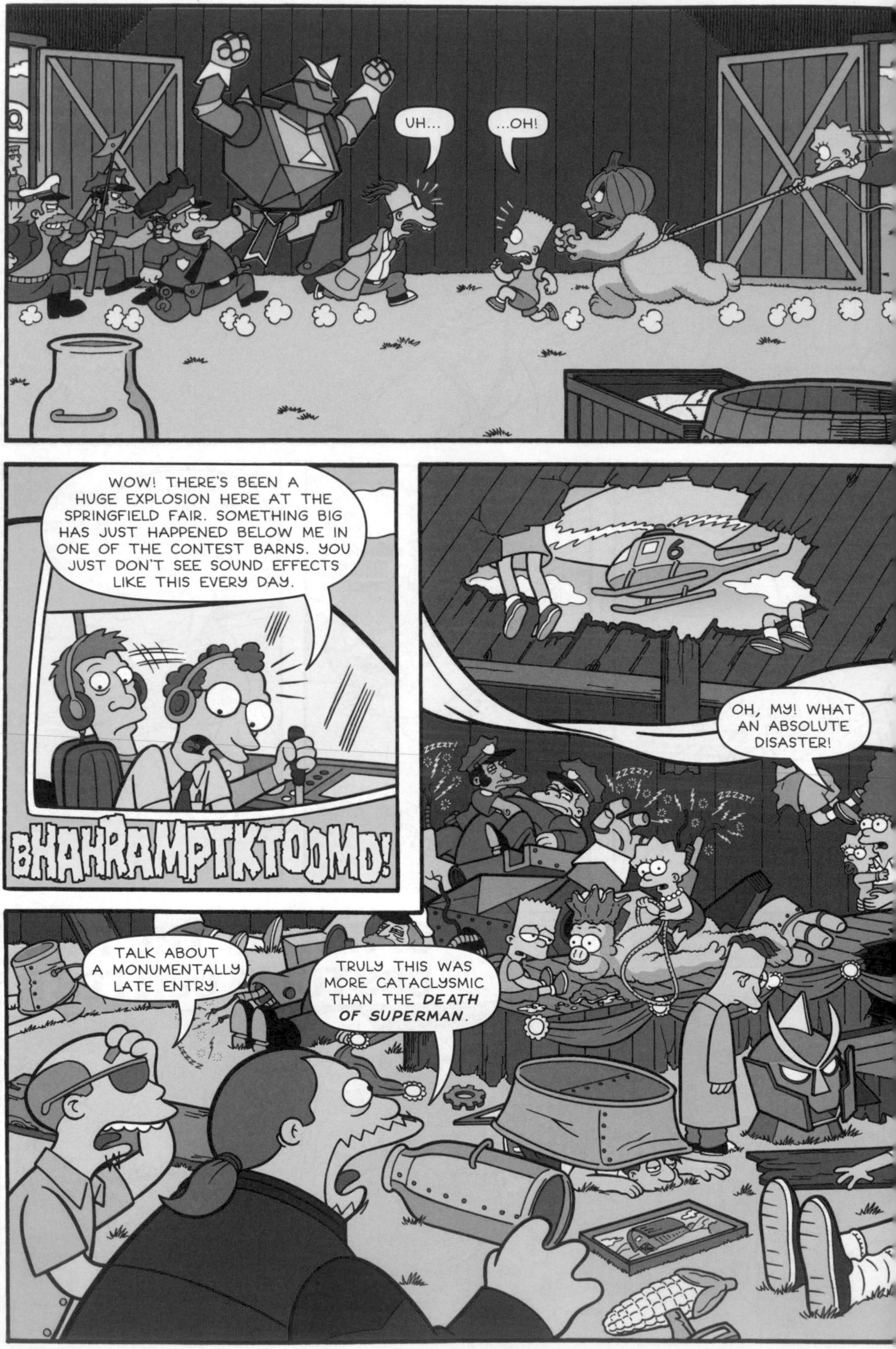
UH...
...OH!
WOW! THERE'S BEEN A HUGE EXPLOSION HERE AT THE SPRINGFIELD FAIR. SOMETHING BIG HAS JUST HAPPENED BELOW ME IN ONE OF THE CONTEST BARNS. YOU JUST DON'T SEE SOUND EFFECTS LIKE THIS EVERY DAY.
BHAHRAMPTKTOOMD!
OH, MY! WHAT AN ABSOLUTE DISASTER!
TALK ABOUT A MONUMENTALLY LATE ENTRY.
TRULY THIS WAS MORE CATACLYSMIC THAN THE *DEATH OF SUPERMAN*.

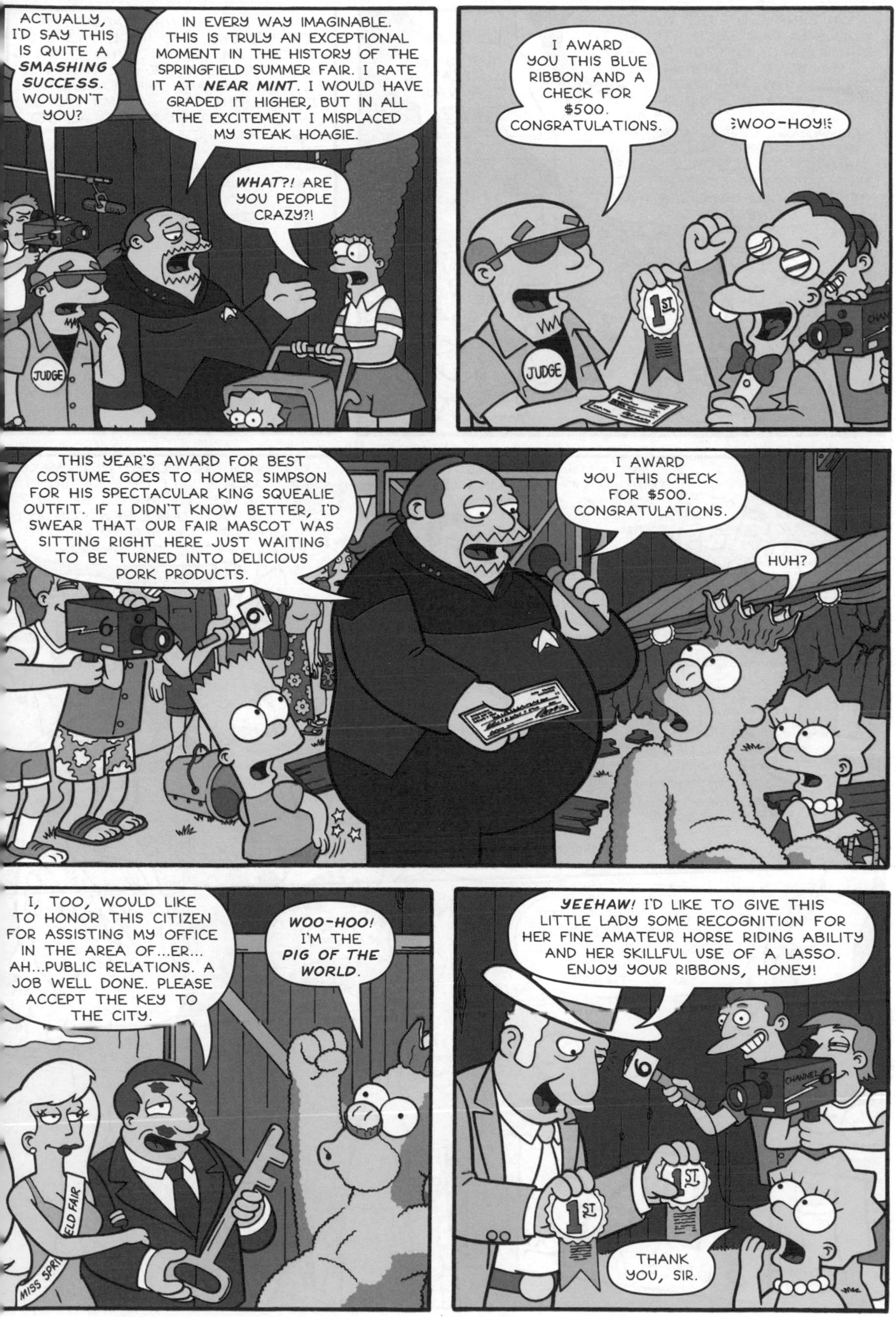
ACTUALLY, I'D SAY THIS IS QUITE A SMASHING SUCCESS. WOULDN'T YOU?
IN EVERY WAY IMAGINABLE. THIS IS TRULY AN EXCEPTIONAL MOMENT IN THE HISTORY OF THE SPRINGFIELD SUMMER FAIR. I RATE IT AT NEAR MINT. I WOULD HAVE GRADED IT HIGHER, BUT IN ALL THE EXCITEMENT I MISPLACED MY STEAK HOAGIE.
WHAT?! ARE YOU PEOPLE CRAZY?!
JUDGE
I AWARD YOU THIS BLUE RIBBON AND A CHECK FOR $500. CONGRATULATIONS.
WOO-HOY!
1ST
JUDGE
THIS YEAR'S AWARD FOR BEST COSTUME GOES TO HOMER SIMPSON FOR HIS SPECTACULAR KING SQUEALIE OUTFIT. IF I DIDN'T KNOW BETTER, I'D SWEAR THAT OUR FAIR MASCOT WAS SITTING RIGHT HERE JUST WAITING TO BE TURNED INTO DELICIOUS PORK PRODUCTS.
I AWARD YOU THIS CHECK FOR $500. CONGRATULATIONS.
HUH?
I, TOO, WOULD LIKE TO HONOR THIS CITIZEN FOR ASSISTING MY OFFICE IN THE AREA OF...ER... AH...PUBLIC RELATIONS. A JOB WELL DONE. PLEASE ACCEPT THE KEY TO THE CITY.
WOO-HOO! I'M THE PIG OF THE WORLD.
MISS SPRI ELD FAIR
YEEHAW! I'D LIKE TO GIVE THIS LITTLE LADY SOME RECOGNITION FOR HER FINE AMATEUR HORSE RIDING ABILITY AND HER SKILLFUL USE OF A LASSO. ENJOY YOUR RIBBONS, HONEY!
CHANNEL 6
1ST
1ST
THANK YOU, SIR.

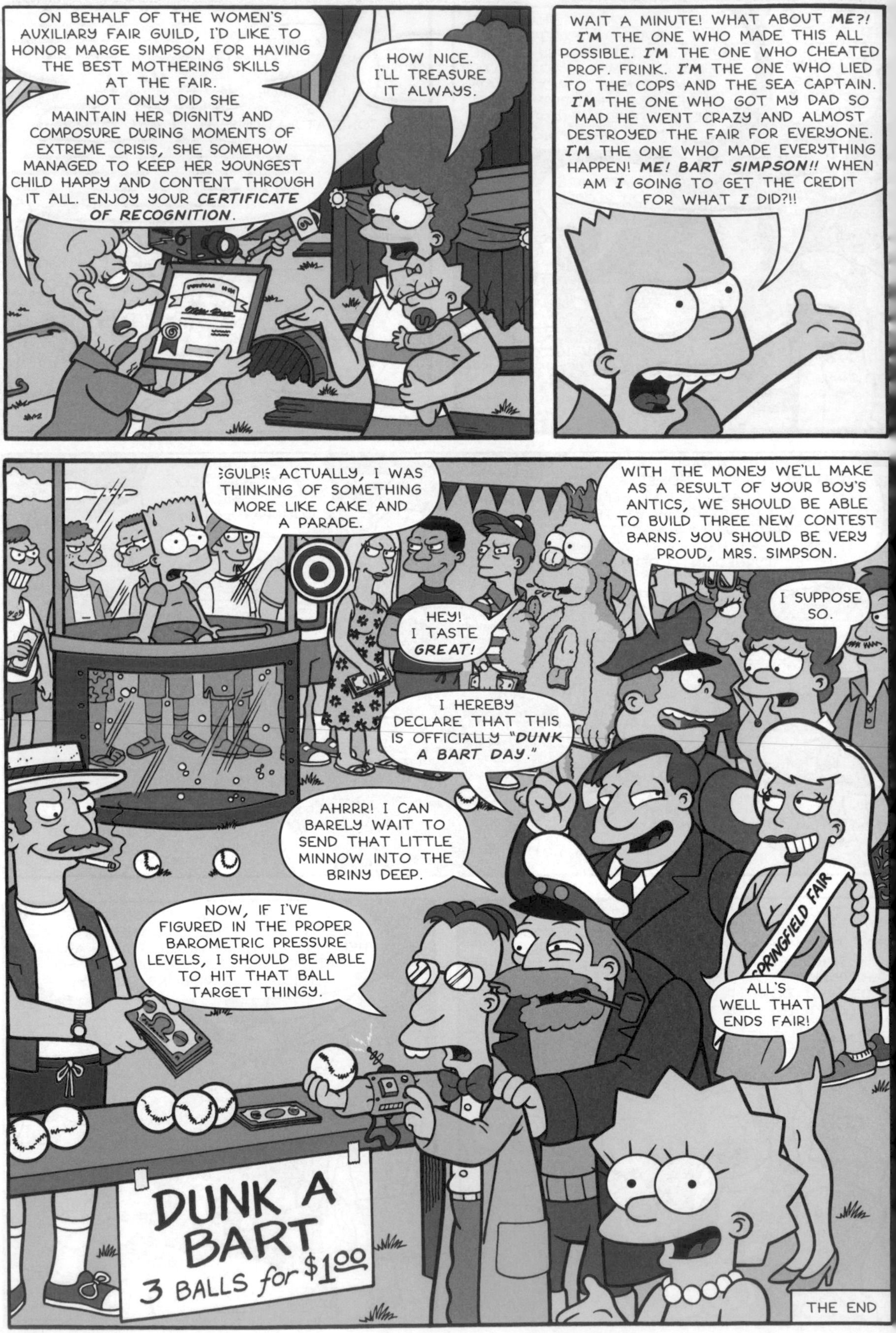
ON BEHALF OF THE WOMEN'S AUXILIARY FAIR GUILD, I'D LIKE TO HONOR MARGE SIMPSON FOR HAVING THE BEST MOTHERING SKILLS AT THE FAIR.
NOT ONLY DID SHE MAINTAIN HER DIGNITY AND COMPOSURE DURING MOMENTS OF EXTREME CRISIS, SHE SOMEHOW MANAGED TO KEEP HER YOUNGEST CHILD HAPPY AND CONTENT THROUGH IT ALL. ENJOY YOUR ***CERTIFICATE OF RECOGNITION***.
HOW NICE. I'LL TREASURE IT ALWAYS.
WAIT A MINUTE! WHAT ABOUT ***ME?!*** ***I'M*** THE ONE WHO MADE THIS ALL POSSIBLE. ***I'M*** THE ONE WHO CHEATED PROF. FRINK. ***I'M*** THE ONE WHO LIED TO THE COPS AND THE SEA CAPTAIN. ***I'M*** THE ONE WHO GOT MY DAD SO MAD HE WENT CRAZY AND ALMOST DESTROYED THE FAIR FOR EVERYONE. ***I'M*** THE ONE WHO MADE EVERYTHING HAPPEN! ***ME! BART SIMPSON!!*** WHEN AM ***I*** GOING TO GET THE CREDIT FOR WHAT ***I*** DID?!!
:GULP!: ACTUALLY, I WAS THINKING OF SOMETHING MORE LIKE CAKE AND A PARADE.
WITH THE MONEY WE'LL MAKE AS A RESULT OF YOUR BOY'S ANTICS, WE SHOULD BE ABLE TO BUILD THREE NEW CONTEST BARNS. YOU SHOULD BE VERY PROUD, MRS. SIMPSON.
I SUPPOSE SO.
HEY! I TASTE ***GREAT!***
I HEREBY DECLARE THAT THIS IS OFFICIALLY "***DUNK A BART DAY***."
AHRRR! I CAN BARELY WAIT TO SEND THAT LITTLE MINNOW INTO THE BRINY DEEP.
NOW, IF I'VE FIGURED IN THE PROPER BAROMETRIC PRESSURE LEVELS, I SHOULD BE ABLE TO HIT THAT BALL TARGET THINGY.
SPRINGFIELD FAIR
ALL'S WELL THAT ENDS FAIR!
DUNK A BART 3 BALLS for $1.00
THE END

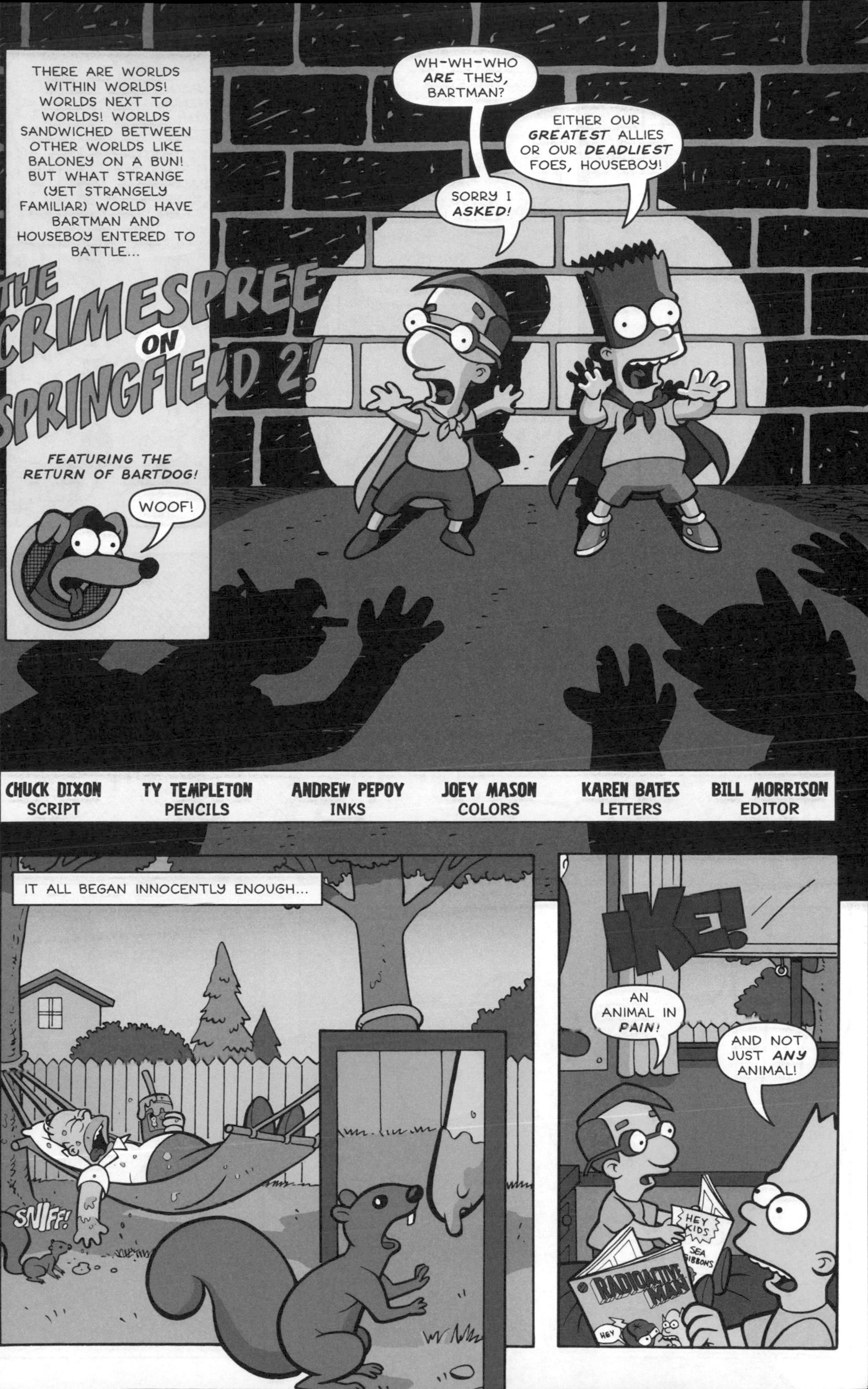
THERE ARE WORLDS WITHIN WORLDS! WORLDS NEXT TO WORLDS! WORLDS SANDWICHED BETWEEN OTHER WORLDS LIKE BALONEY ON A BUN! BUT WHAT STRANGE (YET STRANGELY FAMILIAR) WORLD HAVE BARTMAN AND HOUSEBOY ENTERED TO BATTLE...
WH-WH-WHO ARE THEY, BARTMAN?
EITHER OUR GREATEST ALLIES OR OUR DEADLIEST FOES, HOUSEBOY!
SORRY I ASKED!
THE CRIMESPREE ON SPRINGFIELD 2!
FEATURING THE RETURN OF BARTDOG!
WOOF!
CHUCK DIXON SCRIPT
TY TEMPLETON PENCILS
ANDREW PEPOY INKS
JOEY MASON COLORS
KAREN BATES LETTERS
BILL MORRISON EDITOR
IT ALL BEGAN INNOCENTLY ENOUGH...
SNIFF!
IKE!
AN ANIMAL IN PAIN!
AND NOT JUST ANY ANIMAL!
HEY KIDS
SEA GIBBONS
RADIOACTIVE MAN
HEY

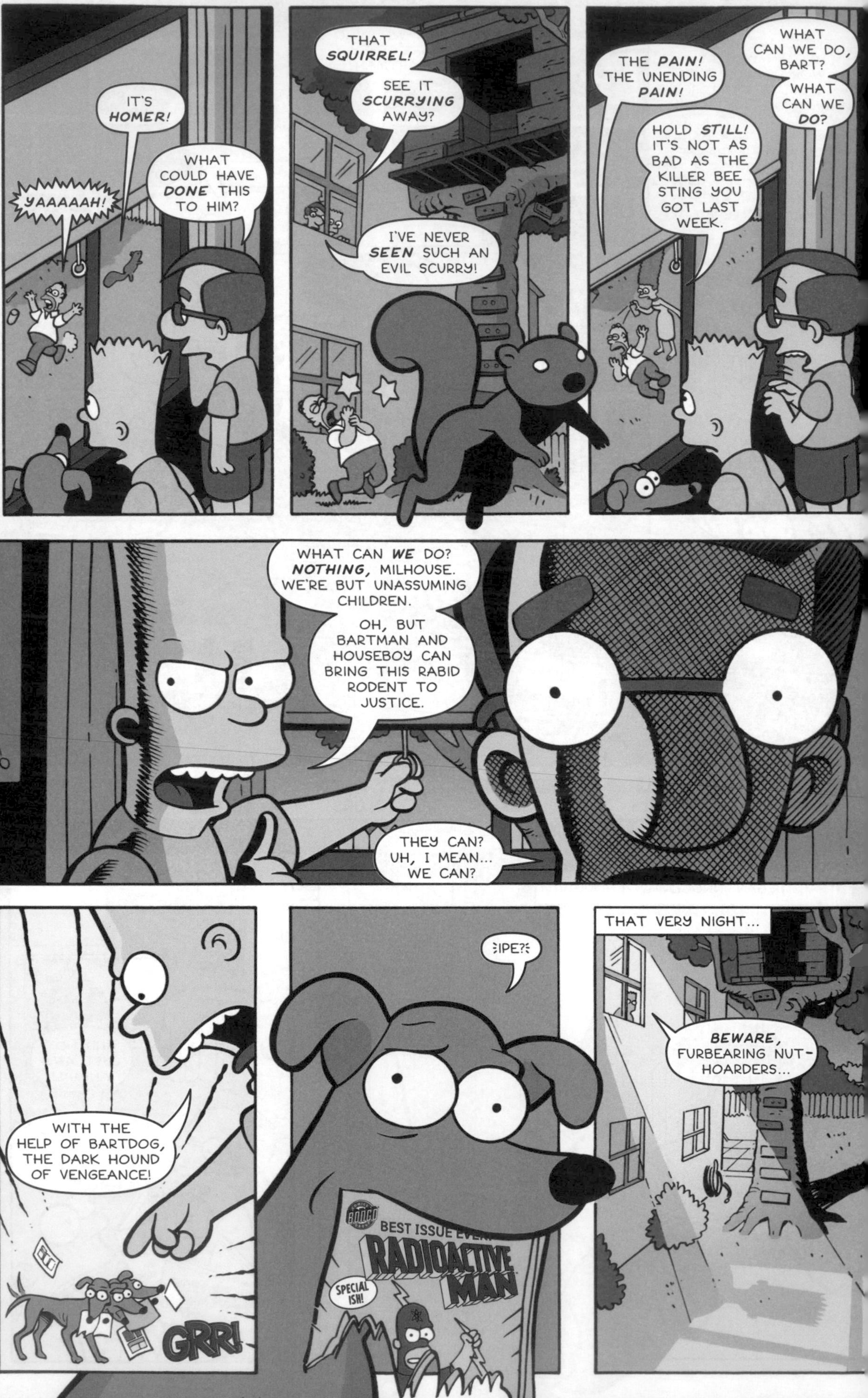
YAAAAAH!
IT'S HOMER!
WHAT COULD HAVE DONE THIS TO HIM?
THAT SQUIRREL!
SEE IT SCURRYING AWAY?
I'VE NEVER SEEN SUCH AN EVIL SCURRY!
THE PAIN! THE UNENDING PAIN!
WHAT CAN WE DO, BART?
WHAT CAN WE DO?
HOLD STILL! IT'S NOT AS BAD AS THE KILLER BEE STING YOU GOT LAST WEEK.
WHAT CAN WE DO? NOTHING, MILHOUSE. WE'RE BUT UNASSUMING CHILDREN.
OH, BUT BARTMAN AND HOUSEBOY CAN BRING THIS RABID RODENT TO JUSTICE.
THEY CAN? UH, I MEAN... WE CAN?
WITH THE HELP OF BARTDOG, THE DARK HOUND OF VENGEANCE!
GRR!
IPE?
RADIOACTIVE MAN
SPECIAL ISH!
THAT VERY NIGHT...
BEWARE, FURBEARING NUT-HOARDERS...

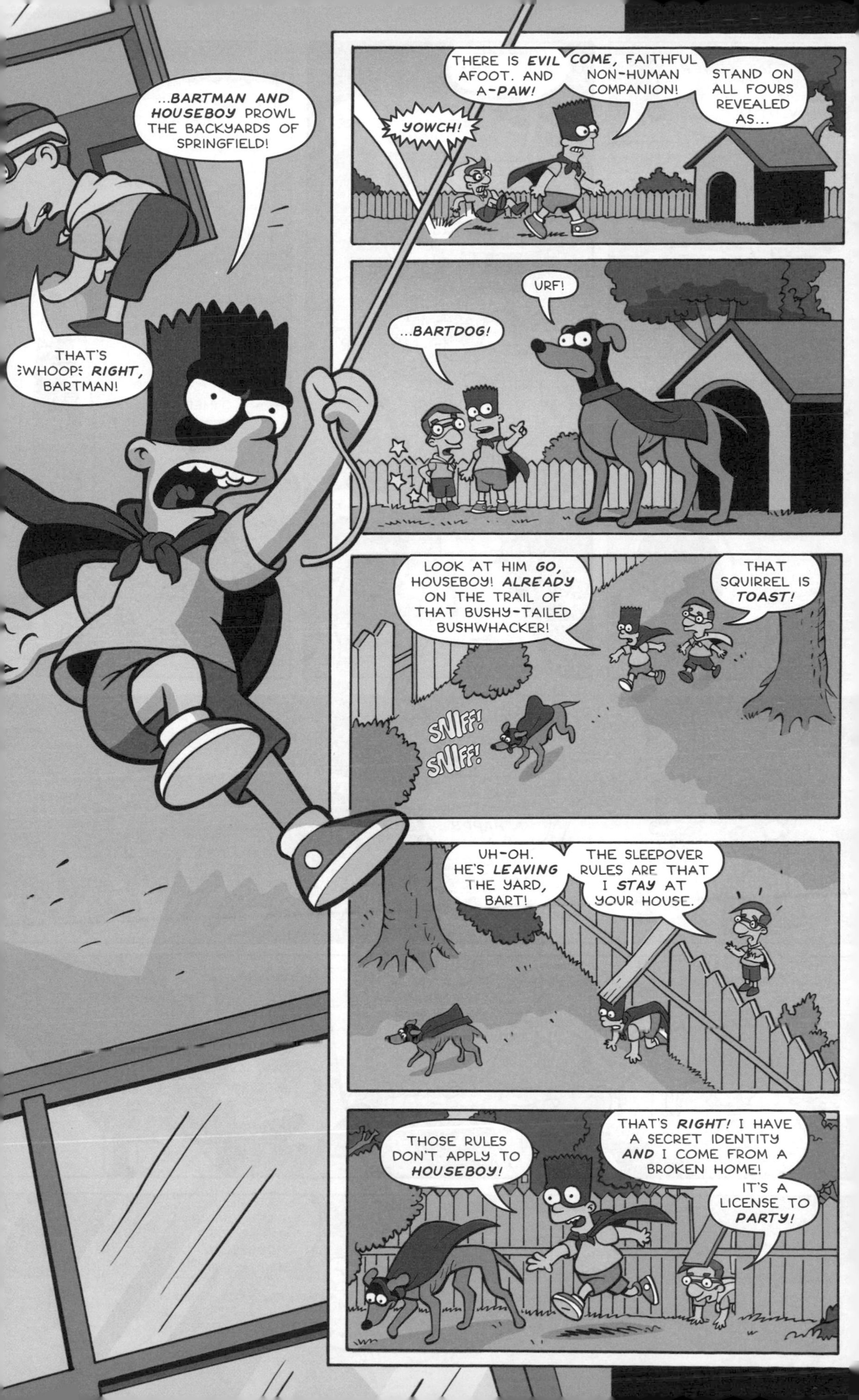
...BARTMAN AND HOUSEBOY PROWL THE BACKYARDS OF SPRINGFIELD!
THAT'S *WHOOP* RIGHT, BARTMAN!
YOWCH!
THERE IS EVIL AFOOT. AND A-PAW!
COME, FAITHFUL NON-HUMAN COMPANION!
STAND ON ALL FOURS REVEALED AS...
...BARTDOG!
URF!
LOOK AT HIM GO, HOUSEBOY! ALREADY ON THE TRAIL OF THAT BUSHY-TAILED BUSHWHACKER!
THAT SQUIRREL IS TOAST!
SNIFF! SNIFF!
UH-OH. HE'S LEAVING THE YARD, BART!
THE SLEEPOVER RULES ARE THAT I STAY AT YOUR HOUSE.
THOSE RULES DON'T APPLY TO HOUSEBOY!
THAT'S RIGHT! I HAVE A SECRET IDENTITY AND I COME FROM A BROKEN HOME!
IT'S A LICENSE TO PARTY!

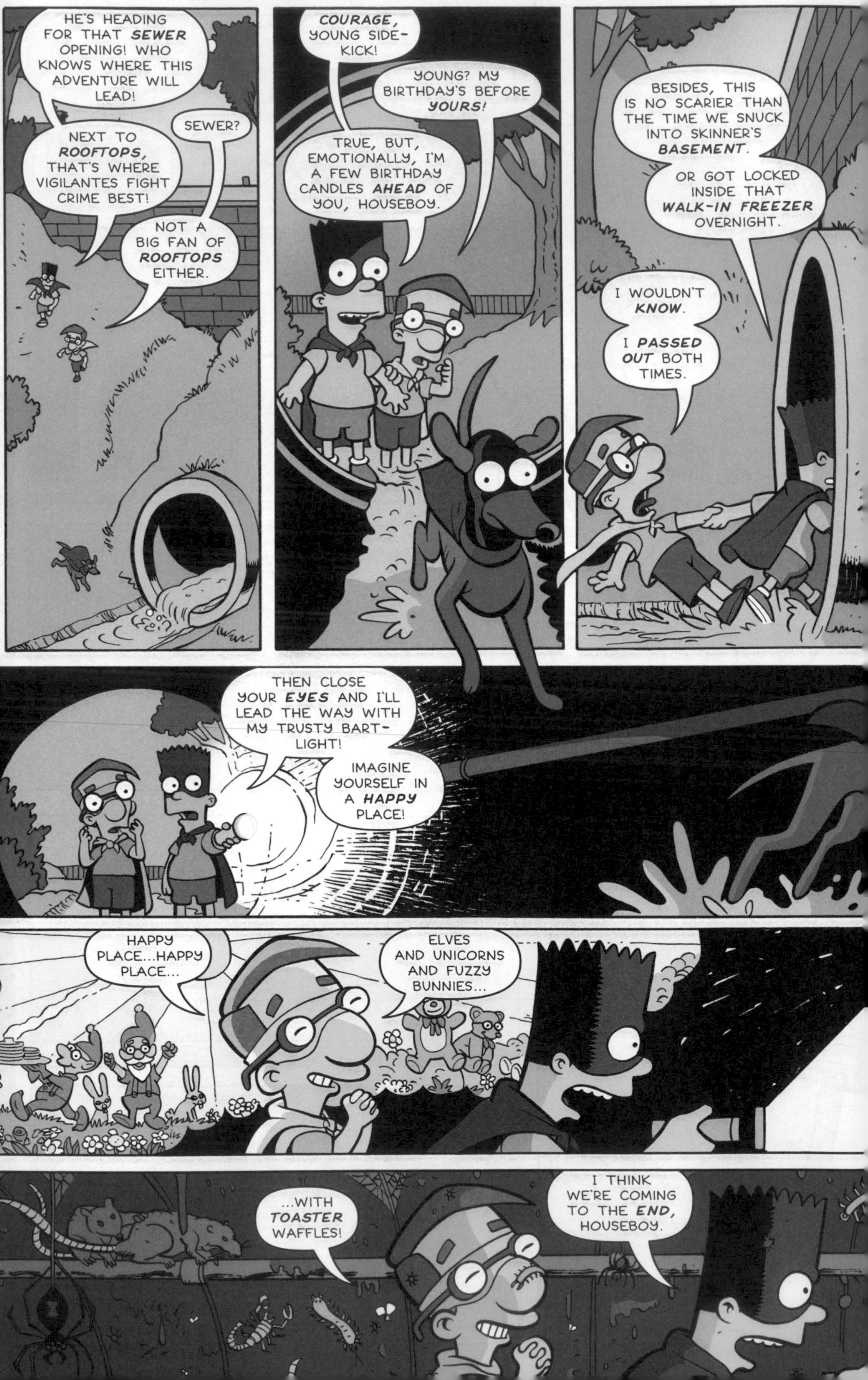
HE'S HEADING FOR THAT SEWER OPENING! WHO KNOWS WHERE THIS ADVENTURE WILL LEAD!
SEWER?
NEXT TO ROOFTOPS, THAT'S WHERE VIGILANTES FIGHT CRIME BEST!
NOT A BIG FAN OF ROOFTOPS EITHER.
COURAGE, YOUNG SIDE-KICK!
YOUNG? MY BIRTHDAY'S BEFORE YOURS!
TRUE, BUT, EMOTIONALLY, I'M A FEW BIRTHDAY CANDLES AHEAD OF YOU, HOUSEBOY.
BESIDES, THIS IS NO SCARIER THAN THE TIME WE SNUCK INTO SKINNER'S BASEMENT.
OR GOT LOCKED INSIDE THAT WALK-IN FREEZER OVERNIGHT.
I WOULDN'T KNOW.
I PASSED OUT BOTH TIMES.
THEN CLOSE YOUR EYES AND I'LL LEAD THE WAY WITH MY TRUSTY BART-LIGHT!
IMAGINE YOURSELF IN A HAPPY PLACE!
HAPPY PLACE...HAPPY PLACE...
ELVES AND UNICORNS AND FUZZY BUNNIES...
...WITH TOASTER WAFFLES!
I THINK WE'RE COMING TO THE END, HOUSEBOY.

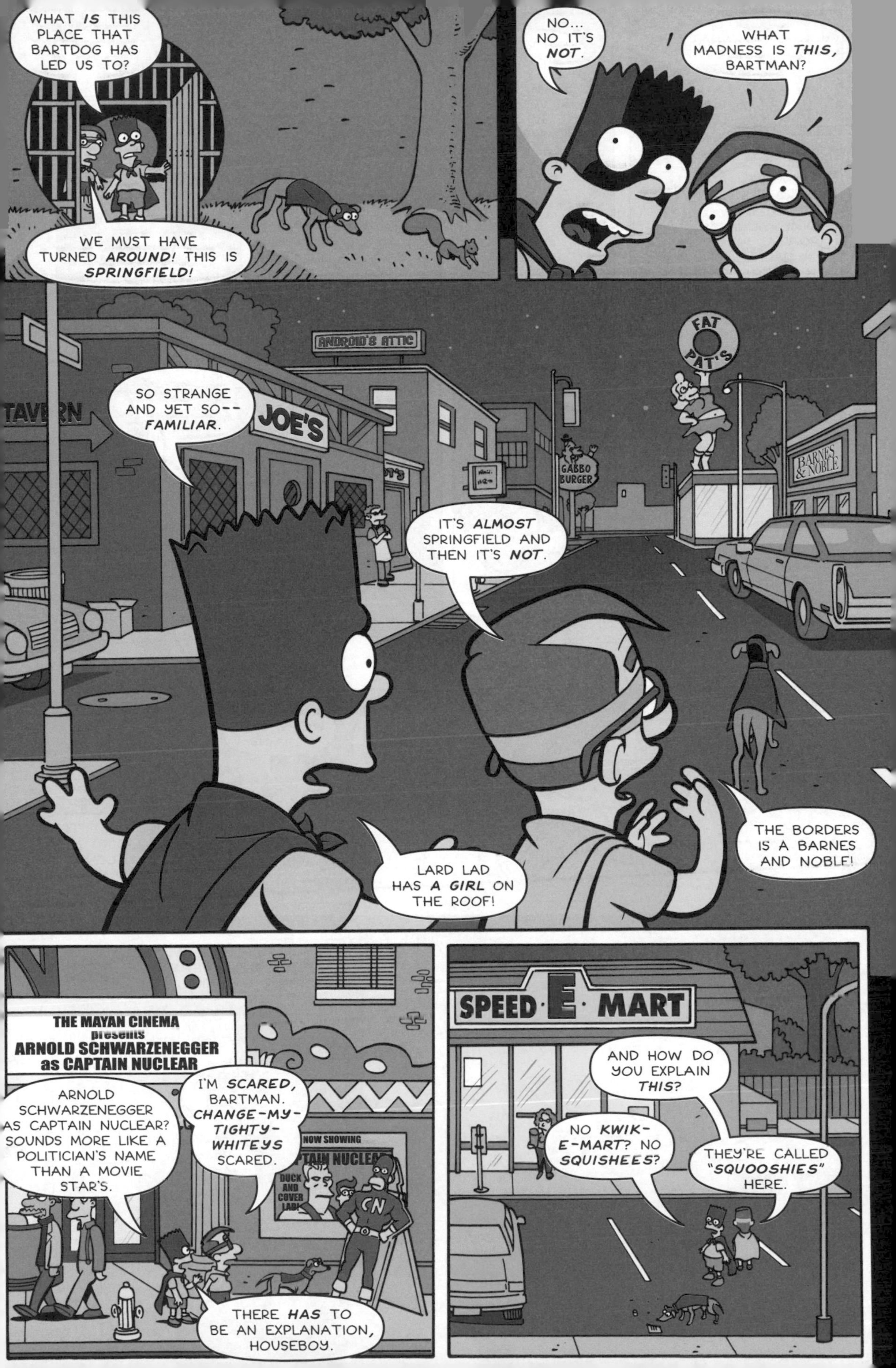
WHAT IS THIS PLACE THAT BARTDOG HAS LED US TO?
WE MUST HAVE TURNED AROUND! THIS IS SPRINGFIELD!
NO... NO IT'S NOT.
WHAT MADNESS IS THIS, BARTMAN?
TAVERN
JOE'S
ANDROID'S ATTIC
FAT PAT'S
GABBO BURGER
BARNES & NOBLE
SO STRANGE AND YET SO--FAMILIAR.
IT'S ALMOST SPRINGFIELD AND THEN IT'S NOT.
LARD LAD HAS A GIRL ON THE ROOF!
THE BORDERS IS A BARNES AND NOBLE!
THE MAYAN CINEMA presents ARNOLD SCHWARZENEGGER as CAPTAIN NUCLEAR
ARNOLD SCHWARZENEGGER AS CAPTAIN NUCLEAR? SOUNDS MORE LIKE A POLITICIAN'S NAME THAN A MOVIE STAR'S.
I'M SCARED, BARTMAN. CHANGE-MY-TIGHTY-WHITEYS SCARED.
NOW SHOWING
DUCK AND COVER LAD!
THERE HAS TO BE AN EXPLANATION, HOUSEBOY.
SPEED·E·MART
AND HOW DO YOU EXPLAIN THIS?
NO KWIK-E-MART? NO SQUISHEES?
THEY'RE CALLED "SQUOOSHIES" HERE.

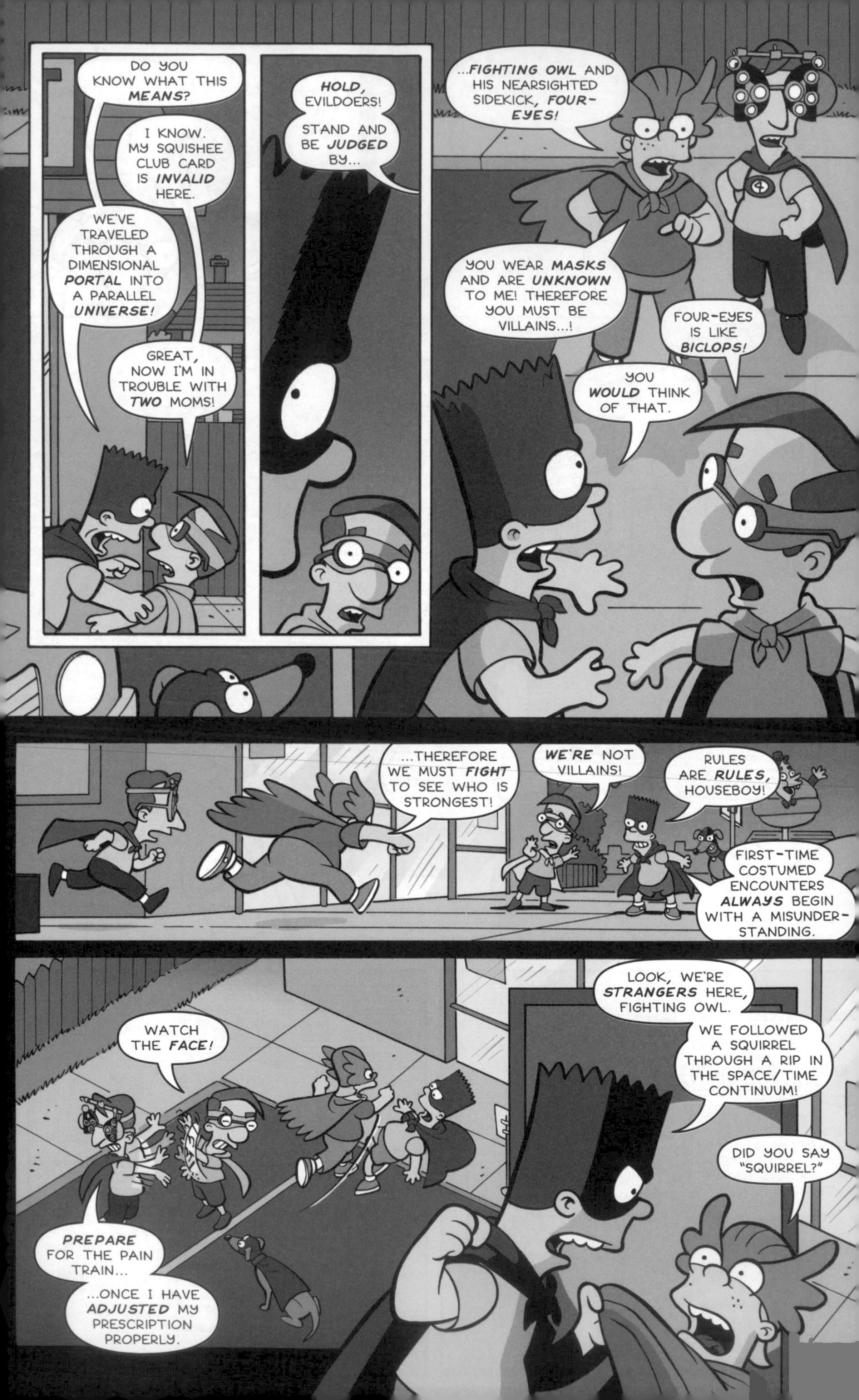

DO YOU KNOW WHAT THIS MEANS?
I KNOW. MY SQUISHEE CLUB CARD IS INVALID HERE.
WE'VE TRAVELED THROUGH A DIMENSIONAL PORTAL INTO A PARALLEL UNIVERSE!
GREAT, NOW I'M IN TROUBLE WITH TWO MOMS!
HOLD, EVILDOERS!
STAND AND BE JUDGED BY...
...FIGHTING OWL AND HIS NEARSIGHTED SIDEKICK, FOUR-EYES!
YOU WEAR MASKS AND ARE UNKNOWN TO ME! THEREFORE YOU MUST BE VILLAINS...!
FOUR-EYES IS LIKE BICLOPS!
YOU WOULD THINK OF THAT.
...THEREFORE WE MUST FIGHT TO SEE WHO IS STRONGEST!
WE'RE NOT VILLAINS!
RULES ARE RULES, HOUSEBOY!
FIRST-TIME COSTUMED ENCOUNTERS ALWAYS BEGIN WITH A MISUNDER-STANDING.
WATCH THE FACE!
PREPARE FOR THE PAIN TRAIN...
...ONCE I HAVE ADJUSTED MY PRESCRIPTION PROPERLY.
LOOK, WE'RE STRANGERS HERE, FIGHTING OWL.
WE FOLLOWED A SQUIRREL THROUGH A RIP IN THE SPACE/TIME CONTINUUM!
DID YOU SAY "SQUIRREL?"

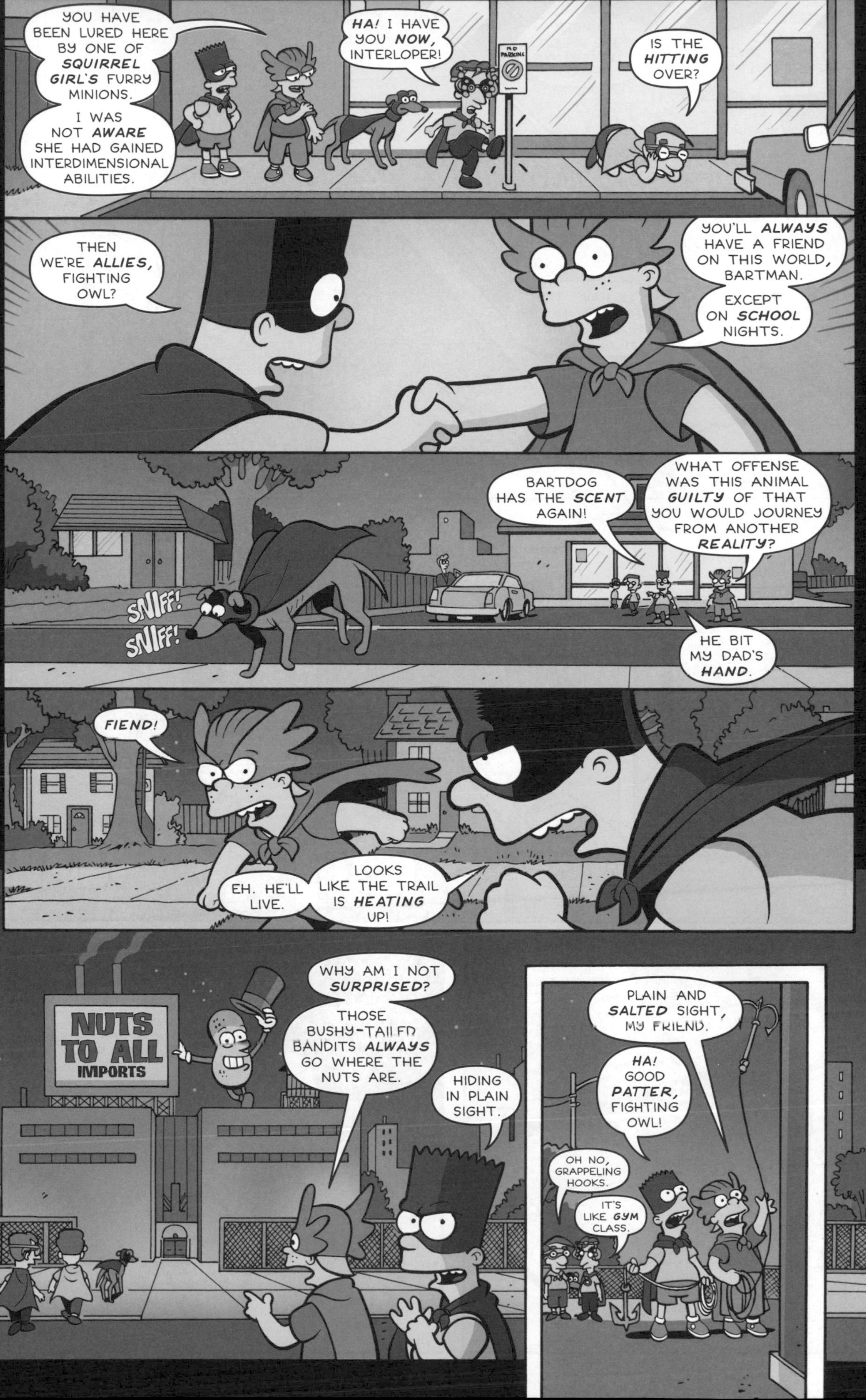

YOU HAVE BEEN LURED HERE BY ONE OF SQUIRREL GIRL'S FURRY MINIONS.
I WAS NOT AWARE SHE HAD GAINED INTERDIMENSIONAL ABILITIES.
HA! I HAVE YOU NOW, INTERLOPER!
NO PARKING
IS THE HITTING OVER?
THEN WE'RE ALLIES, FIGHTING OWL?
YOU'LL ALWAYS HAVE A FRIEND ON THIS WORLD, BARTMAN.
EXCEPT ON SCHOOL NIGHTS.
SNIFF! SNIFF!
BARTDOG HAS THE SCENT AGAIN!
WHAT OFFENSE WAS THIS ANIMAL GUILTY OF THAT YOU WOULD JOURNEY FROM ANOTHER REALITY?
HE BIT MY DAD'S HAND.
FIEND!
EH. HE'LL LIVE.
LOOKS LIKE THE TRAIL IS HEATING UP!
NUTS TO ALL IMPORTS
WHY AM I NOT SURPRISED?
THOSE BUSHY-TAILED BANDITS ALWAYS GO WHERE THE NUTS ARE.
HIDING IN PLAIN SIGHT.
PLAIN AND SALTED SIGHT, MY FRIEND.
HA! GOOD PATTER, FIGHTING OWL!
OH NO, GRAPPELING HOOKS.
IT'S LIKE GYM CLASS.

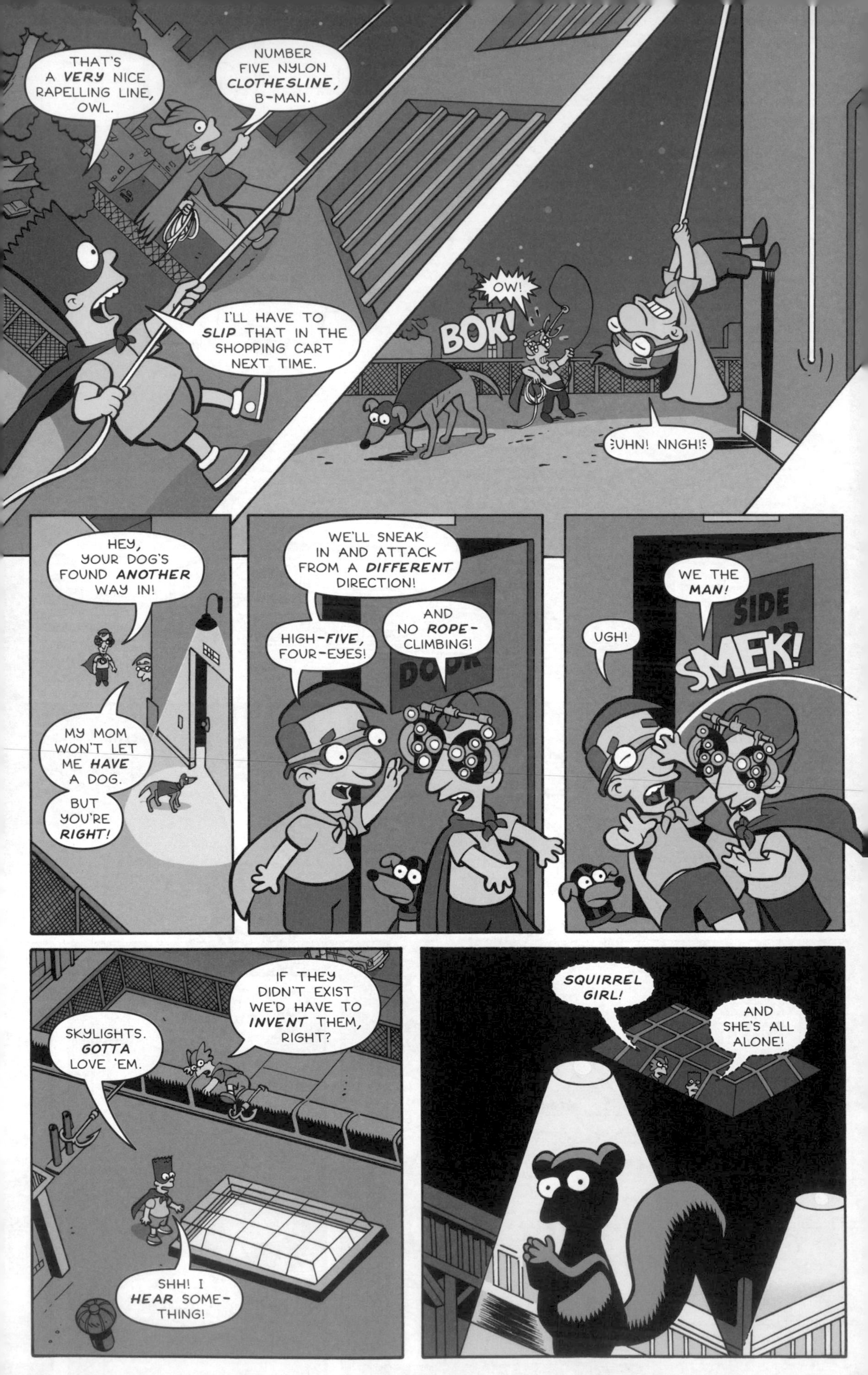

THAT'S A VERY NICE RAPELLING LINE, OWL.
NUMBER FIVE NYLON CLOTHESLINE, B-MAN.
I'LL HAVE TO SLIP THAT IN THE SHOPPING CART NEXT TIME.
OW!
BOK!
UHN! NNGH!
HEY, YOUR DOG'S FOUND ANOTHER WAY IN!
MY MOM WON'T LET ME HAVE A DOG.
BUT YOU'RE RIGHT!
WE'LL SNEAK IN AND ATTACK FROM A DIFFERENT DIRECTION!
HIGH-FIVE, FOUR-EYES!
AND NO ROPE-CLIMBING!
WE THE MAN!
UGH!
SMEK!
SKYLIGHTS. GOTTA LOVE 'EM.
IF THEY DIDN'T EXIST WE'D HAVE TO INVENT THEM, RIGHT?
SHH! I HEAR SOME-THING!
SQUIRREL GIRL!
AND SHE'S ALL ALONE!

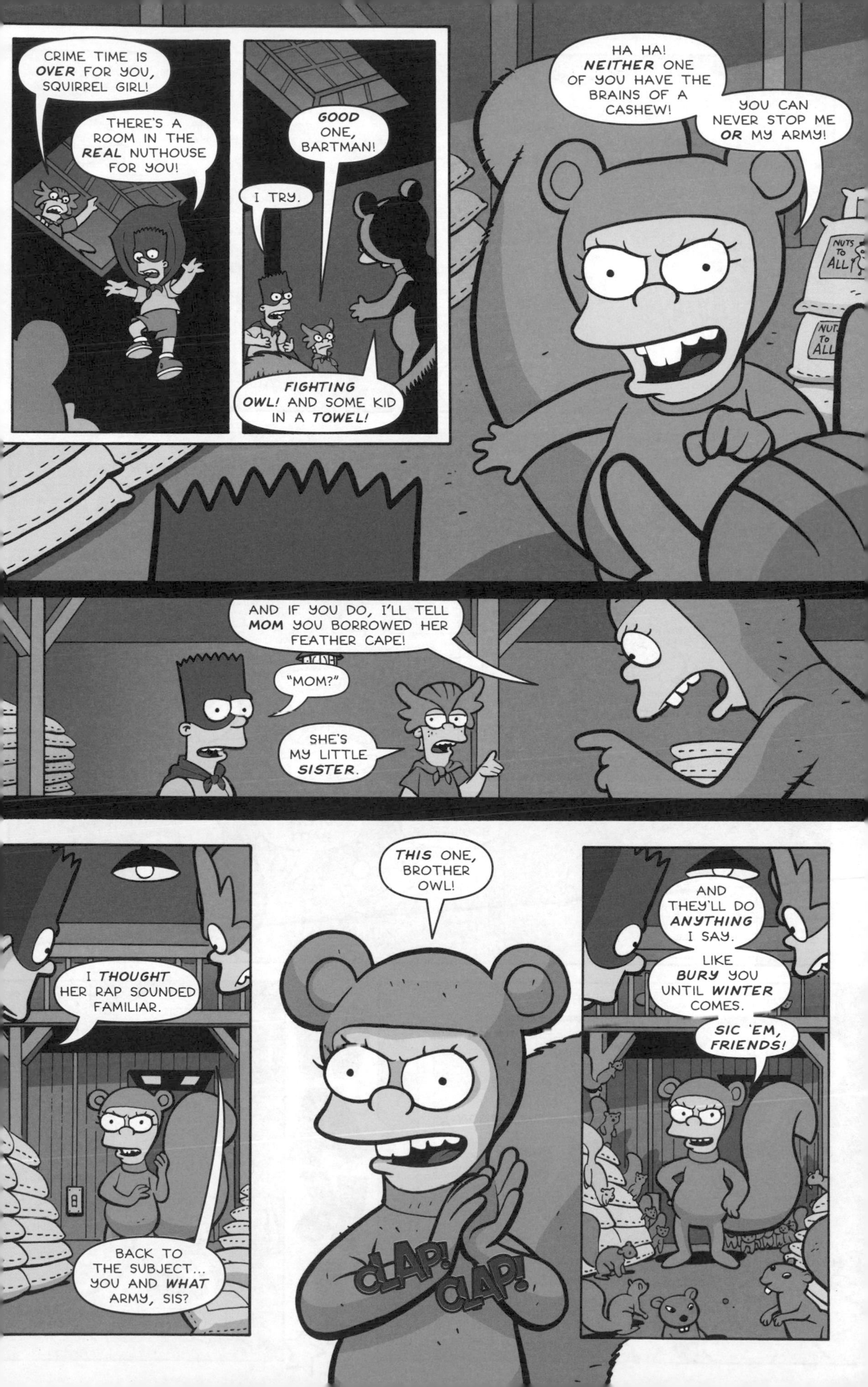
CRIME TIME IS OVER FOR YOU, SQUIRREL GIRL!
THERE'S A ROOM IN THE REAL NUTHOUSE FOR YOU!
GOOD ONE, BARTMAN!
I TRY.
FIGHTING OWL! AND SOME KID IN A TOWEL!
HA HA! NEITHER ONE OF YOU HAVE THE BRAINS OF A CASHEW!
YOU CAN NEVER STOP ME OR MY ARMY!
NUTS TO ALL!
NUTS TO ALL
AND IF YOU DO, I'LL TELL MOM YOU BORROWED HER FEATHER CAPE!
"MOM?"
SHE'S MY LITTLE SISTER.
I THOUGHT HER RAP SOUNDED FAMILIAR.
BACK TO THE SUBJECT... YOU AND WHAT ARMY, SIS?
THIS ONE, BROTHER OWL!
CLAP! CLAP!
AND THEY'LL DO ANYTHING I SAY.
LIKE BURY YOU UNTIL WINTER COMES.
SIC 'EM, FRIENDS!

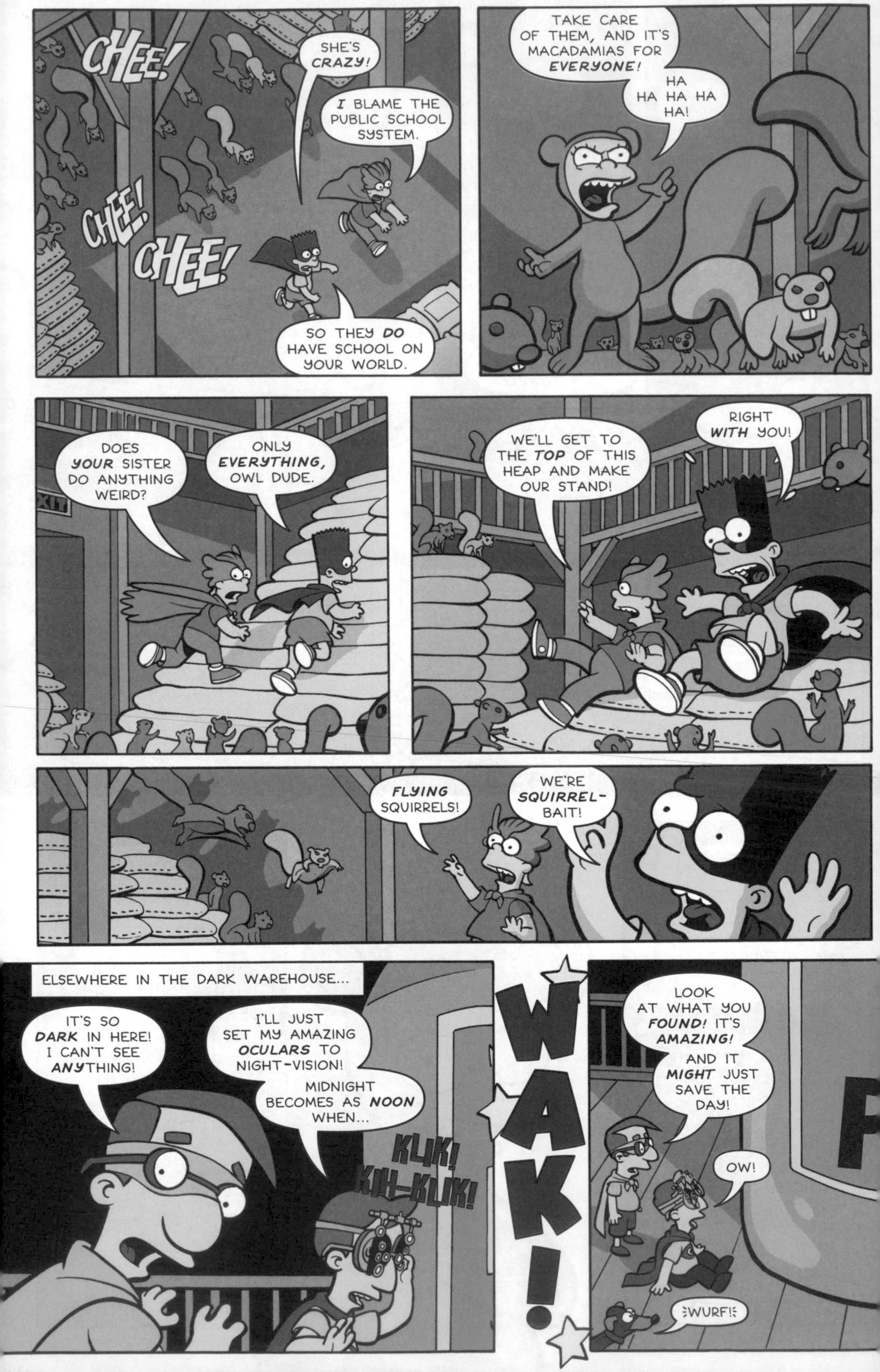
CHEE!
SHE'S CRAZY!
I BLAME THE PUBLIC SCHOOL SYSTEM.
CHEE!
CHEE!
SO THEY DO HAVE SCHOOL ON YOUR WORLD.
TAKE CARE OF THEM, AND IT'S MACADAMIAS FOR EVERYONE!
HA HA HA HA HA!
DOES YOUR SISTER DO ANYTHING WEIRD?
ONLY EVERYTHING, OWL DUDE.
WE'LL GET TO THE TOP OF THIS HEAP AND MAKE OUR STAND!
RIGHT WITH YOU!
FLYING SQUIRRELS!
WE'RE SQUIRREL-BAIT!
ELSEWHERE IN THE DARK WAREHOUSE...
IT'S SO DARK IN HERE! I CAN'T SEE ANYTHING!
I'LL JUST SET MY AMAZING OCULARS TO NIGHT-VISION!
MIDNIGHT BECOMES AS NOON WHEN...
KLIK! KIH-KLIK!
WAK!
LOOK AT WHAT YOU FOUND! IT'S AMAZING!
AND IT MIGHT JUST SAVE THE DAY!
OW!
WURF!

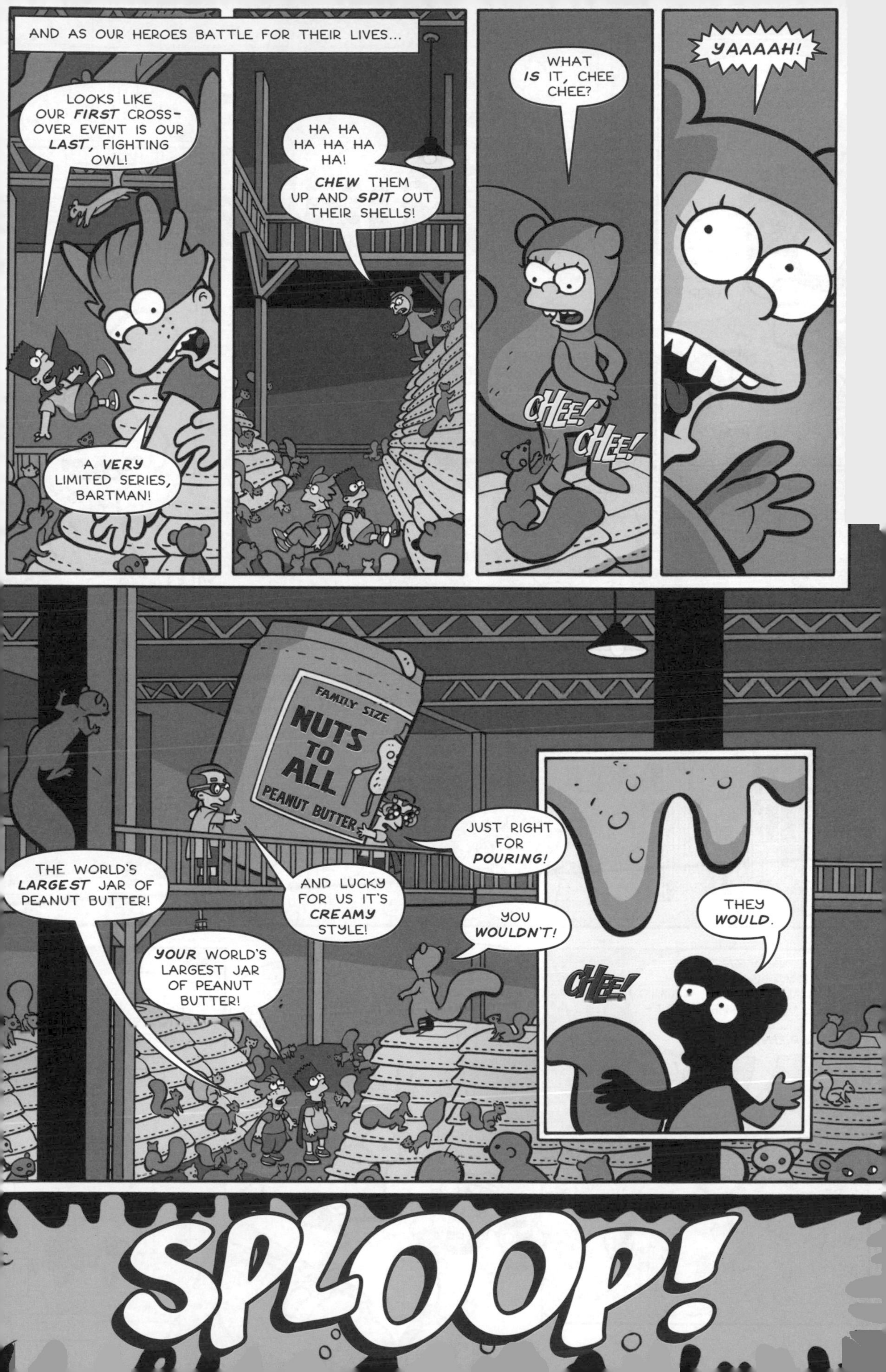

AND AS OUR HEROES BATTLE FOR THEIR LIVES...
LOOKS LIKE OUR FIRST CROSS-OVER EVENT IS OUR LAST, FIGHTING OWL!
A VERY LIMITED SERIES, BARTMAN!
HA HA HA HA HA HA!
CHEW THEM UP AND SPIT OUT THEIR SHELLS!
WHAT IS IT, CHEE CHEE?
CHEE! CHEE!
YAAAAH!
FAMILY SIZE
NUTS TO ALL
PEANUT BUTTER
THE WORLD'S LARGEST JAR OF PEANUT BUTTER!
AND LUCKY FOR US IT'S CREAMY STYLE!
JUST RIGHT FOR POURING!
YOUR WORLD'S LARGEST JAR OF PEANUT BUTTER!
YOU WOULDN'T!
CHEE!
THEY WOULD.
SPLOOP!

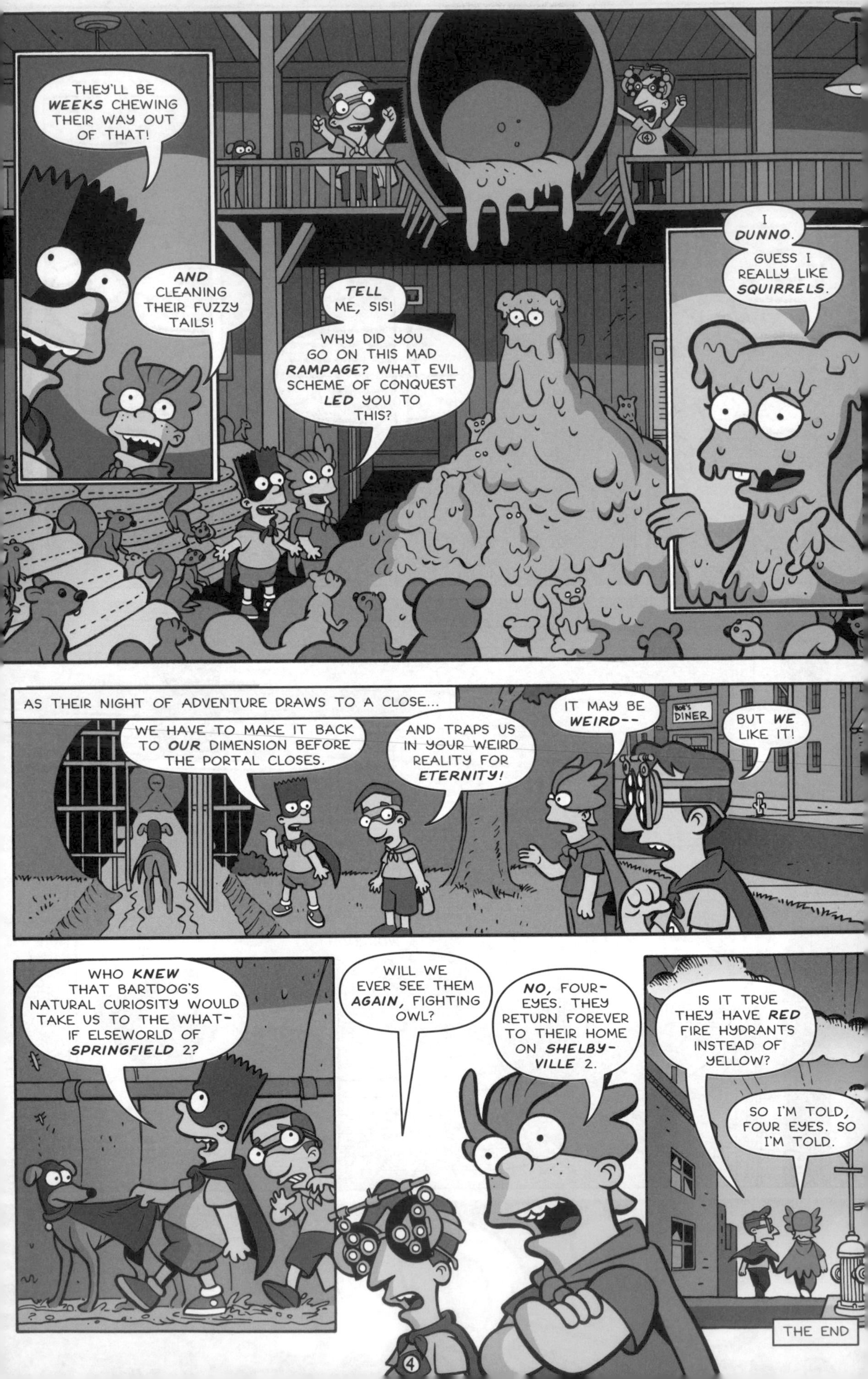

THEY'LL BE WEEKS CHEWING THEIR WAY OUT OF THAT!
AND CLEANING THEIR FUZZY TAILS!
TELL ME, SIS!
WHY DID YOU GO ON THIS MAD RAMPAGE? WHAT EVIL SCHEME OF CONQUEST LED YOU TO THIS?
I DUNNO.
GUESS I REALLY LIKE SQUIRRELS.
AS THEIR NIGHT OF ADVENTURE DRAWS TO A CLOSE...
WE HAVE TO MAKE IT BACK TO OUR DIMENSION BEFORE THE PORTAL CLOSES.
AND TRAPS US IN YOUR WEIRD REALITY FOR ETERNITY!
IT MAY BE WEIRD--
BOB'S DINER
BUT WE LIKE IT!
WHO KNEW THAT BARTDOG'S NATURAL CURIOSITY WOULD TAKE US TO THE WHAT-IF ELSEWORLD OF SPRINGFIELD 2?
WILL WE EVER SEE THEM AGAIN, FIGHTING OWL?
NO, FOUR-EYES. THEY RETURN FOREVER TO THEIR HOME ON SHELBYVILLE 2.
IS IT TRUE THEY HAVE RED FIRE HYDRANTS INSTEAD OF YELLOW?
SO I'M TOLD, FOUR EYES. SO I'M TOLD.
THE END

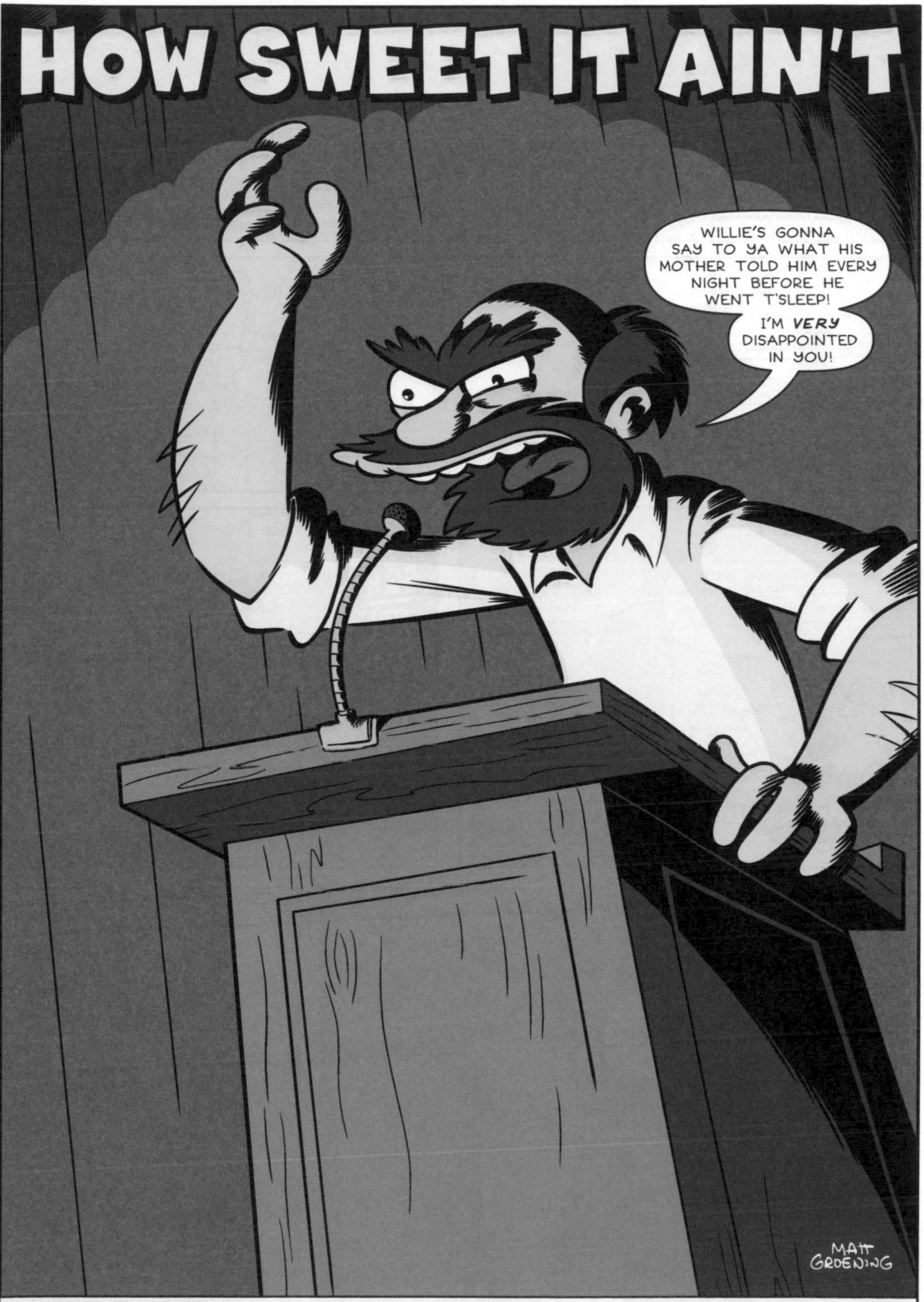
HOW SWEET IT AIN'T
WILLIE'S GONNA SAY TO YA WHAT HIS MOTHER TOLD HIM EVERY NIGHT BEFORE HE WENT T'SLEEP!
I'M **VERY** DISAPPOINTED IN YOU!
MATT GROENING

IAN BOOTHBY SCRIPT | **JOHN DELANEY** PENCILS | **DAN DAVIS** INKS | **ART VILLANUEVA** COLORS | **KAREN BATES** LETTERS | **BILL MORRISON** EDITOR

YOU WEE LADS AND LASSIES ARE ALL IN WORSE SHAPE THAN ME GRANDMA'S BAGPIPES!

"YE CANNA KEEP UP IN GYM CLASS!"

≋WHEEZE≋ ARE WE THERE YET?

NO, IT'S A HUNDRED-YARD DASH! YOU'VE GOT NINETY-FIVE YARDS TO GO!

"THE BULLIES ARE SLACKIN' OFF!"

YEAH, WE STILL WANT YOUR LUNCH MONEY, BUT WE'VE OUTSOURCED THE BEATINGS.

HAND OVER YOUR EUROS, OR I'LL GIVE YOUR TULIPS SUCH A CLOGGING!

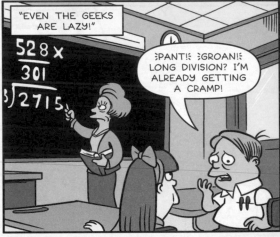

"EVEN THE GEEKS ARE LAZY!"

$$5\,2\,8\,\times$$
$$\overline{3\,0\,1}$$
$$5\,)\overline{2\,7\,1\,5}$$

≋PANT!≋ ≋GROAN!≋ LONG DIVISION? I'M ALREADY GETTING A CRAMP!

I HAVE A TWO-PART QUESTION. ONE...CAN YOU NOT STAND SO CLOSE TO THE EDGE OF THE STAGE IN THAT *KILT*?

AND TWO... MAYBE WE'RE ALL TIRED, BUT WHAT DO YOU WANT US TO *DO* ABOUT IT?

I'LL *TELL* YA, YE FOUR-EYED PANTS-WEARIN' PRISS!

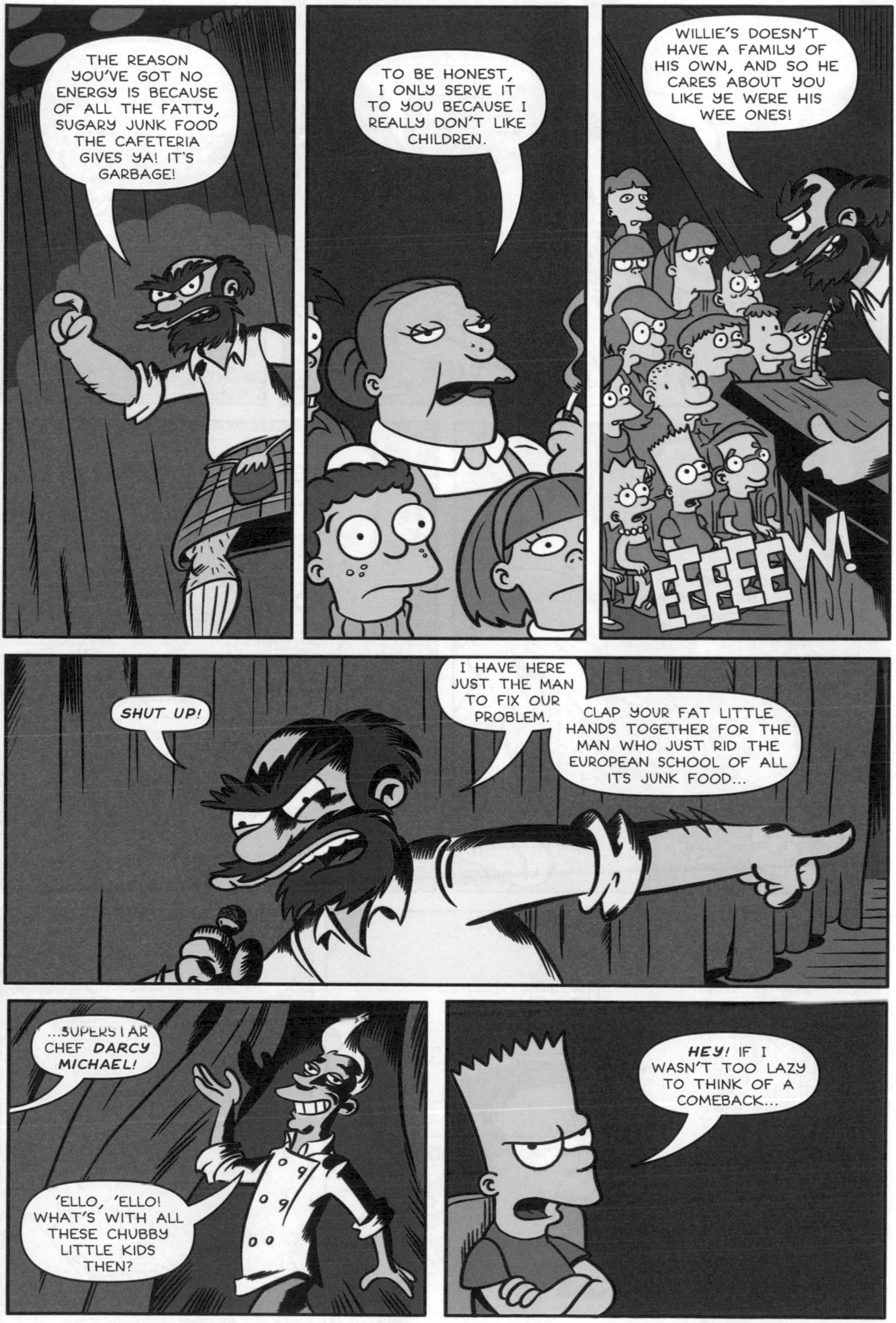
THE REASON YOU'VE GOT NO ENERGY IS BECAUSE OF ALL THE FATTY, SUGARY JUNK FOOD THE CAFETERIA GIVES YA! IT'S GARBAGE!
TO BE HONEST, I ONLY SERVE IT TO YOU BECAUSE I REALLY DON'T LIKE CHILDREN.
WILLIE'S DOESN'T HAVE A FAMILY OF HIS OWN, AND SO HE CARES ABOUT YOU LIKE YE WERE HIS WEE ONES!
EEEEEW!
SHUT UP!
I HAVE HERE JUST THE MAN TO FIX OUR PROBLEM.
CLAP YOUR FAT LITTLE HANDS TOGETHER FOR THE MAN WHO JUST RID THE EUROPEAN SCHOOL OF ALL ITS JUNK FOOD...
...SUPERSTAR CHEF DARCY MICHAEL!
'ELLO, 'ELLO! WHAT'S WITH ALL THESE CHUBBY LITTLE KIDS THEN?
HEY! IF I WASN'T TOO LAZY TO THINK OF A COMEBACK...

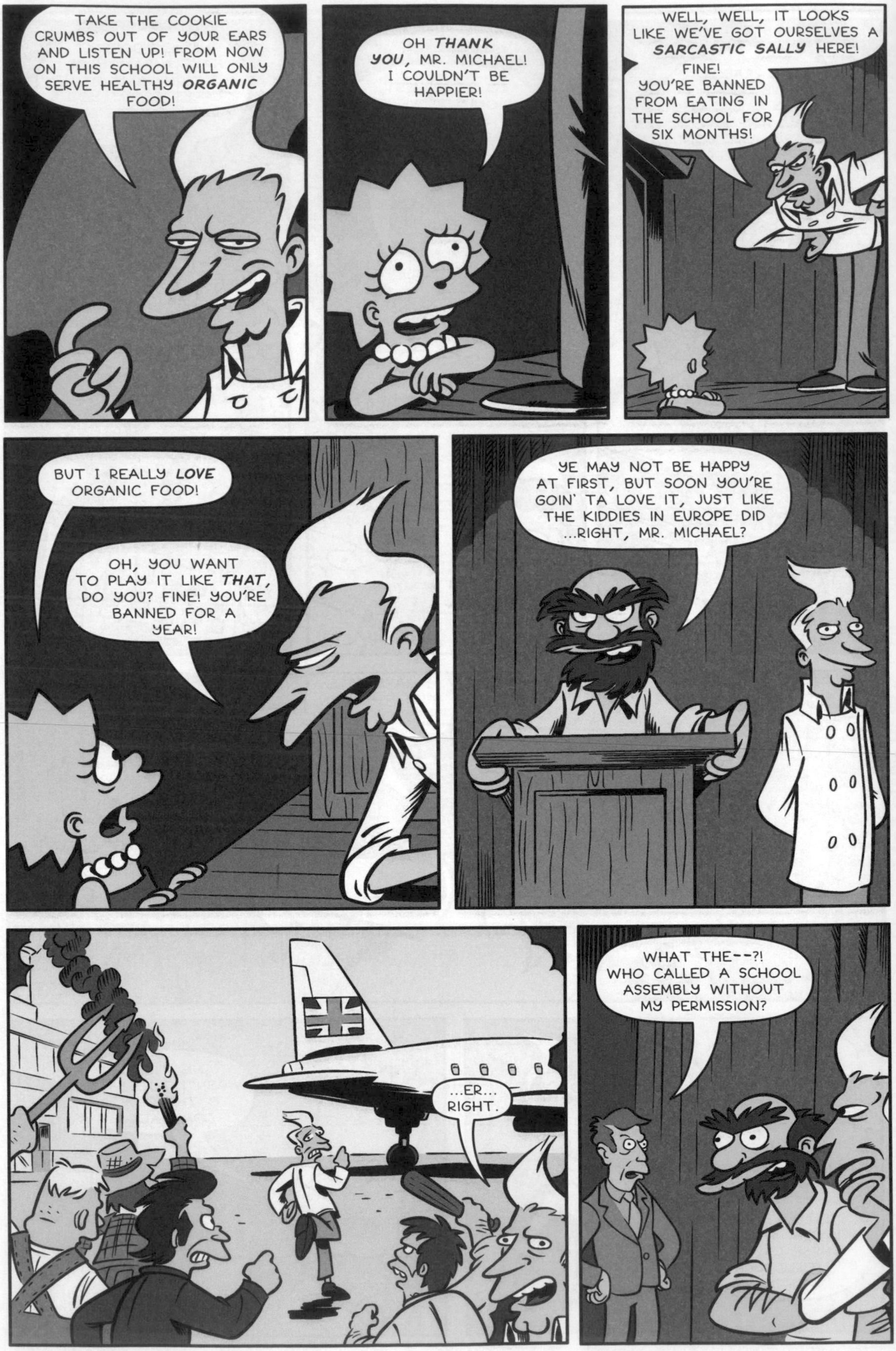
TAKE THE COOKIE CRUMBS OUT OF YOUR EARS AND LISTEN UP! FROM NOW ON THIS SCHOOL WILL ONLY SERVE HEALTHY ORGANIC FOOD!
OH THANK YOU, MR. MICHAEL! I COULDN'T BE HAPPIER!
WELL, WELL, IT LOOKS LIKE WE'VE GOT OURSELVES A SARCASTIC SALLY HERE!
FINE! YOU'RE BANNED FROM EATING IN THE SCHOOL FOR SIX MONTHS!
BUT I REALLY LOVE ORGANIC FOOD!
OH, YOU WANT TO PLAY IT LIKE THAT, DO YOU? FINE! YOU'RE BANNED FOR A YEAR!
YE MAY NOT BE HAPPY AT FIRST, BUT SOON YOU'RE GOIN' TA LOVE IT, JUST LIKE THE KIDDIES IN EUROPE DID ...RIGHT, MR. MICHAEL?
...ER... RIGHT.
WHAT THE--?! WHO CALLED A SCHOOL ASSEMBLY WITHOUT MY PERMISSION?

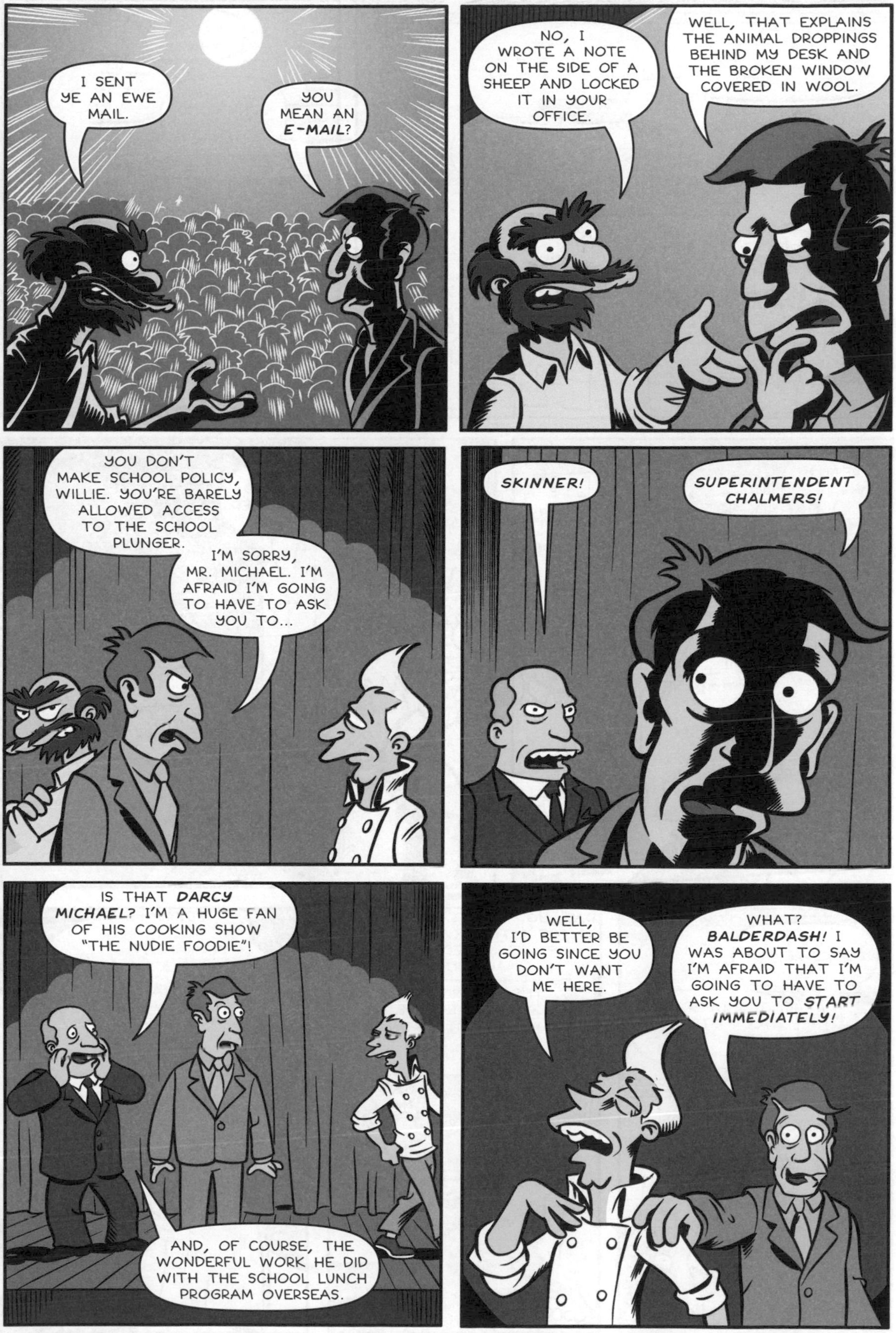
I SENT YE AN EWE MAIL.
YOU MEAN AN E-MAIL?
NO, I WROTE A NOTE ON THE SIDE OF A SHEEP AND LOCKED IT IN YOUR OFFICE.
WELL, THAT EXPLAINS THE ANIMAL DROPPINGS BEHIND MY DESK AND THE BROKEN WINDOW COVERED IN WOOL.
YOU DON'T MAKE SCHOOL POLICY, WILLIE. YOU'RE BARELY ALLOWED ACCESS TO THE SCHOOL PLUNGER.
I'M SORRY, MR. MICHAEL. I'M AFRAID I'M GOING TO HAVE TO ASK YOU TO...
SKINNER!
SUPERINTENDENT CHALMERS!
IS THAT DARCY MICHAEL? I'M A HUGE FAN OF HIS COOKING SHOW "THE NUDIE FOODIE"!
AND, OF COURSE, THE WONDERFUL WORK HE DID WITH THE SCHOOL LUNCH PROGRAM OVERSEAS.
WELL, I'D BETTER BE GOING SINCE YOU DON'T WANT ME HERE.
WHAT? BALDERDASH! I WAS ABOUT TO SAY I'M AFRAID THAT I'M GOING TO HAVE TO ASK YOU TO START IMMEDIATELY!

IT'S NOT FAIR!

LISA'S RIGHT! WE NEED JUNK FOOD!

THAT'S NOT WHAT I--

BANNING JUNK FOOD AT SCHOOL? THAT'S *UNCONSTITUTIONAL*!

REALLY?

NO, NOT REALLY.

WELL, LET'S JUST CHECK THE CONSTITUTION AND SEE.

HERE IT IS, BEHIND THE BOARD GAMES WE BORROWED FROM FLANDERS!

The Constitution of the United States of America

We the people of the United States...

HOLYOPOLY

ANTS IN THE SINNER'S PANTS

THAT LOOKS REALLY OLD.

IT SHOULD, IT WAS WRITTEN IN 1500 OR SOMETHING.

DAD, YOU'RE NOT SAYING THIS IS THE *ACTUAL* CONSTITUTION OF THE UNITED STATES, ARE YOU?

IT'S A LONG STORY. CRAZY ADVENTURE, A FEW CELEBRITY CAMEOS, HMMM...I DON'T SEE IT IN HERE.

BUT IF WE ADD IT IN PERMANENT MARKER! *THAT*, BOY, IS CALLED *AN AMENDMENT*!

¡GASP!¡

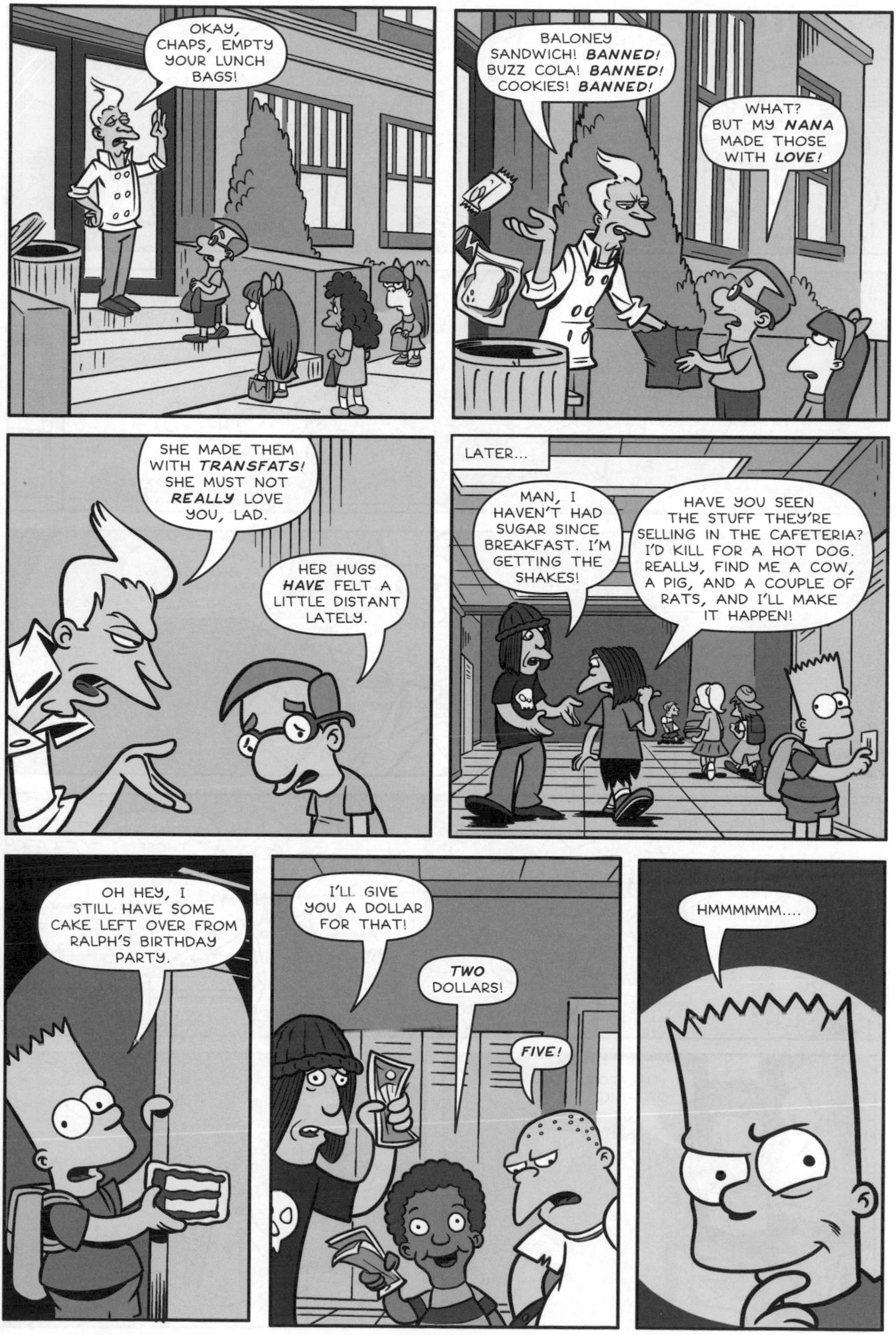
OKAY, CHAPS, EMPTY YOUR LUNCH BAGS!
BALONEY SANDWICH! BANNED! BUZZ COLA! BANNED! COOKIES! BANNED!
WHAT? BUT MY NANA MADE THOSE WITH LOVE!
SHE MADE THEM WITH TRANSFATS! SHE MUST NOT REALLY LOVE YOU, LAD.
HER HUGS HAVE FELT A LITTLE DISTANT LATELY.
LATER...
MAN, I HAVEN'T HAD SUGAR SINCE BREAKFAST. I'M GETTING THE SHAKES!
HAVE YOU SEEN THE STUFF THEY'RE SELLING IN THE CAFETERIA? I'D KILL FOR A HOT DOG. REALLY, FIND ME A COW, A PIG, AND A COUPLE OF RATS, AND I'LL MAKE IT HAPPEN!
OH HEY, I STILL HAVE SOME CAKE LEFT OVER FROM RALPH'S BIRTHDAY PARTY.
I'LL GIVE YOU A DOLLAR FOR THAT!
TWO DOLLARS!
FIVE!
HMMMMMM....

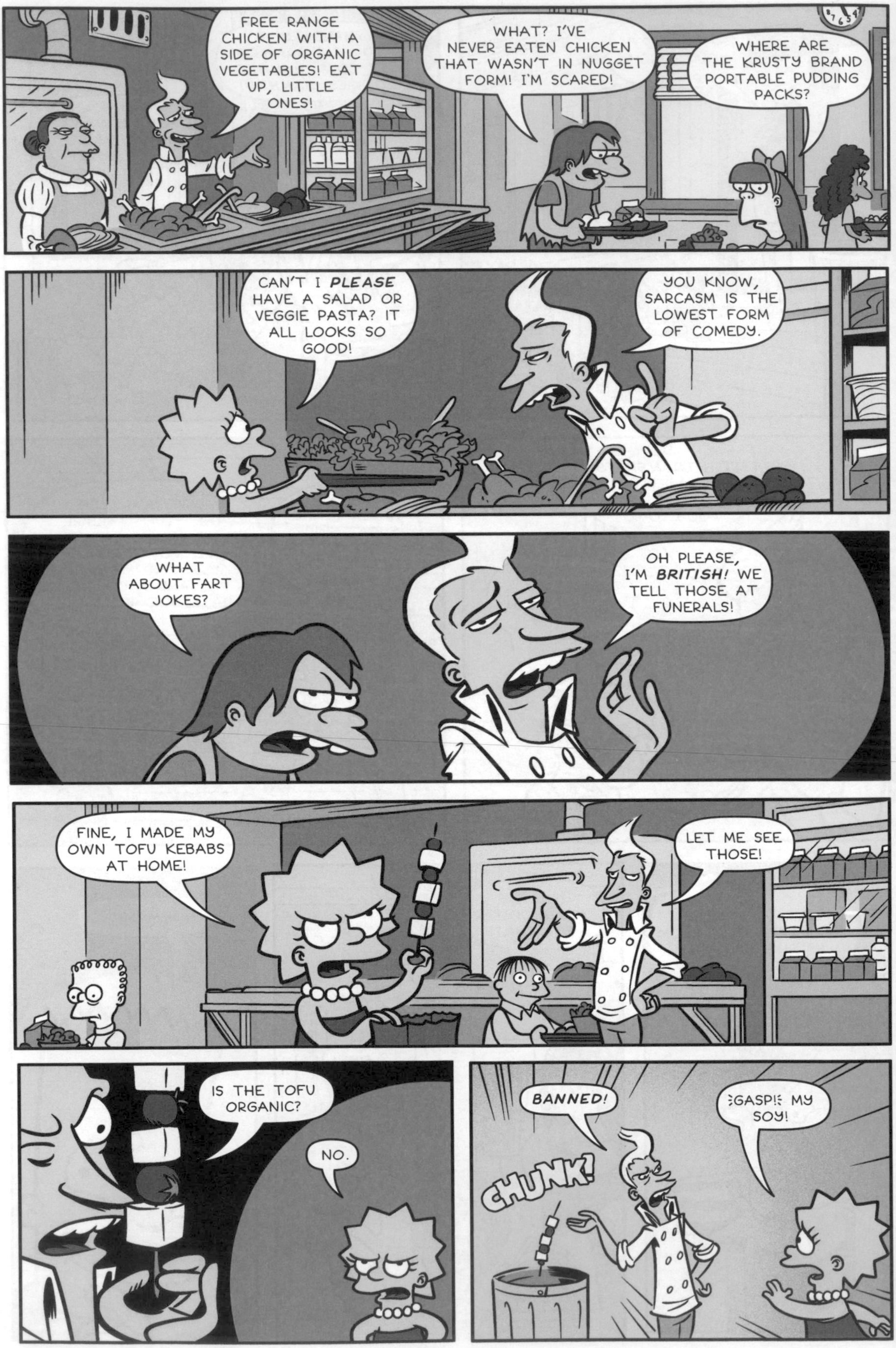
FREE RANGE CHICKEN WITH A SIDE OF ORGANIC VEGETABLES! EAT UP, LITTLE ONES!
WHAT? I'VE NEVER EATEN CHICKEN THAT WASN'T IN NUGGET FORM! I'M SCARED!
WHERE ARE THE KRUSTY BRAND PORTABLE PUDDING PACKS?
CAN'T I *PLEASE* HAVE A SALAD OR VEGGIE PASTA? IT ALL LOOKS SO GOOD!
YOU KNOW, SARCASM IS THE LOWEST FORM OF COMEDY.
WHAT ABOUT FART JOKES?
OH PLEASE, I'M *BRITISH!* WE TELL THOSE AT FUNERALS!
FINE, I MADE MY OWN TOFU KEBABS AT HOME!
LET ME SEE THOSE!
IS THE TOFU ORGANIC?
NO.
BANNED!
CHUNK!
GASP! MY SOY!

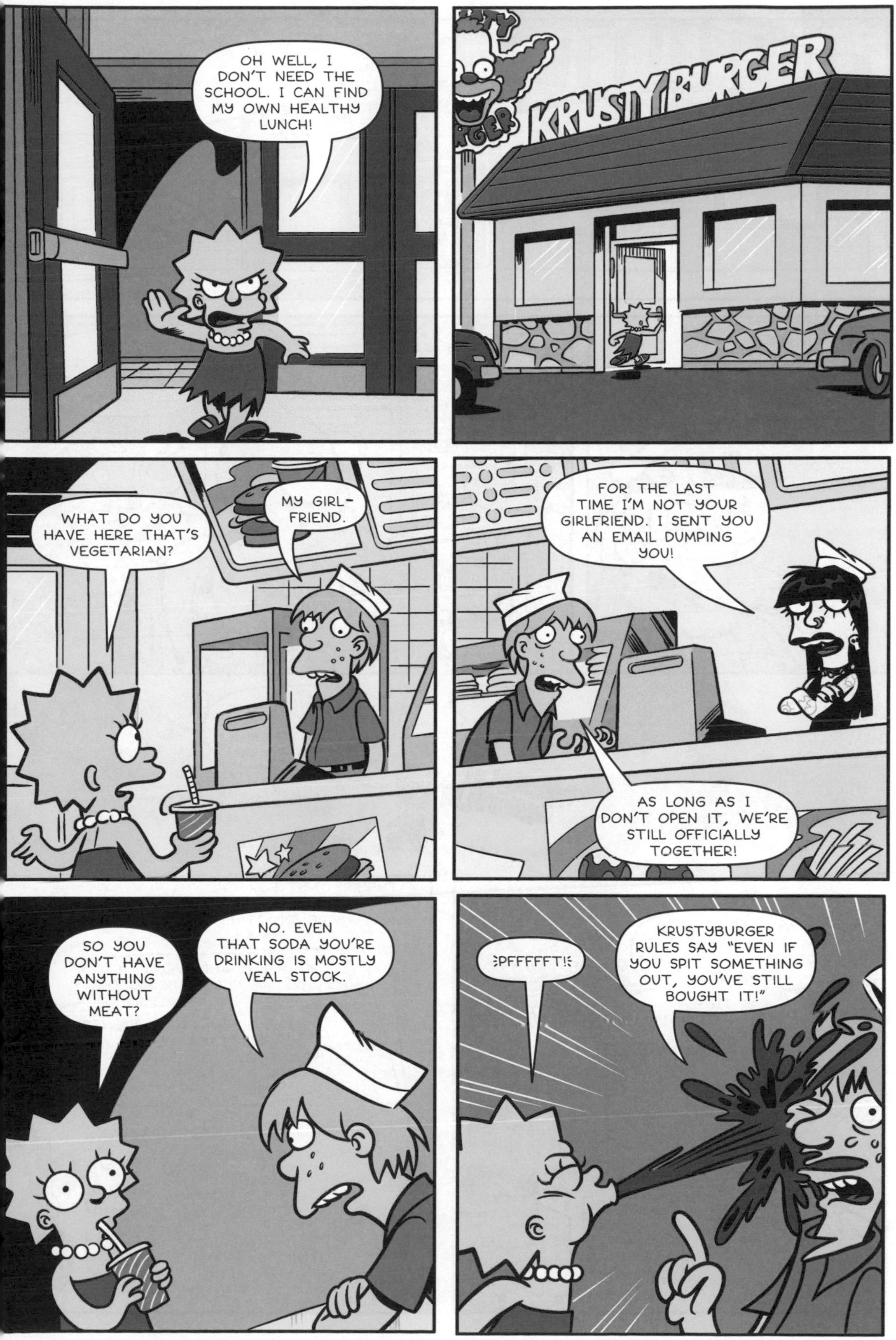
OH WELL, I DON'T NEED THE SCHOOL. I CAN FIND MY OWN HEALTHY LUNCH!
KRUSTY BURGER
WHAT DO YOU HAVE HERE THAT'S VEGETARIAN?
MY GIRL-FRIEND.
FOR THE LAST TIME I'M NOT YOUR GIRLFRIEND. I SENT YOU AN EMAIL DUMPING YOU!
AS LONG AS I DON'T OPEN IT, WE'RE STILL OFFICIALLY TOGETHER!
SO YOU DON'T HAVE ANYTHING WITHOUT MEAT?
NO. EVEN THAT SODA YOU'RE DRINKING IS MOSTLY VEAL STOCK.
PFFFFFT!
KRUSTYBURGER RULES SAY "EVEN IF YOU SPIT SOMETHING OUT, YOU'VE STILL BOUGHT IT!"

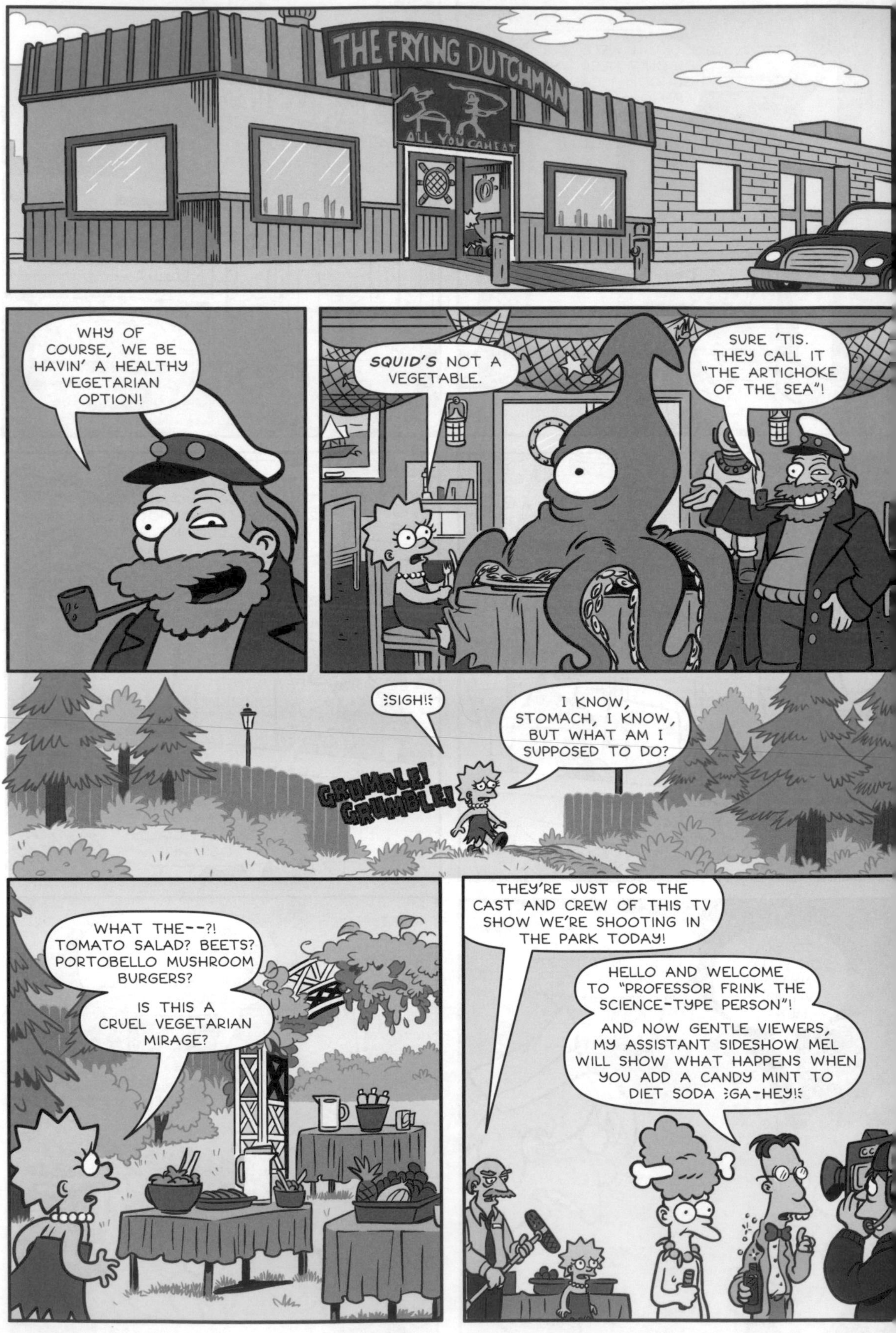
THE FRYING DUTCHMAN
ALL YOU CAN EAT
WHY OF COURSE, WE BE HAVIN' A HEALTHY VEGETARIAN OPTION!
SQUID'S NOT A VEGETABLE.
SURE 'TIS. THEY CALL IT "THE ARTICHOKE OF THE SEA"!
SIGH!
GRUMBLE! GRUMBLE!
I KNOW, STOMACH, I KNOW, BUT WHAT AM I SUPPOSED TO DO?
WHAT THE--?! TOMATO SALAD? BEETS? PORTOBELLO MUSHROOM BURGERS?
IS THIS A CRUEL VEGETARIAN MIRAGE?
THEY'RE JUST FOR THE CAST AND CREW OF THIS TV SHOW WE'RE SHOOTING IN THE PARK TODAY!
HELLO AND WELCOME TO "PROFESSOR FRINK THE SCIENCE-TYPE PERSON"!
AND NOW GENTLE VIEWERS, MY ASSISTANT SIDESHOW MEL WILL SHOW WHAT HAPPENS WHEN YOU ADD A CANDY MINT TO DIET SODA GA-HEY!

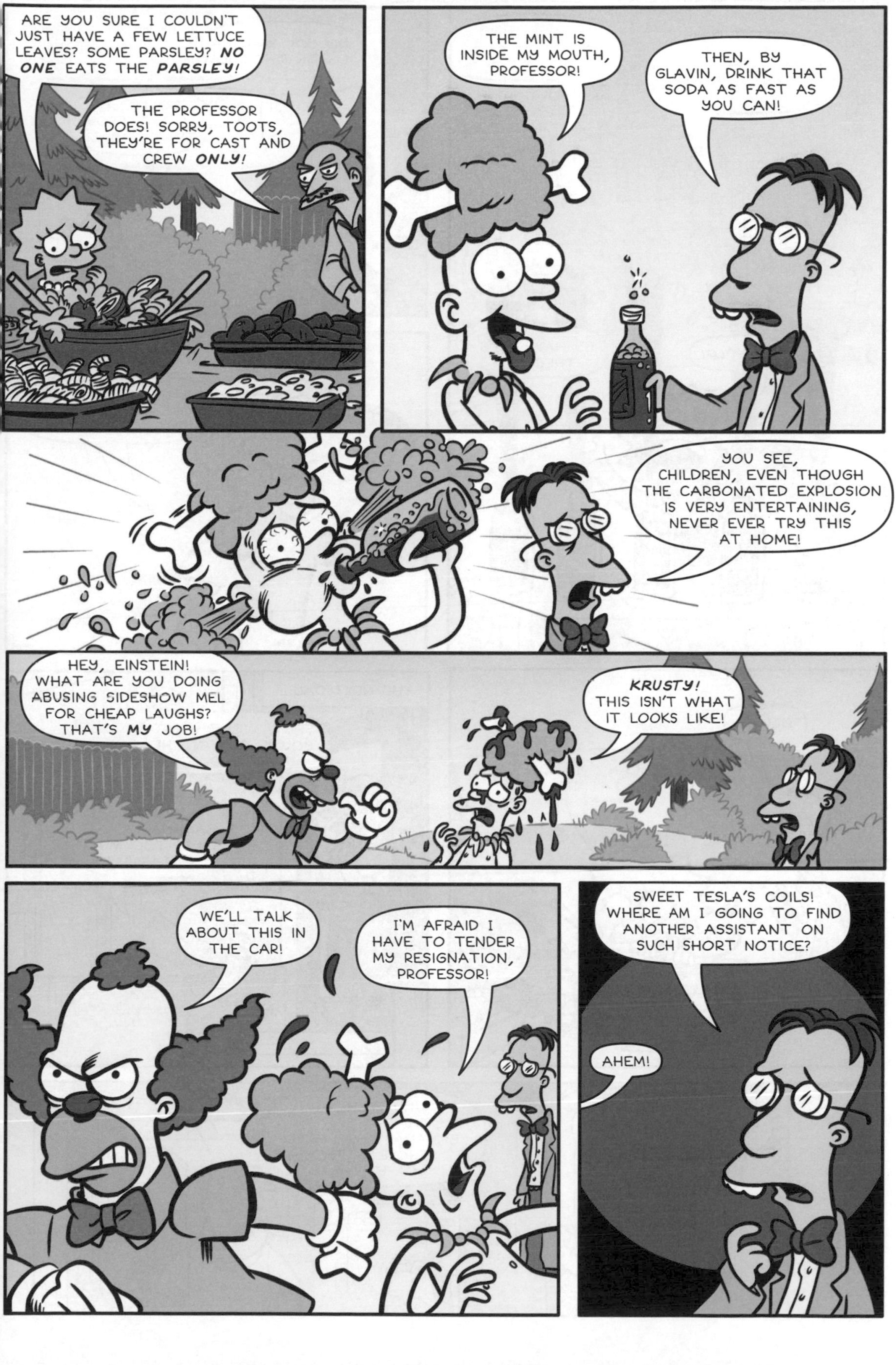

ARE YOU SURE I COULDN'T JUST HAVE A FEW LETTUCE LEAVES? SOME PARSLEY? NO ONE EATS THE PARSLEY!
THE PROFESSOR DOES! SORRY, TOOTS, THEY'RE FOR CAST AND CREW ONLY!
THE MINT IS INSIDE MY MOUTH, PROFESSOR!
THEN, BY GLAVIN, DRINK THAT SODA AS FAST AS YOU CAN!
YOU SEE, CHILDREN, EVEN THOUGH THE CARBONATED EXPLOSION IS VERY ENTERTAINING, NEVER EVER TRY THIS AT HOME!
HEY, EINSTEIN! WHAT ARE YOU DOING ABUSING SIDESHOW MEL FOR CHEAP LAUGHS? THAT'S MY JOB!
KRUSTY! THIS ISN'T WHAT IT LOOKS LIKE!
WE'LL TALK ABOUT THIS IN THE CAR!
I'M AFRAID I HAVE TO TENDER MY RESIGNATION, PROFESSOR!
SWEET TESLA'S COILS! WHERE AM I GOING TO FIND ANOTHER ASSISTANT ON SUCH SHORT NOTICE?
AHEM!

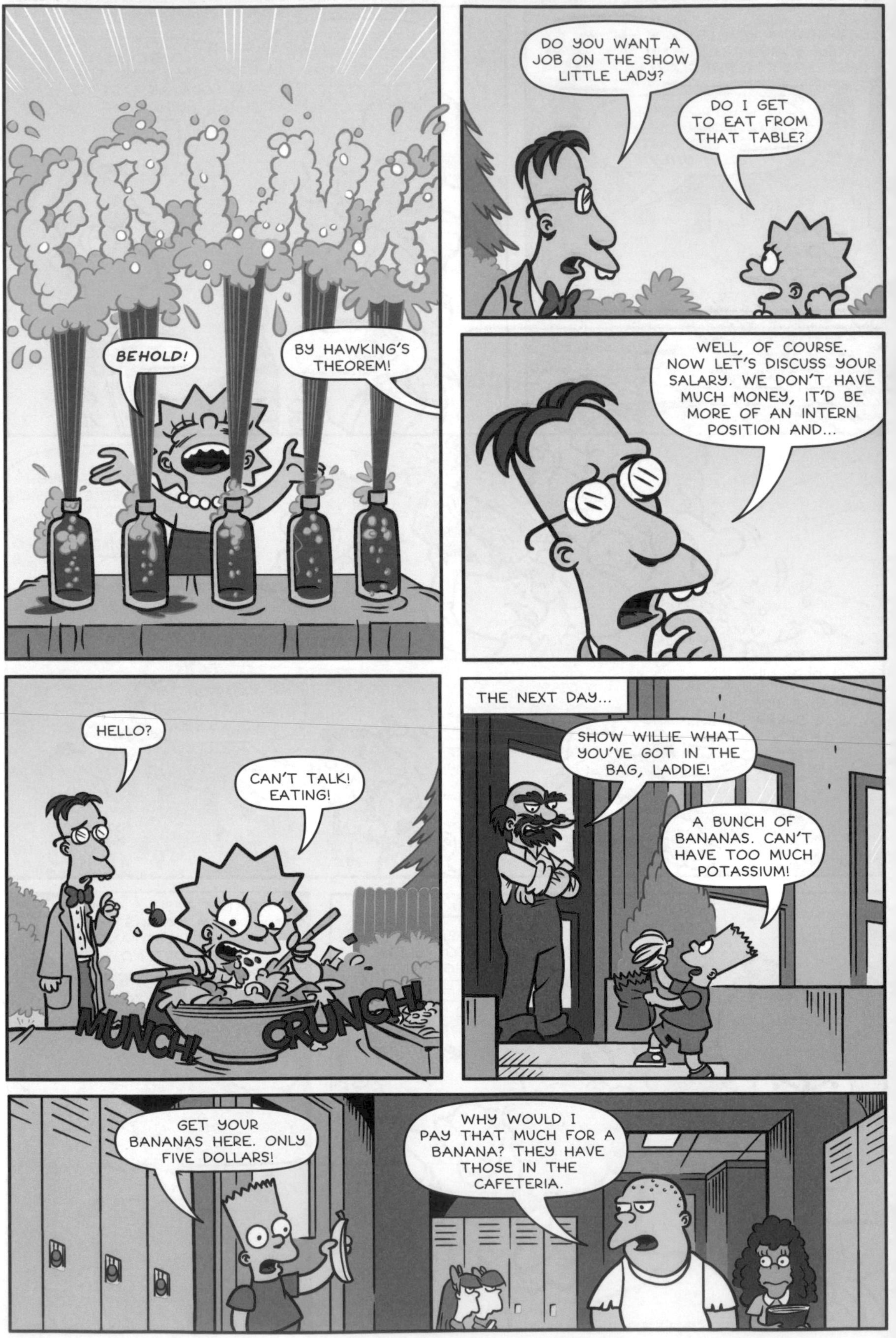
GRINK
BEHOLD!
BY HAWKING'S THEOREM!
DO YOU WANT A JOB ON THE SHOW LITTLE LADY?
DO I GET TO EAT FROM THAT TABLE?
WELL, OF COURSE. NOW LET'S DISCUSS YOUR SALARY. WE DON'T HAVE MUCH MONEY, IT'D BE MORE OF AN INTERN POSITION AND...
HELLO?
CAN'T TALK! EATING!
MUNCH!
CRUNCH!
THE NEXT DAY...
SHOW WILLIE WHAT YOU'VE GOT IN THE BAG, LADDIE!
A BUNCH OF BANANAS. CAN'T HAVE TOO MUCH POTASSIUM!
GET YOUR BANANAS HERE. ONLY FIVE DOLLARS!
WHY WOULD I PAY THAT MUCH FOR A BANANA? THEY HAVE THOSE IN THE CAFETERIA.

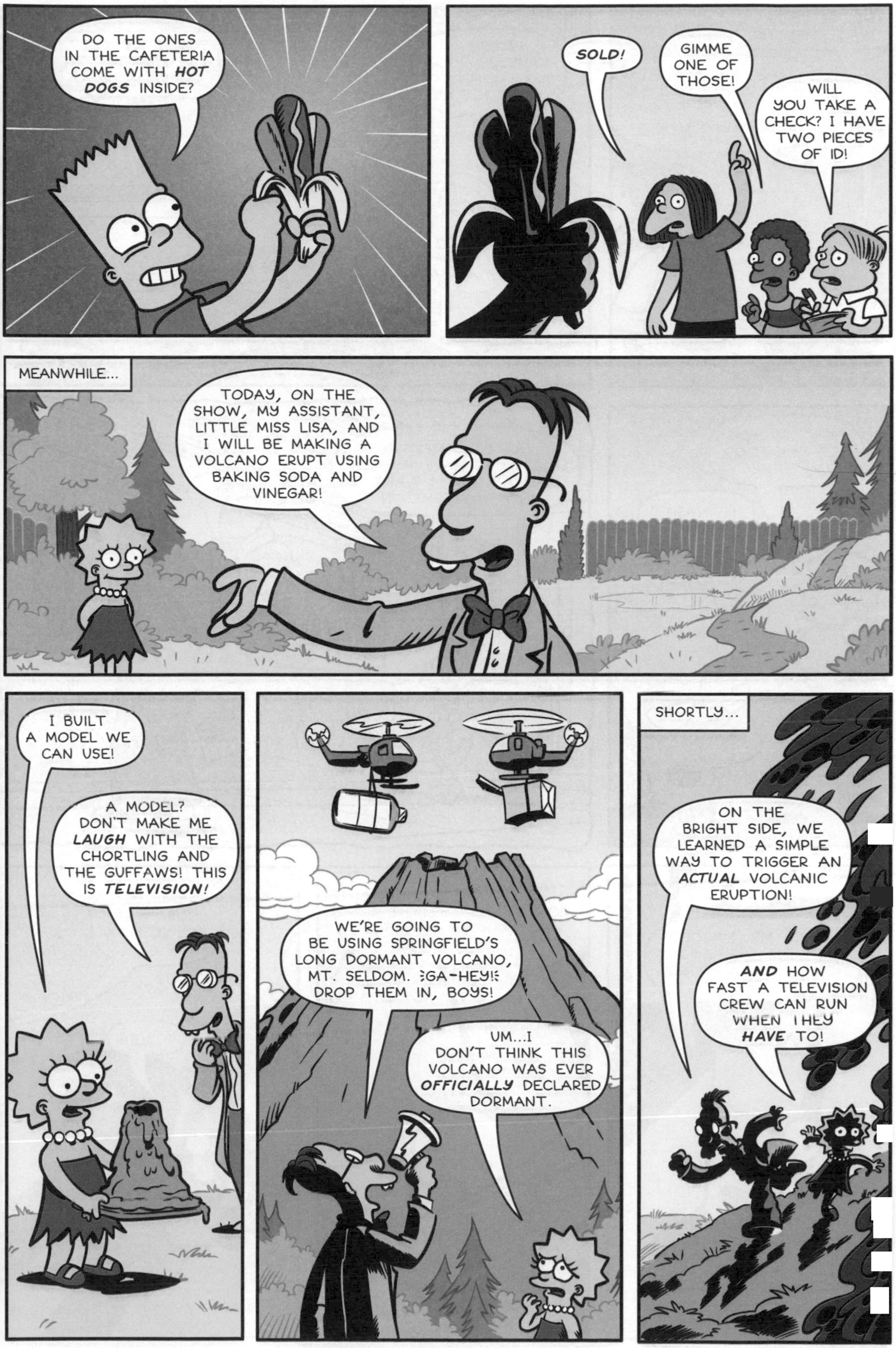
DO THE ONES IN THE CAFETERIA COME WITH HOT DOGS INSIDE?
SOLD!
GIMME ONE OF THOSE!
WILL YOU TAKE A CHECK? I HAVE TWO PIECES OF ID!
MEANWHILE...
TODAY, ON THE SHOW, MY ASSISTANT, LITTLE MISS LISA, AND I WILL BE MAKING A VOLCANO ERUPT USING BAKING SODA AND VINEGAR!
I BUILT A MODEL WE CAN USE!
A MODEL? DON'T MAKE ME LAUGH WITH THE CHORTLING AND THE GUFFAWS! THIS IS TELEVISION!
WE'RE GOING TO BE USING SPRINGFIELD'S LONG DORMANT VOLCANO, MT. SELDOM. GA-HEY! DROP THEM IN, BOYS!
UM...I DON'T THINK THIS VOLCANO WAS EVER OFFICIALLY DECLARED DORMANT.
SHORTLY...
ON THE BRIGHT SIDE, WE LEARNED A SIMPLE WAY TO TRIGGER AN ACTUAL VOLCANIC ERUPTION!
AND HOW FAST A TELEVISION CREW CAN RUN WHEN THEY HAVE TO!

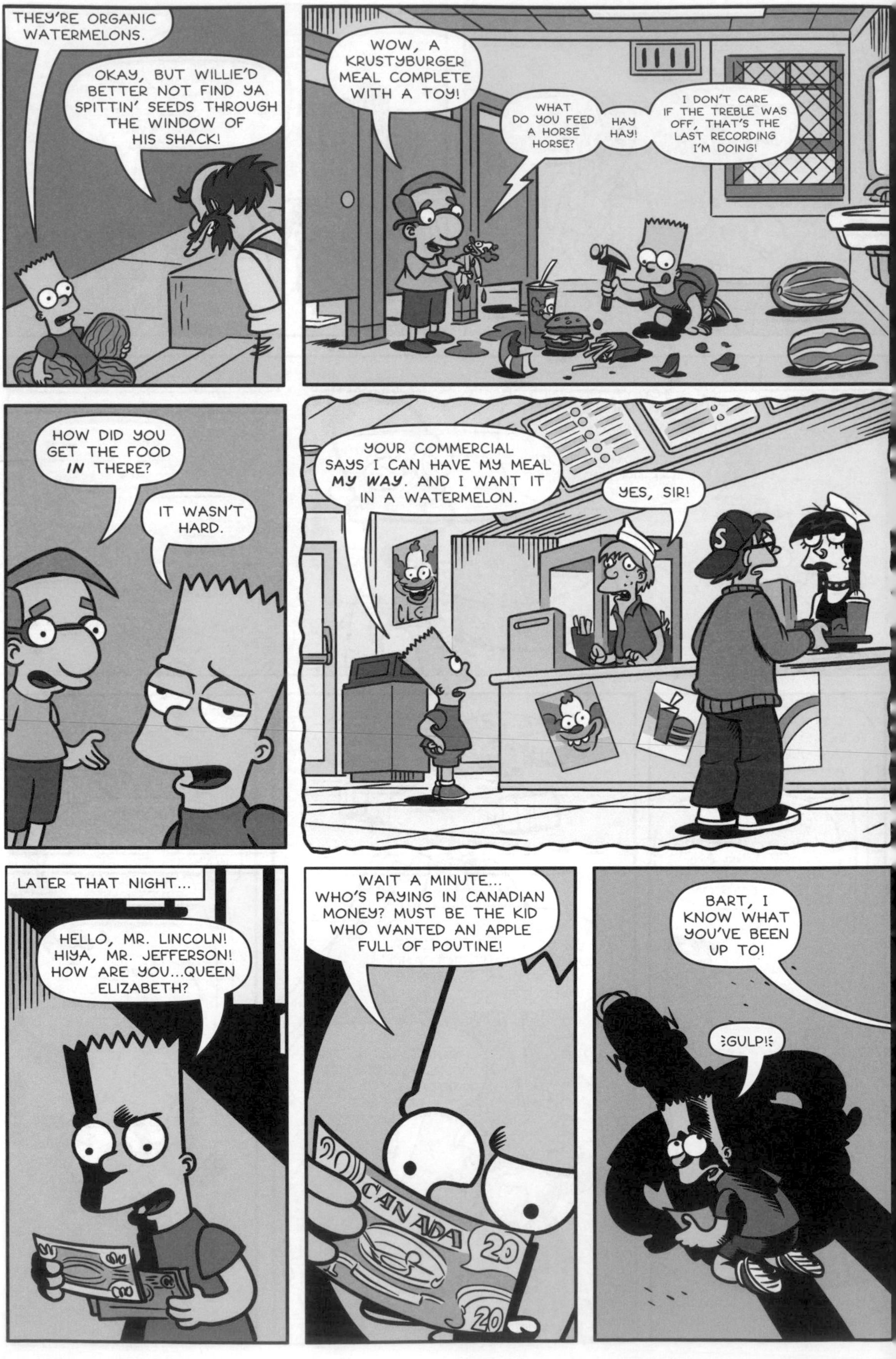
THEY'RE ORGANIC WATERMELONS.
OKAY, BUT WILLIE'D BETTER NOT FIND YA SPITTIN' SEEDS THROUGH THE WINDOW OF HIS SHACK!
WOW, A KRUSTYBURGER MEAL COMPLETE WITH A TOY!
WHAT DO YOU FEED A HORSE HORSE?
HAY HAY!
I DON'T CARE IF THE TREBLE WAS OFF, THAT'S THE LAST RECORDING I'M DOING!
HOW DID YOU GET THE FOOD IN THERE?
IT WASN'T HARD.
YOUR COMMERCIAL SAYS I CAN HAVE MY MEAL MY WAY. AND I WANT IT IN A WATERMELON.
YES, SIR!
LATER THAT NIGHT...
HELLO, MR. LINCOLN! HIYA, MR. JEFFERSON! HOW ARE YOU...QUEEN ELIZABETH?
WAIT A MINUTE... WHO'S PAYING IN CANADIAN MONEY? MUST BE THE KID WHO WANTED AN APPLE FULL OF POUTINE!
CANADA
20
BART, I KNOW WHAT YOU'VE BEEN UP TO!
GULP!

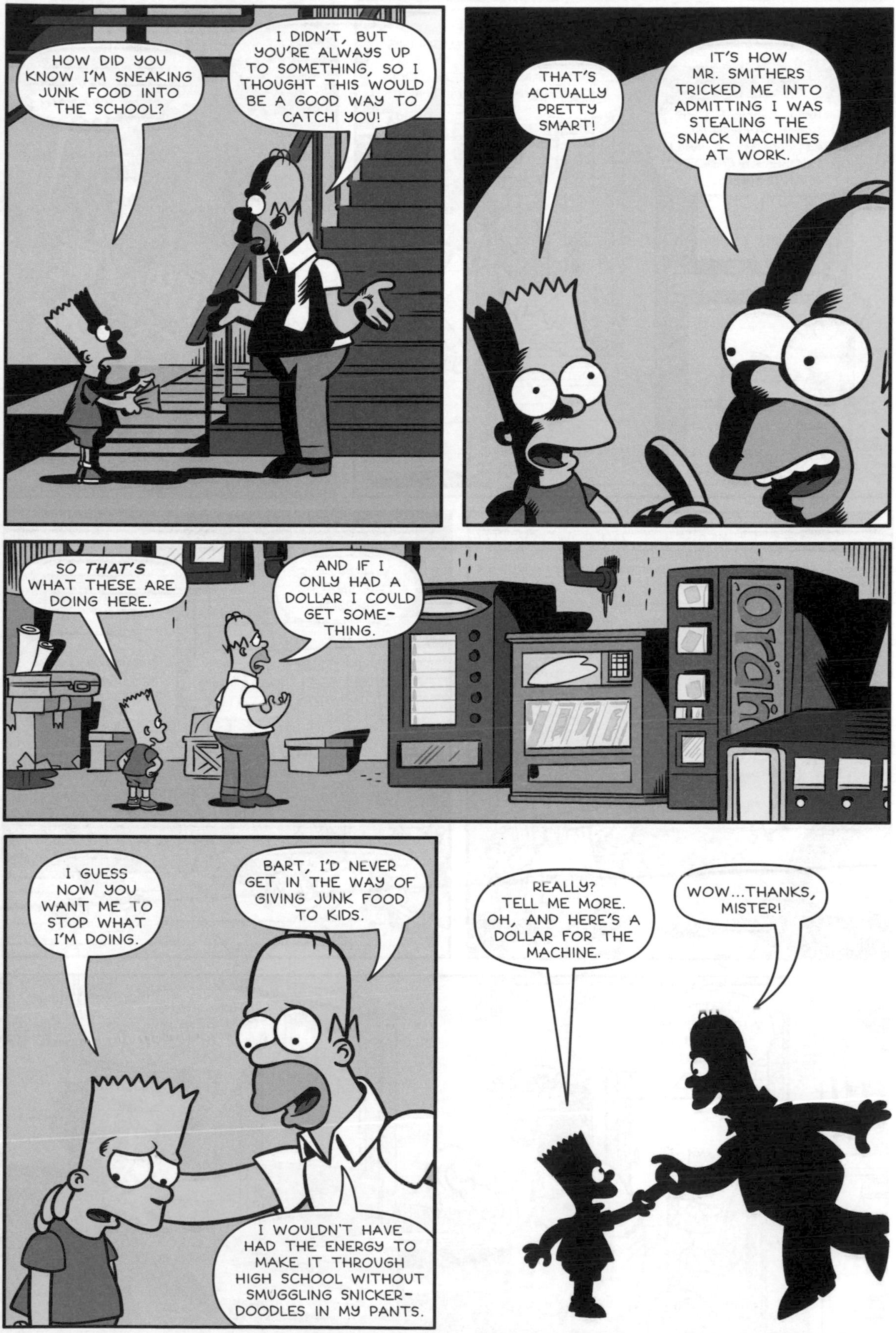
HOW DID YOU KNOW I'M SNEAKING JUNK FOOD INTO THE SCHOOL?
I DIDN'T, BUT YOU'RE ALWAYS UP TO SOMETHING, SO I THOUGHT THIS WOULD BE A GOOD WAY TO CATCH YOU!
THAT'S ACTUALLY PRETTY SMART!
IT'S HOW MR. SMITHERS TRICKED ME INTO ADMITTING I WAS STEALING THE SNACK MACHINES AT WORK.
SO *THAT'S* WHAT THESE ARE DOING HERE.
AND IF I ONLY HAD A DOLLAR I COULD GET SOME-THING.
I GUESS NOW YOU WANT ME TO STOP WHAT I'M DOING.
BART, I'D NEVER GET IN THE WAY OF GIVING JUNK FOOD TO KIDS.
I WOULDN'T HAVE HAD THE ENERGY TO MAKE IT THROUGH HIGH SCHOOL WITHOUT SMUGGLING SNICKER-DOODLES IN MY PANTS.
REALLY? TELL ME MORE. OH, AND HERE'S A DOLLAR FOR THE MACHINE.
WOW...THANKS, MISTER!

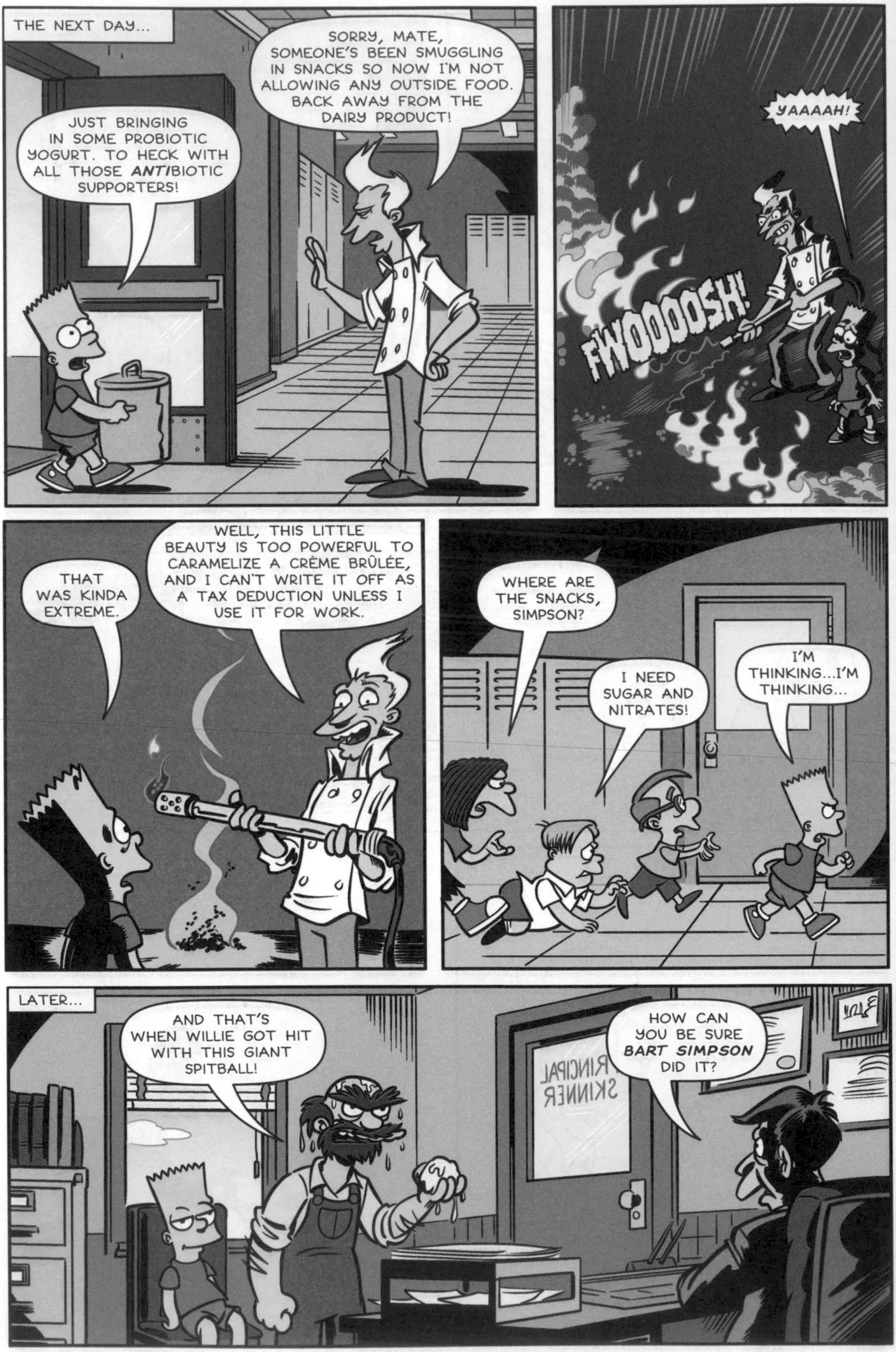
THE NEXT DAY...
JUST BRINGING IN SOME PROBIOTIC YOGURT. TO HECK WITH ALL THOSE *ANTI*BIOTIC SUPPORTERS!
SORRY, MATE, SOMEONE'S BEEN SMUGGLING IN SNACKS SO NOW I'M NOT ALLOWING ANY OUTSIDE FOOD. BACK AWAY FROM THE DAIRY PRODUCT!
YAAAAH!
FWOOOOSH!
THAT WAS KINDA EXTREME.
WELL, THIS LITTLE BEAUTY IS TOO POWERFUL TO CARAMELIZE A CRÈME BRÛLÉE, AND I CAN'T WRITE IT OFF AS A TAX DEDUCTION UNLESS I USE IT FOR WORK.
WHERE ARE THE SNACKS, SIMPSON?
I NEED SUGAR AND NITRATES!
I'M THINKING...I'M THINKING...
LATER...
AND THAT'S WHEN WILLIE GOT HIT WITH THIS GIANT SPITBALL!
HOW CAN YOU BE SURE *BART SIMPSON* DID IT?

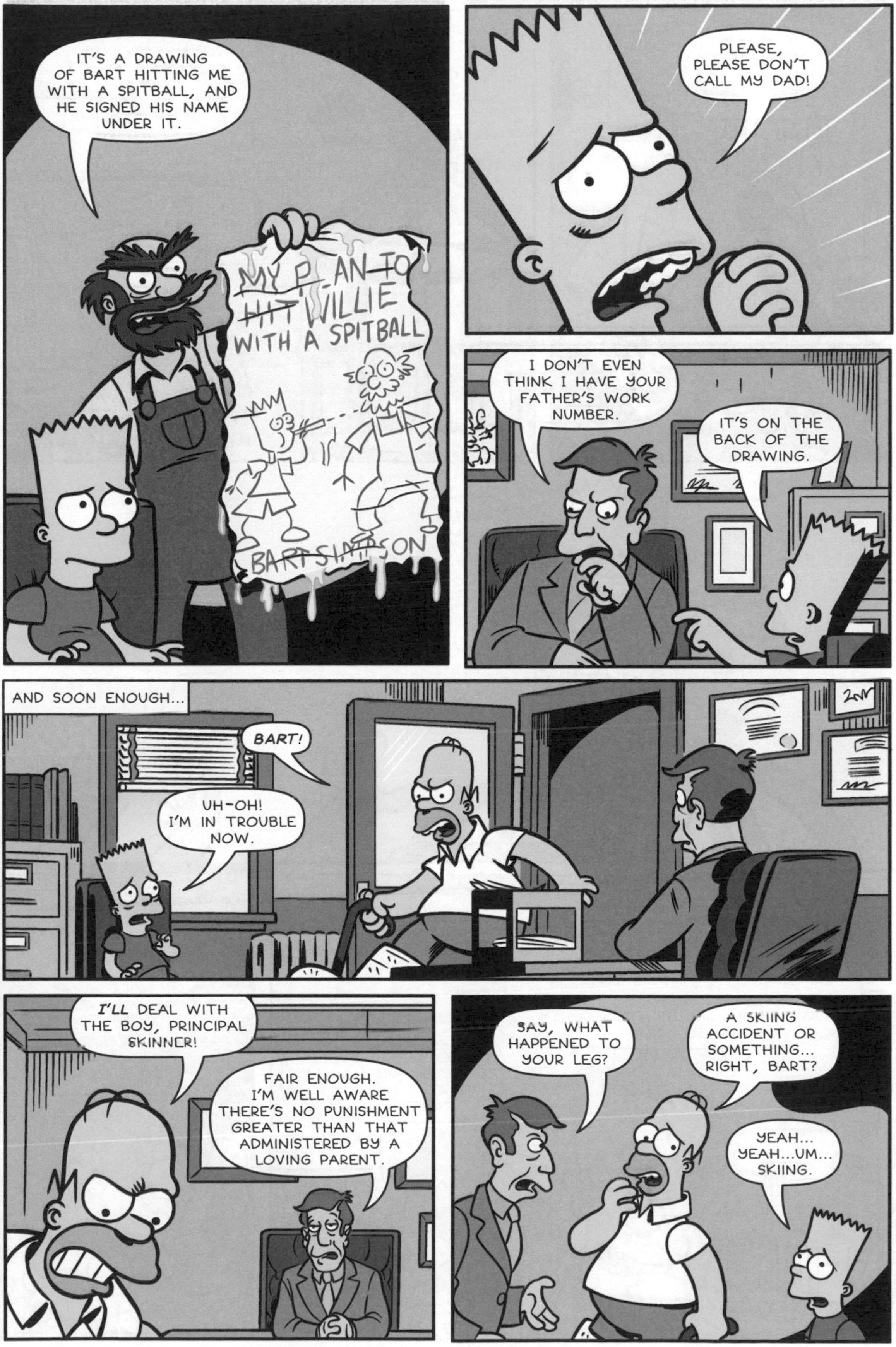
IT'S A DRAWING OF BART HITTING ME WITH A SPITBALL, AND HE SIGNED HIS NAME UNDER IT.
MY PLAN TO HIT WILLIE WITH A SPITBALL
BART SIMPSON
PLEASE, PLEASE DON'T CALL MY DAD!
I DON'T EVEN THINK I HAVE YOUR FATHER'S WORK NUMBER.
IT'S ON THE BACK OF THE DRAWING.
AND SOON ENOUGH...
BART!
UH-OH! I'M IN TROUBLE NOW.
I'LL DEAL WITH THE BOY, PRINCIPAL SKINNER!
FAIR ENOUGH. I'M WELL AWARE THERE'S NO PUNISHMENT GREATER THAN THAT ADMINISTERED BY A LOVING PARENT.
SAY, WHAT HAPPENED TO YOUR LEG?
A SKIING ACCIDENT OR SOMETHING... RIGHT, BART?
YEAH... YEAH...UM... SKIING.

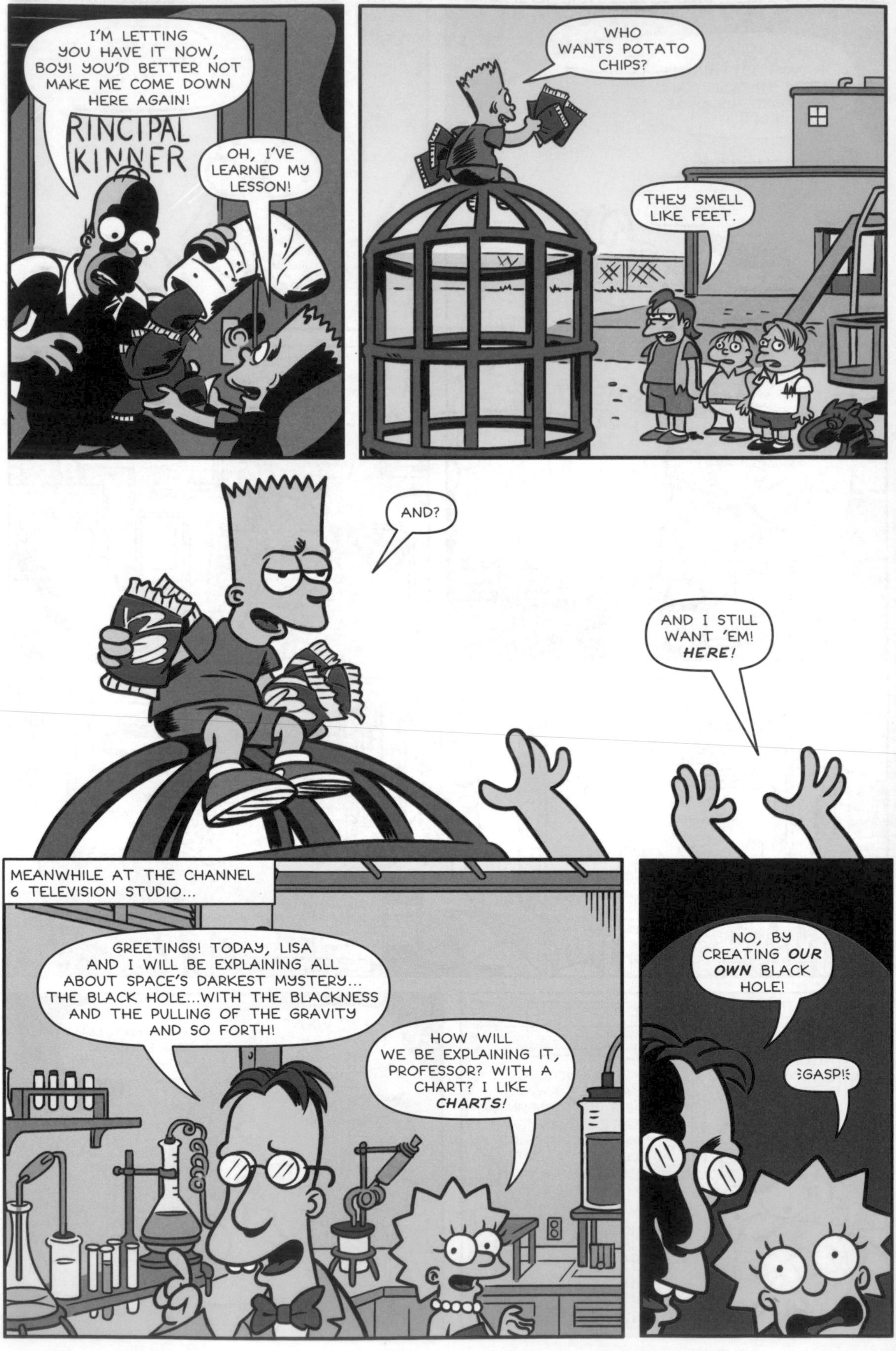
I'M LETTING YOU HAVE IT NOW, BOY! YOU'D BETTER NOT MAKE ME COME DOWN HERE AGAIN!
RINCIPAL KINNER
OH, I'VE LEARNED MY LESSON!
WHO WANTS POTATO CHIPS?
THEY SMELL LIKE FEET.
AND?
AND I STILL WANT 'EM! *HERE!*
MEANWHILE AT THE CHANNEL 6 TELEVISION STUDIO...
GREETINGS! TODAY, LISA AND I WILL BE EXPLAINING ALL ABOUT SPACE'S DARKEST MYSTERY... THE BLACK HOLE...WITH THE BLACKNESS AND THE PULLING OF THE GRAVITY AND SO FORTH!
HOW WILL WE BE EXPLAINING IT, PROFESSOR? WITH A CHART? I LIKE *CHARTS!*
NO, BY CREATING *OUR OWN* BLACK HOLE!
GASP!

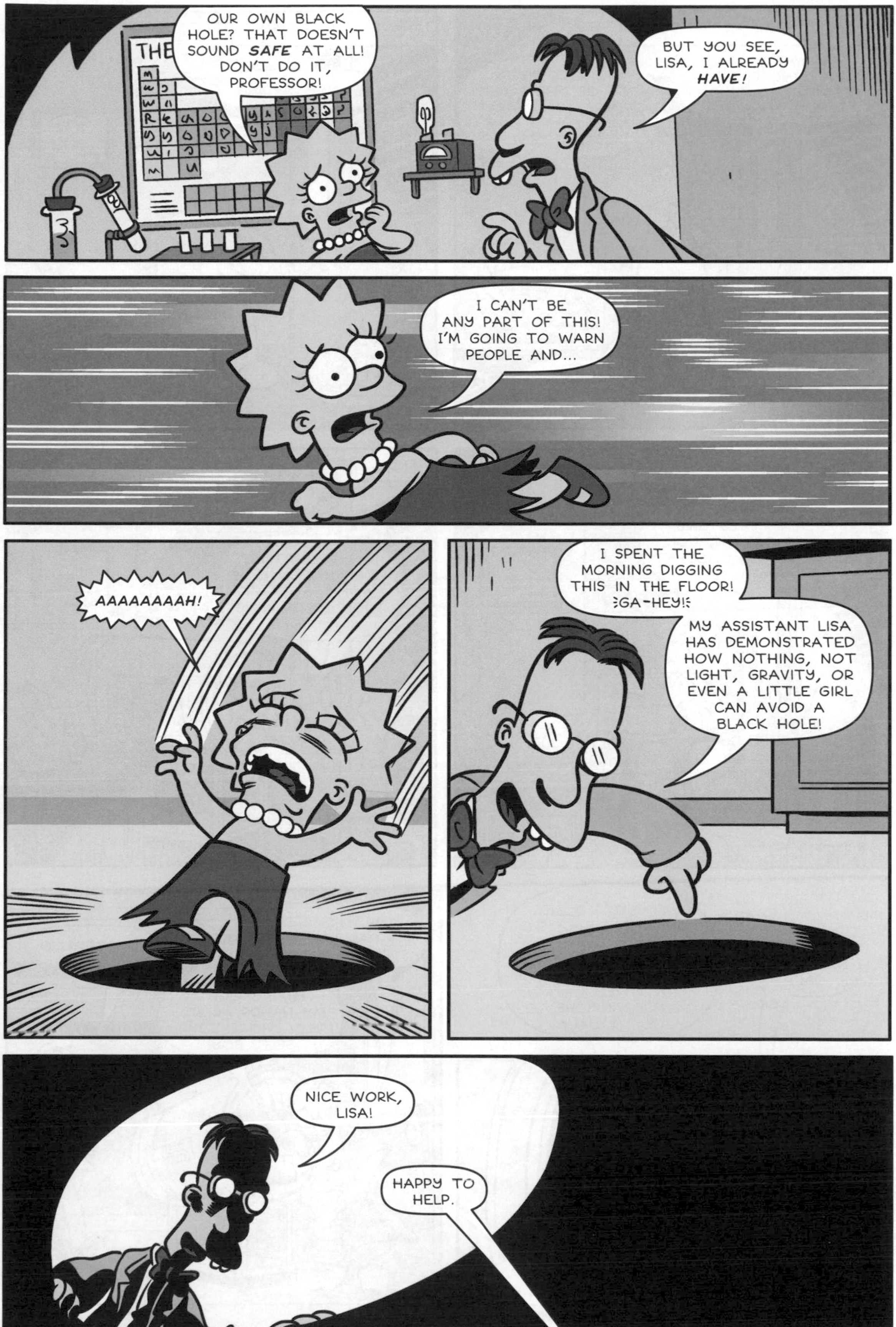
OUR OWN BLACK HOLE? THAT DOESN'T SOUND **SAFE** AT ALL! DON'T DO IT, PROFESSOR!
BUT YOU SEE, LISA, I ALREADY **HAVE**!
I CAN'T BE ANY PART OF THIS! I'M GOING TO WARN PEOPLE AND...
AAAAAAAAH!
I SPENT THE MORNING DIGGING THIS IN THE FLOOR! GA-HEY!
MY ASSISTANT LISA HAS DEMONSTRATED HOW NOTHING, NOT LIGHT, GRAVITY, OR EVEN A LITTLE GIRL CAN AVOID A BLACK HOLE!
NICE WORK, LISA!
HAPPY TO HELP.

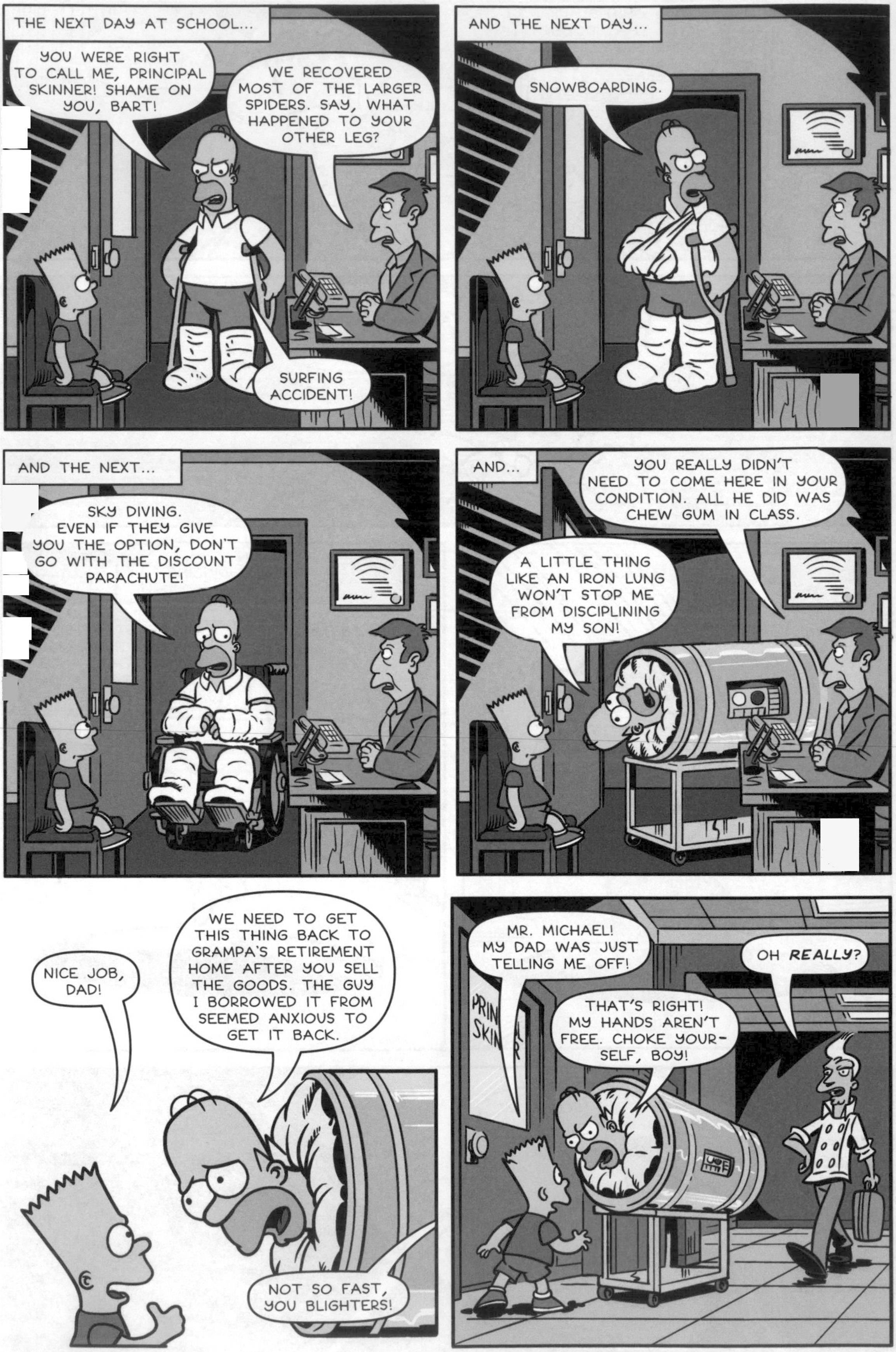

THE NEXT DAY AT SCHOOL...
YOU WERE RIGHT TO CALL ME, PRINCIPAL SKINNER! SHAME ON YOU, BART!
WE RECOVERED MOST OF THE LARGER SPIDERS. SAY, WHAT HAPPENED TO YOUR OTHER LEG?
SURFING ACCIDENT!
AND THE NEXT DAY...
SNOWBOARDING.
AND THE NEXT...
SKY DIVING. EVEN IF THEY GIVE YOU THE OPTION, DON'T GO WITH THE DISCOUNT PARACHUTE!
AND...
YOU REALLY DIDN'T NEED TO COME HERE IN YOUR CONDITION. ALL HE DID WAS CHEW GUM IN CLASS.
A LITTLE THING LIKE AN IRON LUNG WON'T STOP ME FROM DISCIPLINING MY SON!
NICE JOB, DAD!
WE NEED TO GET THIS THING BACK TO GRAMPA'S RETIREMENT HOME AFTER YOU SELL THE GOODS. THE GUY I BORROWED IT FROM SEEMED ANXIOUS TO GET IT BACK.
NOT SO FAST, YOU BLIGHTERS!
MR. MICHAEL! MY DAD WAS JUST TELLING ME OFF!
OH ***REALLY***?
THAT'S RIGHT! MY HANDS AREN'T FREE. CHOKE YOURSELF, BOY!

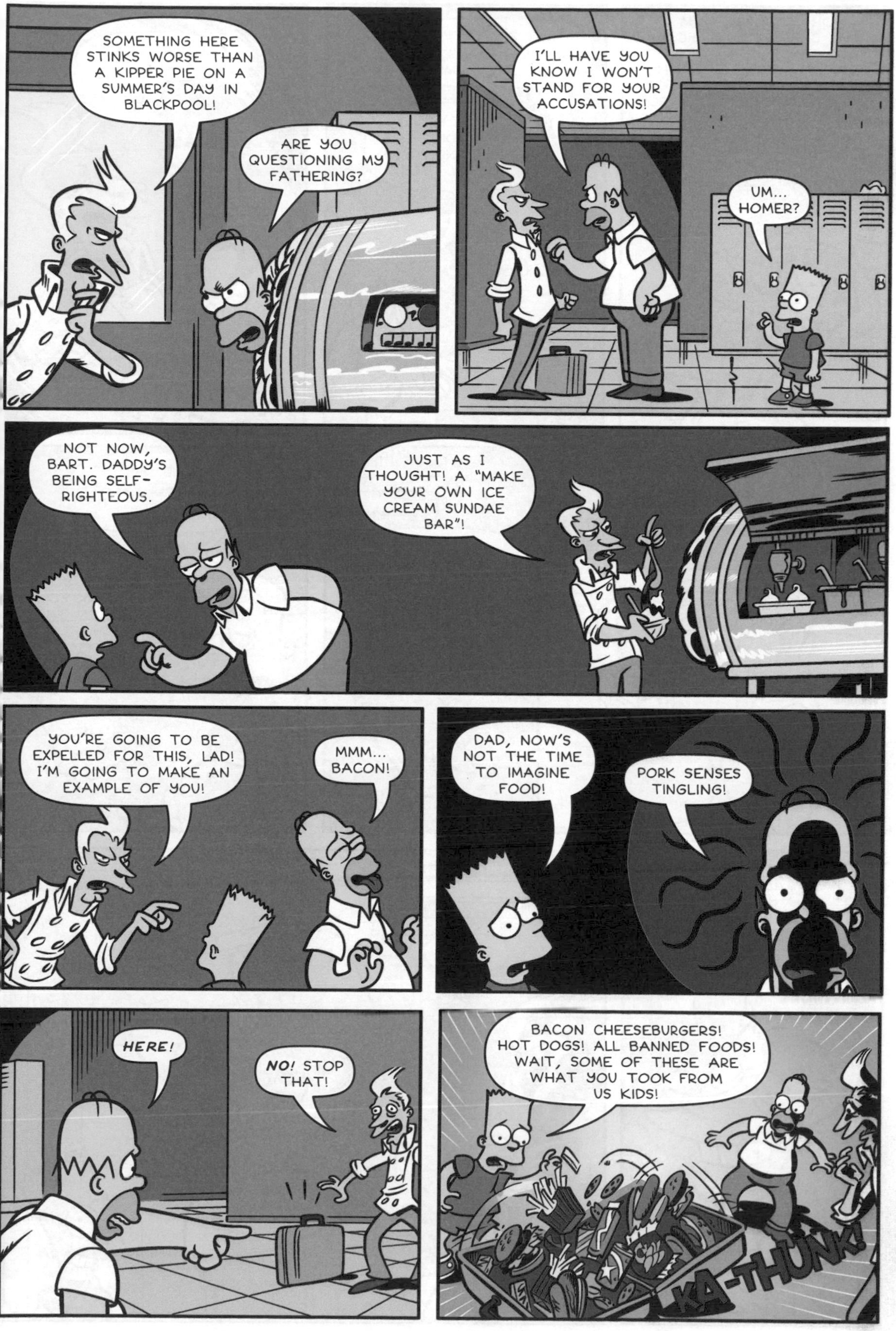
SOMETHING HERE STINKS WORSE THAN A KIPPER PIE ON A SUMMER'S DAY IN BLACKPOOL!
ARE YOU QUESTIONING MY FATHERING?
I'LL HAVE YOU KNOW I WON'T STAND FOR YOUR ACCUSATIONS!
UM... HOMER?
NOT NOW, BART. DADDY'S BEING SELF-RIGHTEOUS.
JUST AS I THOUGHT! A "MAKE YOUR OWN ICE CREAM SUNDAE BAR"!
YOU'RE GOING TO BE EXPELLED FOR THIS, LAD! I'M GOING TO MAKE AN EXAMPLE OF YOU!
MMM... BACON!
DAD, NOW'S NOT THE TIME TO IMAGINE FOOD!
PORK SENSES TINGLING!
HERE!
NO! STOP THAT!
BACON CHEESEBURGERS! HOT DOGS! ALL BANNED FOODS! WAIT, SOME OF THESE ARE WHAT YOU TOOK FROM US KIDS!
KA-THUNK!

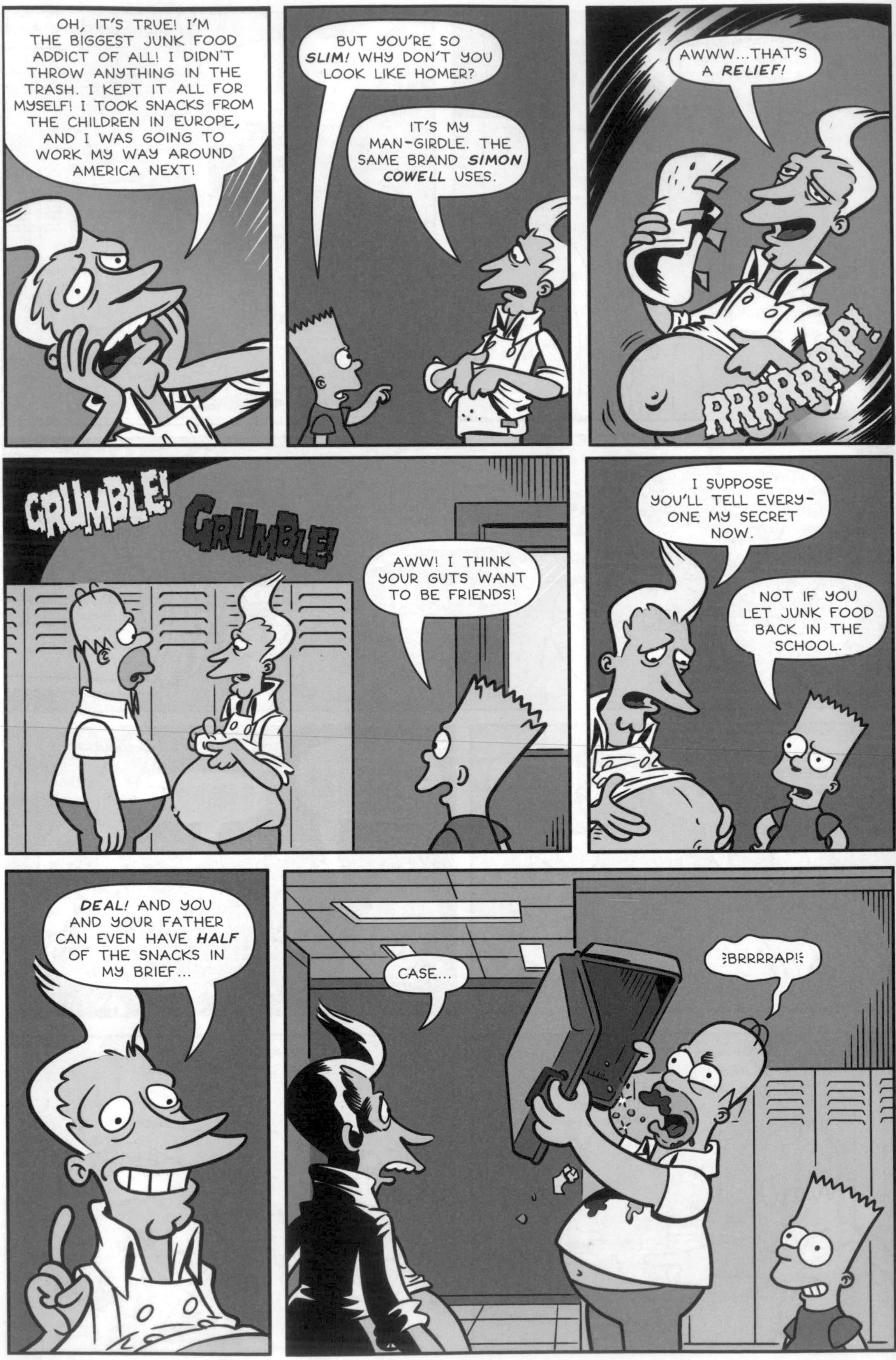
OH, IT'S TRUE! I'M THE BIGGEST JUNK FOOD ADDICT OF ALL! I DIDN'T THROW ANYTHING IN THE TRASH. I KEPT IT ALL FOR MYSELF! I TOOK SNACKS FROM THE CHILDREN IN EUROPE, AND I WAS GOING TO WORK MY WAY AROUND AMERICA NEXT!
BUT YOU'RE SO SLIM! WHY DON'T YOU LOOK LIKE HOMER?
IT'S MY MAN-GIRDLE. THE SAME BRAND SIMON COWELL USES.
AWWW...THAT'S A RELIEF!
RRRRRRIP!
GRUMBLE!
GRUMBLE!
AWW! I THINK YOUR GUTS WANT TO BE FRIENDS!
I SUPPOSE YOU'LL TELL EVERY-ONE MY SECRET NOW.
NOT IF YOU LET JUNK FOOD BACK IN THE SCHOOL.
DEAL! AND YOU AND YOUR FATHER CAN EVEN HAVE HALF OF THE SNACKS IN MY BRIEF...
CASE...
BRRRRAP!

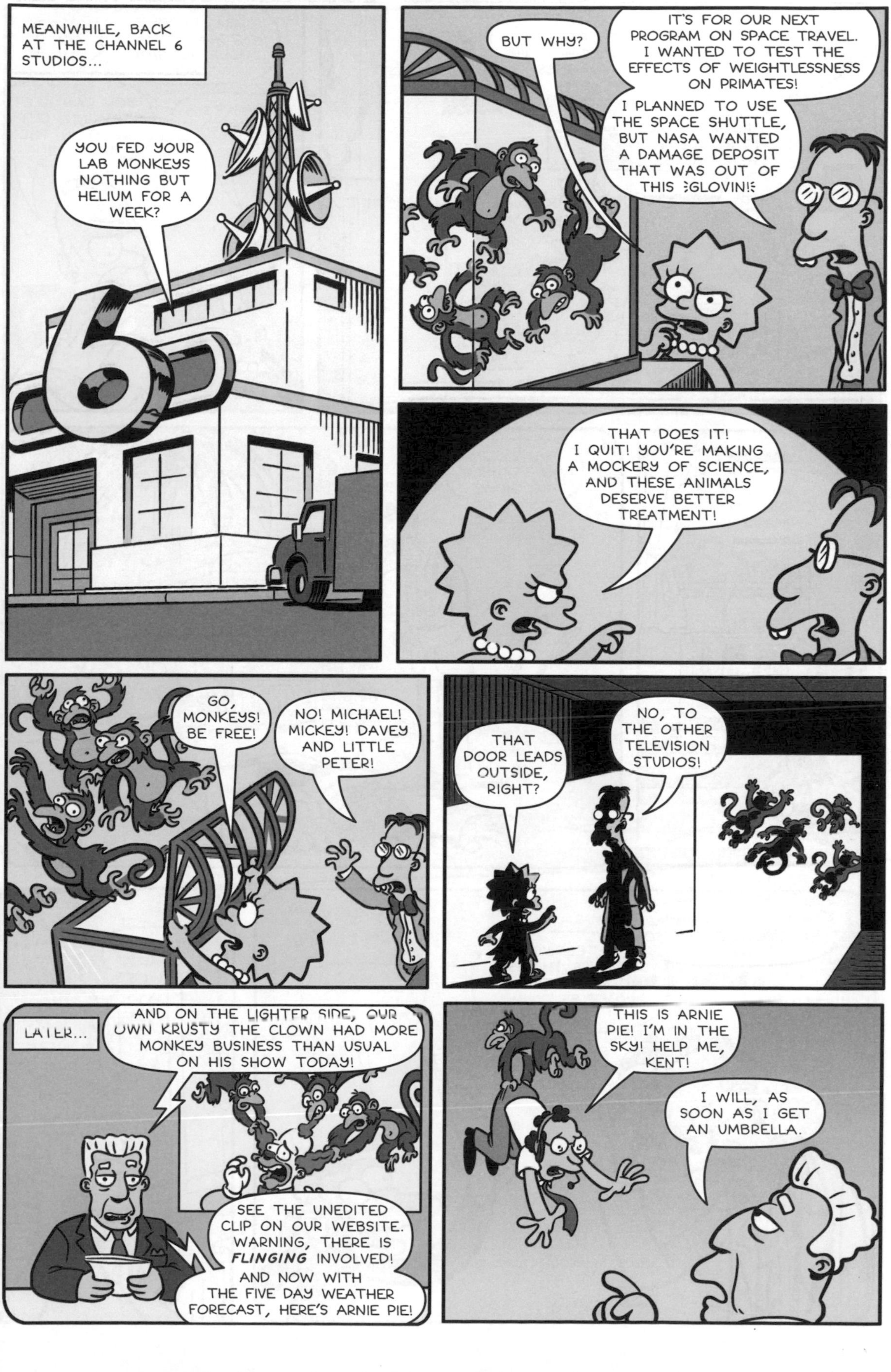

MEANWHILE, BACK AT THE CHANNEL 6 STUDIOS...
YOU FED YOUR LAB MONKEYS NOTHING BUT HELIUM FOR A WEEK?
BUT WHY?
IT'S FOR OUR NEXT PROGRAM ON SPACE TRAVEL. I WANTED TO TEST THE EFFECTS OF WEIGHTLESSNESS ON PRIMATES!
I PLANNED TO USE THE SPACE SHUTTLE, BUT NASA WANTED A DAMAGE DEPOSIT THAT WAS OUT OF THIS GLOVIN!
THAT DOES IT! I QUIT! YOU'RE MAKING A MOCKERY OF SCIENCE, AND THESE ANIMALS DESERVE BETTER TREATMENT!
GO, MONKEYS! BE FREE!
NO! MICHAEL! MICKEY! DAVEY AND LITTLE PETER!
THAT DOOR LEADS OUTSIDE, RIGHT?
NO, TO THE OTHER TELEVISION STUDIOS!
LATER...
AND ON THE LIGHTER SIDE, OUR OWN KRUSTY THE CLOWN HAD MORE MONKEY BUSINESS THAN USUAL ON HIS SHOW TODAY!
SEE THE UNEDITED CLIP ON OUR WEBSITE. WARNING, THERE IS *FLINGING* INVOLVED!
AND NOW WITH THE FIVE DAY WEATHER FORECAST, HERE'S ARNIE PIE!
THIS IS ARNIE PIE! I'M IN THE SKY! HELP ME, KENT!
I WILL, AS SOON AS I GET AN UMBRELLA.

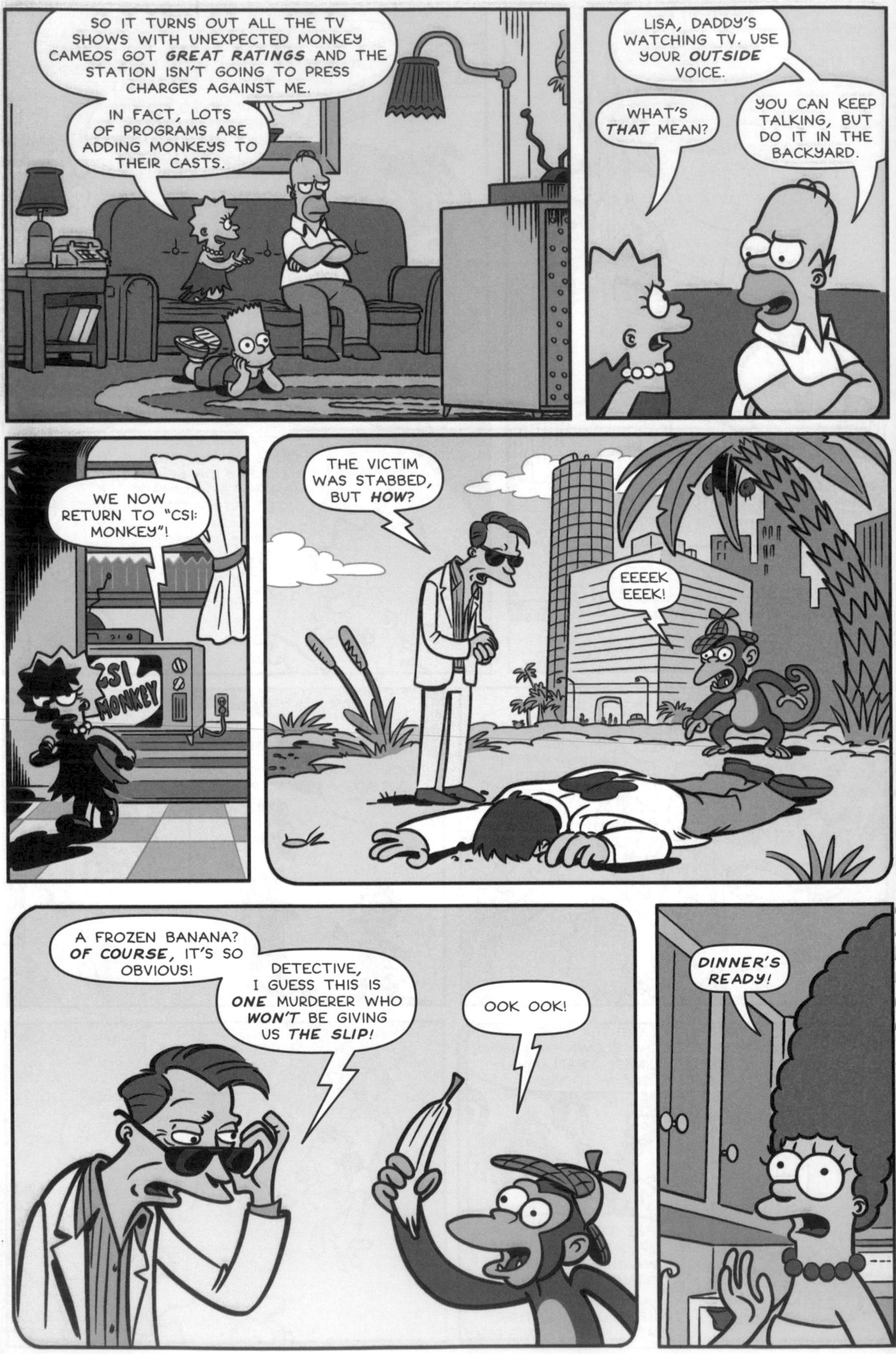
SO IT TURNS OUT ALL THE TV SHOWS WITH UNEXPECTED MONKEY CAMEOS GOT GREAT RATINGS AND THE STATION ISN'T GOING TO PRESS CHARGES AGAINST ME.
IN FACT, LOTS OF PROGRAMS ARE ADDING MONKEYS TO THEIR CASTS.
LISA, DADDY'S WATCHING TV. USE YOUR OUTSIDE VOICE.
WHAT'S THAT MEAN?
YOU CAN KEEP TALKING, BUT DO IT IN THE BACKYARD.
WE NOW RETURN TO "CSI: MONKEY"!
CSI MONKEY
THE VICTIM WAS STABBED, BUT HOW?
EEEEK EEEK!
A FROZEN BANANA? OF COURSE, IT'S SO OBVIOUS!
DETECTIVE, I GUESS THIS IS ONE MURDERER WHO WON'T BE GIVING US THE SLIP!
OOK OOK!
DINNER'S READY!

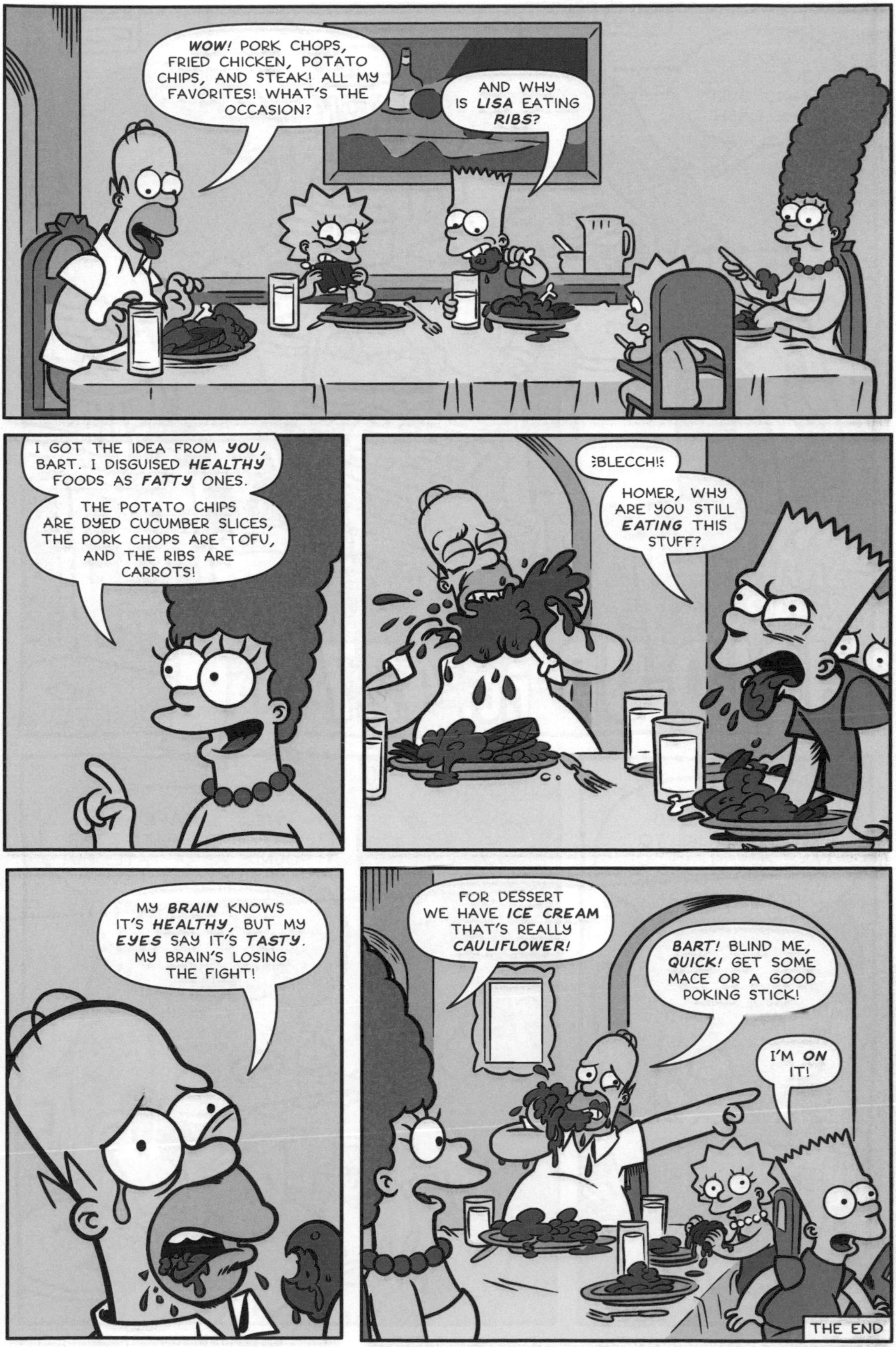
WOW! PORK CHOPS, FRIED CHICKEN, POTATO CHIPS, AND STEAK! ALL MY FAVORITES! WHAT'S THE OCCASION?
AND WHY IS LISA EATING RIBS?
I GOT THE IDEA FROM YOU, BART. I DISGUISED HEALTHY FOODS AS FATTY ONES.
THE POTATO CHIPS ARE DYED CUCUMBER SLICES, THE PORK CHOPS ARE TOFU, AND THE RIBS ARE CARROTS!
BLECCH!
HOMER, WHY ARE YOU STILL EATING THIS STUFF?
MY BRAIN KNOWS IT'S HEALTHY, BUT MY EYES SAY IT'S TASTY. MY BRAIN'S LOSING THE FIGHT!
FOR DESSERT WE HAVE ICE CREAM THAT'S REALLY CAULIFLOWER!
BART! BLIND ME, QUICK! GET SOME MACE OR A GOOD POKING STICK!
I'M ON IT!
THE END

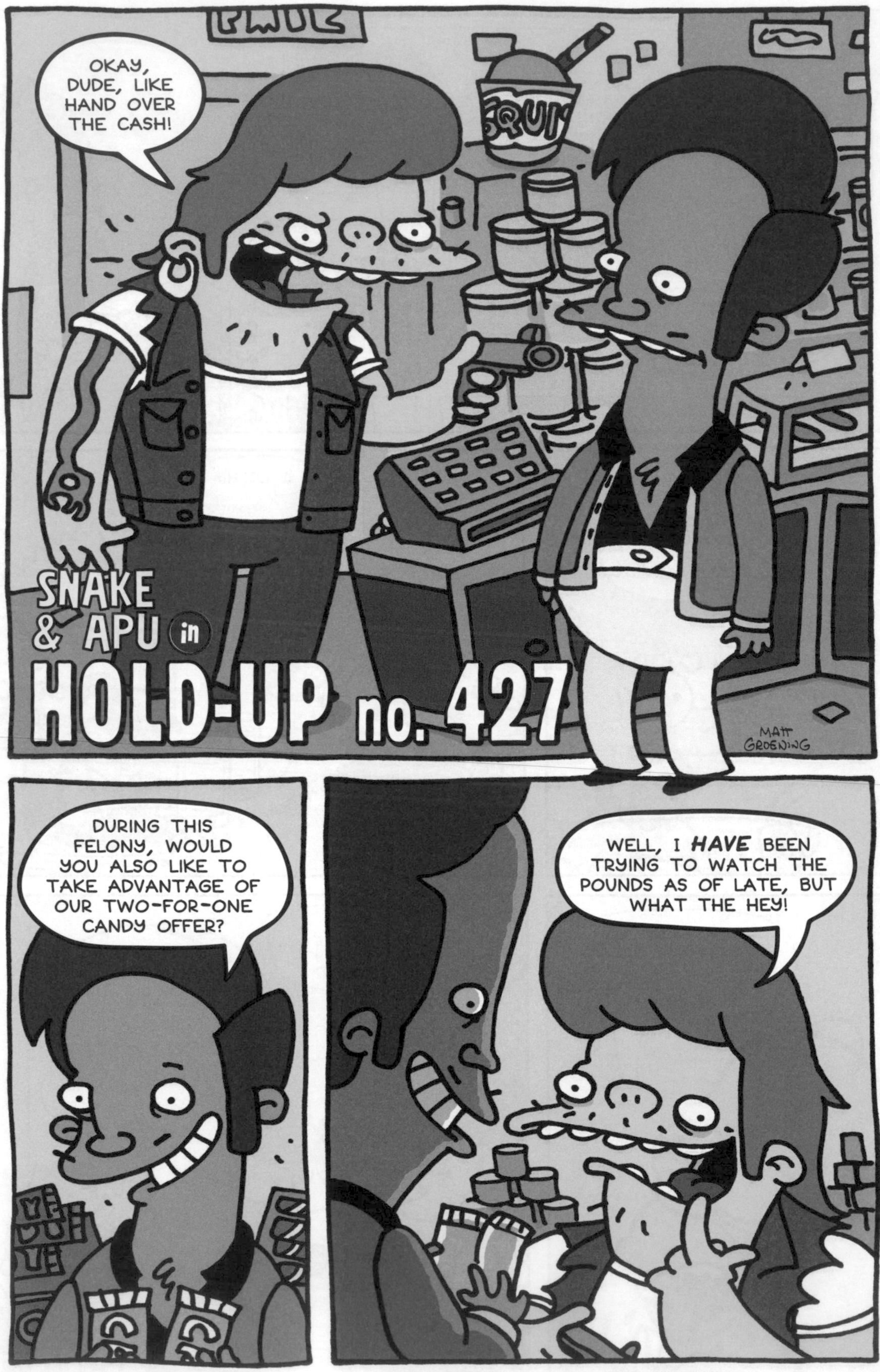
OKAY, DUDE, LIKE HAND OVER THE CASH!
SNAKE & APU in
HOLD-UP no. 427
MATT GROENING
DURING THIS FELONY, WOULD YOU ALSO LIKE TO TAKE ADVANTAGE OF OUR TWO-FOR-ONE CANDY OFFER?
WELL, I ***HAVE*** BEEN TRYING TO WATCH THE POUNDS AS OF LATE, BUT WHAT THE HEY!

DEAN RANKINE STORY & ART *KAREN BATES* LETTERS *BILL MORRISON* EDITOR

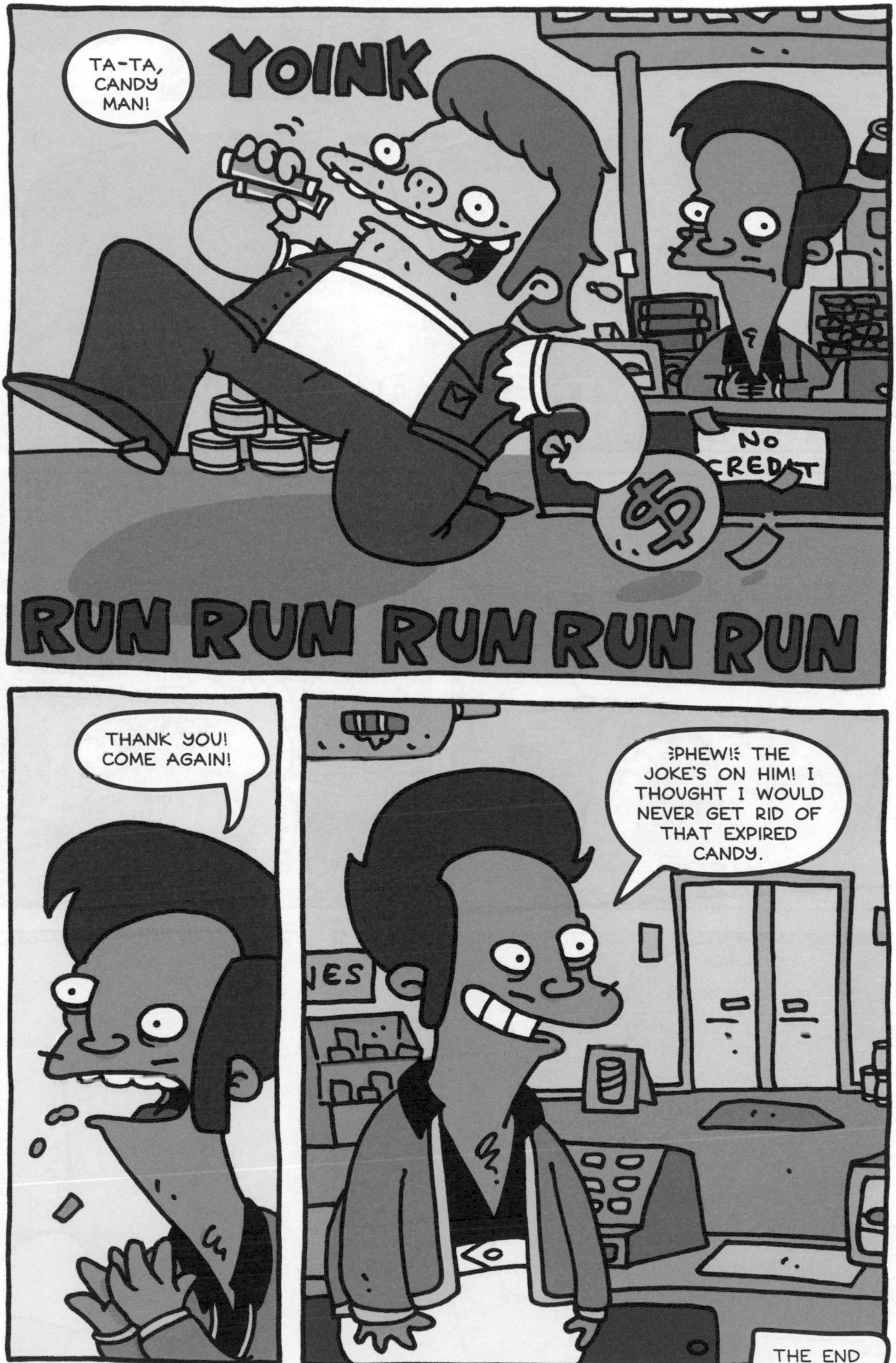
TA-TA, CANDY MAN!
YOINK
NO CREDIT
RUN RUN RUN RUN RUN
THANK YOU! COME AGAIN!
PHEW! THE JOKE'S ON HIM! I THOUGHT I WOULD NEVER GET RID OF THAT EXPIRED CANDY.
THE END

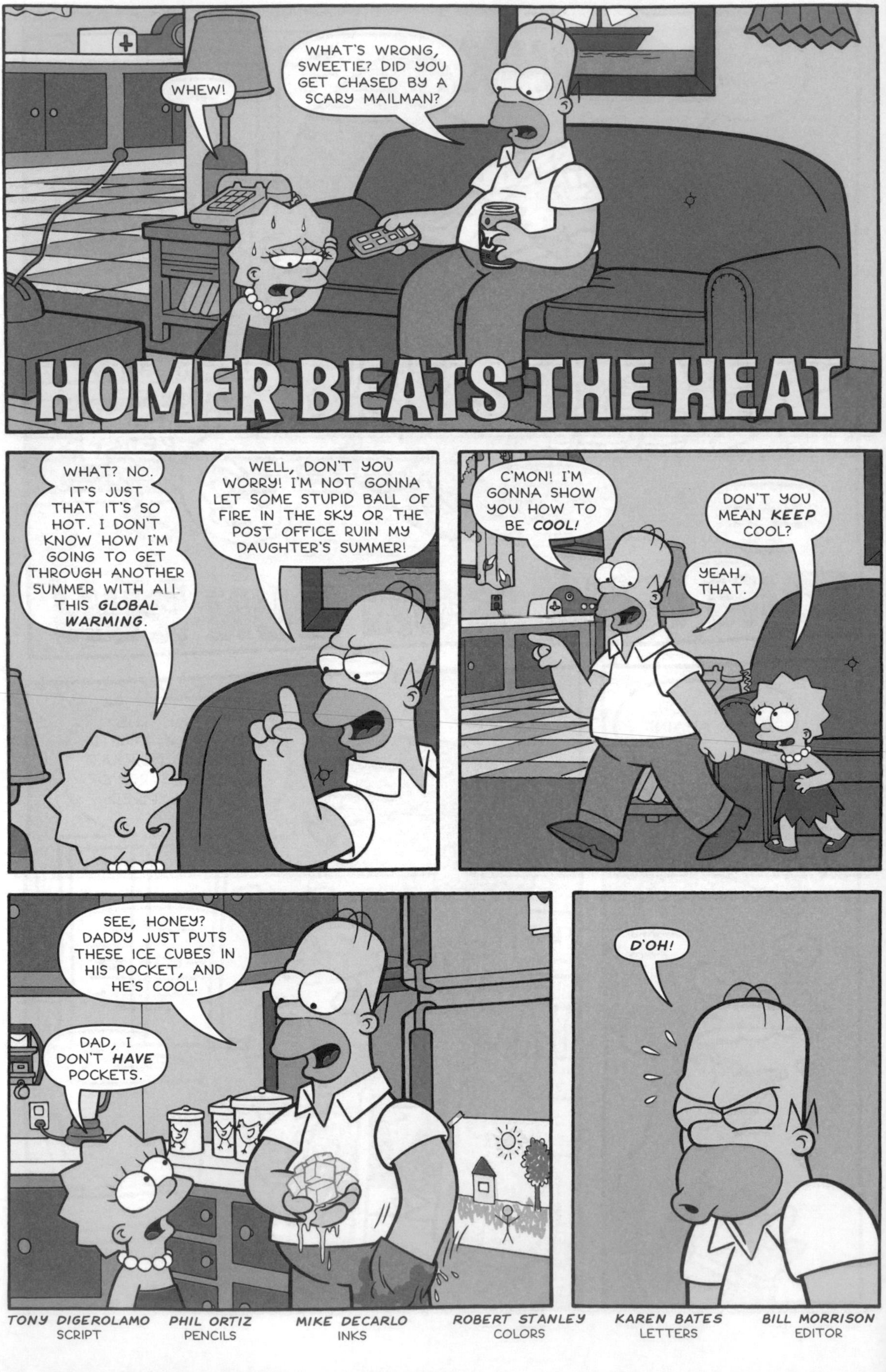
WHEW!
WHAT'S WRONG, SWEETIE? DID YOU GET CHASED BY A SCARY MAILMAN?
HOMER BEATS THE HEAT
WHAT? NO. IT'S JUST THAT IT'S SO HOT. I DON'T KNOW HOW I'M GOING TO GET THROUGH ANOTHER SUMMER WITH ALL THIS **GLOBAL WARMING**.
WELL, DON'T YOU WORRY! I'M NOT GONNA LET SOME STUPID BALL OF FIRE IN THE SKY OR THE POST OFFICE RUIN MY DAUGHTER'S SUMMER!
C'MON! I'M GONNA SHOW YOU HOW TO BE **COOL!**
DON'T YOU MEAN **KEEP** COOL?
YEAH, THAT.
SEE, HONEY? DADDY JUST PUTS THESE ICE CUBES IN HIS POCKET, AND HE'S COOL!
DAD, I DON'T **HAVE** POCKETS.
D'OH!

TONY DIGEROLAMO SCRIPT | *PHIL ORTIZ* PENCILS | *MIKE DECARLO* INKS | *ROBERT STANLEY* COLORS | *KAREN BATES* LETTERS | *BILL MORRISON* EDITOR

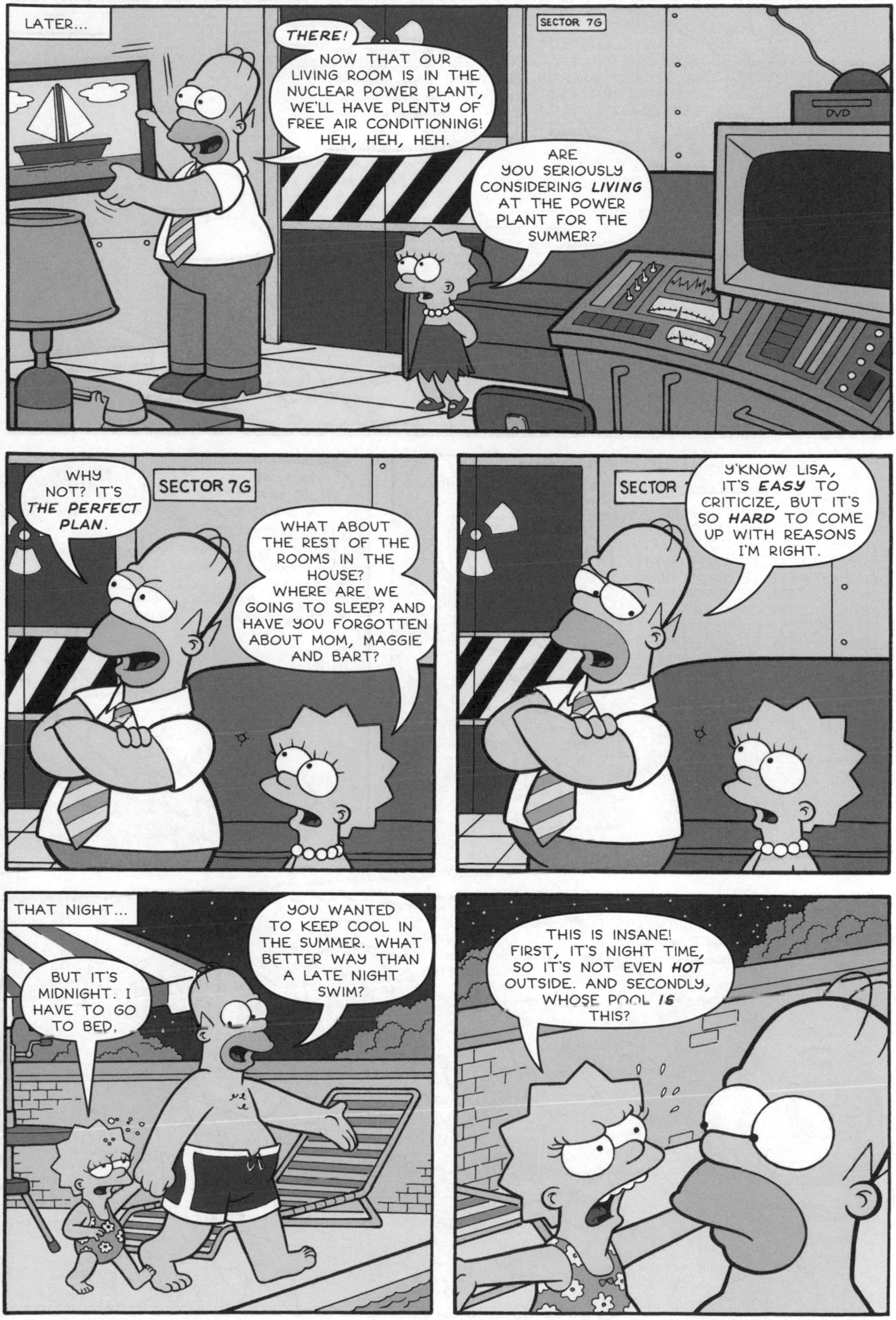
LATER...
THERE! NOW THAT OUR LIVING ROOM IS IN THE NUCLEAR POWER PLANT, WE'LL HAVE PLENTY OF FREE AIR CONDITIONING! HEH, HEH, HEH.
SECTOR 7G
DVD
ARE YOU SERIOUSLY CONSIDERING LIVING AT THE POWER PLANT FOR THE SUMMER?
WHY NOT? IT'S THE PERFECT PLAN.
SECTOR 7G
WHAT ABOUT THE REST OF THE ROOMS IN THE HOUSE? WHERE ARE WE GOING TO SLEEP? AND HAVE YOU FORGOTTEN ABOUT MOM, MAGGIE AND BART?
Y'KNOW LISA, IT'S EASY TO CRITICIZE, BUT IT'S SO HARD TO COME UP WITH REASONS I'M RIGHT.
THAT NIGHT...
YOU WANTED TO KEEP COOL IN THE SUMMER. WHAT BETTER WAY THAN A LATE NIGHT SWIM?
BUT IT'S MIDNIGHT. I HAVE TO GO TO BED.
THIS IS INSANE! FIRST, IT'S NIGHT TIME, SO IT'S NOT EVEN HOT OUTSIDE. AND SECONDLY, WHOSE POOL IS THIS?

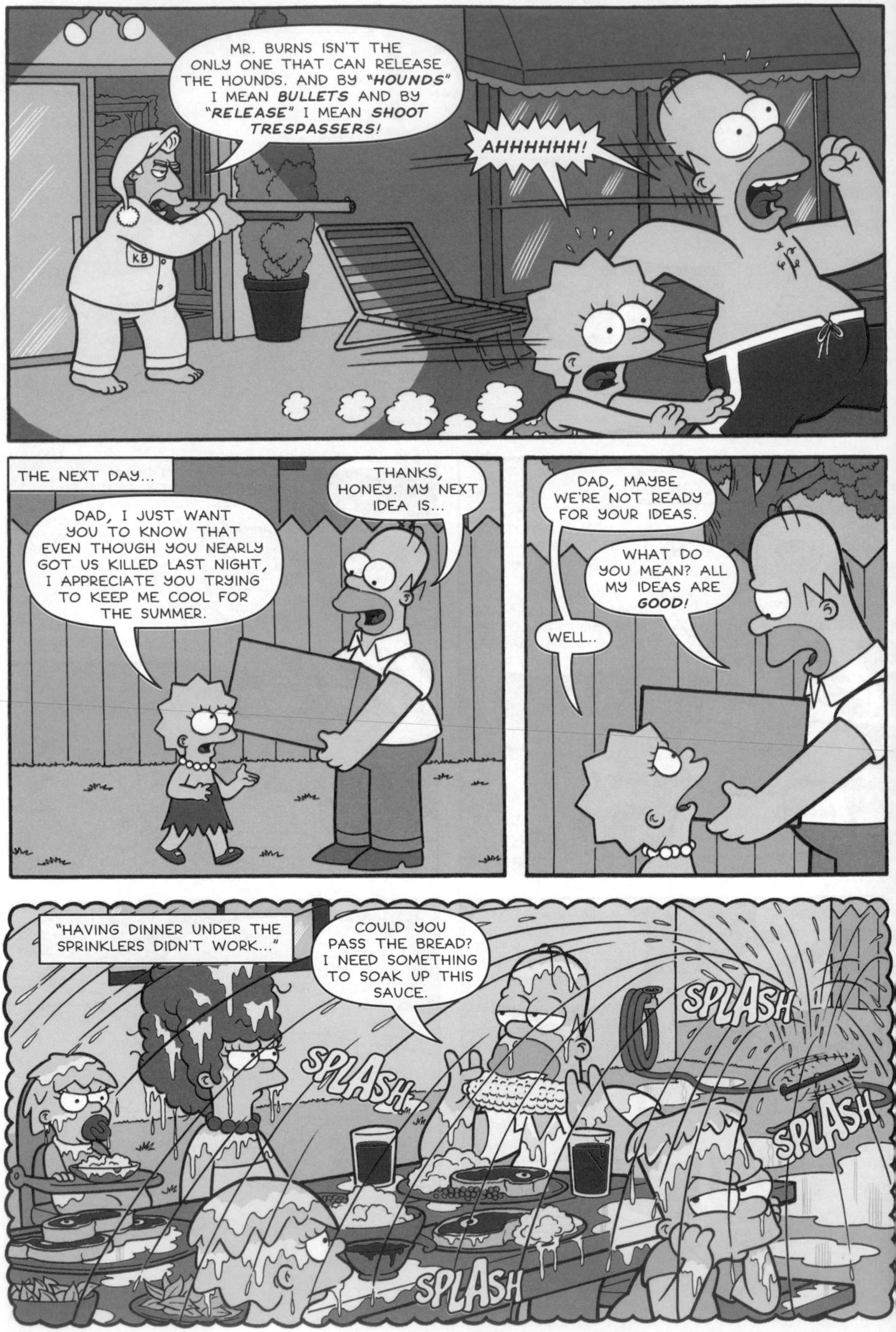

MR. BURNS ISN'T THE ONLY ONE THAT CAN RELEASE THE HOUNDS. AND BY "HOUNDS" I MEAN BULLETS AND BY "RELEASE" I MEAN SHOOT TRESPASSERS!
AHHHHHH!
KB
THE NEXT DAY...
DAD, I JUST WANT YOU TO KNOW THAT EVEN THOUGH YOU NEARLY GOT US KILLED LAST NIGHT, I APPRECIATE YOU TRYING TO KEEP ME COOL FOR THE SUMMER.
THANKS, HONEY. MY NEXT IDEA IS...
DAD, MAYBE WE'RE NOT READY FOR YOUR IDEAS.
WHAT DO YOU MEAN? ALL MY IDEAS ARE GOOD!
WELL..
"HAVING DINNER UNDER THE SPRINKLERS DIDN'T WORK..."
COULD YOU PASS THE BREAD? I NEED SOMETHING TO SOAK UP THIS SAUCE.
SPLASH
SPLASH
SPLASH
SPLASH

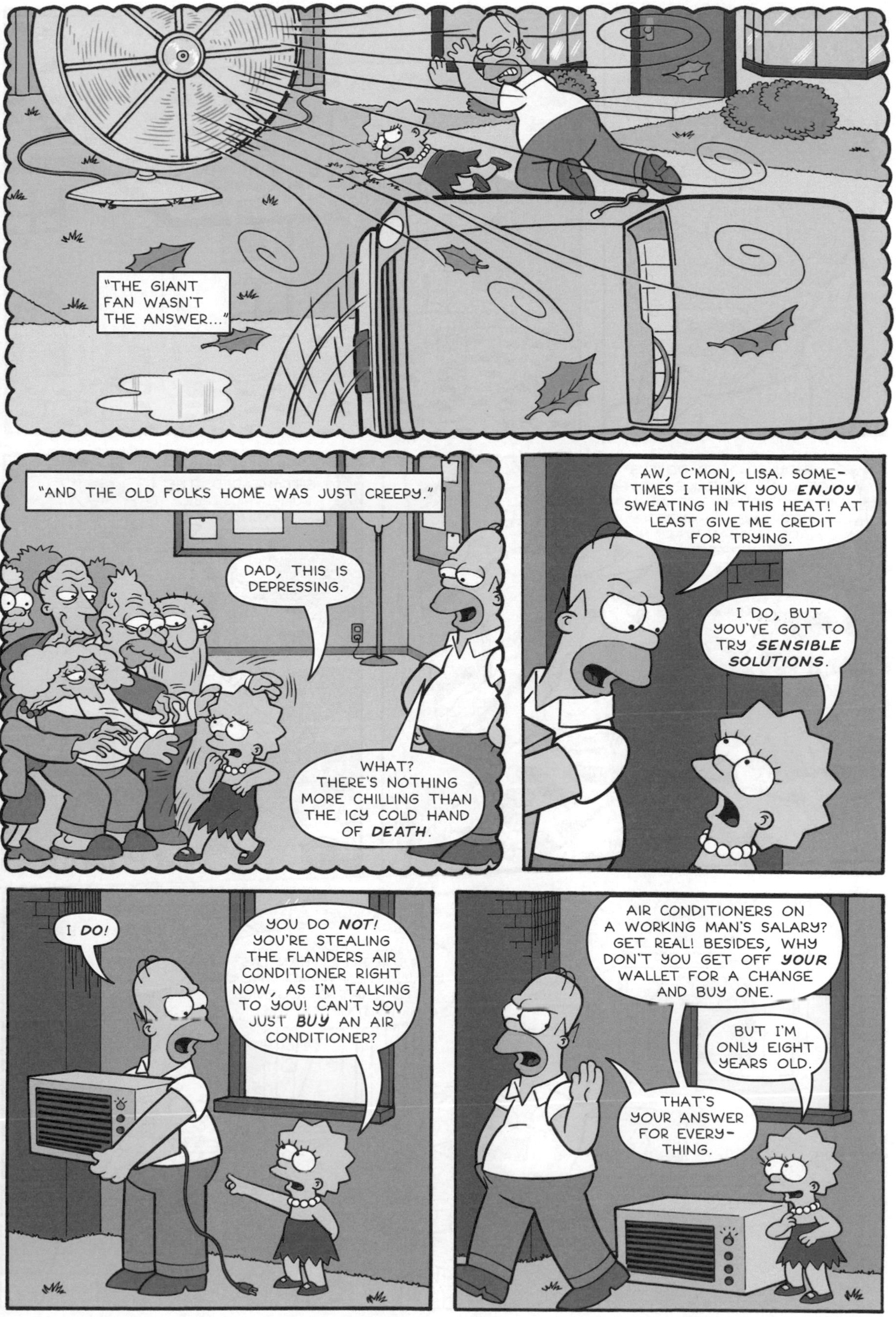
"THE GIANT FAN WASN'T THE ANSWER..."
"AND THE OLD FOLKS HOME WAS JUST CREEPY."
DAD, THIS IS DEPRESSING.
WHAT? THERE'S NOTHING MORE CHILLING THAN THE ICY COLD HAND OF DEATH.
AW, C'MON, LISA. SOMETIMES I THINK YOU ENJOY SWEATING IN THIS HEAT! AT LEAST GIVE ME CREDIT FOR TRYING.
I DO, BUT YOU'VE GOT TO TRY SENSIBLE SOLUTIONS.
I DO!
YOU DO NOT! YOU'RE STEALING THE FLANDERS AIR CONDITIONER RIGHT NOW, AS I'M TALKING TO YOU! CAN'T YOU JUST BUY AN AIR CONDITIONER?
AIR CONDITIONERS ON A WORKING MAN'S SALARY? GET REAL! BESIDES, WHY DON'T YOU GET OFF YOUR WALLET FOR A CHANGE AND BUY ONE.
BUT I'M ONLY EIGHT YEARS OLD.
THAT'S YOUR ANSWER FOR EVERYTHING.

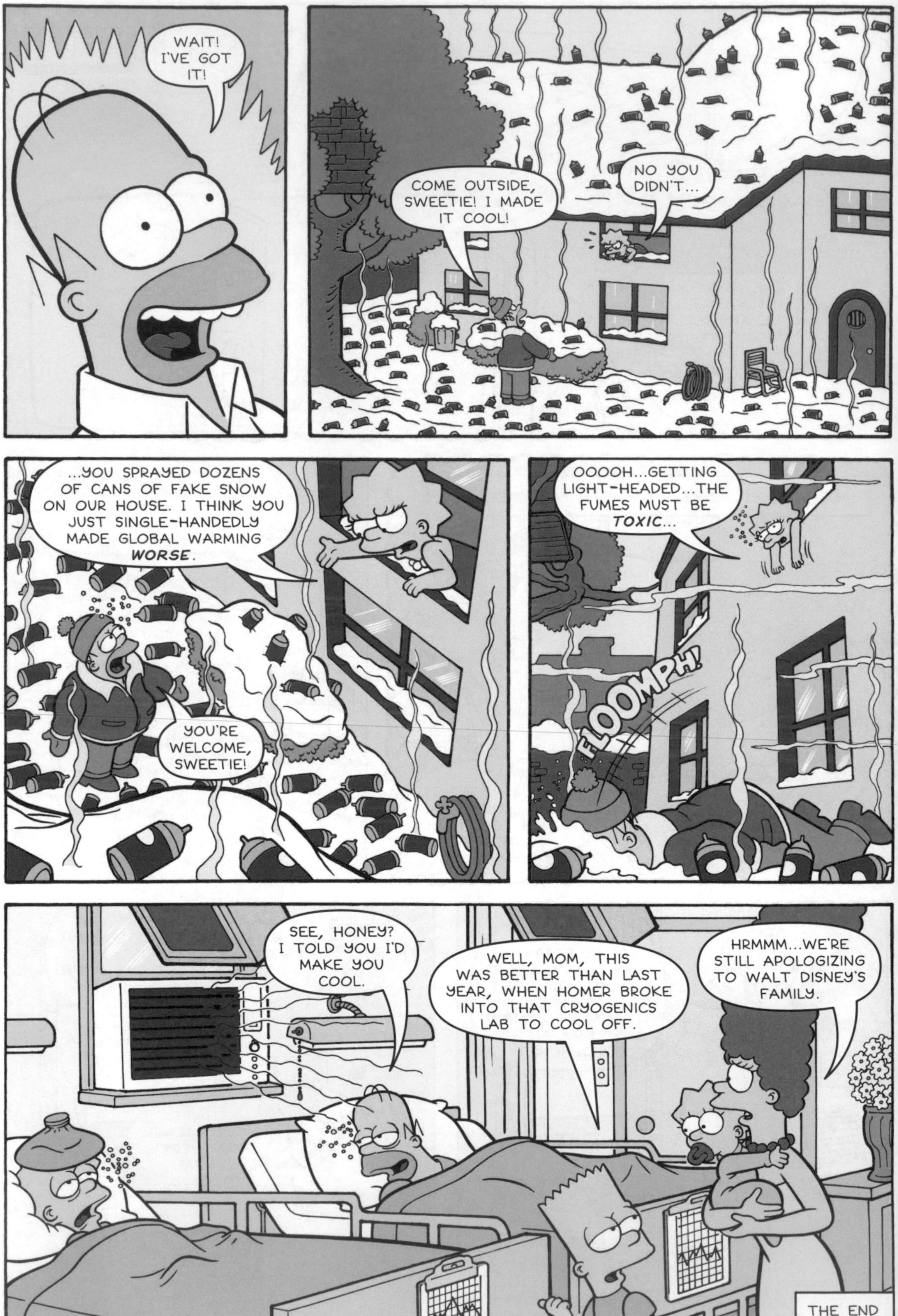

WAIT! I'VE GOT IT!
COME OUTSIDE, SWEETIE! I MADE IT COOL!
NO YOU DIDN'T...
...YOU SPRAYED DOZENS OF CANS OF FAKE SNOW ON OUR HOUSE. I THINK YOU JUST SINGLE-HANDEDLY MADE GLOBAL WARMING **WORSE**.
YOU'RE WELCOME, SWEETIE!
OOOOH...GETTING LIGHT-HEADED...THE FUMES MUST BE *TOXIC*...
FLOOMPH!
SEE, HONEY? I TOLD YOU I'D MAKE YOU COOL.
WELL, MOM, THIS WAS BETTER THAN LAST YEAR, WHEN HOMER BROKE INTO THAT CRYOGENICS LAB TO COOL OFF.
HRMMM...WE'RE STILL APOLOGIZING TO WALT DISNEY'S FAMILY.
THE END

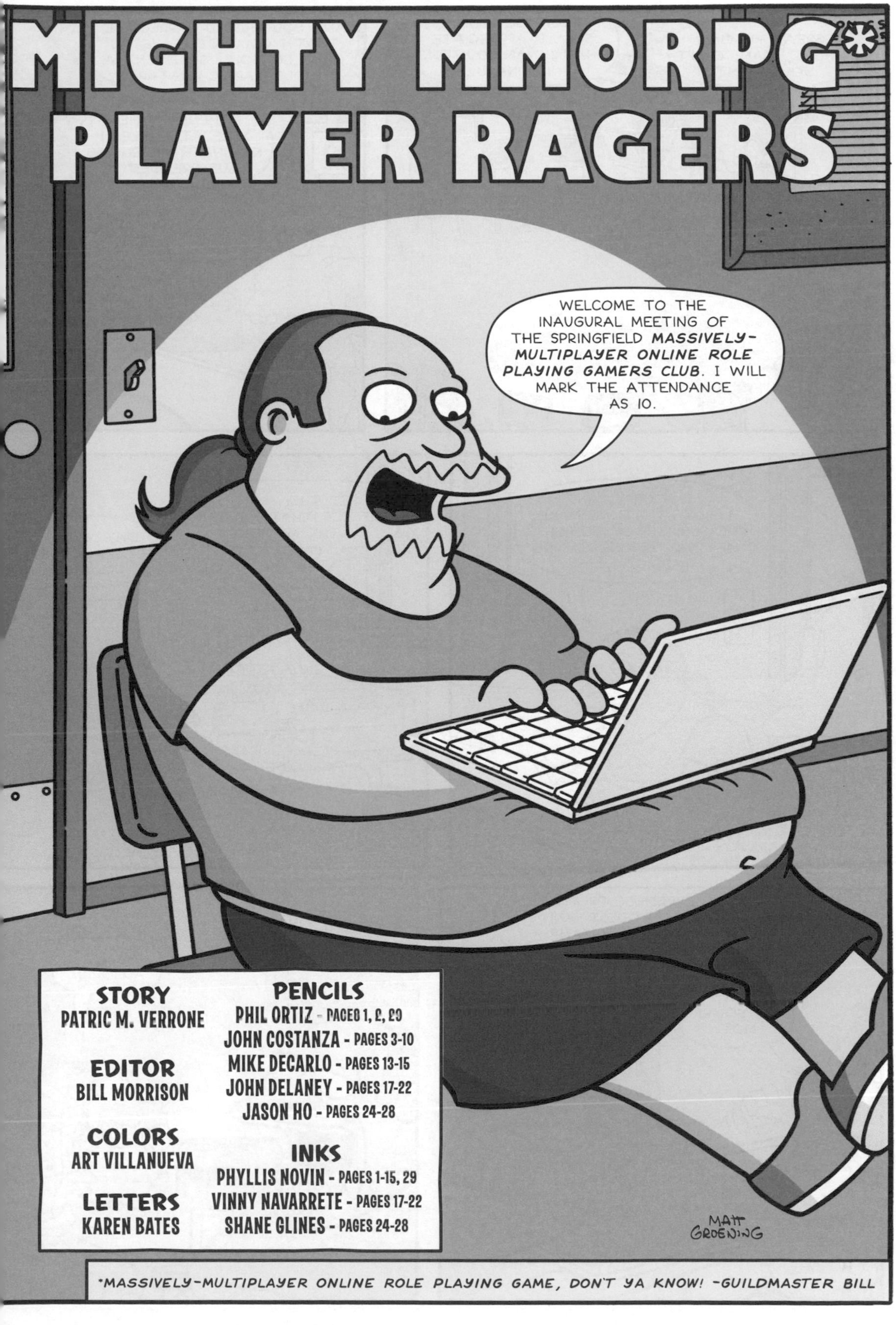
MIGHTY MMORPG* PLAYER RAGERS
WELCOME TO THE INAUGURAL MEETING OF THE SPRINGFIELD MASSIVELY-MULTIPLAYER ONLINE ROLE PLAYING GAMERS CLUB. I WILL MARK THE ATTENDANCE AS 10.
STORY
PATRIC M. VERRONE
EDITOR
BILL MORRISON
COLORS
ART VILLANUEVA
LETTERS
KAREN BATES
PENCILS
PHIL ORTIZ - PAGES 1, 2, 29
JOHN COSTANZA - PAGES 3-10
MIKE DECARLO - PAGES 13-15
JOHN DELANEY - PAGES 17-22
JASON HO - PAGES 24-28
INKS
PHYLLIS NOVIN - PAGES 1-15, 29
VINNY NAVARRETE - PAGES 17-22
SHANE GLINES - PAGES 24-28
MATT GROENING
*MASSIVELY-MULTIPLAYER ONLINE ROLE PLAYING GAME, DON'T YA KNOW! -GUILDMASTER BILL

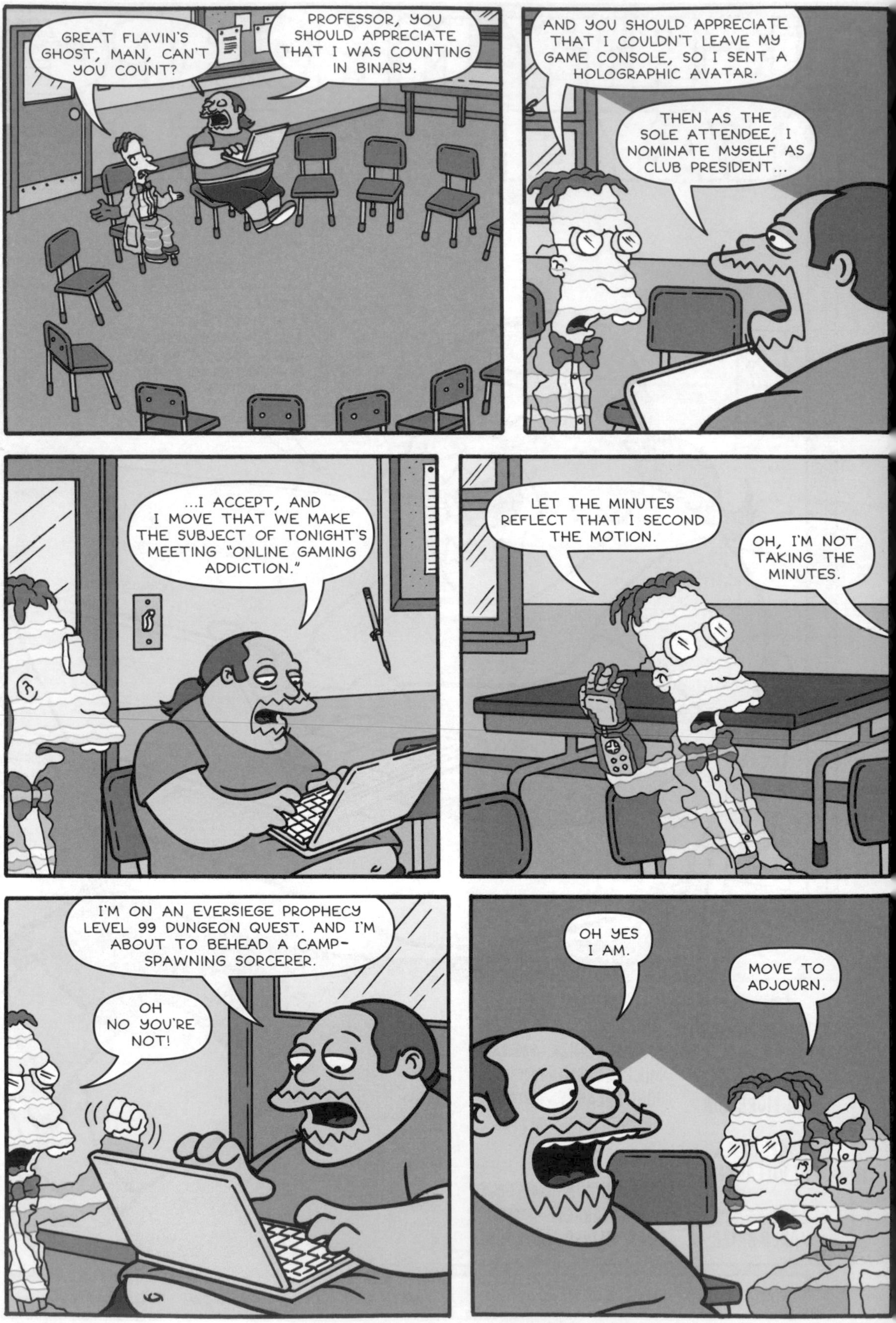
GREAT FLAVIN'S GHOST, MAN, CAN'T YOU COUNT?
PROFESSOR, YOU SHOULD APPRECIATE THAT I WAS COUNTING IN BINARY.
AND YOU SHOULD APPRECIATE THAT I COULDN'T LEAVE MY GAME CONSOLE, SO I SENT A HOLOGRAPHIC AVATAR.
THEN AS THE SOLE ATTENDEE, I NOMINATE MYSELF AS CLUB PRESIDENT...
...I ACCEPT, AND I MOVE THAT WE MAKE THE SUBJECT OF TONIGHT'S MEETING "ONLINE GAMING ADDICTION."
LET THE MINUTES REFLECT THAT I SECOND THE MOTION.
OH, I'M NOT TAKING THE MINUTES.
I'M ON AN EVERSIEGE PROPHECY LEVEL 99 DUNGEON QUEST. AND I'M ABOUT TO BEHEAD A CAMP-SPAWNING SORCERER.
OH NO YOU'RE NOT!
OH YES I AM.
MOVE TO ADJOURN.

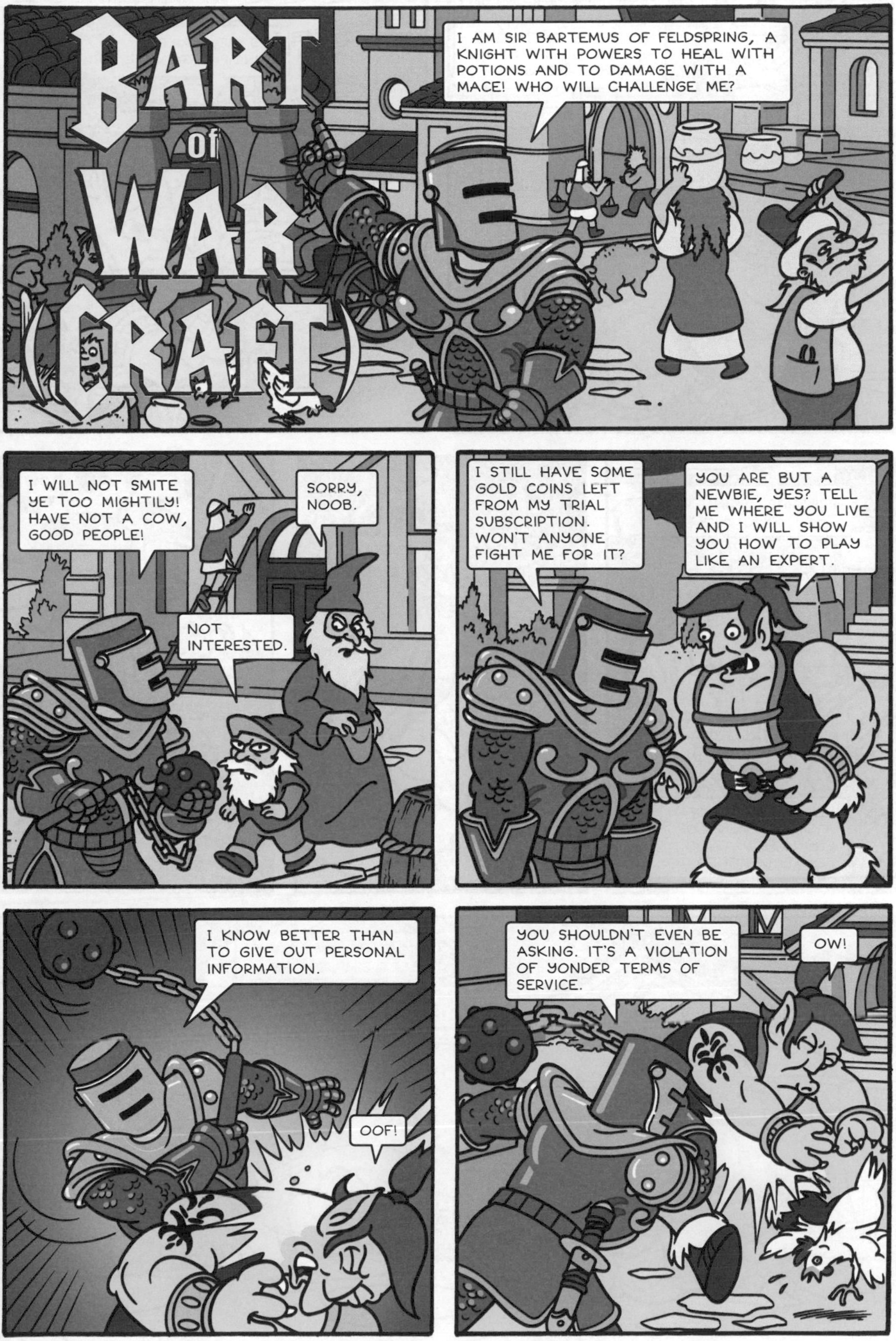
BART of WAR (CRAFT)
I AM SIR BARTEMUS OF FELDSPRING, A KNIGHT WITH POWERS TO HEAL WITH POTIONS AND TO DAMAGE WITH A MACE! WHO WILL CHALLENGE ME?
I WILL NOT SMITE YE TOO MIGHTILY! HAVE NOT A COW, GOOD PEOPLE!
SORRY, NOOB.
NOT INTERESTED.
I STILL HAVE SOME GOLD COINS LEFT FROM MY TRIAL SUBSCRIPTION. WON'T ANYONE FIGHT ME FOR IT?
YOU ARE BUT A NEWBIE, YES? TELL ME WHERE YOU LIVE AND I WILL SHOW YOU HOW TO PLAY LIKE AN EXPERT.
I KNOW BETTER THAN TO GIVE OUT PERSONAL INFORMATION.
OOF!
YOU SHOULDN'T EVEN BE ASKING. IT'S A VIOLATION OF YONDER TERMS OF SERVICE.
OW!

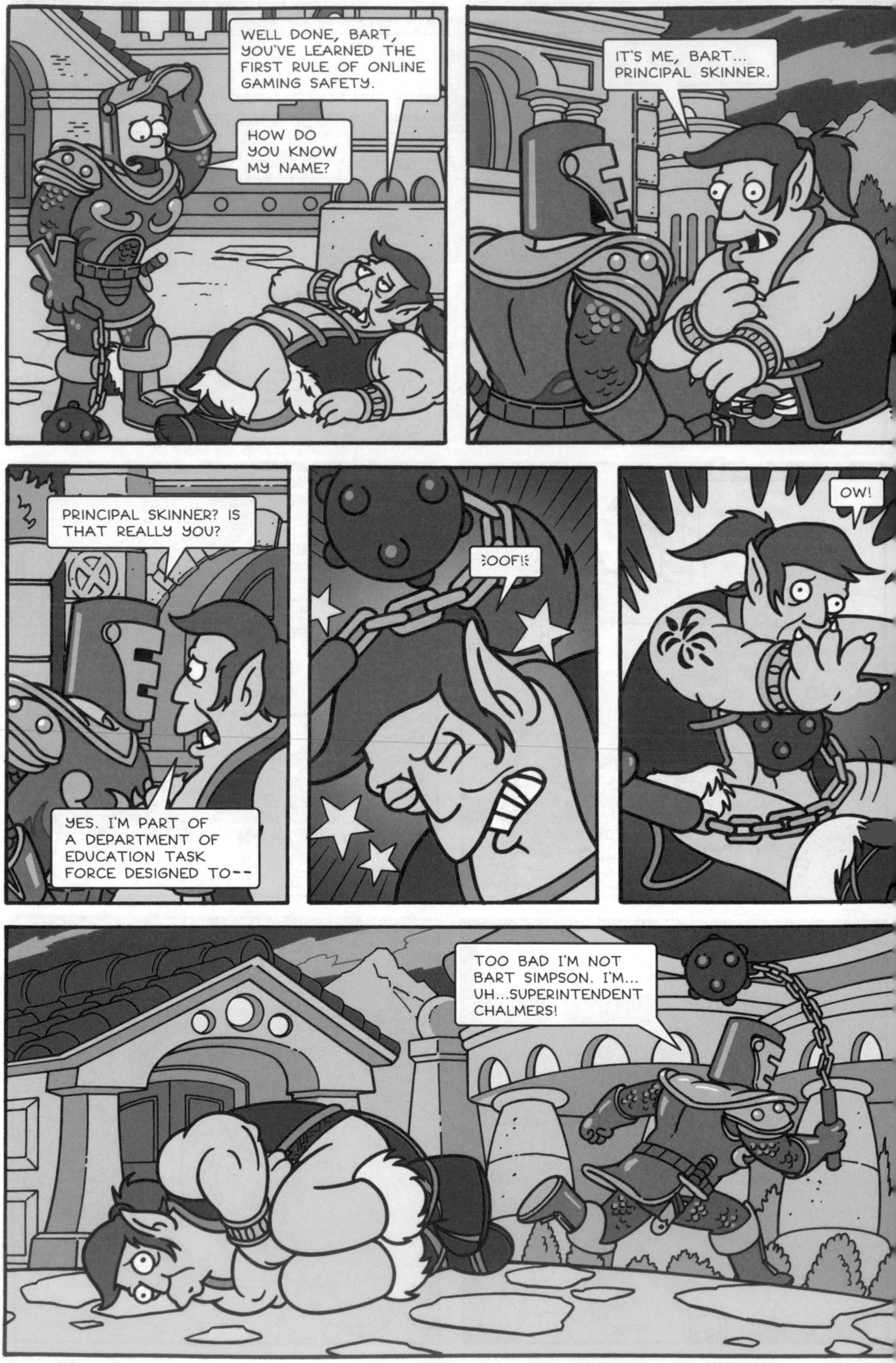
WELL DONE, BART, YOU'VE LEARNED THE FIRST RULE OF ONLINE GAMING SAFETY.
HOW DO YOU KNOW MY NAME?
IT'S ME, BART... PRINCIPAL SKINNER.
PRINCIPAL SKINNER? IS THAT REALLY YOU?
YES. I'M PART OF A DEPARTMENT OF EDUCATION TASK FORCE DESIGNED TO--
OOF!
OW!
TOO BAD I'M NOT BART SIMPSON. I'M... UH...SUPERINTENDENT CHALMERS!

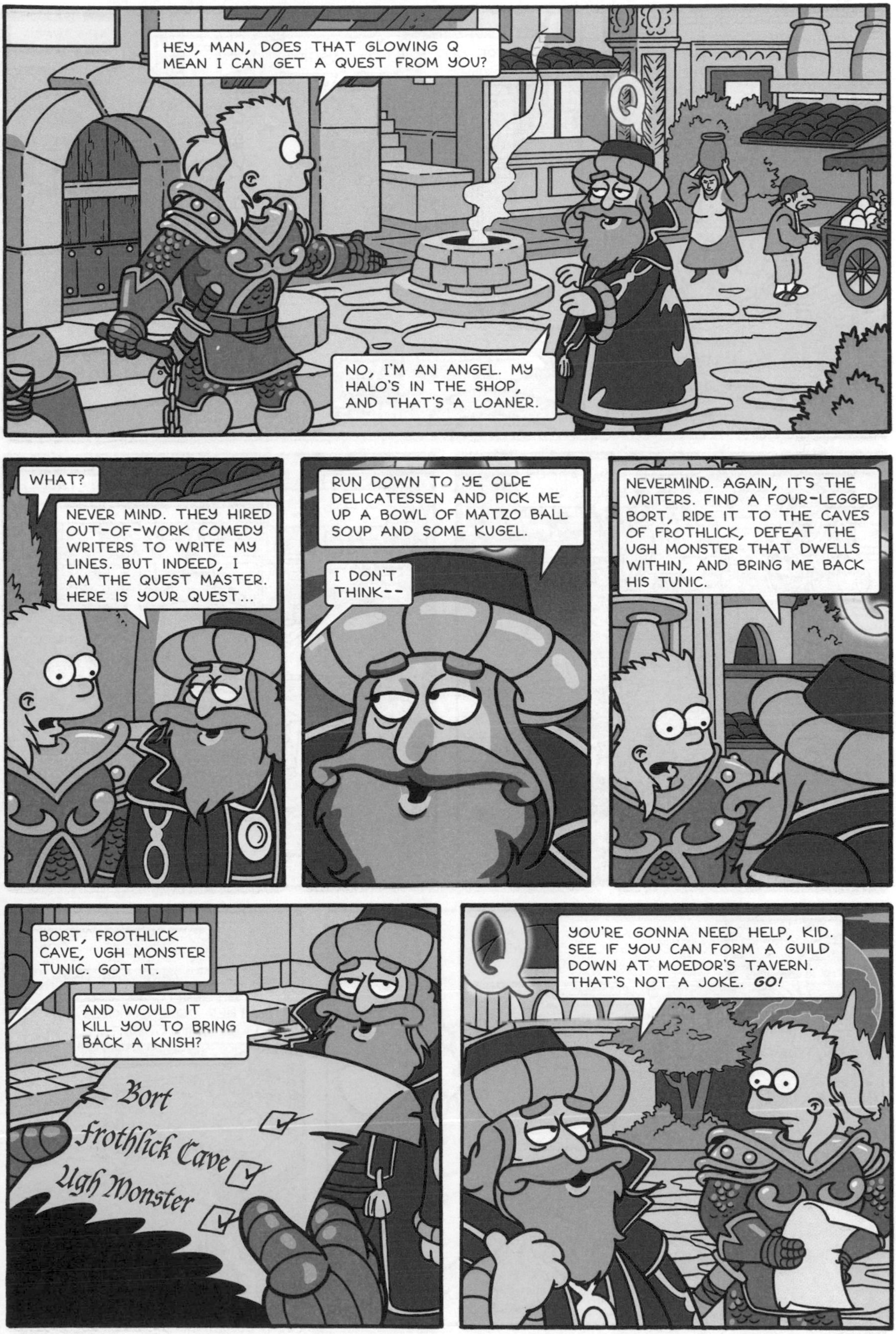
HEY, MAN, DOES THAT GLOWING Q MEAN I CAN GET A QUEST FROM YOU?
NO, I'M AN ANGEL. MY HALO'S IN THE SHOP, AND THAT'S A LOANER.
WHAT?
NEVER MIND. THEY HIRED OUT-OF-WORK COMEDY WRITERS TO WRITE MY LINES. BUT INDEED, I AM THE QUEST MASTER. HERE IS YOUR QUEST...
RUN DOWN TO YE OLDE DELICATESSEN AND PICK ME UP A BOWL OF MATZO BALL SOUP AND SOME KUGEL.
I DON'T THINK--
NEVERMIND. AGAIN, IT'S THE WRITERS. FIND A FOUR-LEGGED BORT, RIDE IT TO THE CAVES OF FROTHLICK, DEFEAT THE UGH MONSTER THAT DWELLS WITHIN, AND BRING ME BACK HIS TUNIC.
BORT, FROTHLICK CAVE, UGH MONSTER TUNIC. GOT IT.
AND WOULD IT KILL YOU TO BRING BACK A KNISH?
Bort
Frothlick Cave
Ugh Monster
YOU'RE GONNA NEED HELP, KID. SEE IF YOU CAN FORM A GUILD DOWN AT MOEDOR'S TAVERN. THAT'S NOT A JOKE. GO!

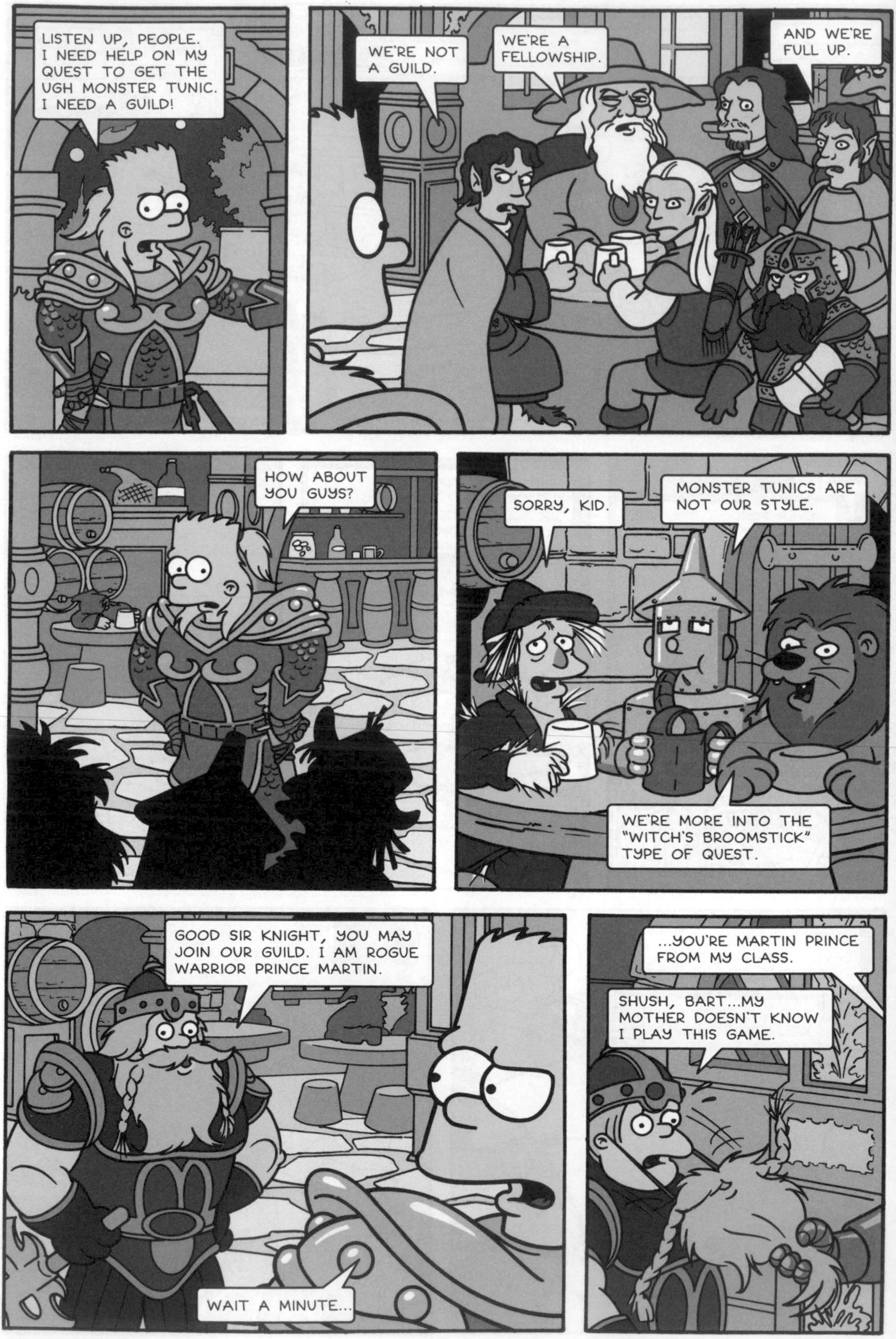
LISTEN UP, PEOPLE. I NEED HELP ON MY QUEST TO GET THE UGH MONSTER TUNIC. I NEED A GUILD!
WE'RE NOT A GUILD.
WE'RE A FELLOWSHIP.
AND WE'RE FULL UP.
HOW ABOUT YOU GUYS?
SORRY, KID.
MONSTER TUNICS ARE NOT OUR STYLE.
WE'RE MORE INTO THE "WITCH'S BROOMSTICK" TYPE OF QUEST.
GOOD SIR KNIGHT, YOU MAY JOIN OUR GUILD. I AM ROGUE WARRIOR PRINCE MARTIN.
WAIT A MINUTE...
...YOU'RE MARTIN PRINCE FROM MY CLASS.
SHUSH, BART...MY MOTHER DOESN'T KNOW I PLAY THIS GAME.

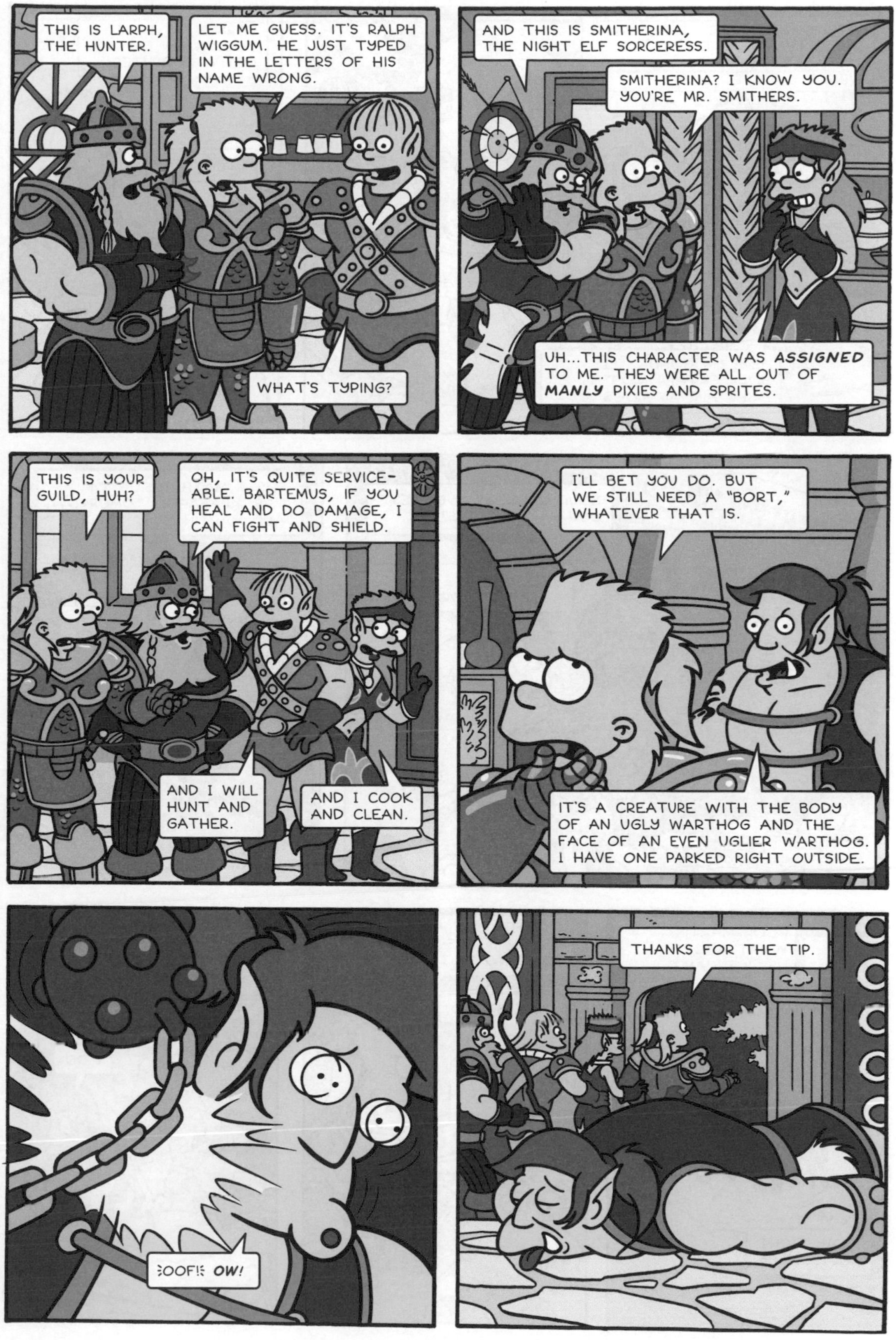
THIS IS LARPH, THE HUNTER.
LET ME GUESS. IT'S RALPH WIGGUM. HE JUST TYPED IN THE LETTERS OF HIS NAME WRONG.
WHAT'S TYPING?
AND THIS IS SMITHERINA, THE NIGHT ELF SORCERESS.
SMITHERINA? I KNOW YOU. YOU'RE MR. SMITHERS.
UH...THIS CHARACTER WAS ASSIGNED TO ME. THEY WERE ALL OUT OF MANLY PIXIES AND SPRITES.
THIS IS YOUR GUILD, HUH?
OH, IT'S QUITE SERVICE-ABLE. BARTEMUS, IF YOU HEAL AND DO DAMAGE, I CAN FIGHT AND SHIELD.
AND I WILL HUNT AND GATHER.
AND I COOK AND CLEAN.
I'LL BET YOU DO. BUT WE STILL NEED A "BORT," WHATEVER THAT IS.
IT'S A CREATURE WITH THE BODY OF AN UGLY WARTHOG AND THE FACE OF AN EVEN UGLIER WARTHOG. I HAVE ONE PARKED RIGHT OUTSIDE.
OOF! OW!
THANKS FOR THE TIP.

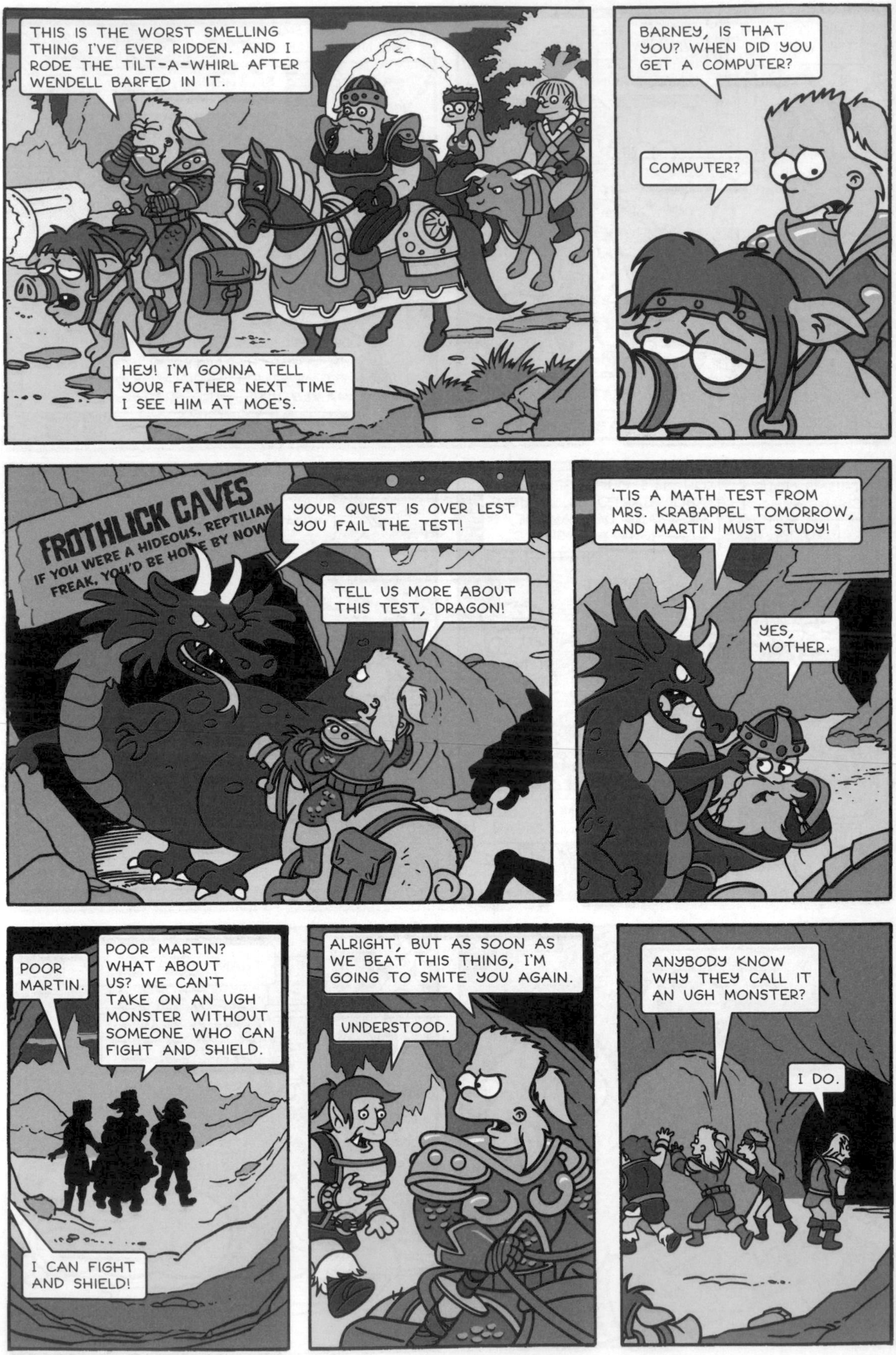
THIS IS THE WORST SMELLING THING I'VE EVER RIDDEN. AND I RODE THE TILT-A-WHIRL AFTER WENDELL BARFED IN IT.
HEY! I'M GONNA TELL YOUR FATHER NEXT TIME I SEE HIM AT MOE'S.
BARNEY, IS THAT YOU? WHEN DID YOU GET A COMPUTER?
COMPUTER?
FROTHLICK CAVES
IF YOU WERE A HIDEOUS, REPTILIAN FREAK, YOU'D BE HOME BY NOW.
YOUR QUEST IS OVER LEST YOU FAIL THE TEST!
TELL US MORE ABOUT THIS TEST, DRAGON!
'TIS A MATH TEST FROM MRS. KRABAPPEL TOMORROW, AND MARTIN MUST STUDY!
YES, MOTHER.
POOR MARTIN.
POOR MARTIN? WHAT ABOUT US? WE CAN'T TAKE ON AN UGH MONSTER WITHOUT SOMEONE WHO CAN FIGHT AND SHIELD.
I CAN FIGHT AND SHIELD!
ALRIGHT, BUT AS SOON AS WE BEAT THIS THING, I'M GOING TO SMITE YOU AGAIN.
UNDERSTOOD.
ANYBODY KNOW WHY THEY CALL IT AN UGH MONSTER?
I DO.

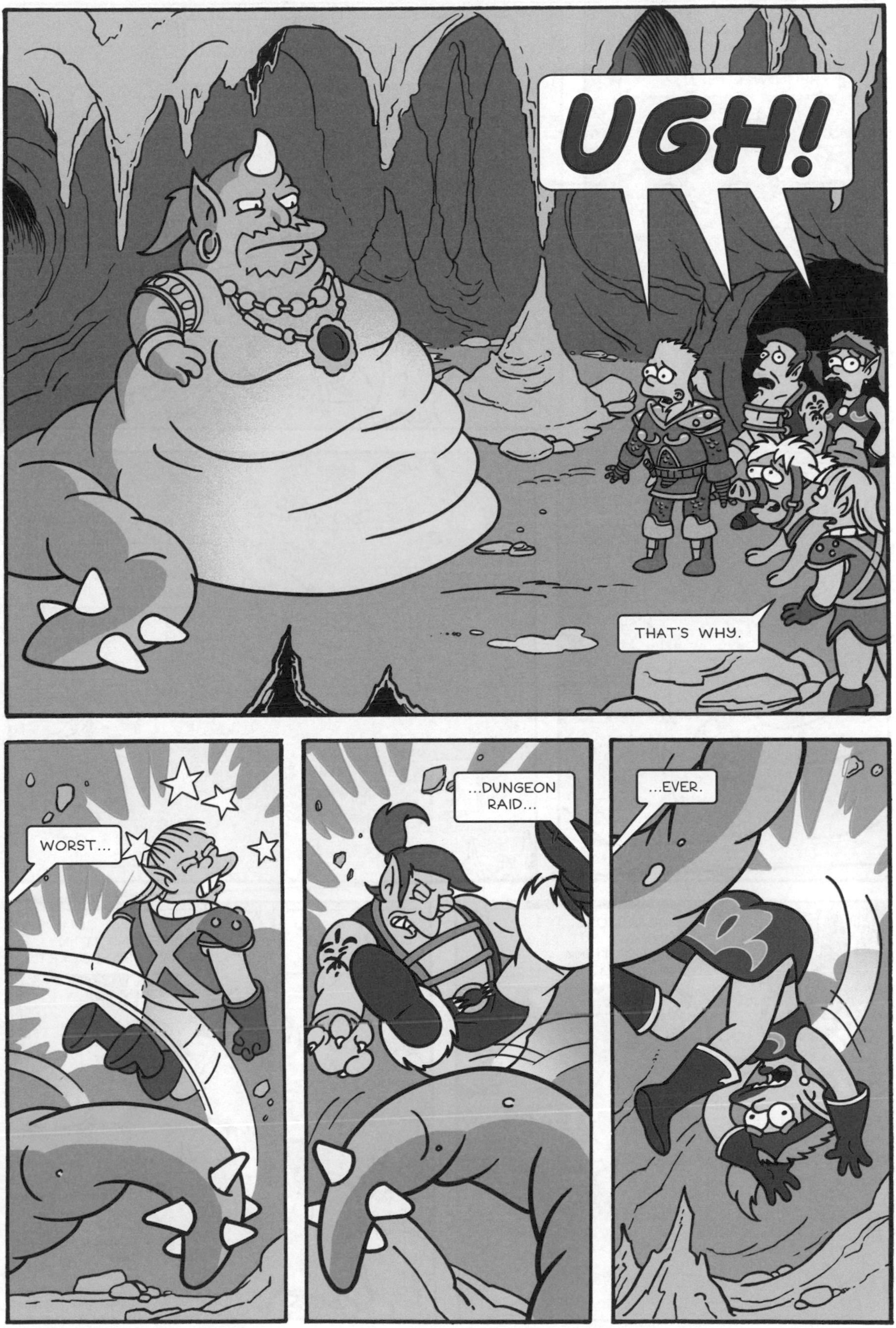
UGH!
THAT'S WHY.
WORST...
...DUNGEON RAID...
...EVER.

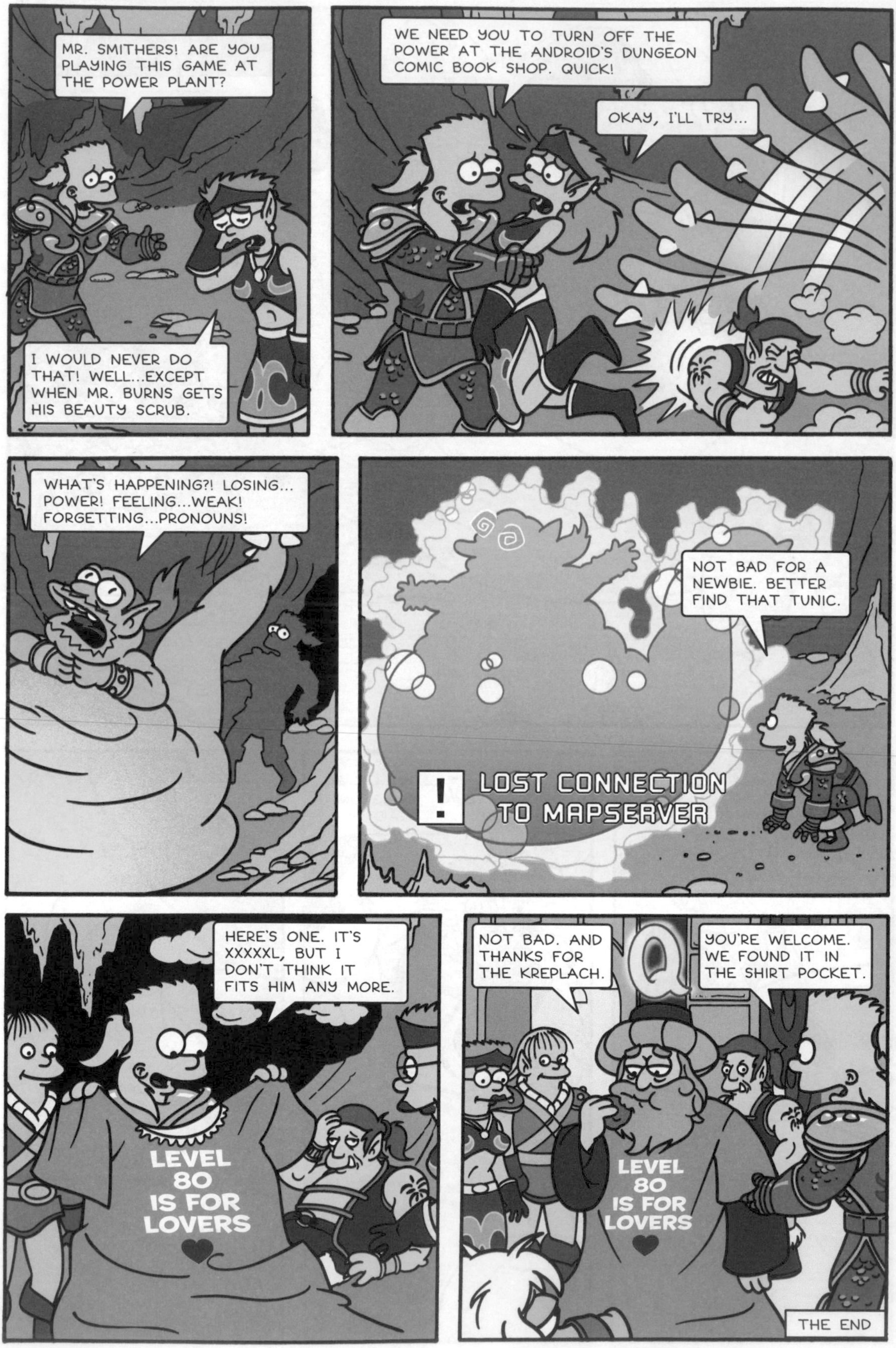
MR. SMITHERS! ARE YOU PLAYING THIS GAME AT THE POWER PLANT?
I WOULD NEVER DO THAT! WELL...EXCEPT WHEN MR. BURNS GETS HIS BEAUTY SCRUB.
WE NEED YOU TO TURN OFF THE POWER AT THE ANDROID'S DUNGEON COMIC BOOK SHOP. QUICK!
OKAY, I'LL TRY...
WHAT'S HAPPENING?! LOSING... POWER! FEELING...WEAK! FORGETTING...PRONOUNS!
NOT BAD FOR A NEWBIE. BETTER FIND THAT TUNIC.
! LOST CONNECTION TO MAPSERVER
HERE'S ONE. IT'S XXXXXL, BUT I DON'T THINK IT FITS HIM ANY MORE.
LEVEL 80 IS FOR LOVERS
NOT BAD. AND THANKS FOR THE KREPLACH.
YOU'RE WELCOME. WE FOUND IT IN THE SHIRT POCKET.
LEVEL 80 IS FOR LOVERS
THE END

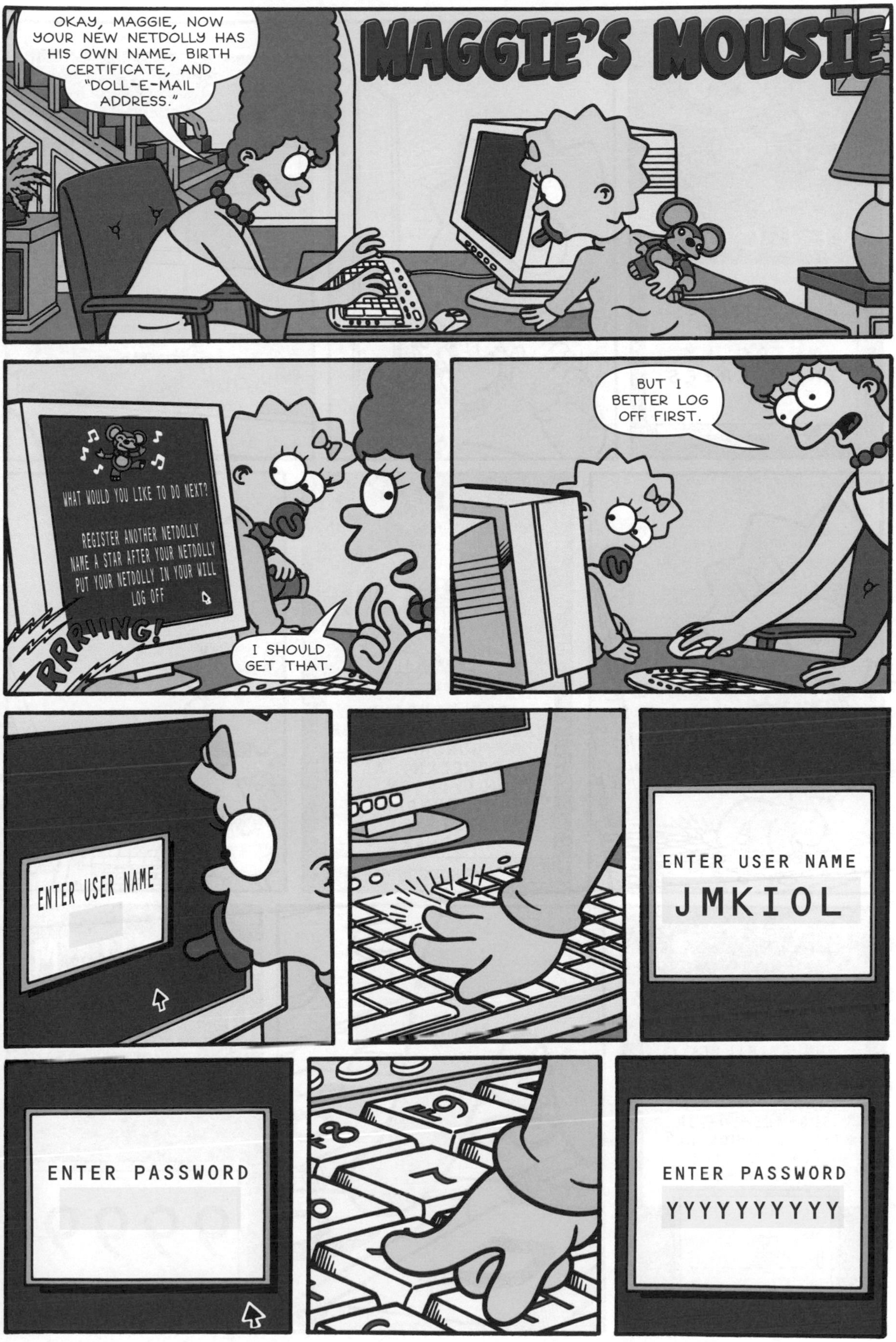
MAGGIE'S MOUSIE
OKAY, MAGGIE, NOW YOUR NEW NETDOLLY HAS HIS OWN NAME, BIRTH CERTIFICATE, AND "DOLL-E-MAIL ADDRESS."
WHAT WOULD YOU LIKE TO DO NEXT?
REGISTER ANOTHER NETDOLLY
NAME A STAR AFTER YOUR NETDOLLY
PUT YOUR NETDOLLY IN YOUR WILL
LOG OFF
RRRIIING!
I SHOULD GET THAT.
BUT I BETTER LOG OFF FIRST.
ENTER USER NAME
ENTER USER NAME
JMKIOL
ENTER PASSWORD
ENTER PASSWORD
YYYYYYYYYY

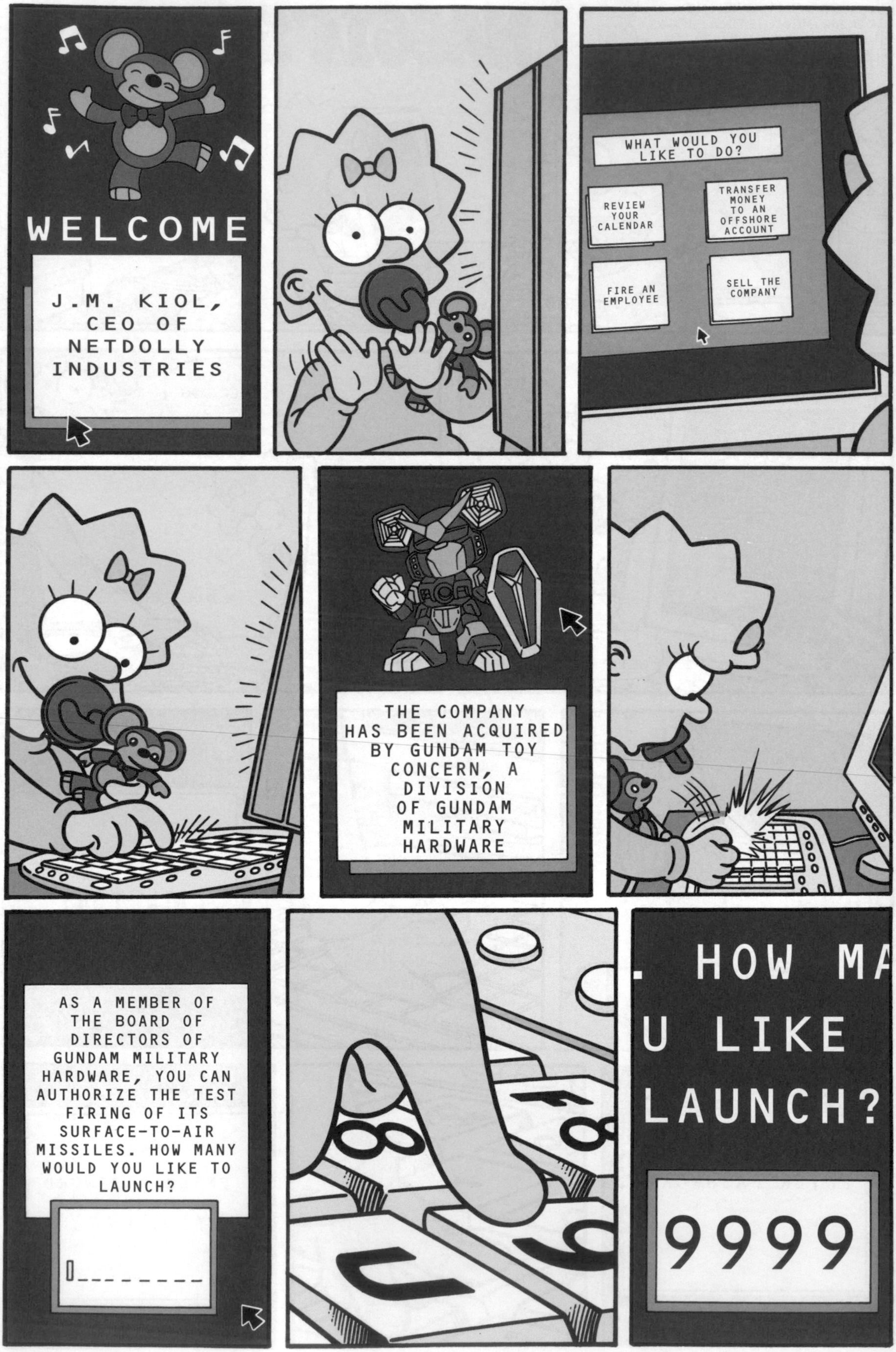
WELCOME
J.M. KIOL, CEO OF NETDOLLY INDUSTRIES
WHAT WOULD YOU LIKE TO DO?
REVIEW YOUR CALENDAR
TRANSFER MONEY TO AN OFFSHORE ACCOUNT
FIRE AN EMPLOYEE
SELL THE COMPANY
THE COMPANY HAS BEEN ACQUIRED BY GUNDAM TOY CONCERN, A DIVISION OF GUNDAM MILITARY HARDWARE
AS A MEMBER OF THE BOARD OF DIRECTORS OF GUNDAM MILITARY HARDWARE, YOU CAN AUTHORIZE THE TEST FIRING OF ITS SURFACE-TO-AIR MISSILES. HOW MANY WOULD YOU LIKE TO LAUNCH?
. HOW MA
U LIKE
LAUNCH?
9999

IN LIGHT OF THE OVERWHELMING SHOW OF FORCE, THE NORTH KOREAN GOVERNMENT HAS SURRENDERED. NO MISSILES WERE FIRED. CONGRATULATIONS, PREMIER KIOL

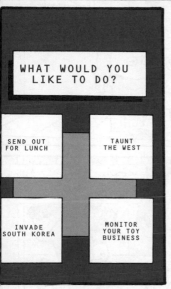

WHAT WOULD YOU LIKE TO DO?

SEND OUT FOR LUNCH

TAUNT THE WEST

INVADE SOUTH KOREA

MONITOR YOUR TOY BUSINESS

WHAT WOULD YOU LIKE TO DO NEXT?

REGISTER A NETDOLLY

NAME A STAR AFTER YOUR NETDOLLY

PUT YOUR NETDOLLY IN YOUR WILL

LAUNCH 9999 MISSILES AT THE U.S.

LOG OFF

I THOUGHT I LOGGED OFF THIS SITE.

I HAVE TO WATCH YOU EVERY MINUTE. YOU COULD HAVE SPENT $6 ON ANOTHER DOLL!

THE END

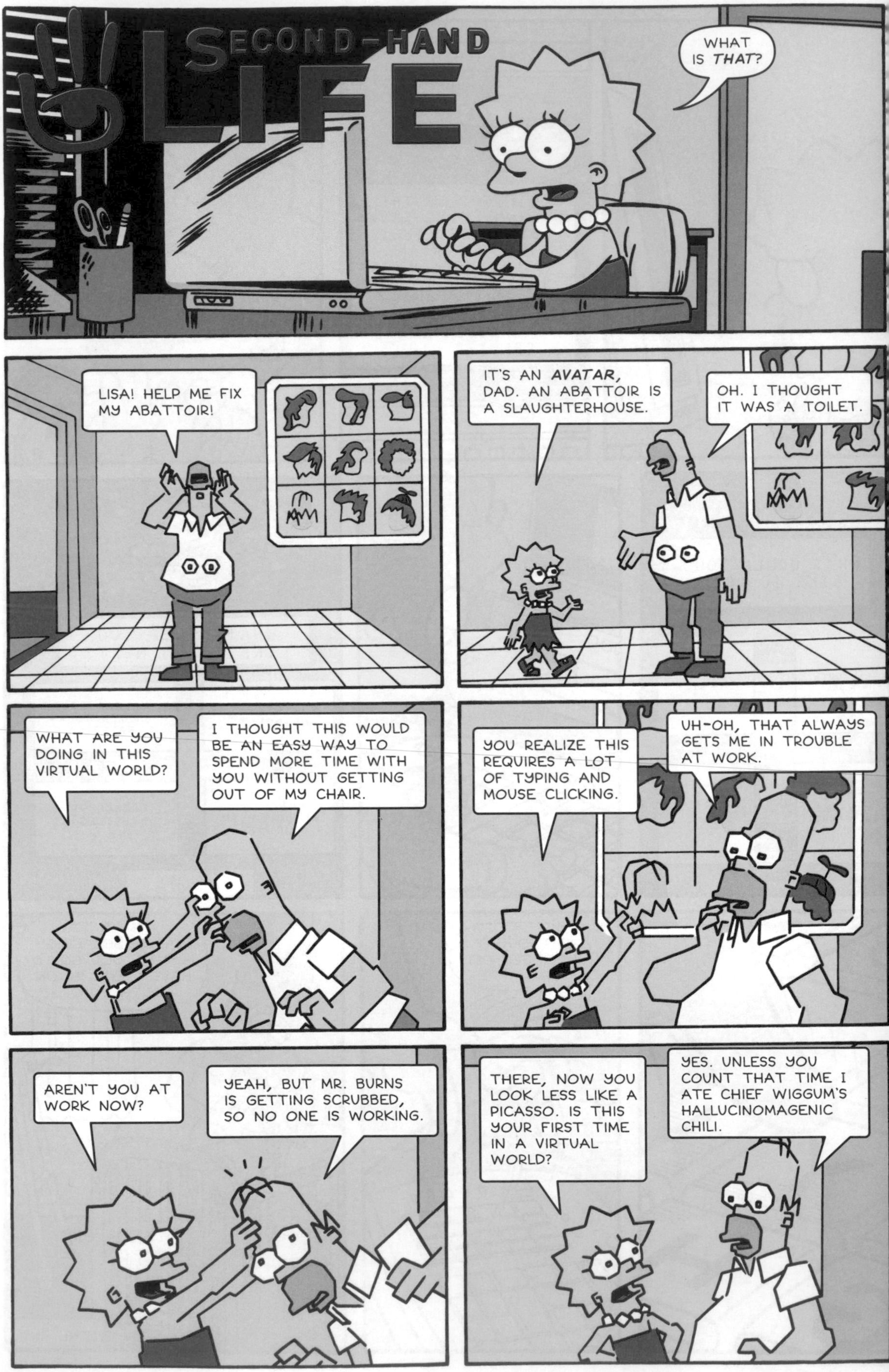
SECOND-HAND LIFE
WHAT IS *THAT*?
LISA! HELP ME FIX MY ABATTOIR!
IT'S AN ***AVATAR,*** DAD. AN ABATTOIR IS A SLAUGHTERHOUSE.
OH. I THOUGHT IT WAS A TOILET.
WHAT ARE YOU DOING IN THIS VIRTUAL WORLD?
I THOUGHT THIS WOULD BE AN EASY WAY TO SPEND MORE TIME WITH YOU WITHOUT GETTING OUT OF MY CHAIR.
YOU REALIZE THIS REQUIRES A LOT OF TYPING AND MOUSE CLICKING.
UH-OH, THAT ALWAYS GETS ME IN TROUBLE AT WORK.
AREN'T YOU AT WORK NOW?
YEAH, BUT MR. BURNS IS GETTING SCRUBBED, SO NO ONE IS WORKING.
THERE, NOW YOU LOOK LESS LIKE A PICASSO. IS THIS YOUR FIRST TIME IN A VIRTUAL WORLD?
YES. UNLESS YOU COUNT THAT TIME I ATE CHIEF WIGGUM'S HALLUCINOMAGENIC CHILI.

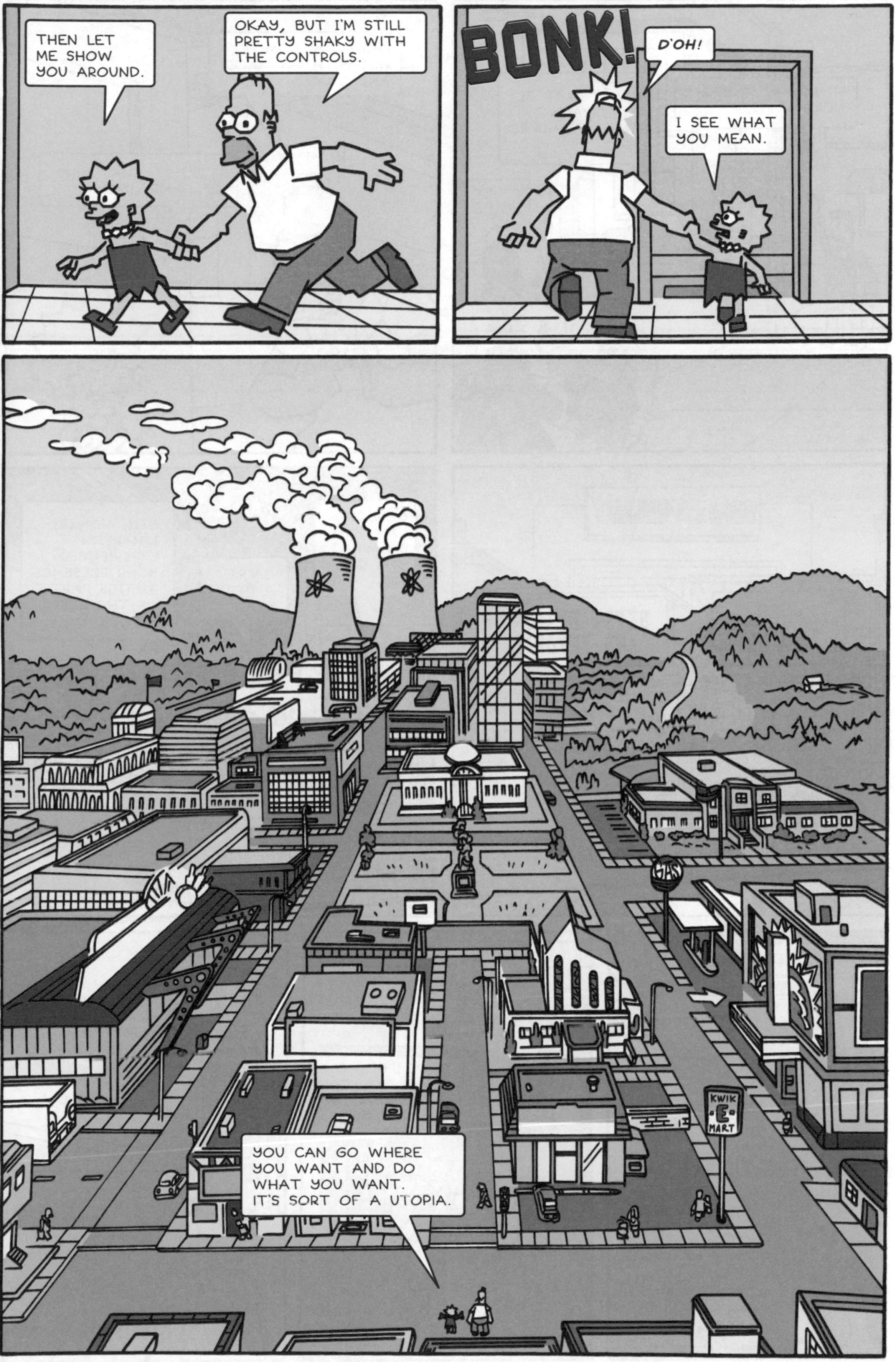
THEN LET ME SHOW YOU AROUND.
OKAY, BUT I'M STILL PRETTY SHAKY WITH THE CONTROLS.
BONK!
D'OH!
I SEE WHAT YOU MEAN.
GAS
KWIK E MART
YOU CAN GO WHERE YOU WANT AND DO WHAT YOU WANT. IT'S SORT OF A UTOPIA.

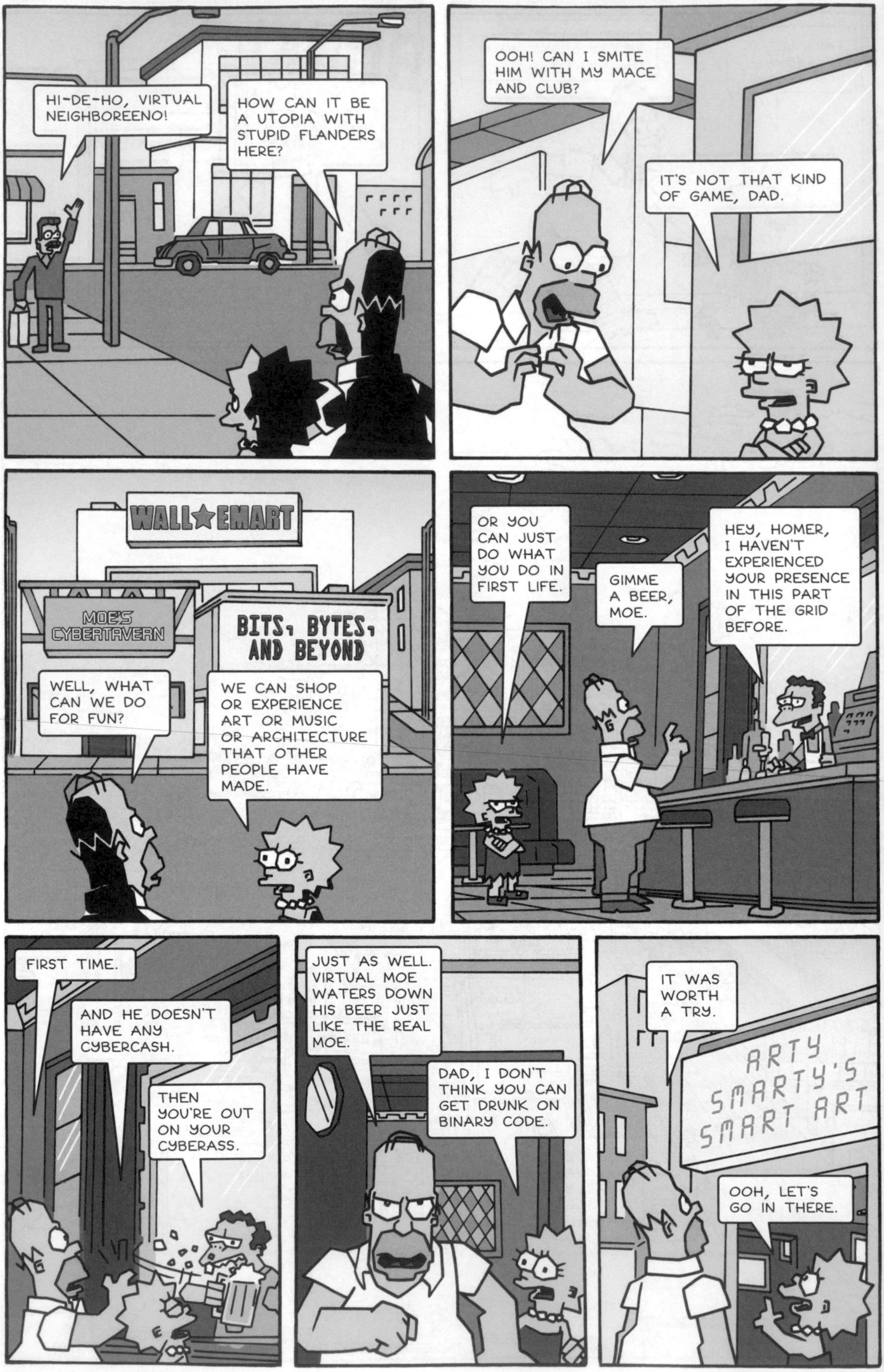
HI-DE-HO, VIRTUAL NEIGHBOREENO!
HOW CAN IT BE A UTOPIA WITH STUPID FLANDERS HERE?
OOH! CAN I SMITE HIM WITH MY MACE AND CLUB?
IT'S NOT THAT KIND OF GAME, DAD.
WALL★EMART
MOE'S CYBERTAVERN
BITS, BYTES, AND BEYOND
WELL, WHAT CAN WE DO FOR FUN?
WE CAN SHOP OR EXPERIENCE ART OR MUSIC OR ARCHITECTURE THAT OTHER PEOPLE HAVE MADE.
OR YOU CAN JUST DO WHAT YOU DO IN FIRST LIFE.
GIMME A BEER, MOE.
HEY, HOMER, I HAVEN'T EXPERIENCED YOUR PRESENCE IN THIS PART OF THE GRID BEFORE.
FIRST TIME.
AND HE DOESN'T HAVE ANY CYBERCASH.
THEN YOU'RE OUT ON YOUR CYBERASS.
JUST AS WELL. VIRTUAL MOE WATERS DOWN HIS BEER JUST LIKE THE REAL MOE.
DAD, I DON'T THINK YOU CAN GET DRUNK ON BINARY CODE.
IT WAS WORTH A TRY.
ARTY SMARTY'S SMART ART
OOH, LET'S GO IN THERE.

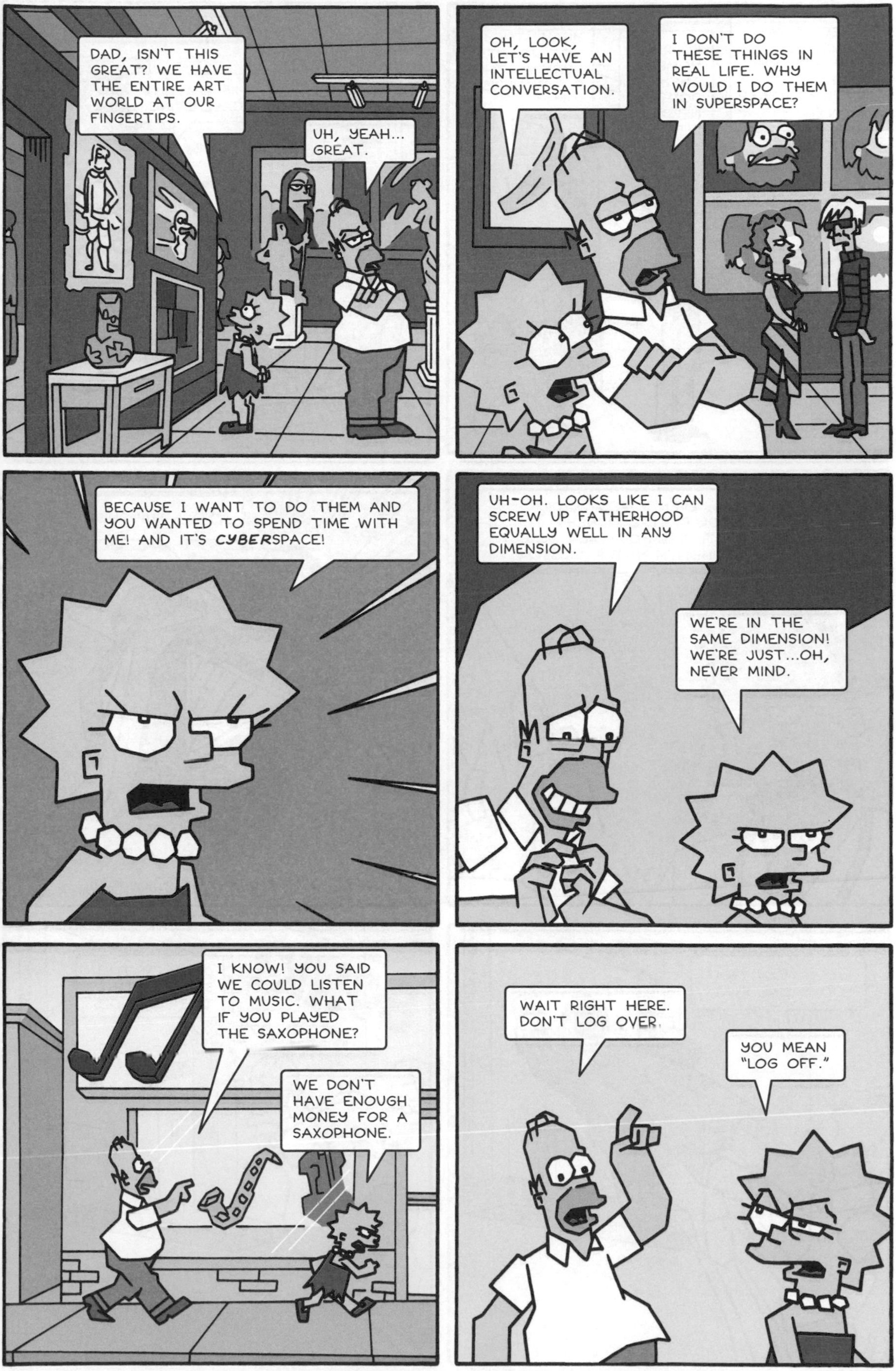

DAD, ISN'T THIS GREAT? WE HAVE THE ENTIRE ART WORLD AT OUR FINGERTIPS.
UH, YEAH... GREAT.
OH, LOOK, LET'S HAVE AN INTELLECTUAL CONVERSATION.
I DON'T DO THESE THINGS IN REAL LIFE. WHY WOULD I DO THEM IN SUPERSPACE?
BECAUSE I WANT TO DO THEM AND YOU WANTED TO SPEND TIME WITH ME! AND IT'S *CYBER*SPACE!
UH-OH. LOOKS LIKE I CAN SCREW UP FATHERHOOD EQUALLY WELL IN ANY DIMENSION.
WE'RE IN THE SAME DIMENSION! WE'RE JUST...OH, NEVER MIND.
I KNOW! YOU SAID WE COULD LISTEN TO MUSIC. WHAT IF YOU PLAYED THE SAXOPHONE?
WE DON'T HAVE ENOUGH MONEY FOR A SAXOPHONE.
WAIT RIGHT HERE. DON'T LOG OVER.
YOU MEAN "LOG OFF."

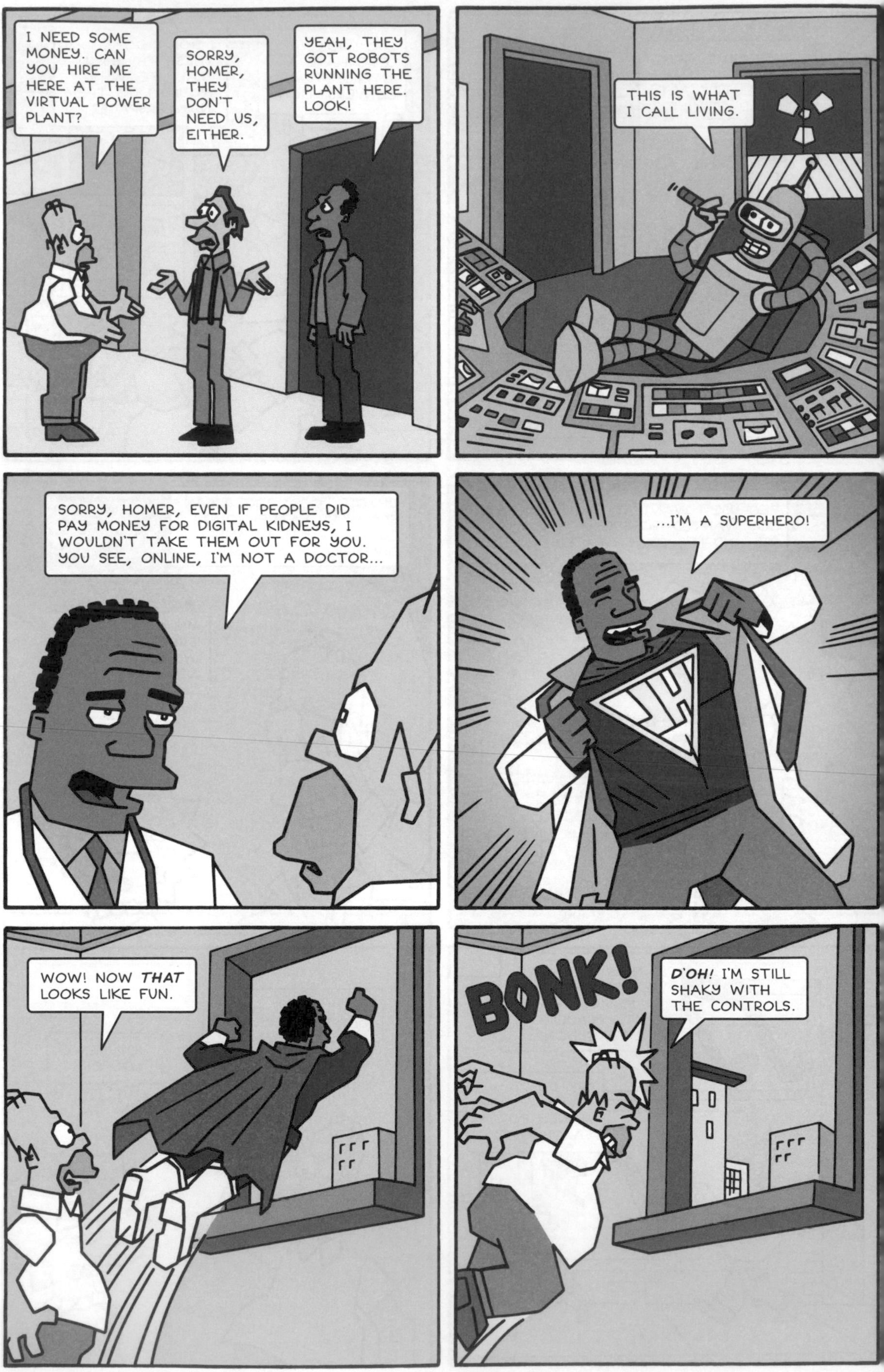
I NEED SOME MONEY. CAN YOU HIRE ME HERE AT THE VIRTUAL POWER PLANT?
SORRY, HOMER, THEY DON'T NEED US, EITHER.
YEAH, THEY GOT ROBOTS RUNNING THE PLANT HERE. LOOK!
THIS IS WHAT I CALL LIVING.
SORRY, HOMER, EVEN IF PEOPLE DID PAY MONEY FOR DIGITAL KIDNEYS, I WOULDN'T TAKE THEM OUT FOR YOU. YOU SEE, ONLINE, I'M NOT A DOCTOR...
...I'M A SUPERHERO!
WOW! NOW *THAT* LOOKS LIKE FUN.
BONK!
D'OH! I'M STILL SHAKY WITH THE CONTROLS.

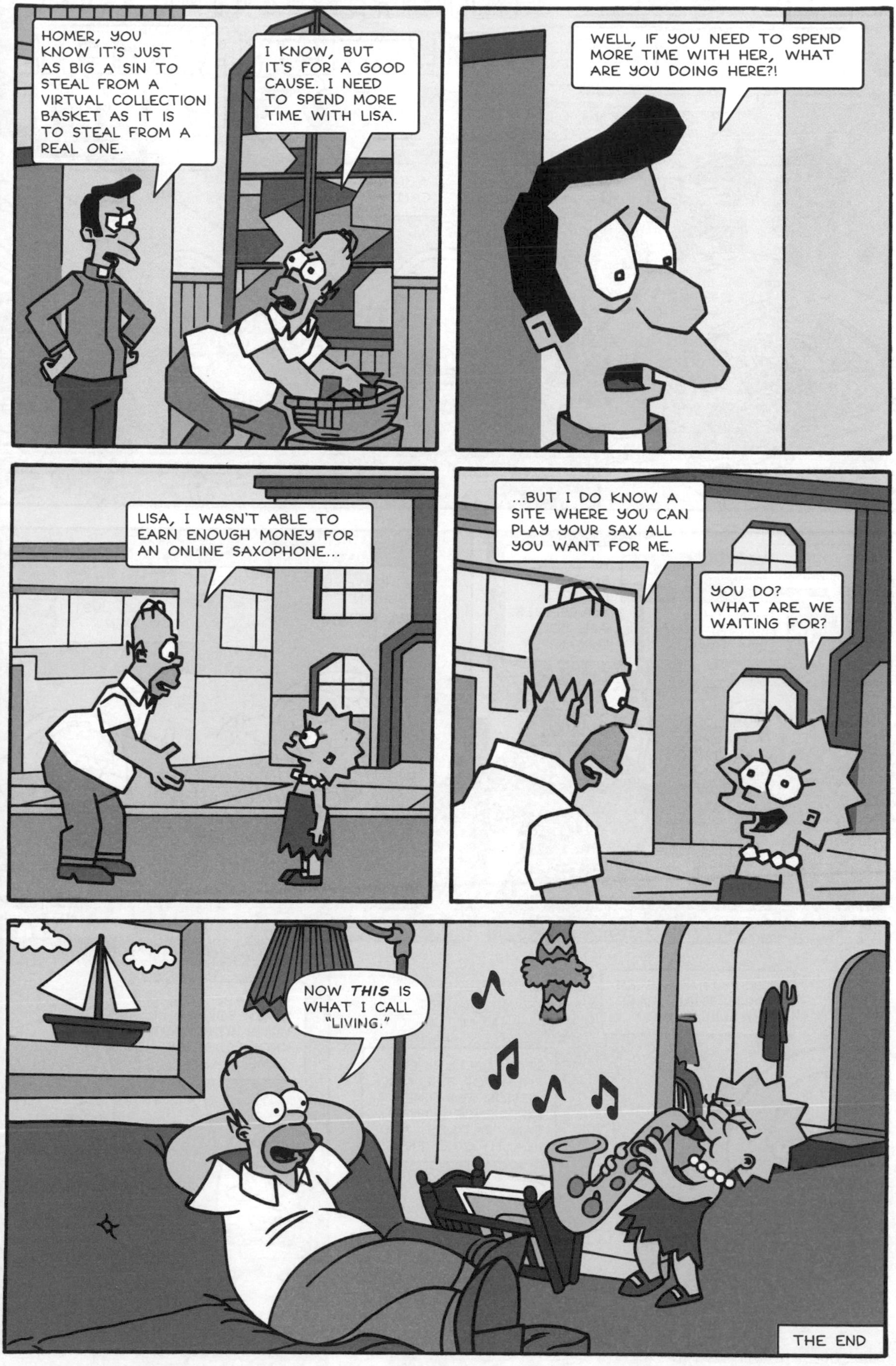
HOMER, YOU KNOW IT'S JUST AS BIG A SIN TO STEAL FROM A VIRTUAL COLLECTION BASKET AS IT IS TO STEAL FROM A REAL ONE.
I KNOW, BUT IT'S FOR A GOOD CAUSE. I NEED TO SPEND MORE TIME WITH LISA.
WELL, IF YOU NEED TO SPEND MORE TIME WITH HER, WHAT ARE YOU DOING HERE?!
LISA, I WASN'T ABLE TO EARN ENOUGH MONEY FOR AN ONLINE SAXOPHONE...
...BUT I DO KNOW A SITE WHERE YOU CAN PLAY YOUR SAX ALL YOU WANT FOR ME.
YOU DO? WHAT ARE WE WAITING FOR?
NOW *THIS* IS WHAT I CALL "LIVING."
THE END

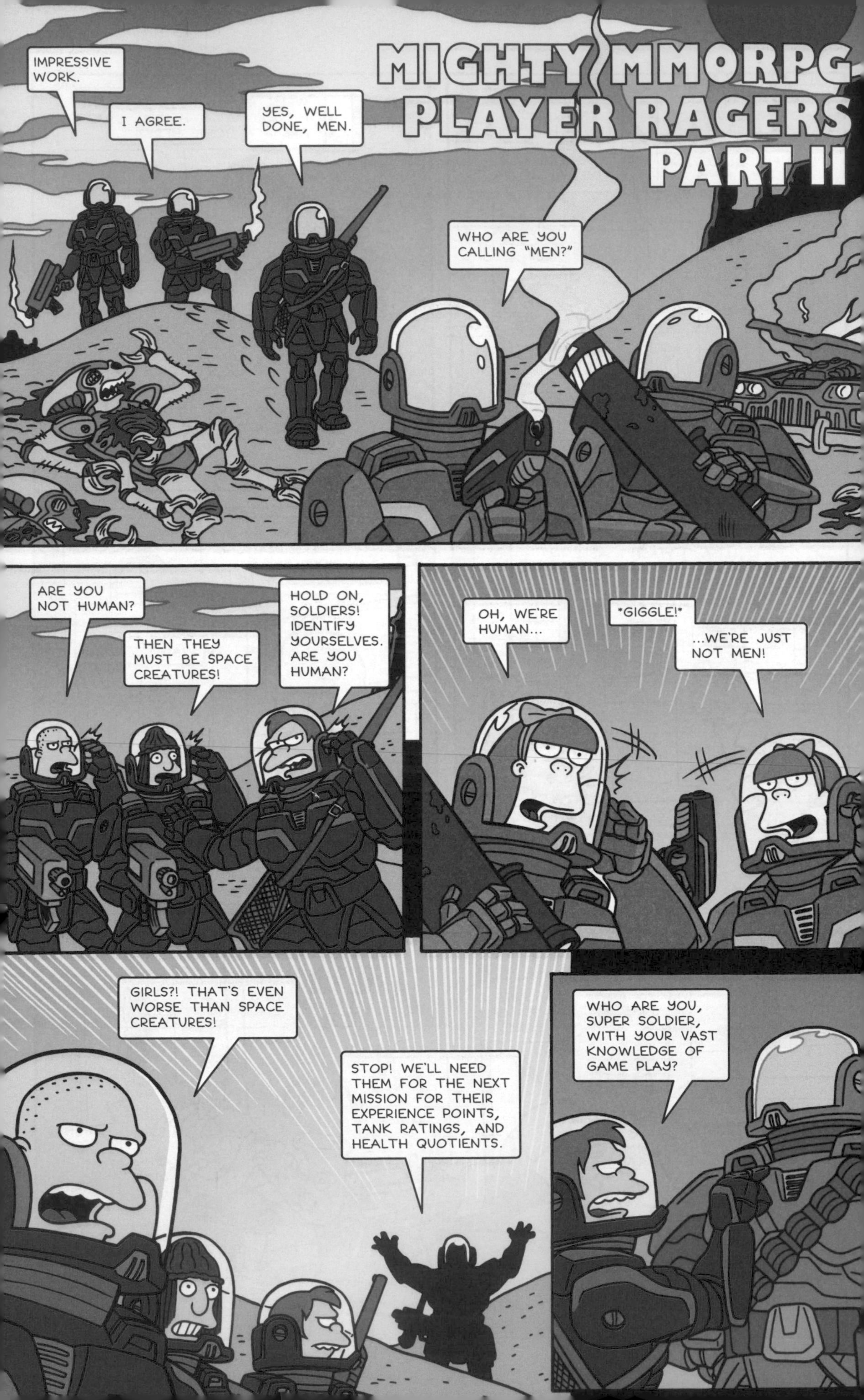
MIGHTY MMORPG PLAYER RAGERS PART II
IMPRESSIVE WORK.
I AGREE.
YES, WELL DONE, MEN.
WHO ARE YOU CALLING "MEN?"
ARE YOU NOT HUMAN?
THEN THEY MUST BE SPACE CREATURES!
HOLD ON, SOLDIERS! IDENTIFY YOURSELVES. ARE YOU HUMAN?
OH, WE'RE HUMAN...
GIGGLE!
...WE'RE JUST NOT MEN!
GIRLS?! THAT'S EVEN WORSE THAN SPACE CREATURES!
STOP! WE'LL NEED THEM FOR THE NEXT MISSION FOR THEIR EXPERIENCE POINTS, TANK RATINGS, AND HEALTH QUOTIENTS.
WHO ARE YOU, SUPER SOLDIER, WITH YOUR VAST KNOWLEDGE OF GAME PLAY?

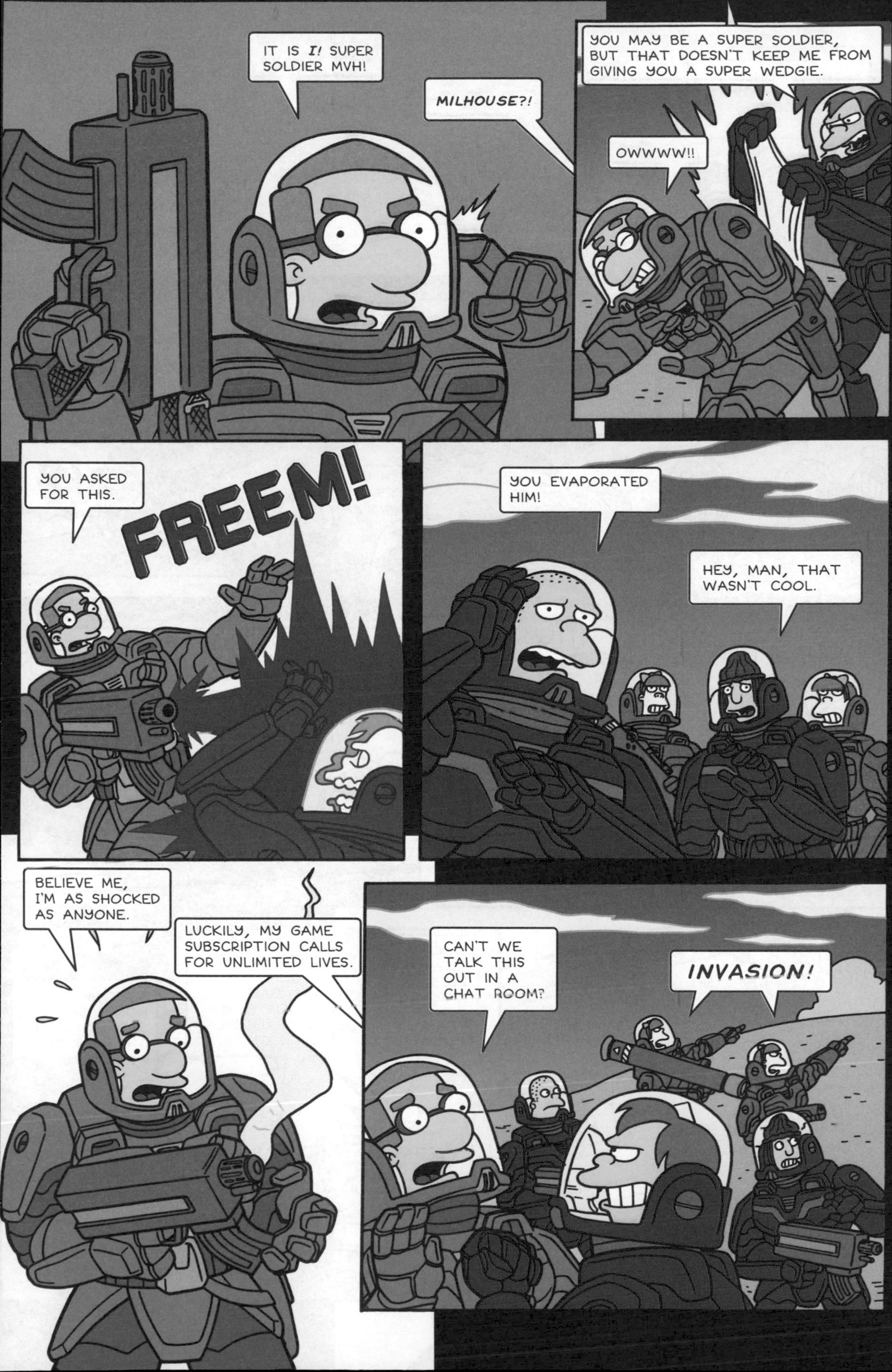
IT IS *I!* SUPER SOLDIER MVH!
MILHOUSE?!
YOU MAY BE A SUPER SOLDIER, BUT THAT DOESN'T KEEP ME FROM GIVING YOU A SUPER WEDGIE.
OWWWW!!
YOU ASKED FOR THIS.
FREEM!
YOU EVAPORATED HIM!
HEY, MAN, THAT WASN'T COOL.
BELIEVE ME, I'M AS SHOCKED AS ANYONE.
LUCKILY, MY GAME SUBSCRIPTION CALLS FOR UNLIMITED LIVES.
CAN'T WE TALK THIS OUT IN A CHAT ROOM?
INVASION!

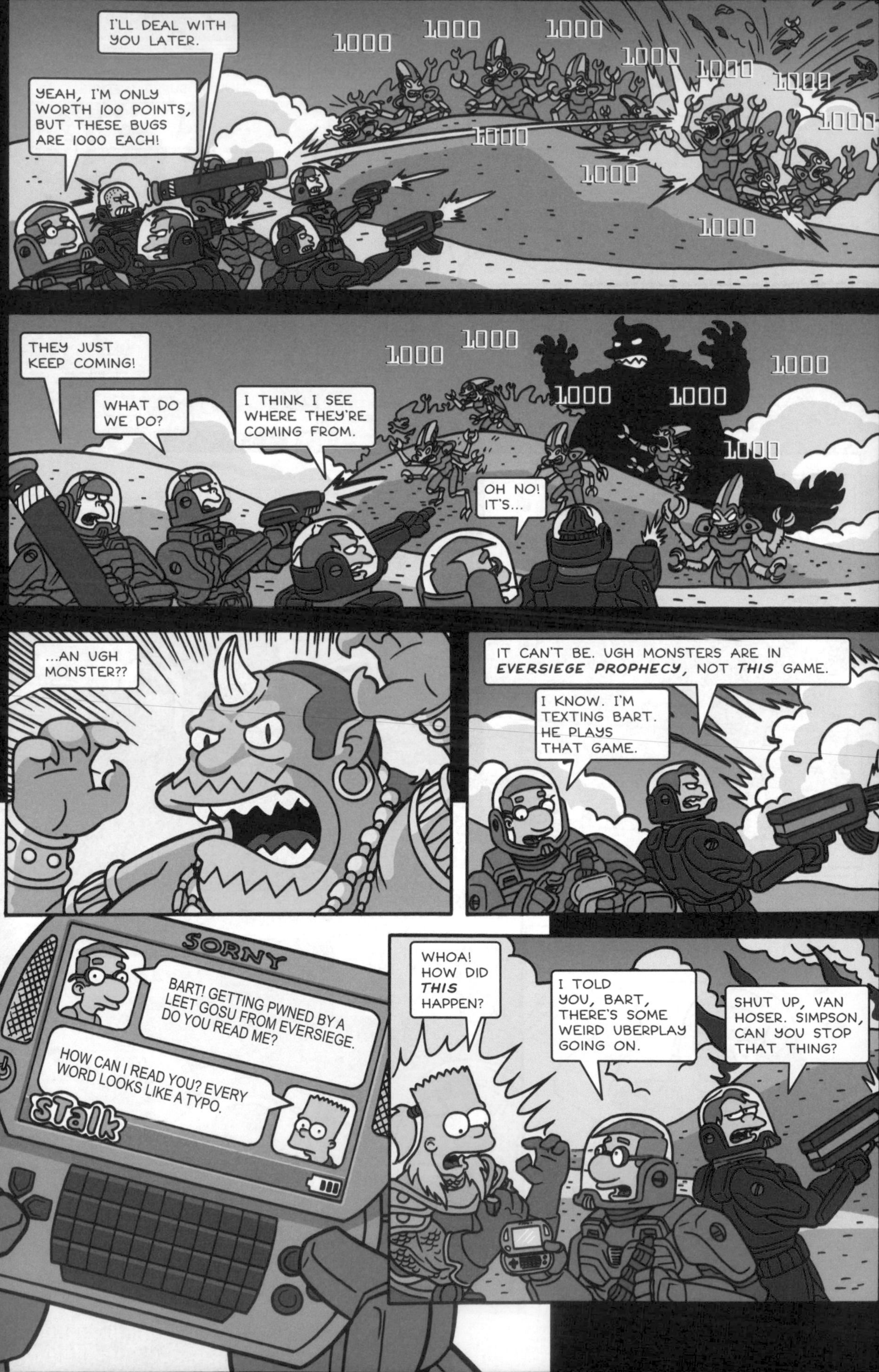

I'LL DEAL WITH YOU LATER.
YEAH, I'M ONLY WORTH 100 POINTS, BUT THESE BUGS ARE 1000 EACH!
1000
THEY JUST KEEP COMING!
WHAT DO WE DO?
I THINK I SEE WHERE THEY'RE COMING FROM.
OH NO! IT'S...
...AN UGH MONSTER??
IT CAN'T BE. UGH MONSTERS ARE IN ***EVERSIEGE PROPHECY***, NOT ***THIS*** GAME.
I KNOW. I'M TEXTING BART. HE PLAYS THAT GAME.
SORNY
BART! GETTING PWNED BY A LEET GOSU FROM EVERSIEGE. DO YOU READ ME?
HOW CAN I READ YOU? EVERY WORD LOOKS LIKE A TYPO.
STalk
WHOA! HOW DID ***THIS*** HAPPEN?
I TOLD YOU, BART, THERE'S SOME WEIRD UBERPLAY GOING ON.
SHUT UP, VAN HOSER. SIMPSON, CAN YOU STOP THAT THING?

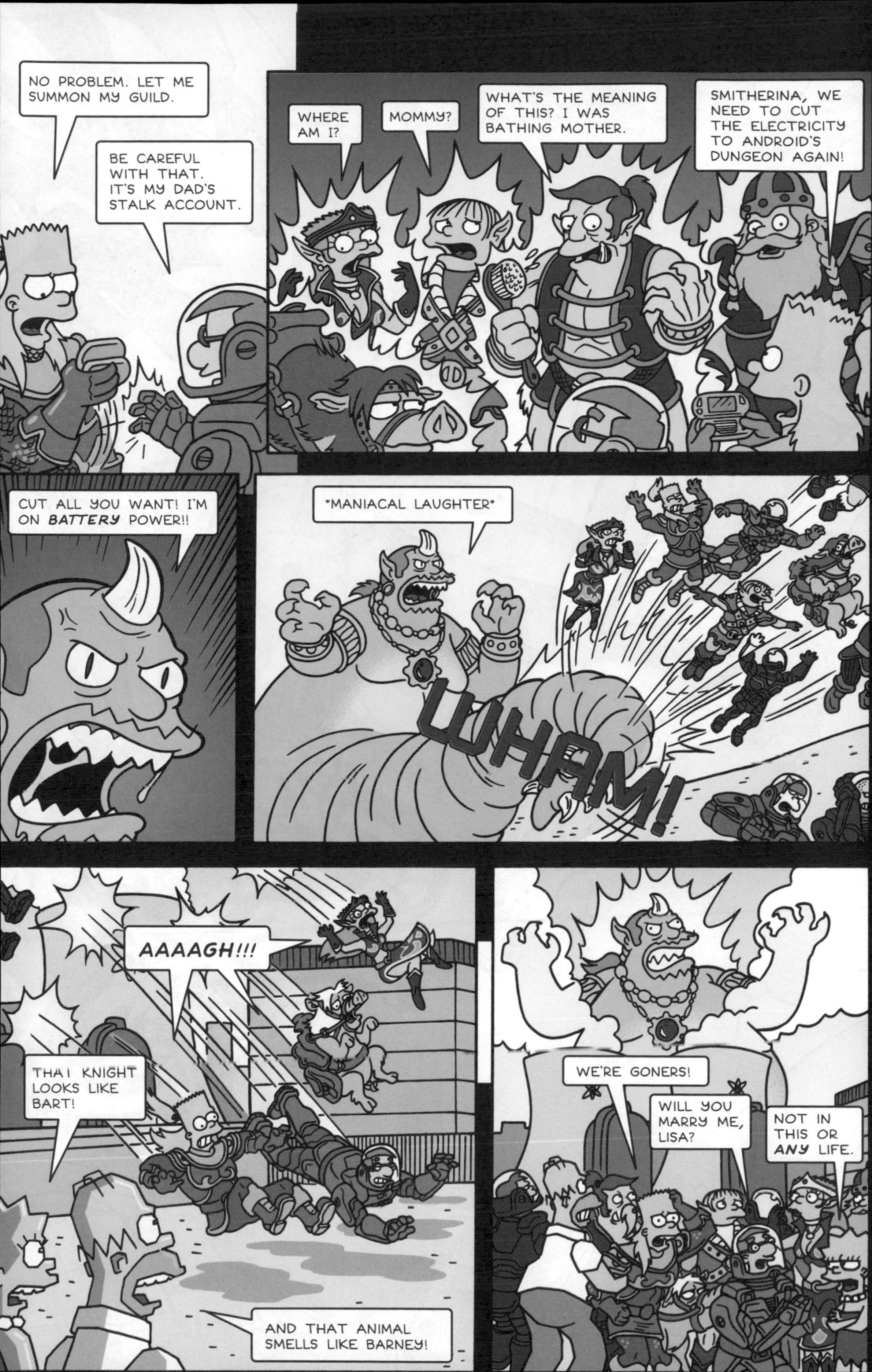
NO PROBLEM. LET ME SUMMON MY GUILD.
BE CAREFUL WITH THAT. IT'S MY DAD'S STALK ACCOUNT.
WHERE AM I?
MOMMY?
WHAT'S THE MEANING OF THIS? I WAS BATHING MOTHER.
SMITHERINA, WE NEED TO CUT THE ELECTRICITY TO ANDROID'S DUNGEON AGAIN!
CUT ALL YOU WANT! I'M ON BATTERY POWER!!
MANIACAL LAUGHTER
WHAM!
AAAAGH!!!
THAT KNIGHT LOOKS LIKE BART!
AND THAT ANIMAL SMELLS LIKE BARNEY!
WE'RE GONERS!
WILL YOU MARRY ME, LISA?
NOT IN THIS OR ANY LIFE.

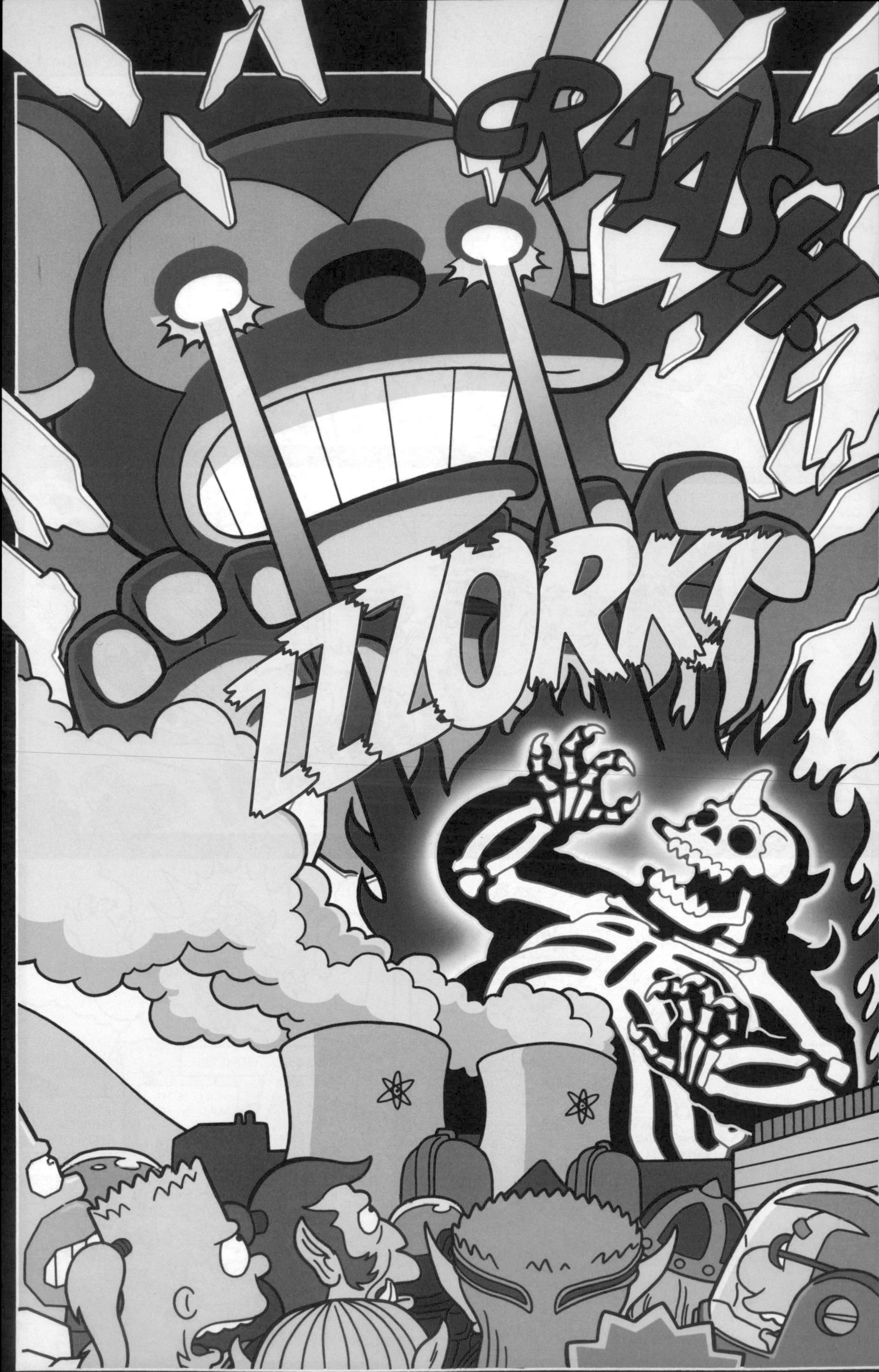
CRAASH
ZZZORK!

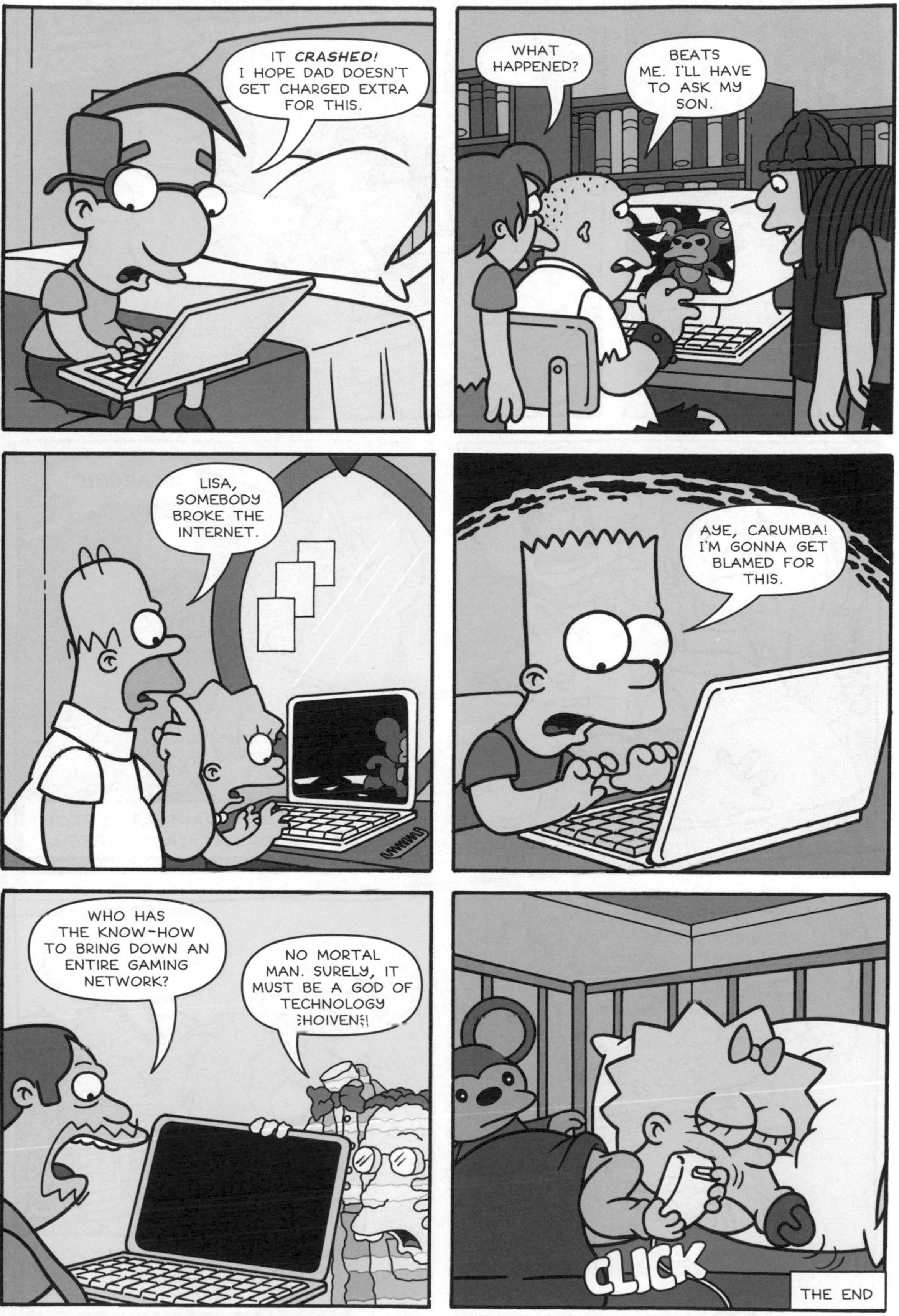
IT CRASHED! I HOPE DAD DOESN'T GET CHARGED EXTRA FOR THIS.
WHAT HAPPENED?
BEATS ME. I'LL HAVE TO ASK MY SON.
LISA, SOMEBODY BROKE THE INTERNET.
AYE, CARUMBA! I'M GONNA GET BLAMED FOR THIS.
WHO HAS THE KNOW-HOW TO BRING DOWN AN ENTIRE GAMING NETWORK?
NO MORTAL MAN. SURELY, IT MUST BE A GOD OF TECHNOLOGY
HOIVEN!
CLICK
THE END

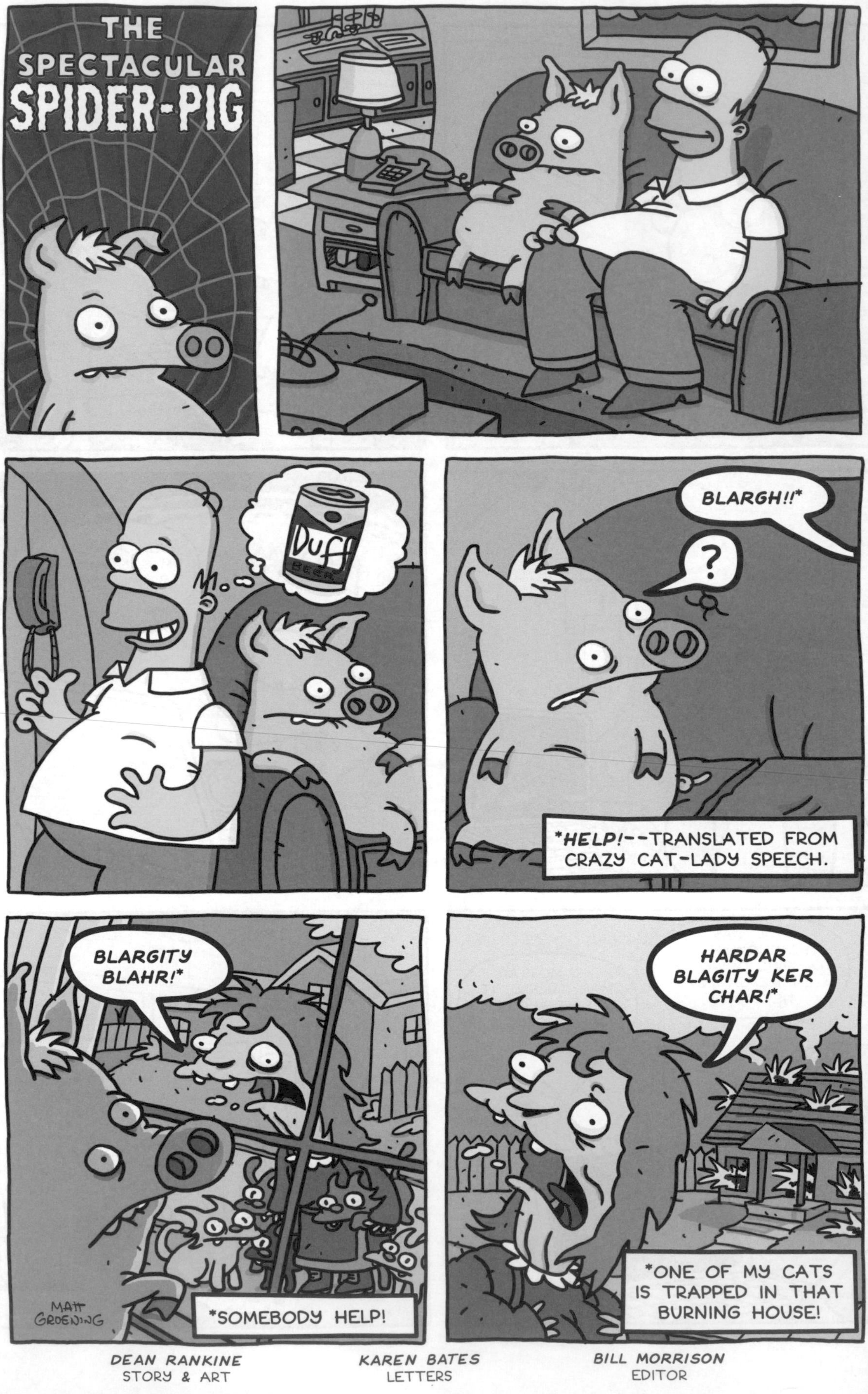
THE SPECTACULAR SPIDER-PIG
Duff BEER
BLARGH!!*
?
*HELP!--TRANSLATED FROM CRAZY CAT-LADY SPEECH.
BLARGITY BLAHR!*
MATT GROENING
*SOMEBODY HELP!
HARDAR BLAGITY KER CHAR!*
*ONE OF MY CATS IS TRAPPED IN THAT BURNING HOUSE!

DEAN RANKINE
STORY & ART

KAREN BATES
LETTERS

BILL MORRISON
EDITOR

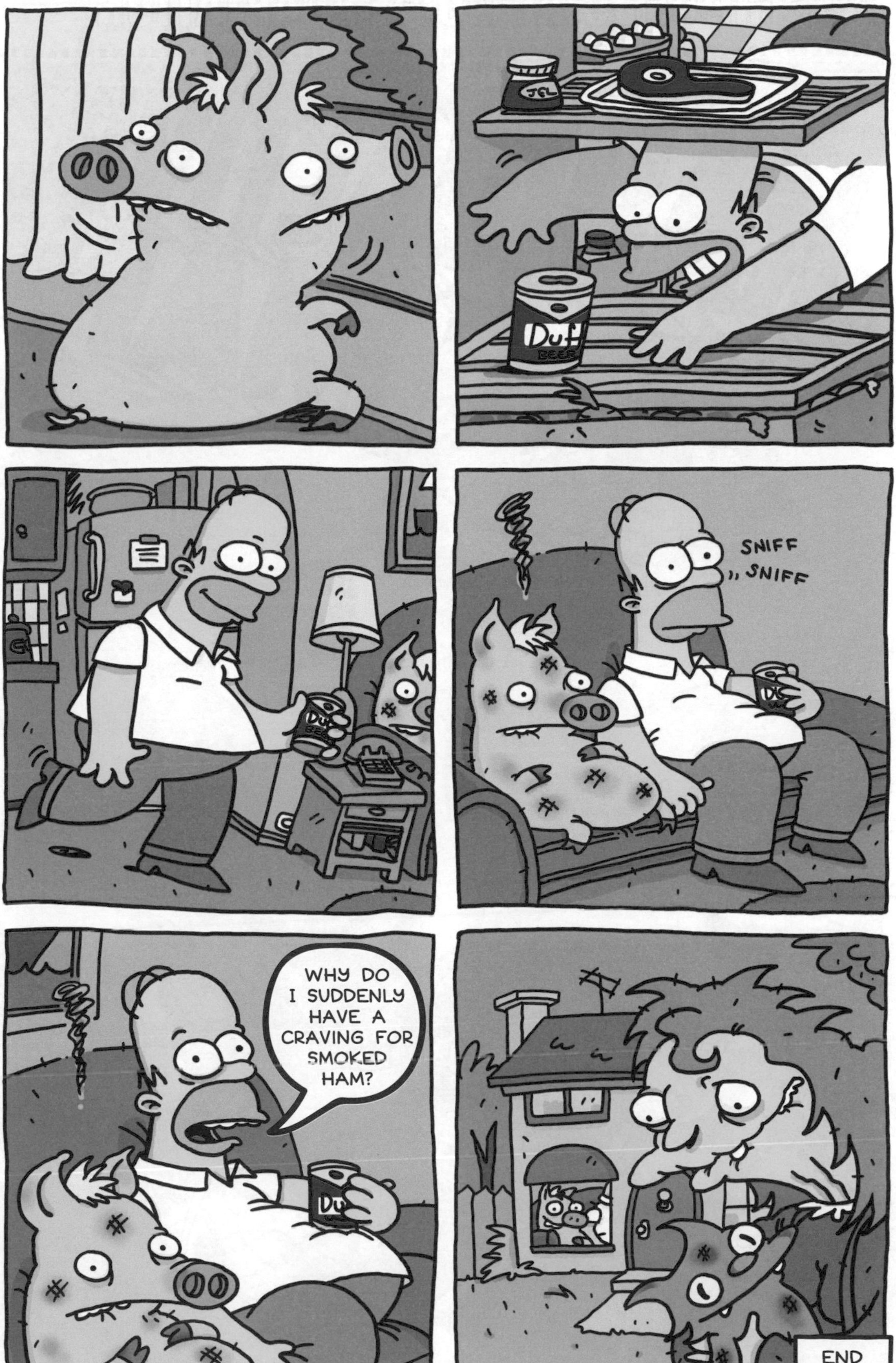

JEL
DUFF BEER
SNIFF SNIFF
WHY DO I SUDDENLY HAVE A CRAVING FOR SMOKED HAM?
END

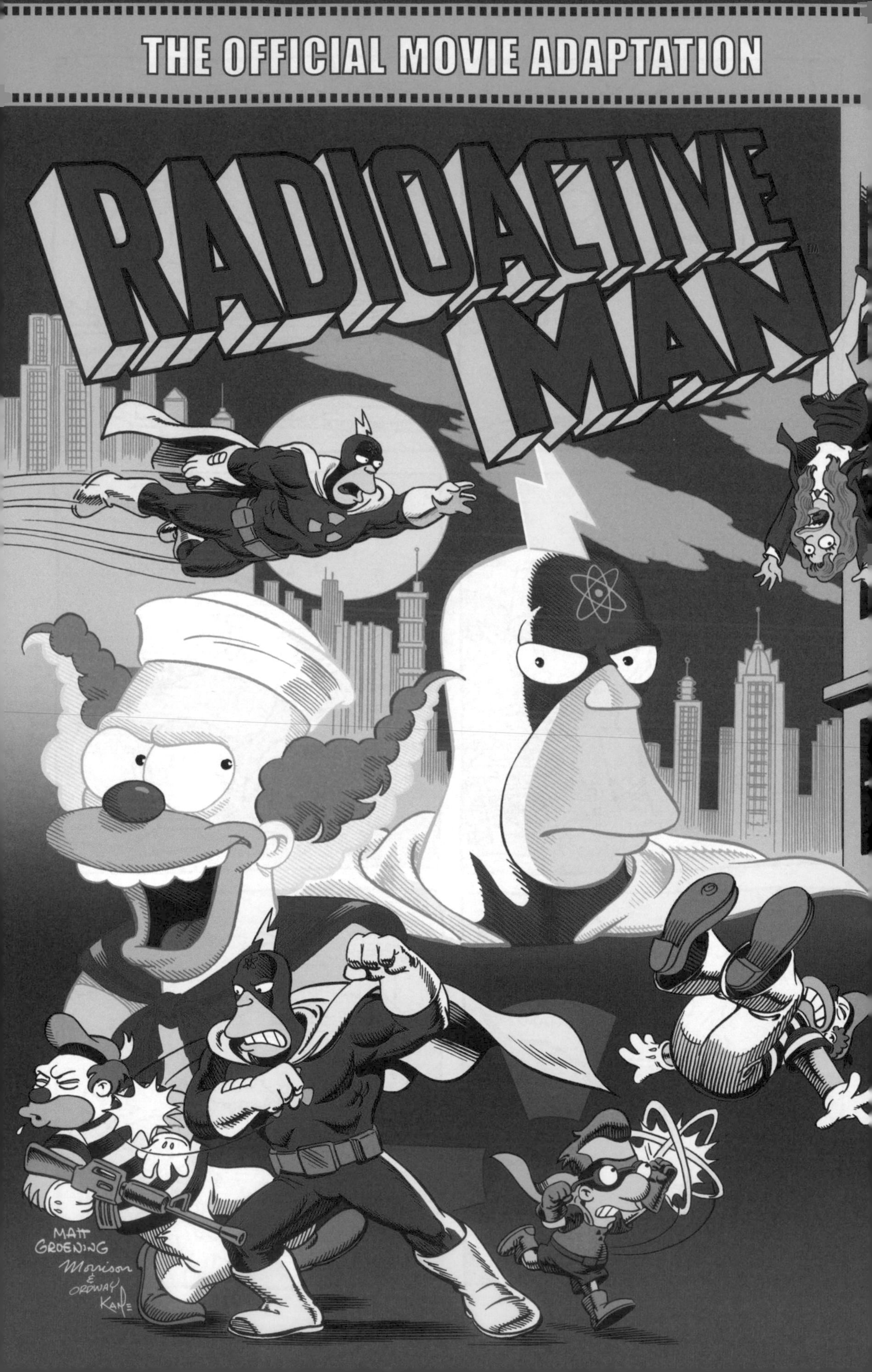
THE OFFICIAL MOVIE ADAPTATION
RADIOACTIVE MAN™
MATT GROENING
Morrison & Ordway
KANE

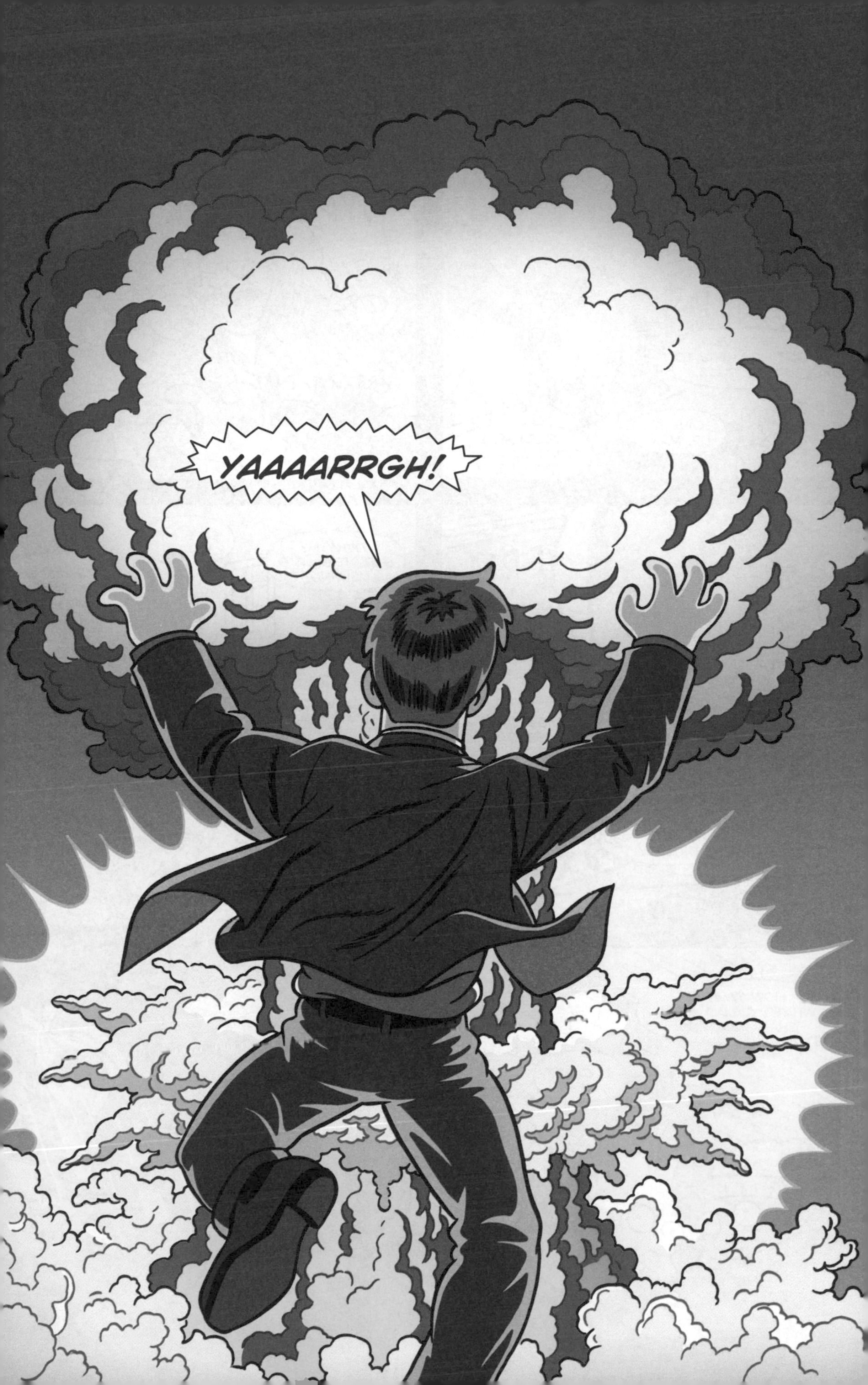
YAAAARRGH!

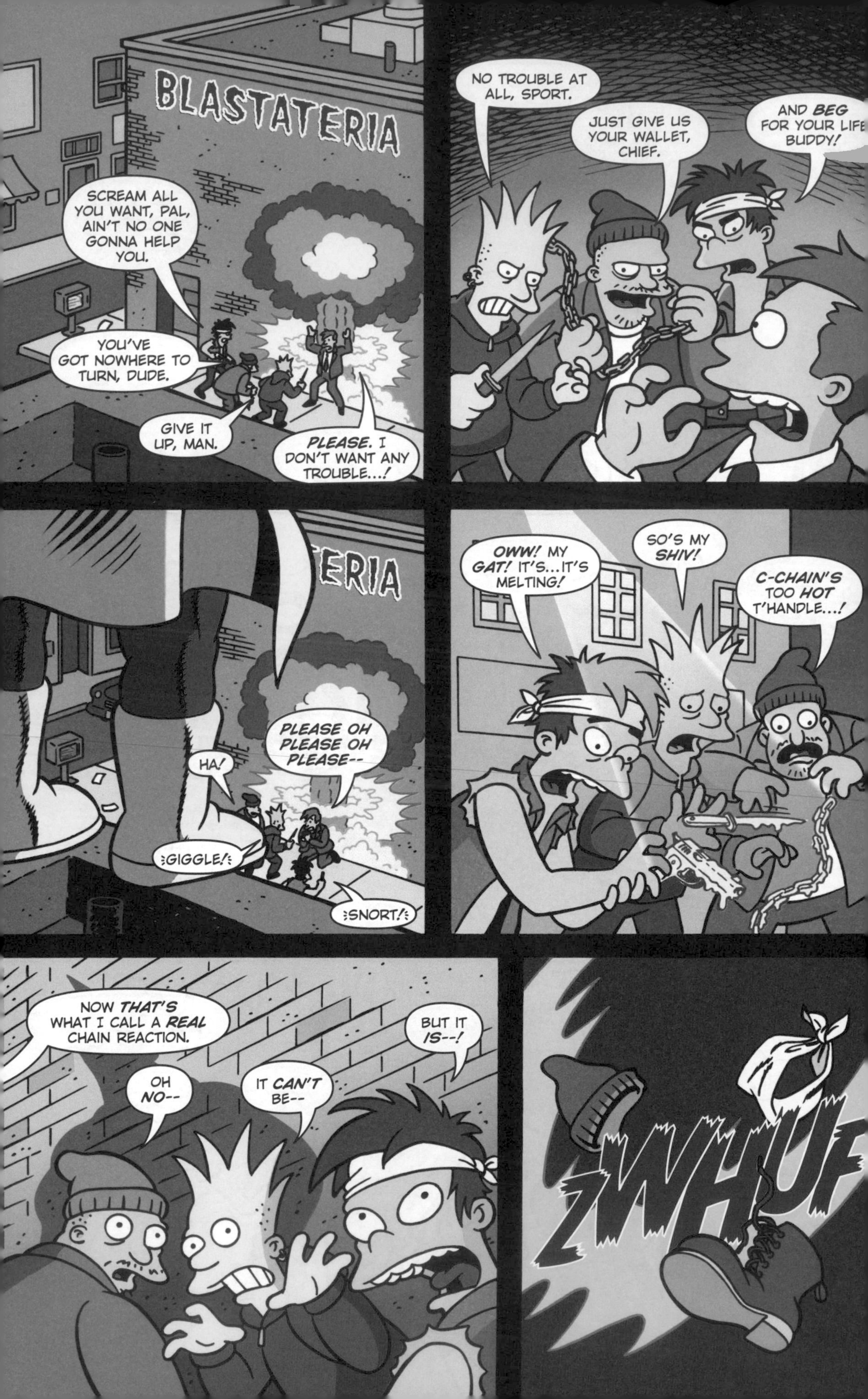
BLASTATERIA
SCREAM ALL YOU WANT, PAL, AIN'T NO ONE GONNA HELP YOU.
YOU'VE GOT NOWHERE TO TURN, DUDE.
GIVE IT UP, MAN.
PLEASE. I DON'T WANT ANY TROUBLE...!
NO TROUBLE AT ALL, SPORT.
JUST GIVE US YOUR WALLET, CHIEF.
AND BEG FOR YOUR LIFE BUDDY!
ERIA
HA!
PLEASE OH PLEASE OH PLEASE--
GIGGLE!
SNORT!
OWW! MY GAT! IT'S...IT'S MELTING!
SO'S MY SHIV!
C-CHAIN'S TOO HOT T'HANDLE...!
NOW THAT'S WHAT I CALL A REAL CHAIN REACTION.
OH NO--
IT CAN'T BE--
BUT IT IS--!
WHUF

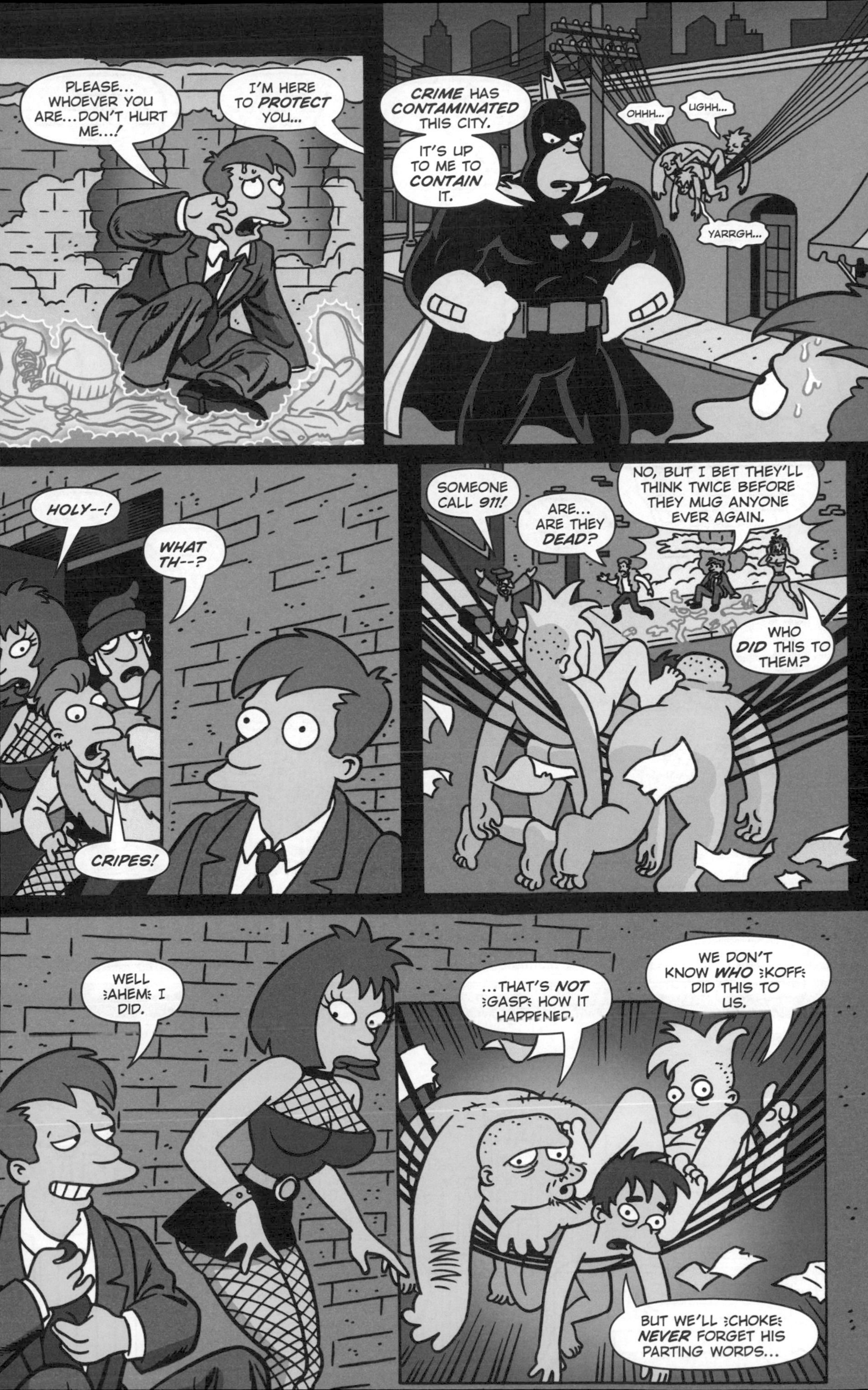

PLEASE... WHOEVER YOU ARE...DON'T HURT ME...!
I'M HERE TO PROTECT YOU...
CRIME HAS CONTAMINATED THIS CITY.
IT'S UP TO ME TO CONTAIN IT.
OHHH...
UGHH...
YARRGH...
HOLY--!
WHAT TH--?
CRIPES!
SOMEONE CALL 911!
ARE... ARE THEY DEAD?
NO, BUT I BET THEY'LL THINK TWICE BEFORE THEY MUG ANYONE EVER AGAIN.
WHO DID THIS TO THEM?
WELL :AHEM: I DID.
...THAT'S NOT :GASP: HOW IT HAPPENED.
WE DON'T KNOW WHO :KOFF: DID THIS TO US.
BUT WE'LL :CHOKE: NEVER FORGET HIS PARTING WORDS...

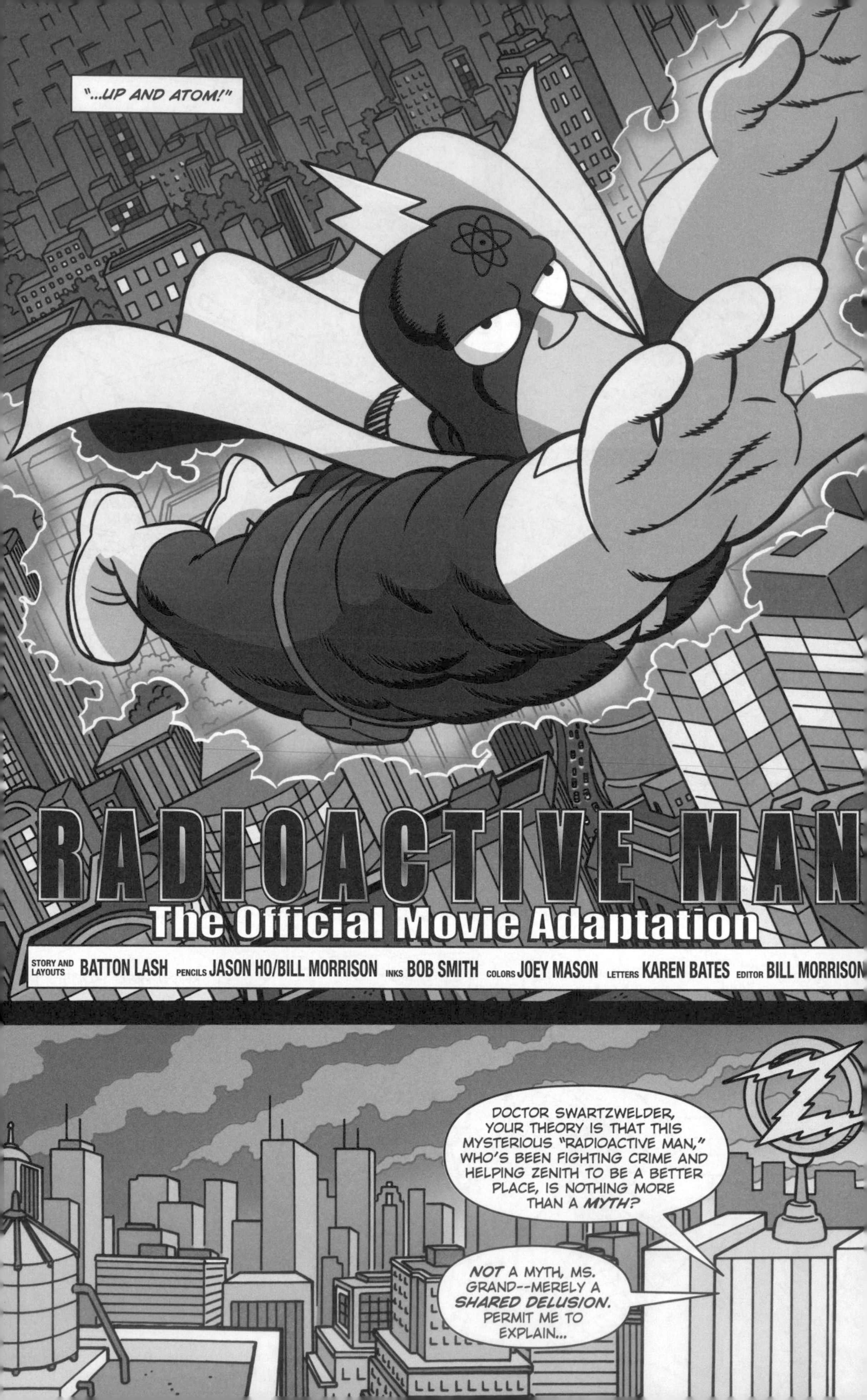

"...UP AND ATOM!"
RADIOACTIVE MAN
The Official Movie Adaptation
STORY AND LAYOUTS BATTON LASH PENCILS JASON HO/BILL MORRISON INKS BOB SMITH COLORS JOEY MASON LETTERS KAREN BATES EDITOR BILL MORRISON
DOCTOR SWARTZWELDER, YOUR THEORY IS THAT THIS MYSTERIOUS "RADIOACTIVE MAN," WHO'S BEEN FIGHTING CRIME AND HELPING ZENITH TO BE A BETTER PLACE, IS NOTHING MORE THAN A *MYTH*?
NOT A MYTH, MS. GRAND--MERELY A *SHARED DELUSION*. PERMIT ME TO EXPLAIN...

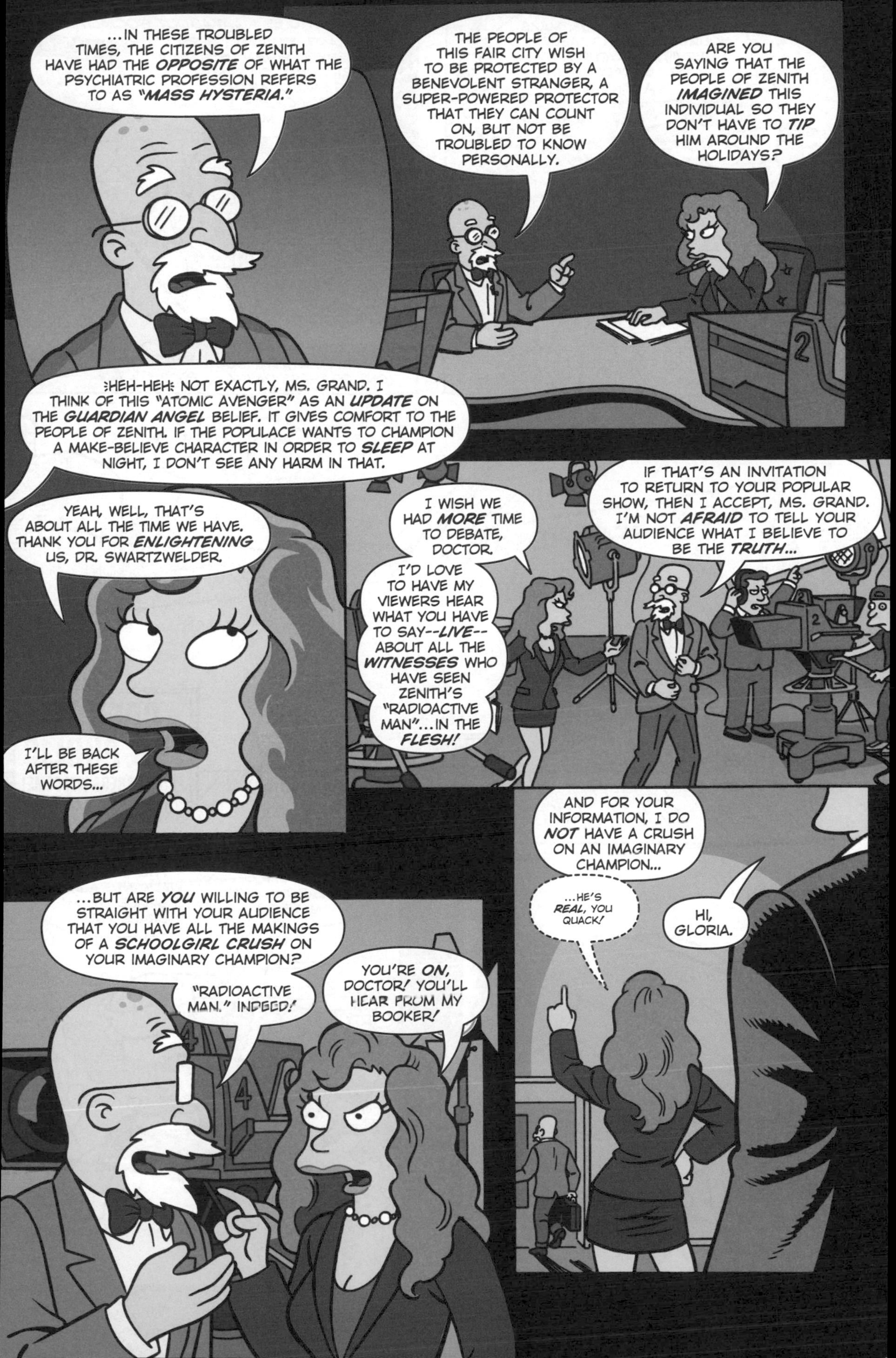
...IN THESE TROUBLED TIMES, THE CITIZENS OF ZENITH HAVE HAD THE OPPOSITE OF WHAT THE PSYCHIATRIC PROFESSION REFERS TO AS "MASS HYSTERIA."
THE PEOPLE OF THIS FAIR CITY WISH TO BE PROTECTED BY A BENEVOLENT STRANGER, A SUPER-POWERED PROTECTOR THAT THEY CAN COUNT ON, BUT NOT BE TROUBLED TO KNOW PERSONALLY.
ARE YOU SAYING THAT THE PEOPLE OF ZENITH IMAGINED THIS INDIVIDUAL SO THEY DON'T HAVE TO TIP HIM AROUND THE HOLIDAYS?
HEH-HEH NOT EXACTLY, MS. GRAND. I THINK OF THIS "ATOMIC AVENGER" AS AN UPDATE ON THE GUARDIAN ANGEL BELIEF. IT GIVES COMFORT TO THE PEOPLE OF ZENITH. IF THE POPULACE WANTS TO CHAMPION A MAKE-BELIEVE CHARACTER IN ORDER TO SLEEP AT NIGHT, I DON'T SEE ANY HARM IN THAT.
YEAH, WELL, THAT'S ABOUT ALL THE TIME WE HAVE. THANK YOU FOR ENLIGHTENING US, DR. SWARTZWELDER.
I'LL BE BACK AFTER THESE WORDS...
I WISH WE HAD MORE TIME TO DEBATE, DOCTOR.
I'D LOVE TO HAVE MY VIEWERS HEAR WHAT YOU HAVE TO SAY--LIVE--ABOUT ALL THE WITNESSES WHO HAVE SEEN ZENITH'S "RADIOACTIVE MAN"...IN THE FLESH!
IF THAT'S AN INVITATION TO RETURN TO YOUR POPULAR SHOW, THEN I ACCEPT, MS. GRAND. I'M NOT AFRAID TO TELL YOUR AUDIENCE WHAT I BELIEVE TO BE THE TRUTH...
...BUT ARE YOU WILLING TO BE STRAIGHT WITH YOUR AUDIENCE THAT YOU HAVE ALL THE MAKINGS OF A SCHOOLGIRL CRUSH ON YOUR IMAGINARY CHAMPION?
"RADIOACTIVE MAN." INDEED!
YOU'RE ON, DOCTOR! YOU'LL HEAR FROM MY BOOKER!
AND FOR YOUR INFORMATION, I DO NOT HAVE A CRUSH ON AN IMAGINARY CHAMPION...
...HE'S REAL, YOU QUACK!
HI, GLORIA.

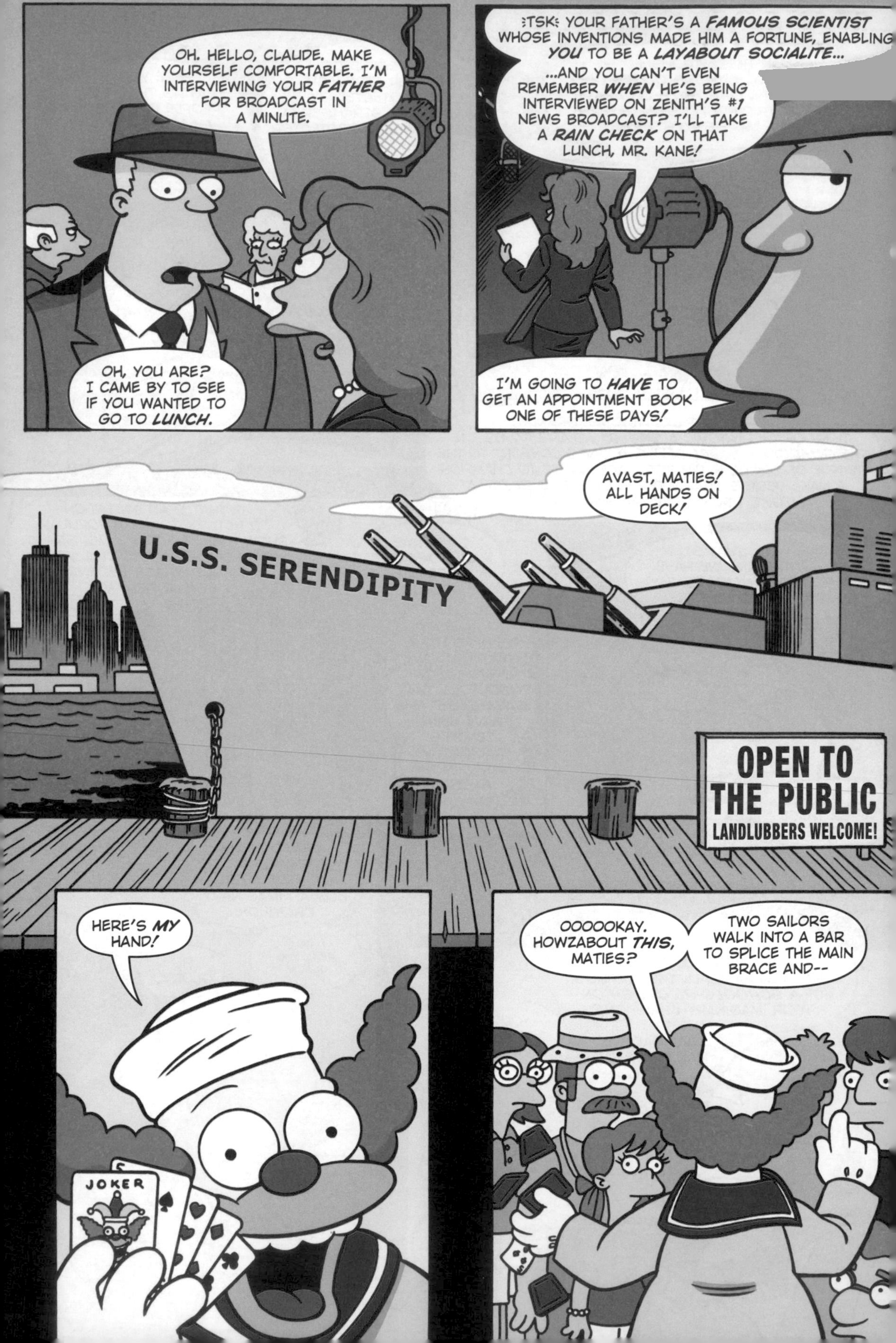
OH. HELLO, CLAUDE. MAKE YOURSELF COMFORTABLE. I'M INTERVIEWING YOUR FATHER FOR BROADCAST IN A MINUTE.
OH, YOU ARE? I CAME BY TO SEE IF YOU WANTED TO GO TO LUNCH.
:TSK: YOUR FATHER'S A FAMOUS SCIENTIST WHOSE INVENTIONS MADE HIM A FORTUNE, ENABLING YOU TO BE A LAYABOUT SOCIALITE...
...AND YOU CAN'T EVEN REMEMBER WHEN HE'S BEING INTERVIEWED ON ZENITH'S #1 NEWS BROADCAST? I'LL TAKE A RAIN CHECK ON THAT LUNCH, MR. KANE!
I'M GOING TO HAVE TO GET AN APPOINTMENT BOOK ONE OF THESE DAYS!
U.S.S. SERENDIPITY
AVAST, MATIES! ALL HANDS ON DECK!
OPEN TO THE PUBLIC
LANDLUBBERS WELCOME!
HERE'S MY HAND!
JOKER
OOOOOKAY. HOWZABOUT THIS, MATIES?
TWO SAILORS WALK INTO A BAR TO SPLICE THE MAIN BRACE AND--

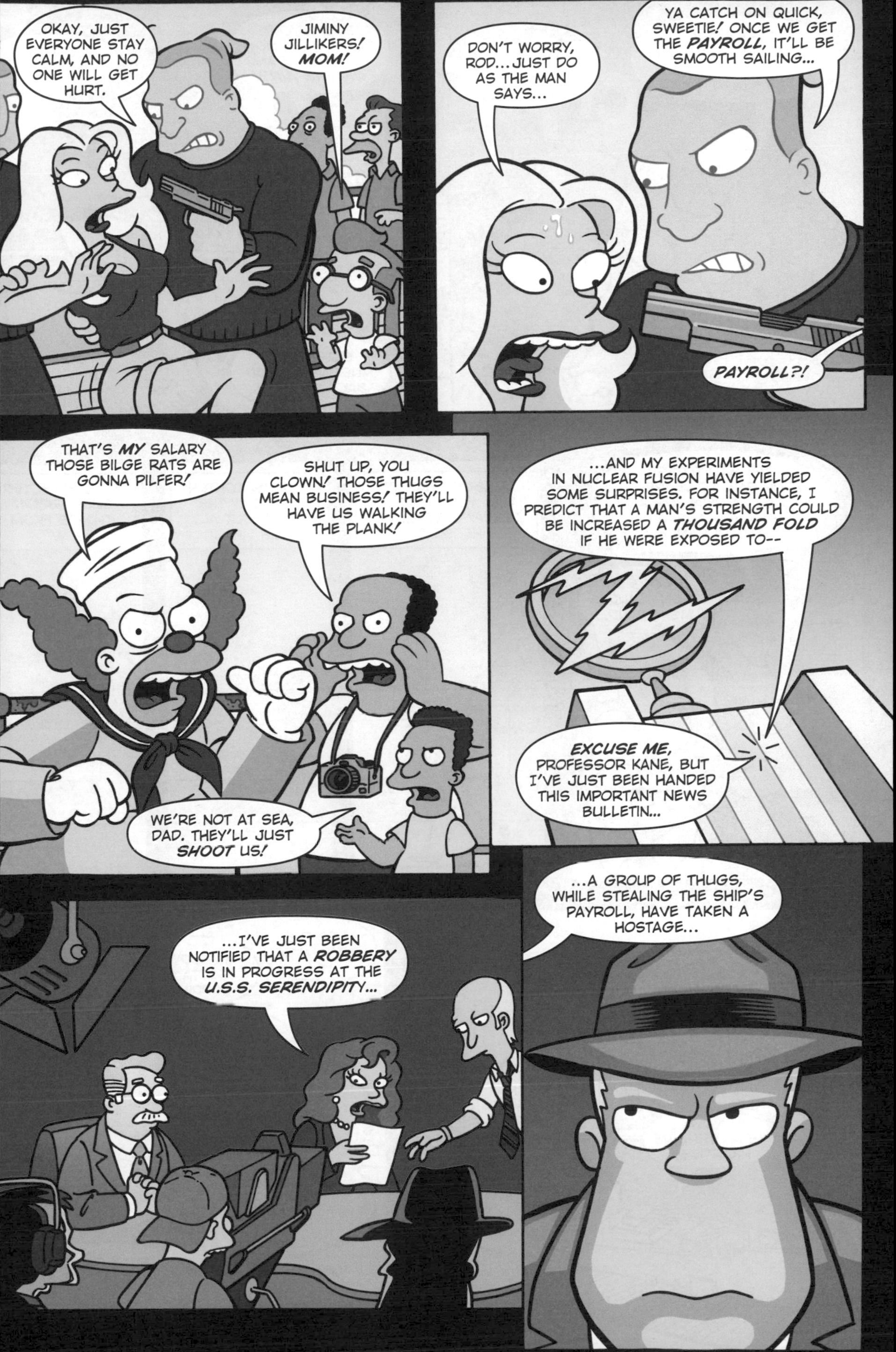
OKAY, JUST EVERYONE STAY CALM, AND NO ONE WILL GET HURT.
JIMINY JILLIKERS! MOM!
DON'T WORRY, ROD... JUST DO AS THE MAN SAYS...
YA CATCH ON QUICK, SWEETIE! ONCE WE GET THE PAYROLL, IT'LL BE SMOOTH SAILING...
PAYROLL?!
THAT'S MY SALARY THOSE BILGE RATS ARE GONNA PILFER!
SHUT UP, YOU CLOWN! THOSE THUGS MEAN BUSINESS! THEY'LL HAVE US WALKING THE PLANK!
WE'RE NOT AT SEA, DAD. THEY'LL JUST SHOOT US!
...AND MY EXPERIMENTS IN NUCLEAR FUSION HAVE YIELDED SOME SURPRISES. FOR INSTANCE, I PREDICT THAT A MAN'S STRENGTH COULD BE INCREASED A THOUSAND FOLD IF HE WERE EXPOSED TO--
EXCUSE ME, PROFESSOR KANE, BUT I'VE JUST BEEN HANDED THIS IMPORTANT NEWS BULLETIN...
...I'VE JUST BEEN NOTIFIED THAT A ROBBERY IS IN PROGRESS AT THE U.S.S. SERENDIPITY...
...A GROUP OF THUGS, WHILE STEALING THE SHIP'S PAYROLL, HAVE TAKEN A HOSTAGE...

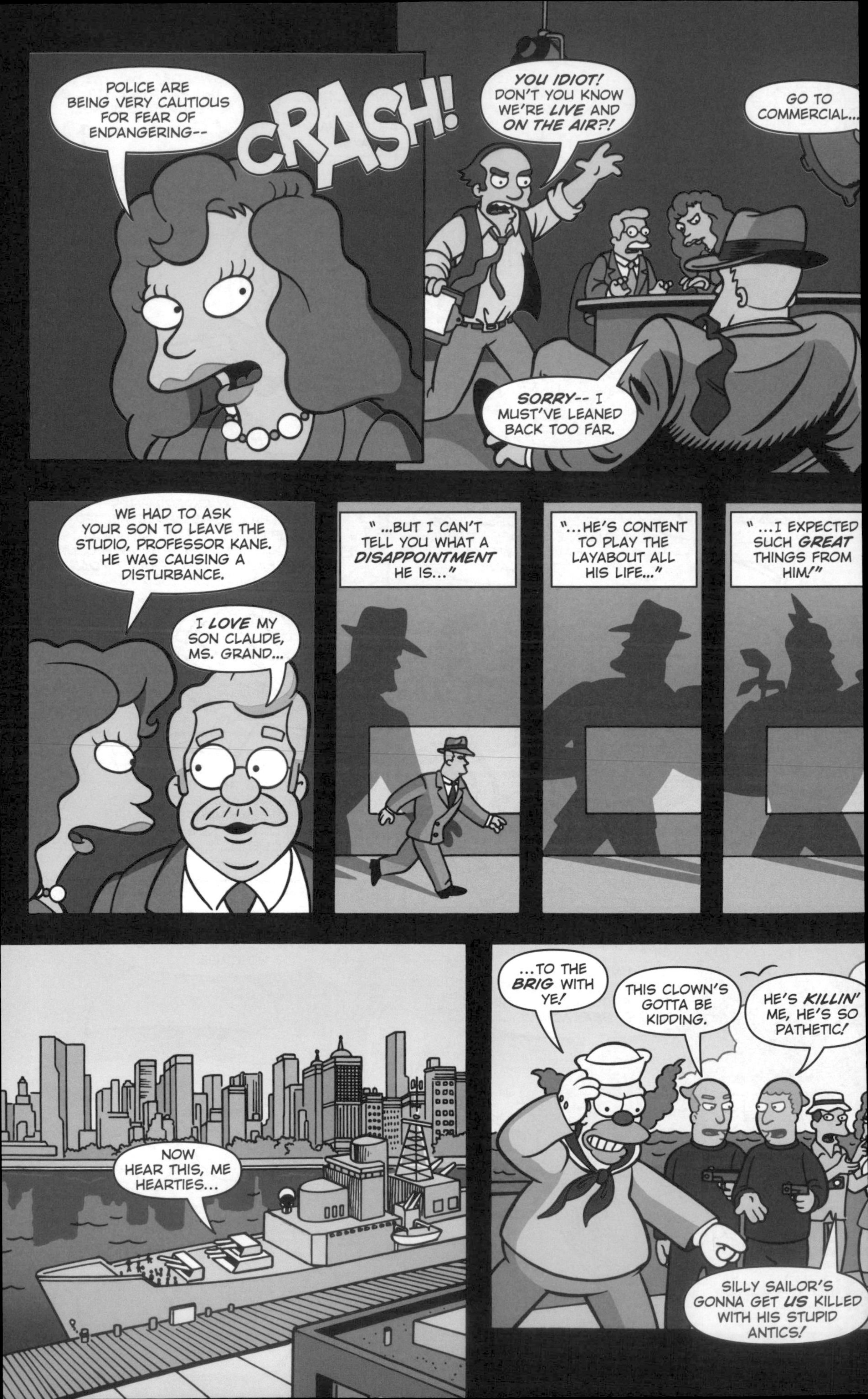

POLICE ARE BEING VERY CAUTIOUS FOR FEAR OF ENDANGERING--
CRASH!
YOU IDIOT! DON'T YOU KNOW WE'RE LIVE AND ON THE AIR?!
GO TO COMMERCIAL...
SORRY-- I MUST'VE LEANED BACK TOO FAR.
WE HAD TO ASK YOUR SON TO LEAVE THE STUDIO, PROFESSOR KANE. HE WAS CAUSING A DISTURBANCE.
I LOVE MY SON CLAUDE, MS. GRAND...
"...BUT I CAN'T TELL YOU WHAT A DISAPPOINTMENT HE IS..."
"...HE'S CONTENT TO PLAY THE LAYABOUT ALL HIS LIFE..."
"...I EXPECTED SUCH GREAT THINGS FROM HIM!"
NOW HEAR THIS, ME HEARTIES...
...TO THE BRIG WITH YE!
THIS CLOWN'S GOTTA BE KIDDING.
HE'S KILLIN' ME, HE'S SO PATHETIC!
SILLY SAILOR'S GONNA GET US KILLED WITH HIS STUPID ANTICS!

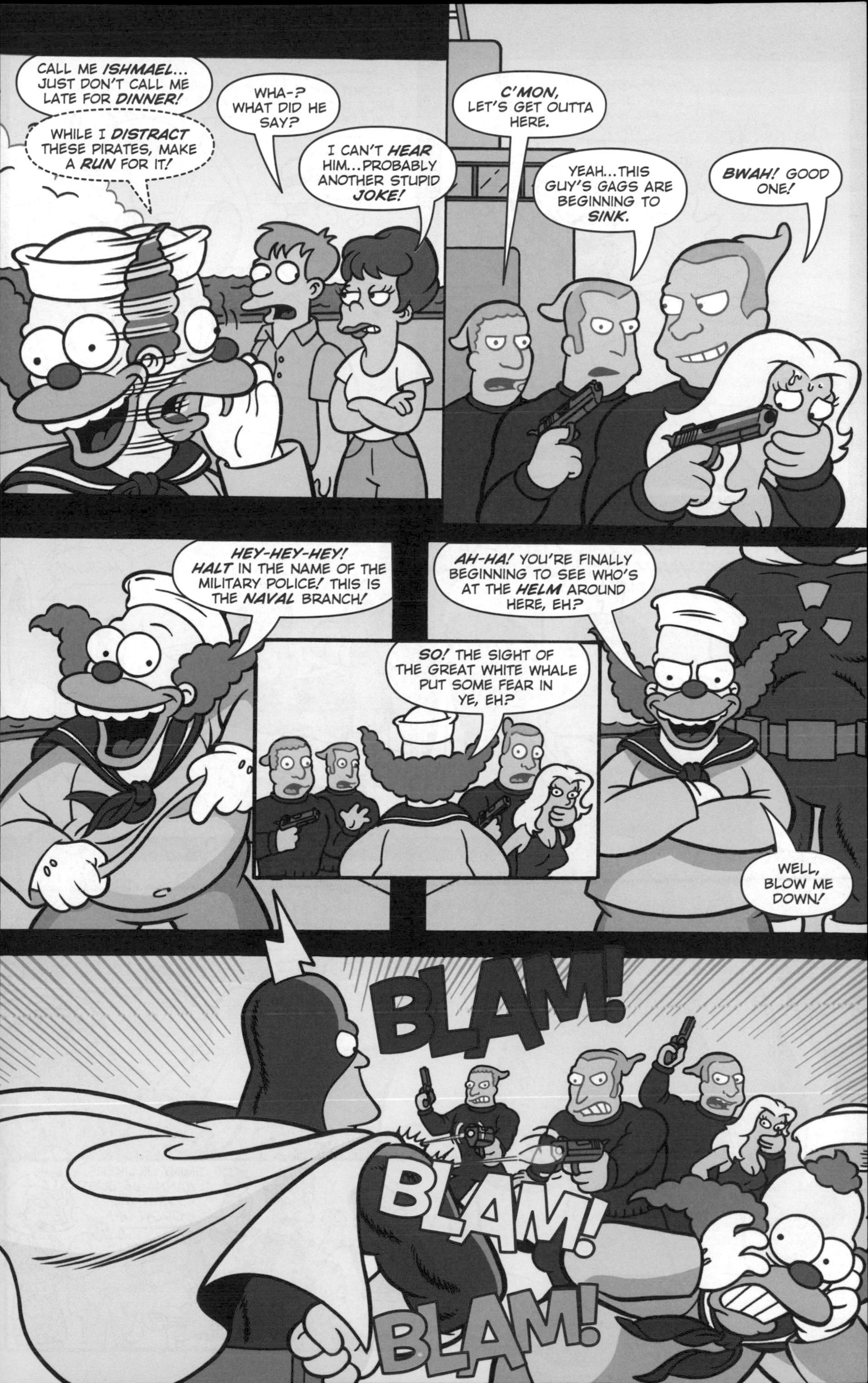
CALL ME ISHMAEL... JUST DON'T CALL ME LATE FOR DINNER!
WHILE I DISTRACT THESE PIRATES, MAKE A RUN FOR IT!
WHA-? WHAT DID HE SAY?
I CAN'T HEAR HIM...PROBABLY ANOTHER STUPID JOKE!
C'MON, LET'S GET OUTTA HERE.
YEAH...THIS GUY'S GAGS ARE BEGINNING TO SINK.
BWAH! GOOD ONE!
HEY-HEY-HEY! HALT IN THE NAME OF THE MILITARY POLICE! THIS IS THE NAVAL BRANCH!
SO! THE SIGHT OF THE GREAT WHITE WHALE PUT SOME FEAR IN YE, EH?
AH-HA! YOU'RE FINALLY BEGINNING TO SEE WHO'S AT THE HELM AROUND HERE, EH?
WELL, BLOW ME DOWN!
BLAM!
BLAM!
BLAM!

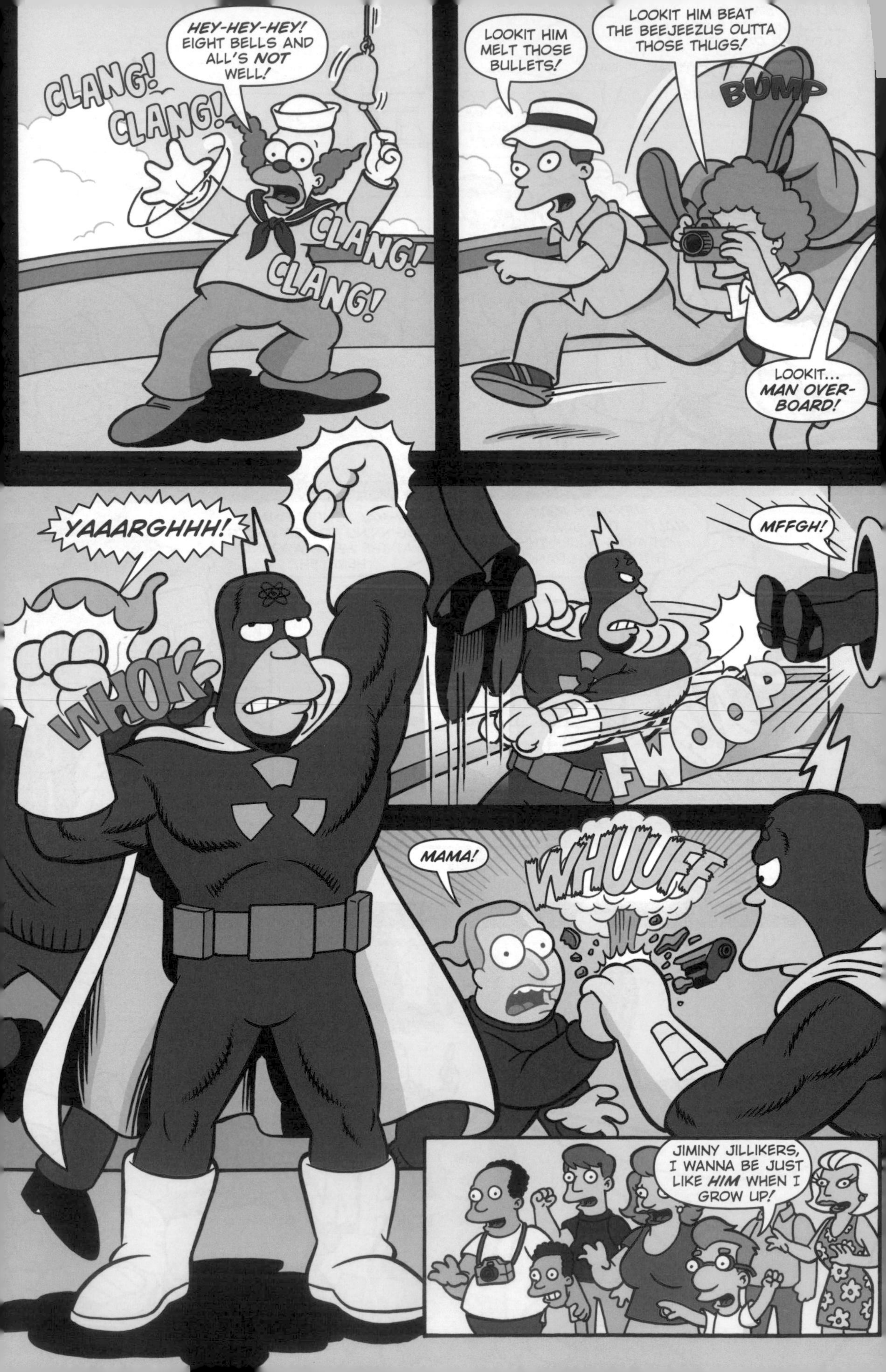

HEY-HEY-HEY! EIGHT BELLS AND ALL'S NOT WELL!
CLANG! CLANG!
CLANG! CLANG!
LOOKIT HIM MELT THOSE BULLETS!
LOOKIT HIM BEAT THE BEEJEEZUS OUTTA THOSE THUGS!
BUMP
LOOKIT... MAN OVER-BOARD!
YAAARGHHH!
WHOK
MFFGH!
FWOOP
MAMA!
WHUUFF
JIMINY JILLIKERS, I WANNA BE JUST LIKE HIM WHEN I GROW UP!

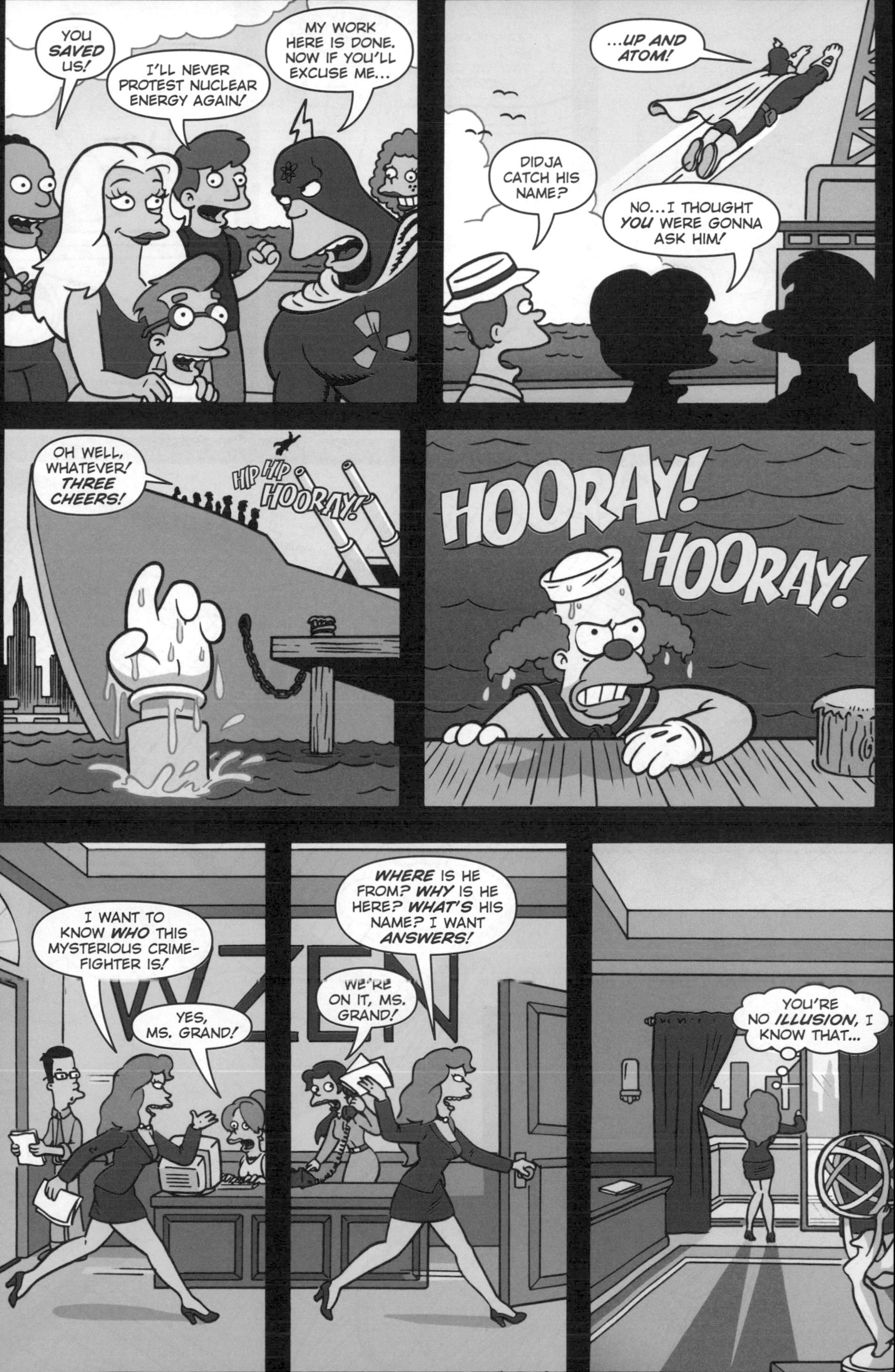

YOU SAVED US!
I'LL NEVER PROTEST NUCLEAR ENERGY AGAIN!
MY WORK HERE IS DONE. NOW IF YOU'LL EXCUSE ME...
...UP AND ATOM!
DIDJA CATCH HIS NAME?
NO...I THOUGHT YOU WERE GONNA ASK HIM!
OH WELL, WHATEVER! THREE CHEERS!
HIP HIP HOORAY!
HOORAY!
HOORAY!
I WANT TO KNOW WHO THIS MYSTERIOUS CRIME-FIGHTER IS!
YES, MS. GRAND!
WHERE IS HE FROM? WHY IS HE HERE? WHAT'S HIS NAME? I WANT ANSWERS!
WE'RE ON IT, MS. GRAND!
YOU'RE NO ILLUSION, I KNOW THAT...

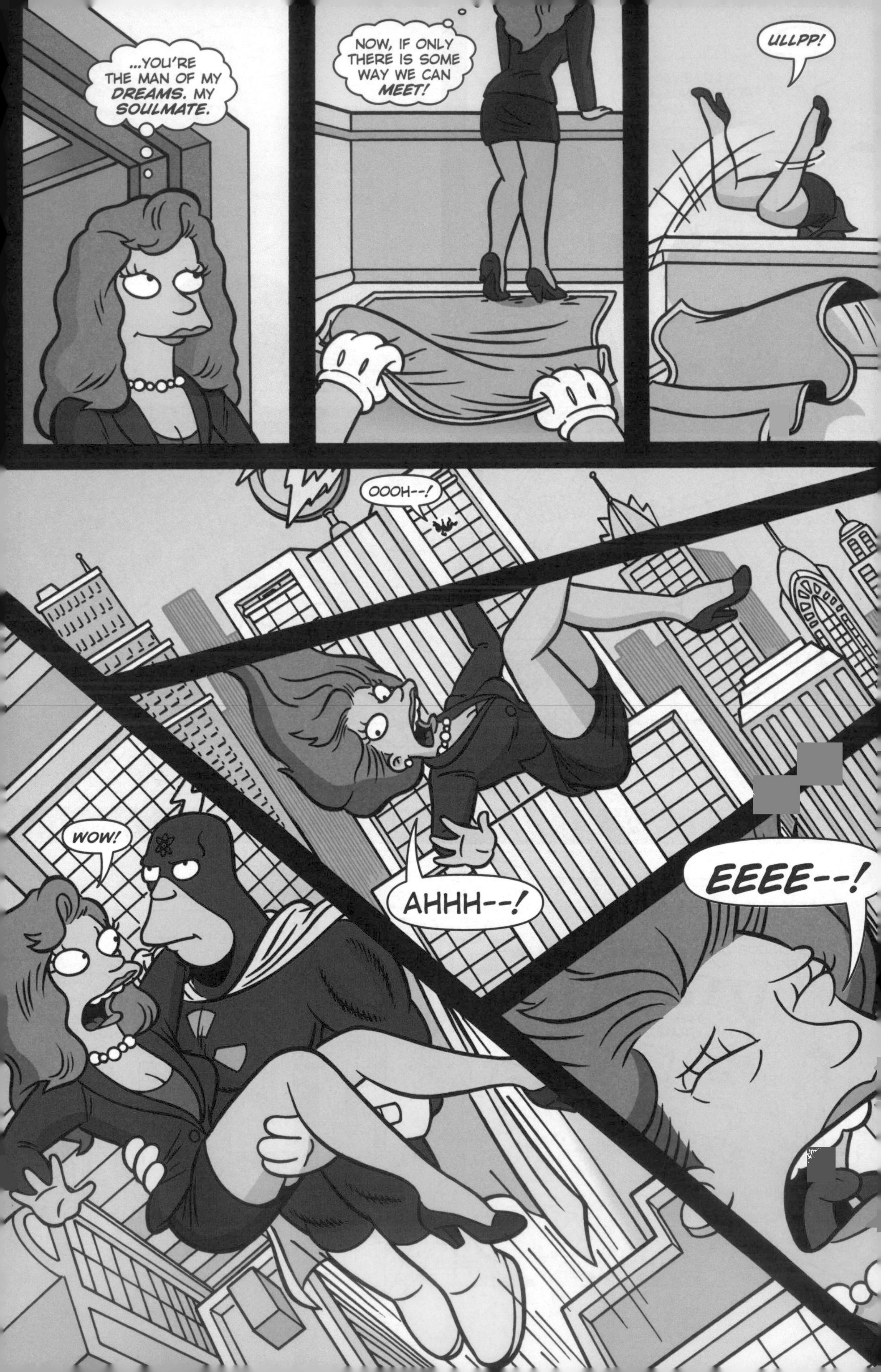
...YOU'RE THE MAN OF MY *DREAMS*. MY *SOULMATE*.
NOW, IF ONLY THERE IS SOME WAY WE CAN *MEET!*
ULLPP!
OOOH--!
AHHH--!
EEEE--!
WOW!

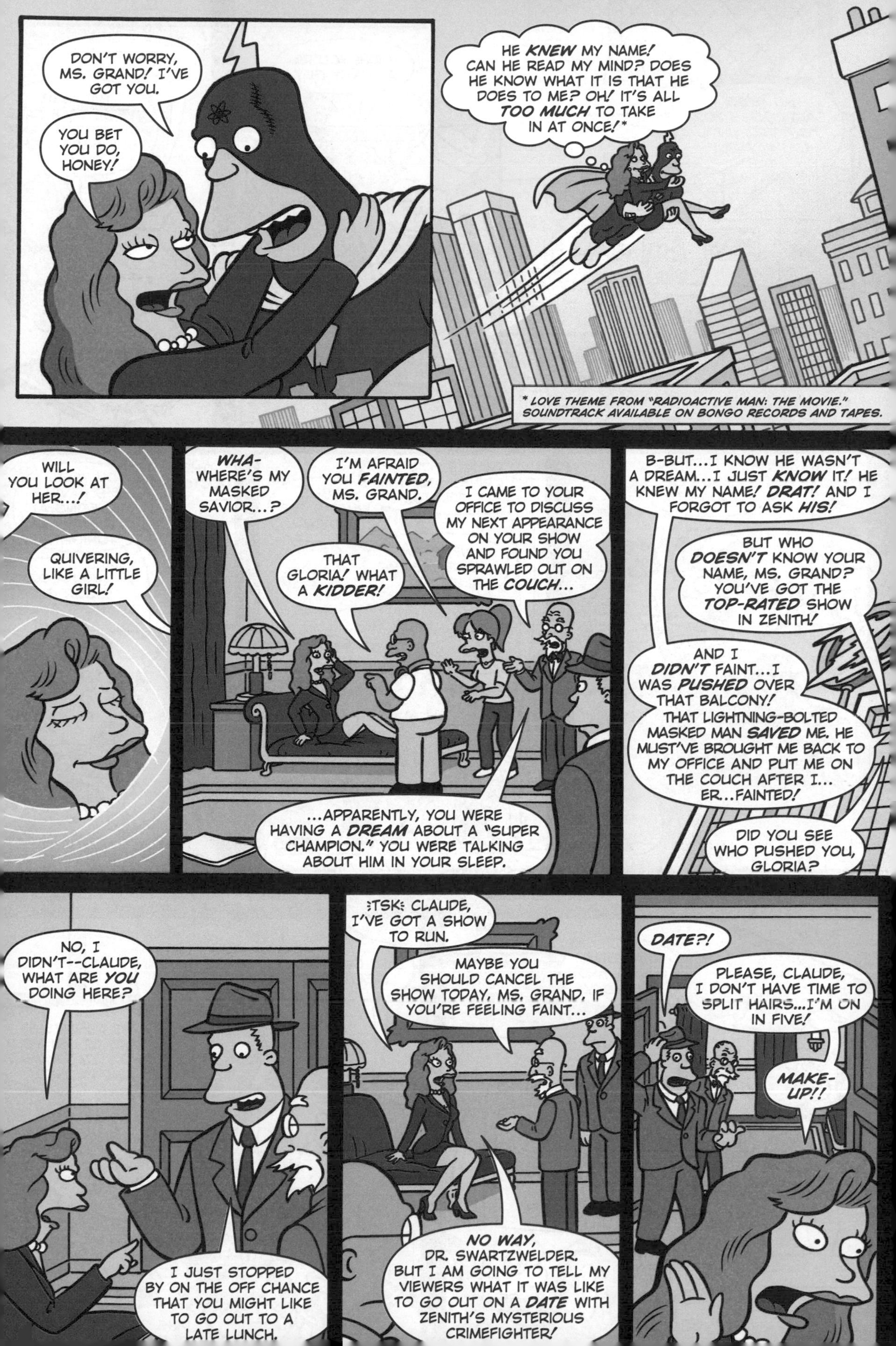
DON'T WORRY, MS. GRAND! I'VE GOT YOU.
YOU BET YOU DO, HONEY!
HE KNEW MY NAME! CAN HE READ MY MIND? DOES HE KNOW WHAT IT IS THAT HE DOES TO ME? OH! IT'S ALL TOO MUCH TO TAKE IN AT ONCE!*
* LOVE THEME FROM "RADIOACTIVE MAN: THE MOVIE." SOUNDTRACK AVAILABLE ON BONGO RECORDS AND TAPES.
WILL YOU LOOK AT HER...!
QUIVERING, LIKE A LITTLE GIRL!
WHA- WHERE'S MY MASKED SAVIOR...?
I'M AFRAID YOU FAINTED, MS. GRAND.
THAT GLORIA! WHAT A KIDDER!
I CAME TO YOUR OFFICE TO DISCUSS MY NEXT APPEARANCE ON YOUR SHOW AND FOUND YOU SPRAWLED OUT ON THE COUCH...
...APPARENTLY, YOU WERE HAVING A DREAM ABOUT A "SUPER CHAMPION." YOU WERE TALKING ABOUT HIM IN YOUR SLEEP.
B-BUT...I KNOW HE WASN'T A DREAM...I JUST KNOW IT! HE KNEW MY NAME! DRAT! AND I FORGOT TO ASK HIS!
BUT WHO DOESN'T KNOW YOUR NAME, MS. GRAND? YOU'VE GOT THE TOP-RATED SHOW IN ZENITH!
AND I DIDN'T FAINT...I WAS PUSHED OVER THAT BALCONY!
THAT LIGHTNING-BOLTED MASKED MAN SAVED ME. HE MUST'VE BROUGHT ME BACK TO MY OFFICE AND PUT ME ON THE COUCH AFTER I... ER...FAINTED!
DID YOU SEE WHO PUSHED YOU, GLORIA?
NO, I DIDN'T--CLAUDE, WHAT ARE YOU DOING HERE?
I JUST STOPPED BY ON THE OFF CHANCE THAT YOU MIGHT LIKE TO GO OUT TO A LATE LUNCH.
:TSK: CLAUDE, I'VE GOT A SHOW TO RUN.
MAYBE YOU SHOULD CANCEL THE SHOW TODAY, MS. GRAND, IF YOU'RE FEELING FAINT...
NO WAY, DR. SWARTZWELDER. BUT I AM GOING TO TELL MY VIEWERS WHAT IT WAS LIKE TO GO OUT ON A DATE WITH ZENITH'S MYSTERIOUS CRIMEFIGHTER!
DATE?!
PLEASE, CLAUDE, I DON'T HAVE TIME TO SPLIT HAIRS...I'M ON IN FIVE!
MAKE-UP!!

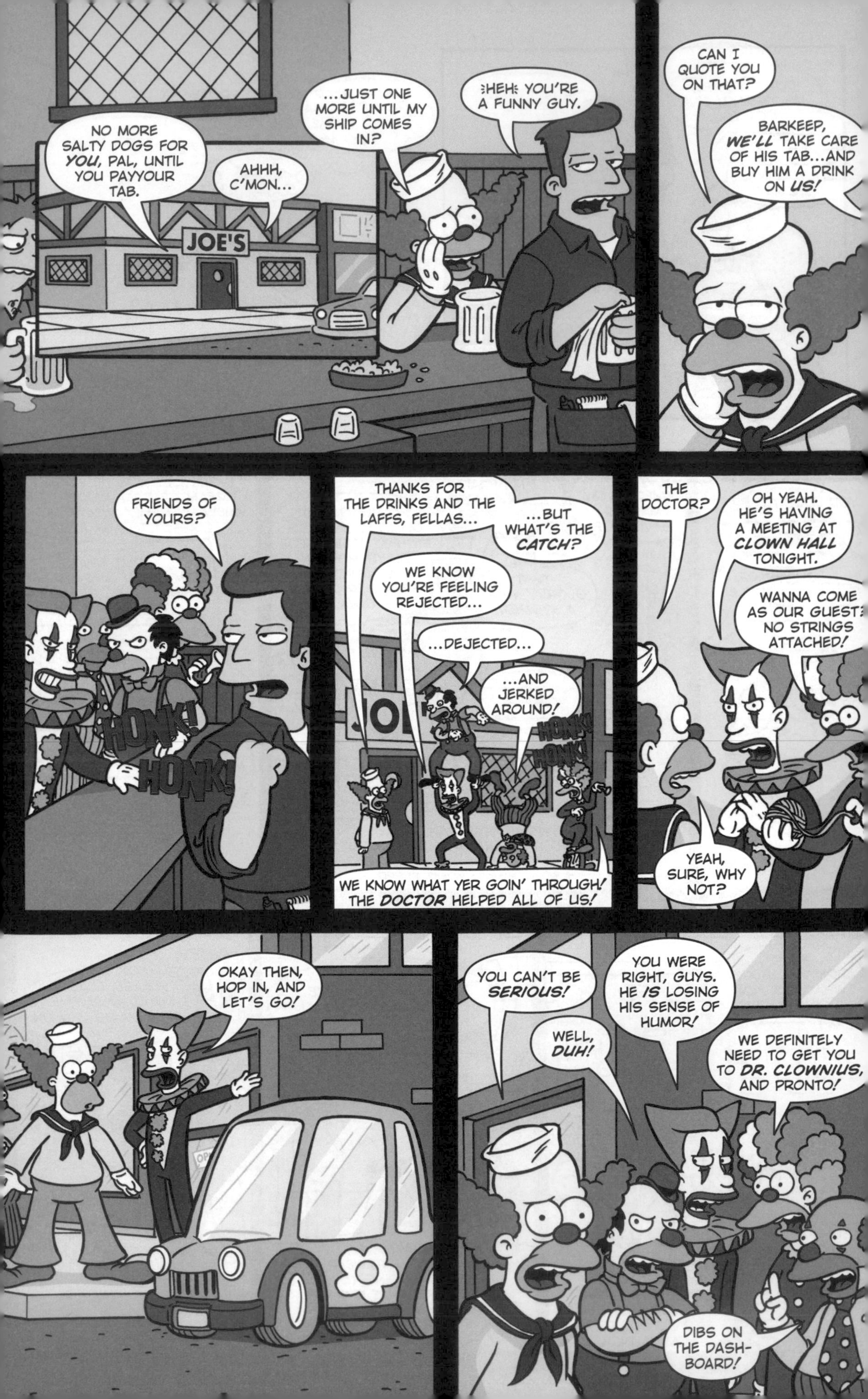

NO MORE SALTY DOGS FOR YOU, PAL, UNTIL YOU PAYYOUR TAB.
AHHH, C'MON...
JOE'S
...JUST ONE MORE UNTIL MY SHIP COMES IN?
HEH YOU'RE A FUNNY GUY.
CAN I QUOTE YOU ON THAT?
BARKEEP, WE'LL TAKE CARE OF HIS TAB...AND BUY HIM A DRINK ON US!
FRIENDS OF YOURS?
HONK!
HONK!
THANKS FOR THE DRINKS AND THE LAFFS, FELLAS...
...BUT WHAT'S THE CATCH?
WE KNOW YOU'RE FEELING REJECTED...
...DEJECTED...
...AND JERKED AROUND!
HONK!
HONK!
WE KNOW WHAT YER GOIN' THROUGH! THE DOCTOR HELPED ALL OF US!
THE DOCTOR?
OH YEAH. HE'S HAVING A MEETING AT CLOWN HALL TONIGHT.
WANNA COME AS OUR GUEST? NO STRINGS ATTACHED!
YEAH, SURE, WHY NOT?
OKAY THEN, HOP IN, AND LET'S GO!
YOU CAN'T BE SERIOUS!
WELL, DUH!
YOU WERE RIGHT, GUYS. HE IS LOSING HIS SENSE OF HUMOR!
WE DEFINITELY NEED TO GET YOU TO DR. CLOWNIUS, AND PRONTO!
DIBS ON THE DASH-BOARD!

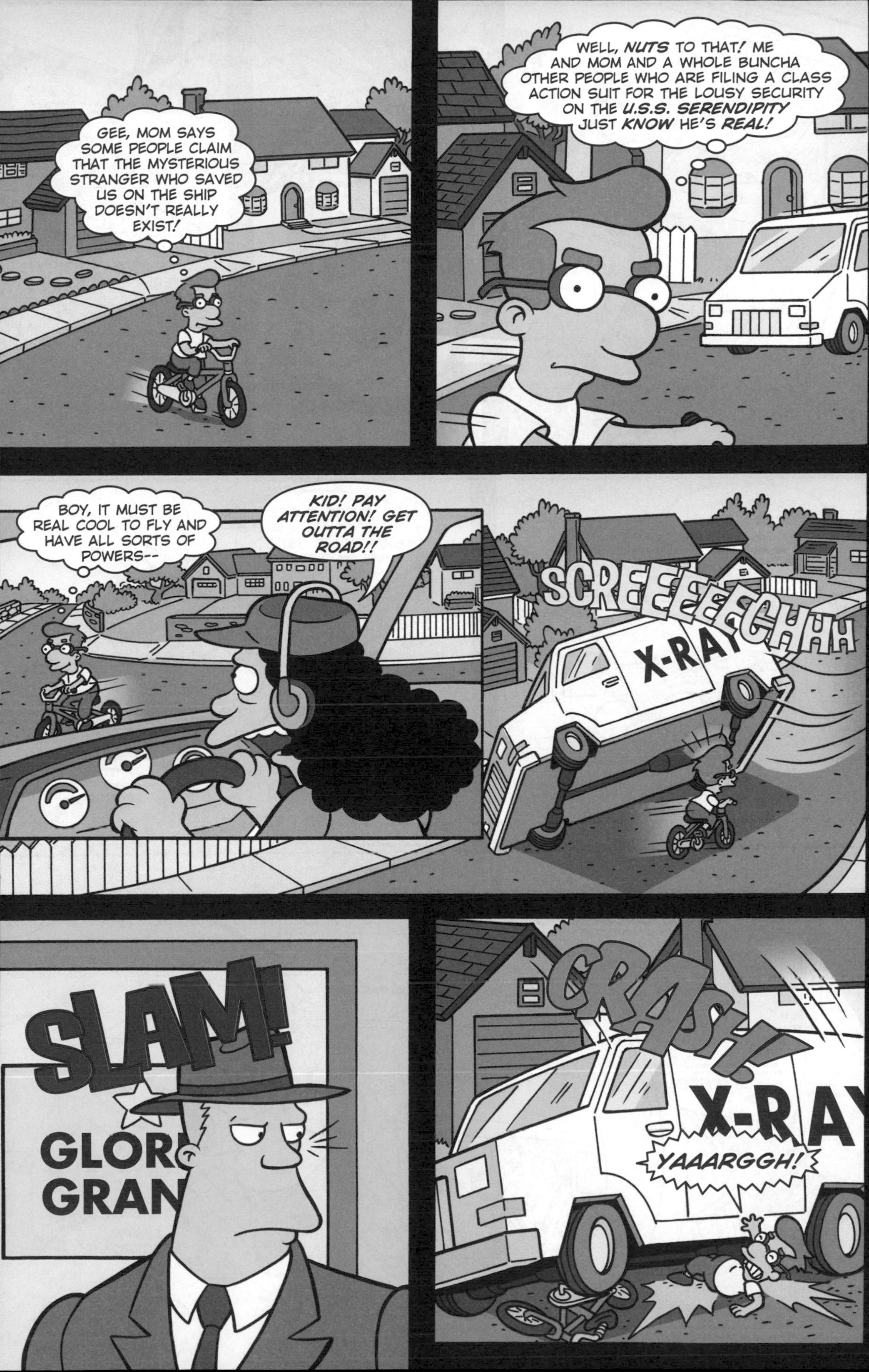

GEE, MOM SAYS SOME PEOPLE CLAIM THAT THE MYSTERIOUS STRANGER WHO SAVED US ON THE SHIP DOESN'T REALLY EXIST!
WELL, NUTS TO THAT! ME AND MOM AND A WHOLE BUNCHA OTHER PEOPLE WHO ARE FILING A CLASS ACTION SUIT FOR THE LOUSY SECURITY ON THE U.S.S. SERENDIPITY JUST KNOW HE'S REAL!
BOY, IT MUST BE REAL COOL TO FLY AND HAVE ALL SORTS OF POWERS--
KID! PAY ATTENTION! GET OUTTA THE ROAD!!
SCREEEEECHHH
X-RAY
SLAM!
GLOR
GRAN
CRASH!
X-RAY
YAAARGGH!

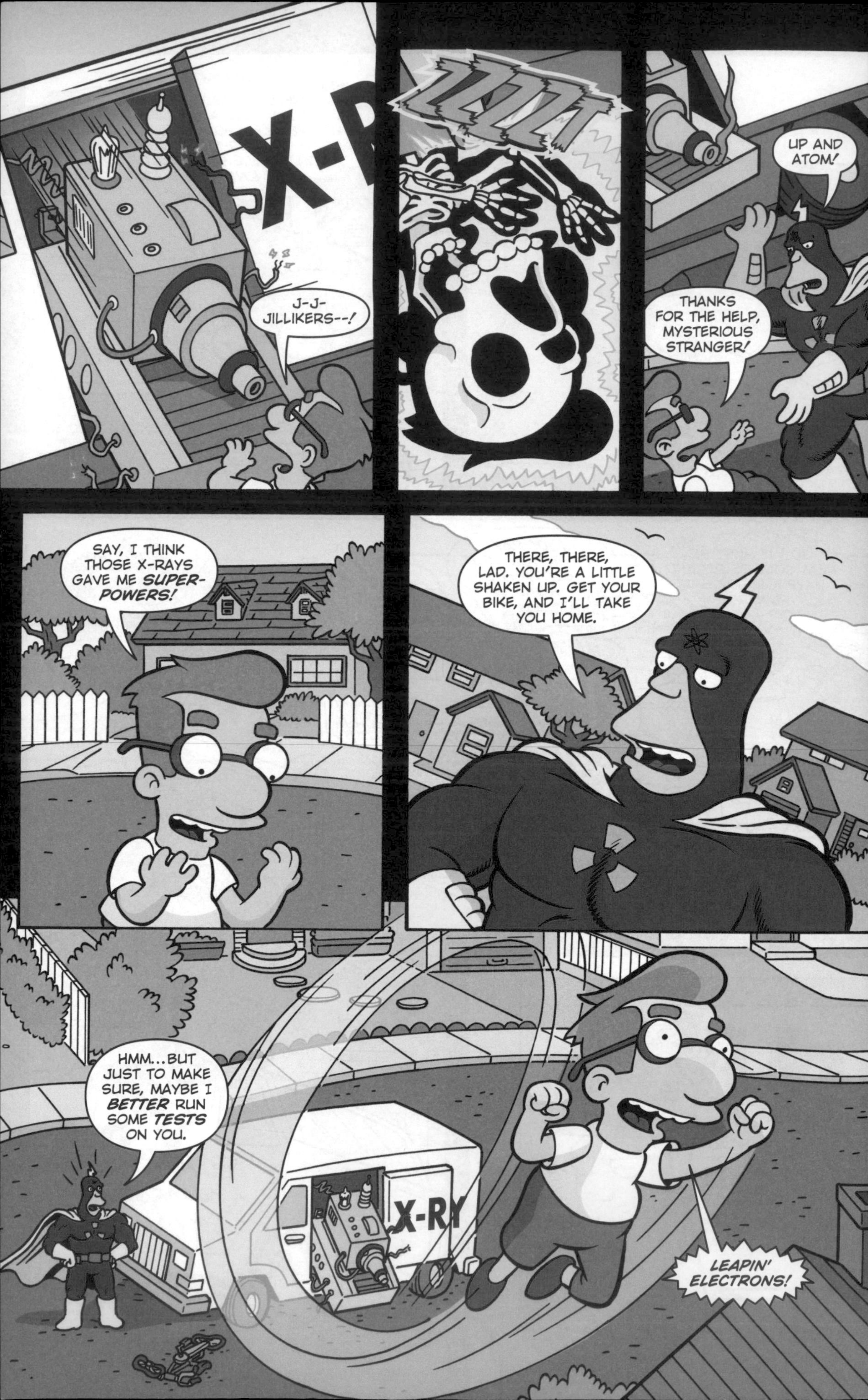
X-R
J-J-JILLIKERS--!
ZZZT
UP AND ATOM!
THANKS FOR THE HELP, MYSTERIOUS STRANGER!
SAY, I THINK THOSE X-RAYS GAVE ME SUPER-POWERS!
THERE, THERE, LAD. YOU'RE A LITTLE SHAKEN UP. GET YOUR BIKE, AND I'LL TAKE YOU HOME.
HMM...BUT JUST TO MAKE SURE, MAYBE I BETTER RUN SOME TESTS ON YOU.
X-RY
LEAPIN' ELECTRONS!

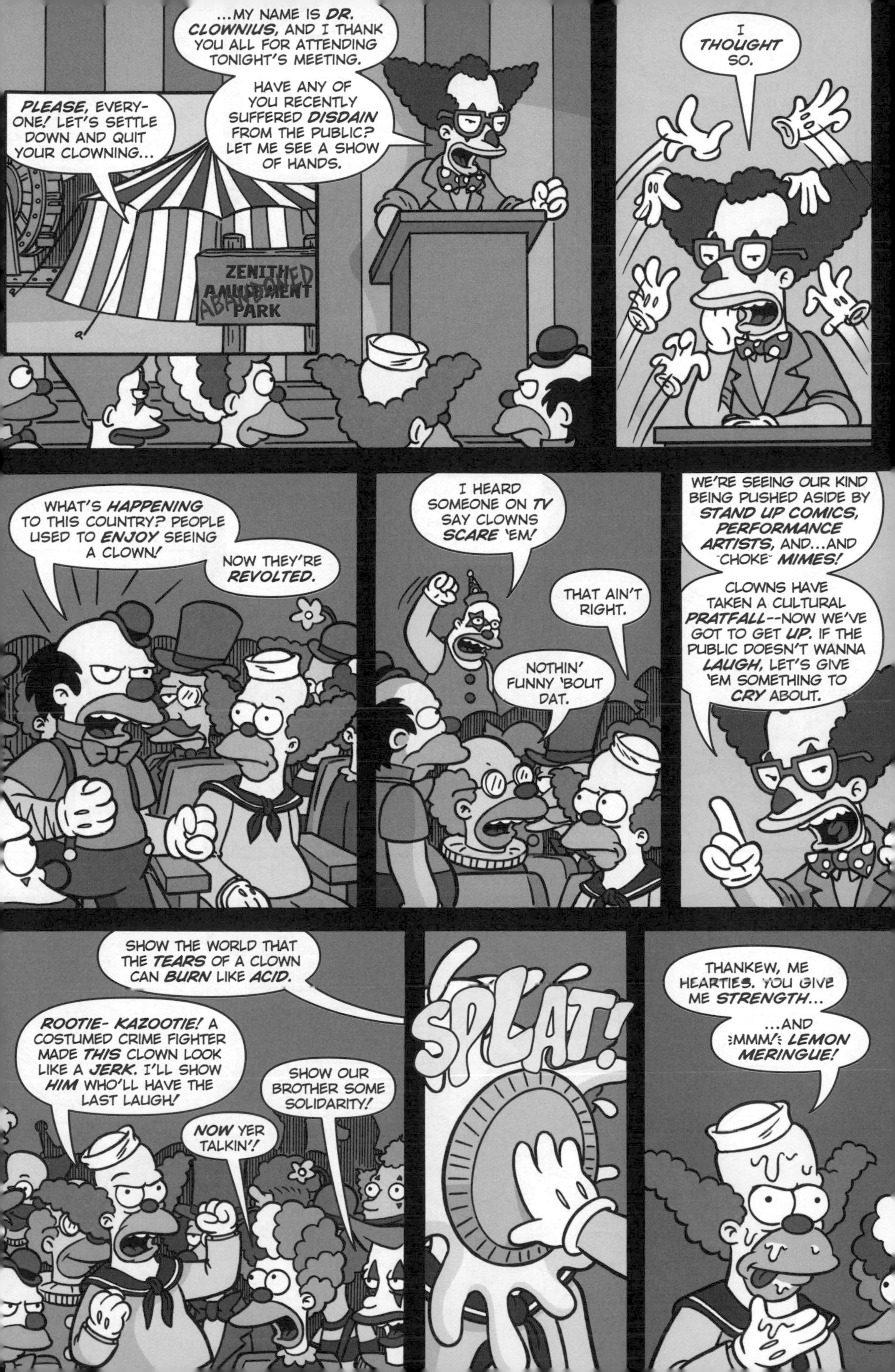

PLEASE, EVERYONE! LET'S SETTLE DOWN AND QUIT YOUR CLOWNING...
...MY NAME IS DR. CLOWNIUS, AND I THANK YOU ALL FOR ATTENDING TONIGHT'S MEETING.
HAVE ANY OF YOU RECENTLY SUFFERED DISDAIN FROM THE PUBLIC? LET ME SEE A SHOW OF HANDS.
ZENITH ABANDONED AMUSEMENT PARK
I THOUGHT SO.
WHAT'S HAPPENING TO THIS COUNTRY? PEOPLE USED TO ENJOY SEEING A CLOWN!
NOW THEY'RE REVOLTED.
I HEARD SOMEONE ON TV SAY CLOWNS SCARE 'EM!
THAT AIN'T RIGHT.
NOTHIN' FUNNY 'BOUT DAT.
WE'RE SEEING OUR KIND BEING PUSHED ASIDE BY STAND UP COMICS, PERFORMANCE ARTISTS, AND...AND *CHOKE* MIMES!
CLOWNS HAVE TAKEN A CULTURAL PRATFALL--NOW WE'VE GOT TO GET UP. IF THE PUBLIC DOESN'T WANNA LAUGH, LET'S GIVE 'EM SOMETHING TO CRY ABOUT.
SHOW THE WORLD THAT THE TEARS OF A CLOWN CAN BURN LIKE ACID.
ROOTIE- KAZOOTIE! A COSTUMED CRIME FIGHTER MADE THIS CLOWN LOOK LIKE A JERK. I'LL SHOW HIM WHO'LL HAVE THE LAST LAUGH!
SHOW OUR BROTHER SOME SOLIDARITY!
NOW YER TALKIN'!
SPLAT!
THANKEW, ME HEARTIES. YOU GIVE ME STRENGTH...
...AND *MMM!* LEMON MERINGUE!

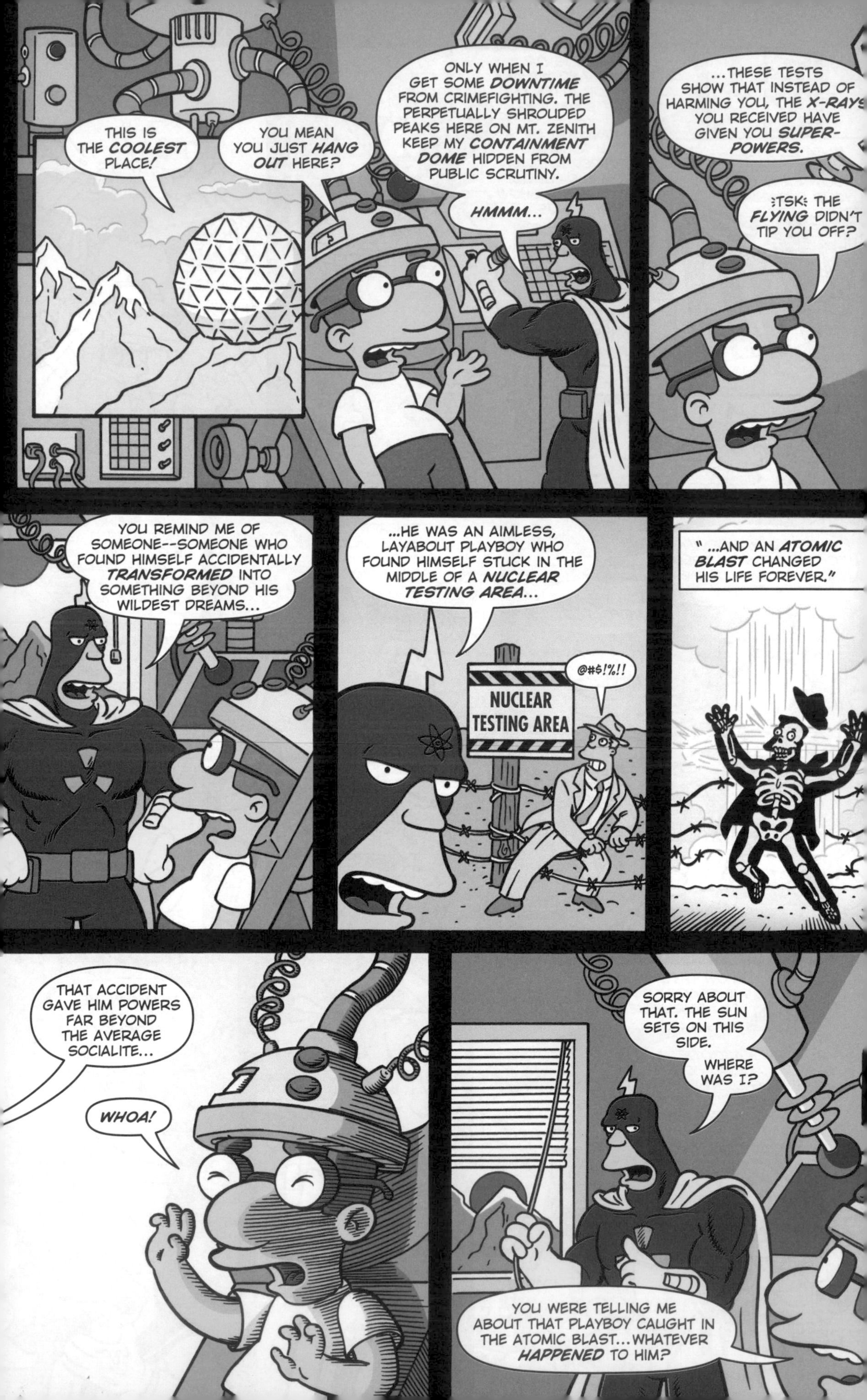
THIS IS THE COOLEST PLACE!
YOU MEAN YOU JUST HANG OUT HERE?
ONLY WHEN I GET SOME DOWNTIME FROM CRIMEFIGHTING. THE PERPETUALLY SHROUDED PEAKS HERE ON MT. ZENITH KEEP MY CONTAINMENT DOME HIDDEN FROM PUBLIC SCRUTINY.
HMMM...
...THESE TESTS SHOW THAT INSTEAD OF HARMING YOU, THE X-RAYS YOU RECEIVED HAVE GIVEN YOU SUPER-POWERS.
TSK THE FLYING DIDN'T TIP YOU OFF?
YOU REMIND ME OF SOMEONE--SOMEONE WHO FOUND HIMSELF ACCIDENTALLY TRANSFORMED INTO SOMETHING BEYOND HIS WILDEST DREAMS...
...HE WAS AN AIMLESS, LAYABOUT PLAYBOY WHO FOUND HIMSELF STUCK IN THE MIDDLE OF A NUCLEAR TESTING AREA...
NUCLEAR TESTING AREA
@#$!%!!
"...AND AN ATOMIC BLAST CHANGED HIS LIFE FOREVER."
THAT ACCIDENT GAVE HIM POWERS FAR BEYOND THE AVERAGE SOCIALITE...
WHOA!
SORRY ABOUT THAT. THE SUN SETS ON THIS SIDE.
WHERE WAS I?
YOU WERE TELLING ME ABOUT THAT PLAYBOY CAUGHT IN THE ATOMIC BLAST...WHATEVER HAPPENED TO HIM?

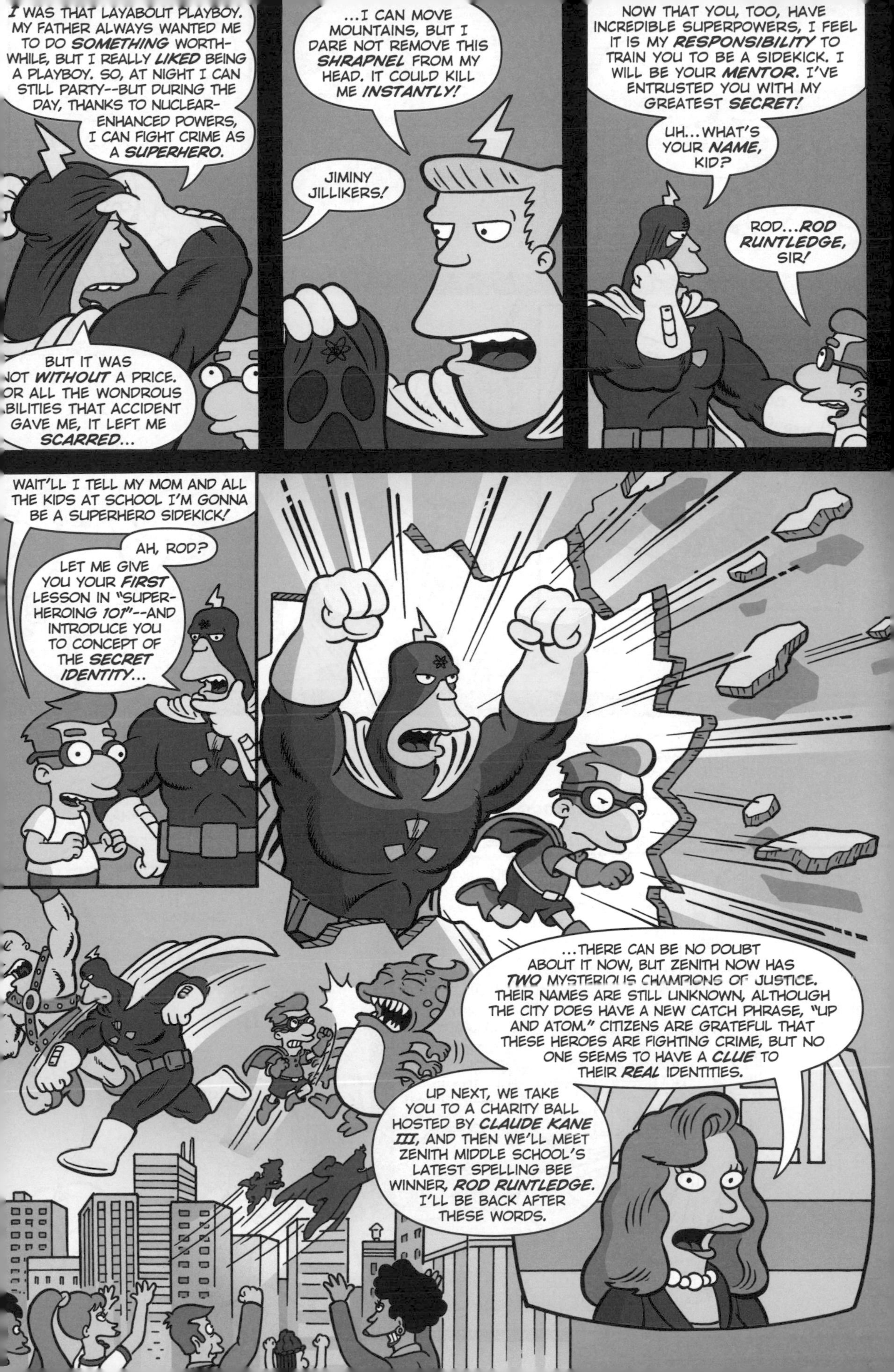
I WAS THAT LAYABOUT PLAYBOY. MY FATHER ALWAYS WANTED ME TO DO SOMETHING WORTHWHILE, BUT I REALLY LIKED BEING A PLAYBOY. SO, AT NIGHT I CAN STILL PARTY--BUT DURING THE DAY, THANKS TO NUCLEAR-ENHANCED POWERS, I CAN FIGHT CRIME AS A SUPERHERO.
BUT IT WAS OT WITHOUT A PRICE. OR ALL THE WONDROUS BILITIES THAT ACCIDENT GAVE ME, IT LEFT ME SCARRED...
...I CAN MOVE MOUNTAINS, BUT I DARE NOT REMOVE THIS SHRAPNEL FROM MY HEAD. IT COULD KILL ME INSTANTLY!
JIMINY JILLIKERS!
NOW THAT YOU, TOO, HAVE INCREDIBLE SUPERPOWERS, I FEEL IT IS MY RESPONSIBILITY TO TRAIN YOU TO BE A SIDEKICK. I WILL BE YOUR MENTOR. I'VE ENTRUSTED YOU WITH MY GREATEST SECRET!
UH...WHAT'S YOUR NAME, KID?
ROD...ROD RUNTLEDGE, SIR!
WAIT'LL I TELL MY MOM AND ALL THE KIDS AT SCHOOL I'M GONNA BE A SUPERHERO SIDEKICK!
AH, ROD?
LET ME GIVE YOU YOUR FIRST LESSON IN "SUPERHEROING 101"--AND INTRODUCE YOU TO CONCEPT OF THE SECRET IDENTITY...
...THERE CAN BE NO DOUBT ABOUT IT NOW, BUT ZENITH NOW HAS TWO MYSTERIOUS CHAMPIONS OF JUSTICE. THEIR NAMES ARE STILL UNKNOWN, ALTHOUGH THE CITY DOES HAVE A NEW CATCH PHRASE, "UP AND ATOM." CITIZENS ARE GRATEFUL THAT THESE HEROES ARE FIGHTING CRIME, BUT NO ONE SEEMS TO HAVE A CLUE TO THEIR REAL IDENTITIES.
UP NEXT, WE TAKE YOU TO A CHARITY BALL HOSTED BY CLAUDE KANE III, AND THEN WE'LL MEET ZENITH MIDDLE SCHOOL'S LATEST SPELLING BEE WINNER, ROD RUNTLEDGE. I'LL BE BACK AFTER THESE WORDS.

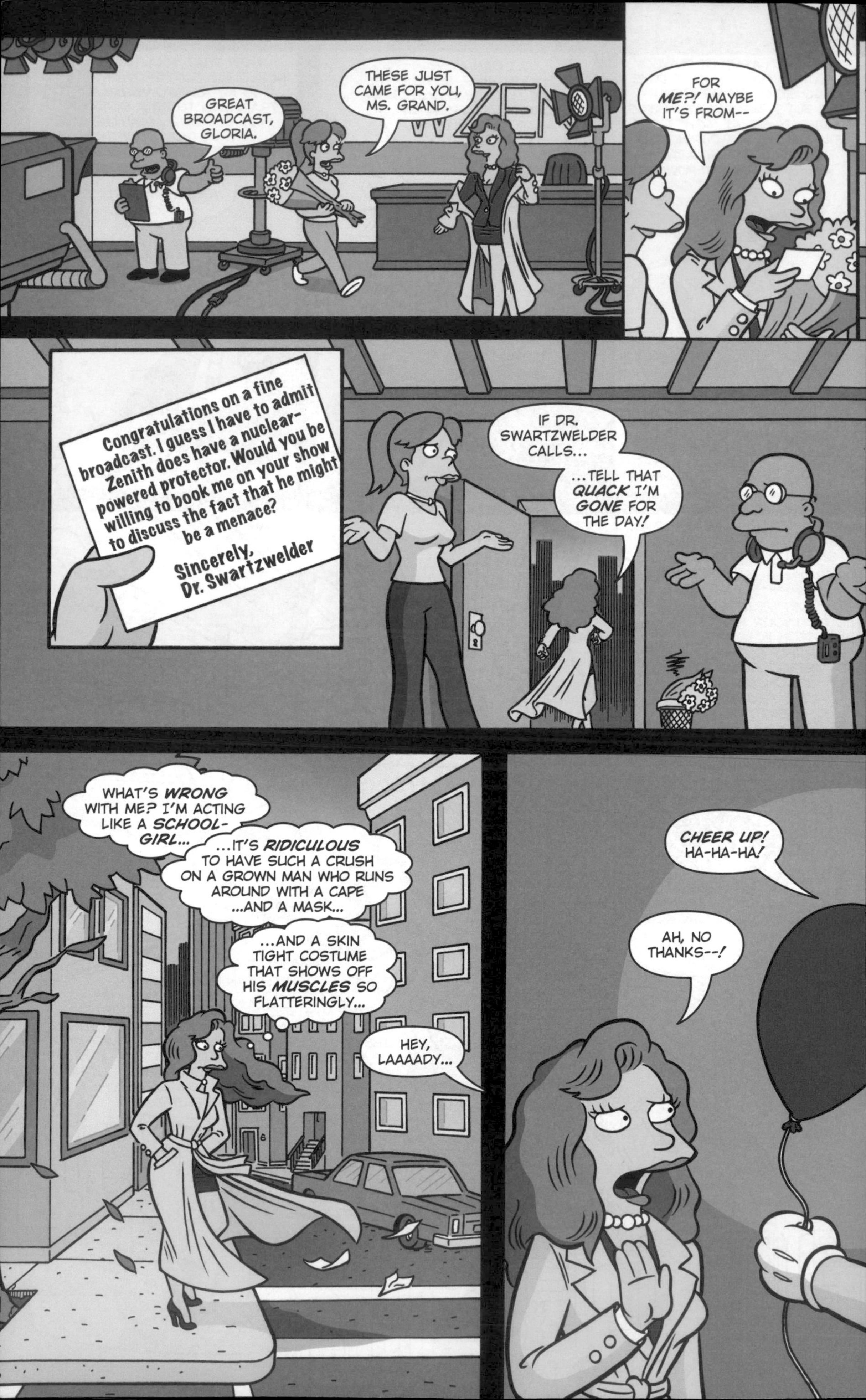

GREAT BROADCAST, GLORIA.
THESE JUST CAME FOR YOU, MS. GRAND.
FOR ME?! MAYBE IT'S FROM--
Congratulations on a fine broadcast. I guess I have to admit Zenith does have a nuclear-powered protector. Would you be willing to book me on your show to discuss the fact that he might be a menace?
Sincerely, Dr. Swartzwelder
IF DR. SWARTZWELDER CALLS...
...TELL THAT QUACK I'M GONE FOR THE DAY!
WHAT'S WRONG WITH ME? I'M ACTING LIKE A SCHOOL-GIRL...
...IT'S RIDICULOUS TO HAVE SUCH A CRUSH ON A GROWN MAN WHO RUNS AROUND WITH A CAPE ...AND A MASK...
...AND A SKIN TIGHT COSTUME THAT SHOWS OFF HIS MUSCLES SO FLATTERINGLY...
HEY, LAAAADY...
CHEER UP! HA-HA-HA!
AH, NO THANKS--!

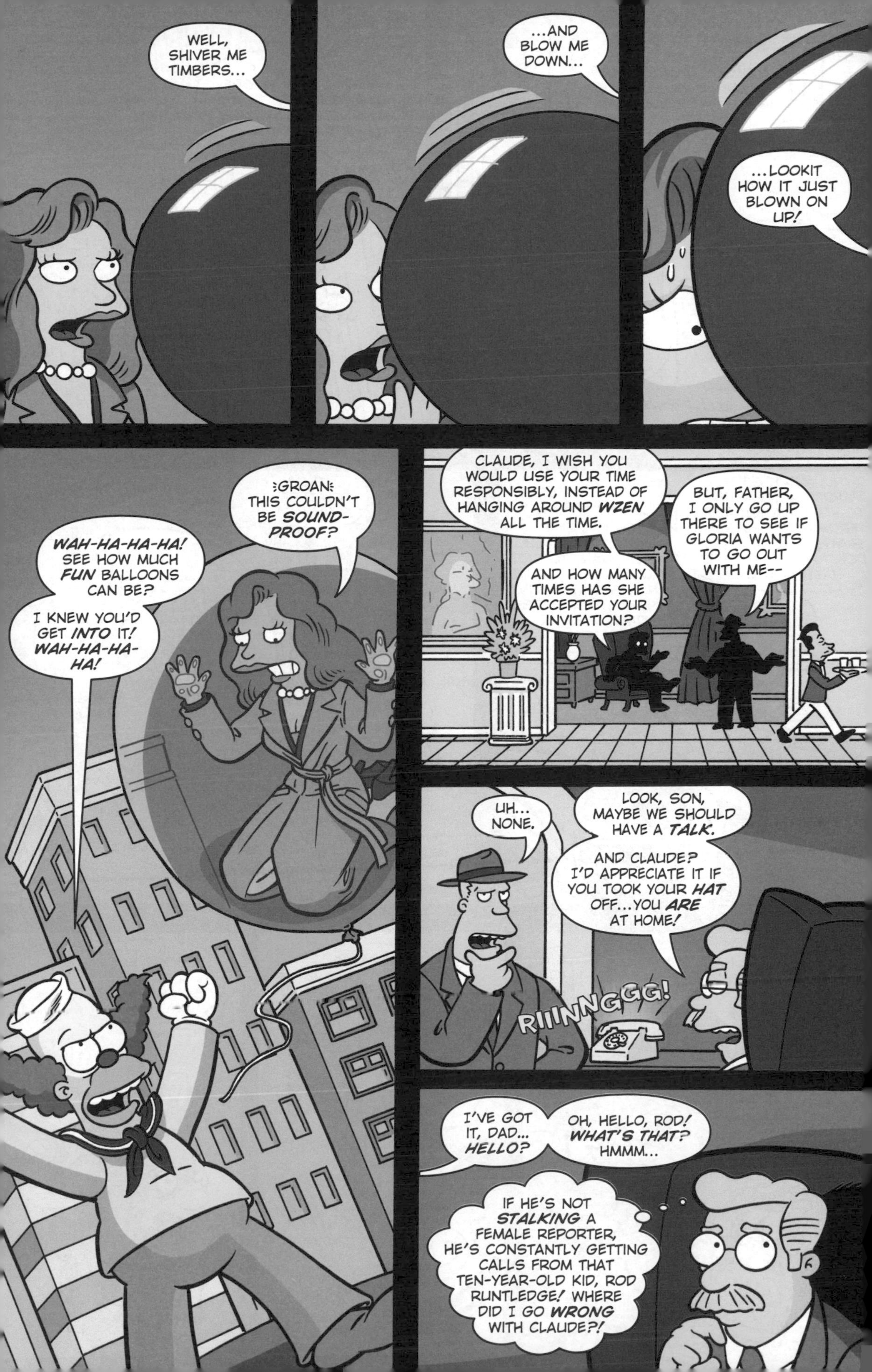
WELL, SHIVER ME TIMBERS...
...AND BLOW ME DOWN...
...LOOKIT HOW IT JUST BLOWN ON UP!
WAH-HA-HA-HA! SEE HOW MUCH FUN BALLOONS CAN BE?
I KNEW YOU'D GET INTO IT! WAH-HA-HA-HA!
GROAN THIS COULDN'T BE SOUND-PROOF?
CLAUDE, I WISH YOU WOULD USE YOUR TIME RESPONSIBLY, INSTEAD OF HANGING AROUND WZEN ALL THE TIME.
BUT, FATHER, I ONLY GO UP THERE TO SEE IF GLORIA WANTS TO GO OUT WITH ME--
AND HOW MANY TIMES HAS SHE ACCEPTED YOUR INVITATION?
UH... NONE.
LOOK, SON, MAYBE WE SHOULD HAVE A TALK.
AND CLAUDE? I'D APPRECIATE IT IF YOU TOOK YOUR HAT OFF...YOU ARE AT HOME!
RIIINNGGG!
I'VE GOT IT, DAD... HELLO?
OH, HELLO, ROD! WHAT'S THAT? HMMM...
IF HE'S NOT STALKING A FEMALE REPORTER, HE'S CONSTANTLY GETTING CALLS FROM THAT TEN-YEAR-OLD KID, ROD RUNTLEDGE! WHERE DID I GO WRONG WITH CLAUDE?!

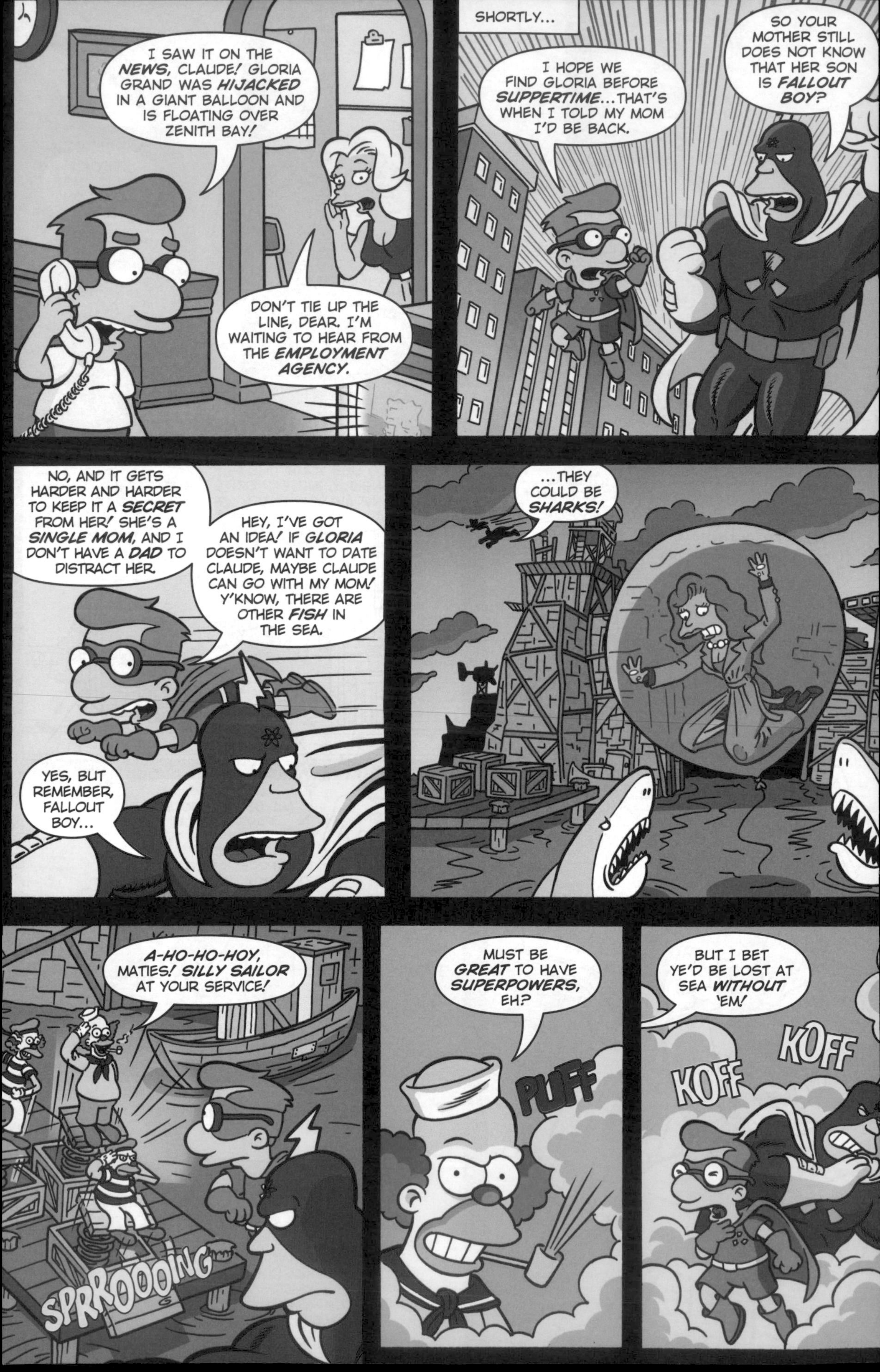
I SAW IT ON THE NEWS, CLAUDE! GLORIA GRAND WAS HIJACKED IN A GIANT BALLOON AND IS FLOATING OVER ZENITH BAY!
DON'T TIE UP THE LINE, DEAR. I'M WAITING TO HEAR FROM THE EMPLOYMENT AGENCY.
SHORTLY...
I HOPE WE FIND GLORIA BEFORE SUPPERTIME...THAT'S WHEN I TOLD MY MOM I'D BE BACK.
SO YOUR MOTHER STILL DOES NOT KNOW THAT HER SON IS FALLOUT BOY?
NO, AND IT GETS HARDER AND HARDER TO KEEP IT A SECRET FROM HER! SHE'S A SINGLE MOM, AND I DON'T HAVE A DAD TO DISTRACT HER.
HEY, I'VE GOT AN IDEA! IF GLORIA DOESN'T WANT TO DATE CLAUDE, MAYBE CLAUDE CAN GO WITH MY MOM! Y'KNOW, THERE ARE OTHER FISH IN THE SEA.
YES, BUT REMEMBER, FALLOUT BOY...
...THEY COULD BE SHARKS!
A-HO-HO-HOY, MATIES! SILLY SAILOR AT YOUR SERVICE!
SPRROOOING
MUST BE GREAT TO HAVE SUPERPOWERS, EH?
PUFF
BUT I BET YE'D BE LOST AT SEA WITHOUT 'EM!
KOFF
KOFF

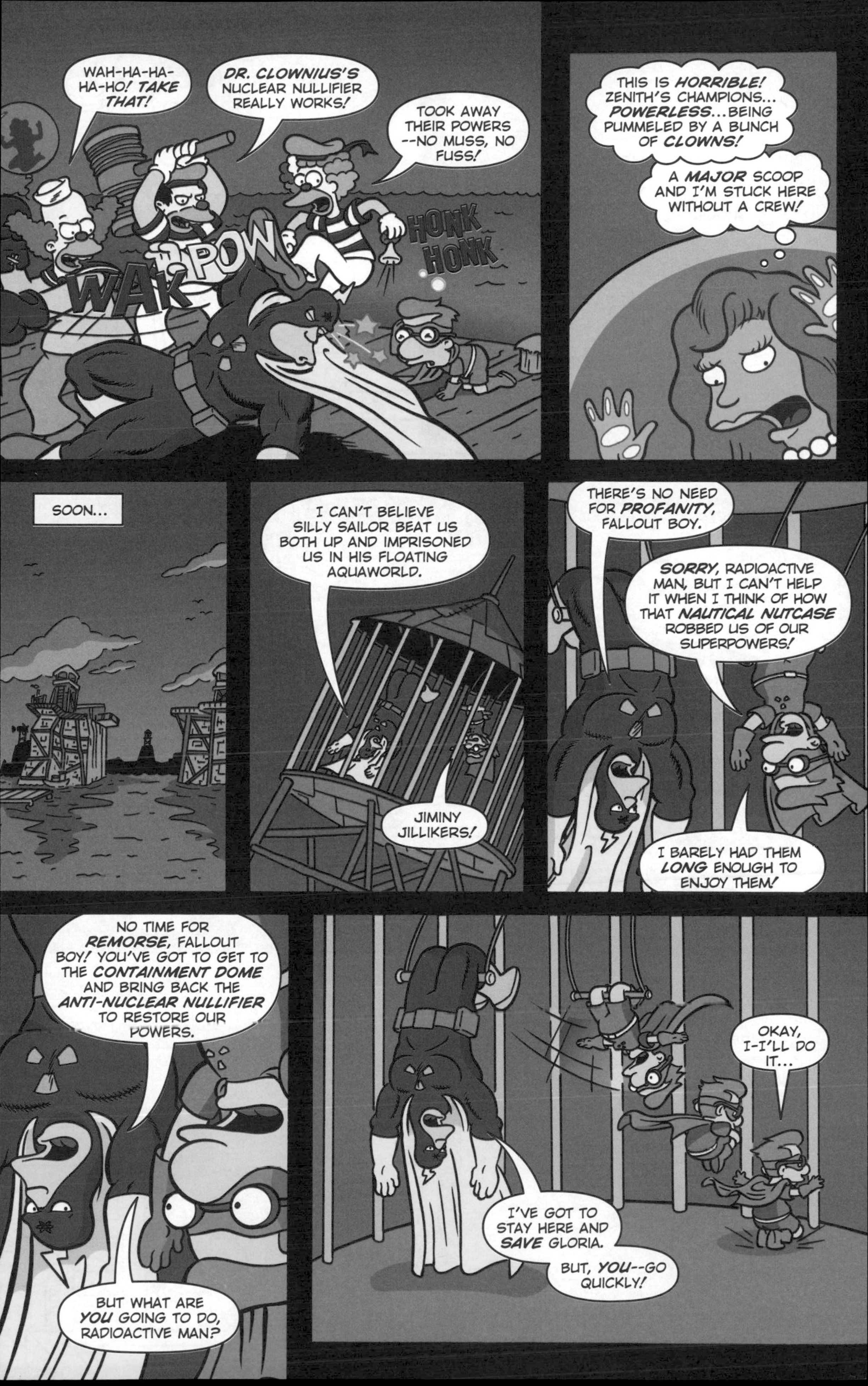
WAH-HA-HA-HA-HO! TAKE THAT!
DR. CLOWNIUS'S NUCLEAR NULLIFIER REALLY WORKS!
TOOK AWAY THEIR POWERS --NO MUSS, NO FUSS!
WAK
POW
HONK HONK
THIS IS HORRIBLE! ZENITH'S CHAMPIONS... POWERLESS...BEING PUMMELED BY A BUNCH OF CLOWNS!
A MAJOR SCOOP AND I'M STUCK HERE WITHOUT A CREW!
SOON...
I CAN'T BELIEVE SILLY SAILOR BEAT US BOTH UP AND IMPRISONED US IN HIS FLOATING AQUAWORLD.
JIMINY JILLIKERS!
THERE'S NO NEED FOR PROFANITY, FALLOUT BOY.
SORRY, RADIOACTIVE MAN, BUT I CAN'T HELP IT WHEN I THINK OF HOW THAT NAUTICAL NUTCASE ROBBED US OF OUR SUPERPOWERS!
I BARELY HAD THEM LONG ENOUGH TO ENJOY THEM!
NO TIME FOR REMORSE, FALLOUT BOY! YOU'VE GOT TO GET TO THE CONTAINMENT DOME AND BRING BACK THE ANTI-NUCLEAR NULLIFIER TO RESTORE OUR POWERS.
BUT WHAT ARE YOU GOING TO DO, RADIOACTIVE MAN?
I'VE GOT TO STAY HERE AND SAVE GLORIA.
BUT, YOU--GO QUICKLY!
OKAY, I-I'LL DO IT...

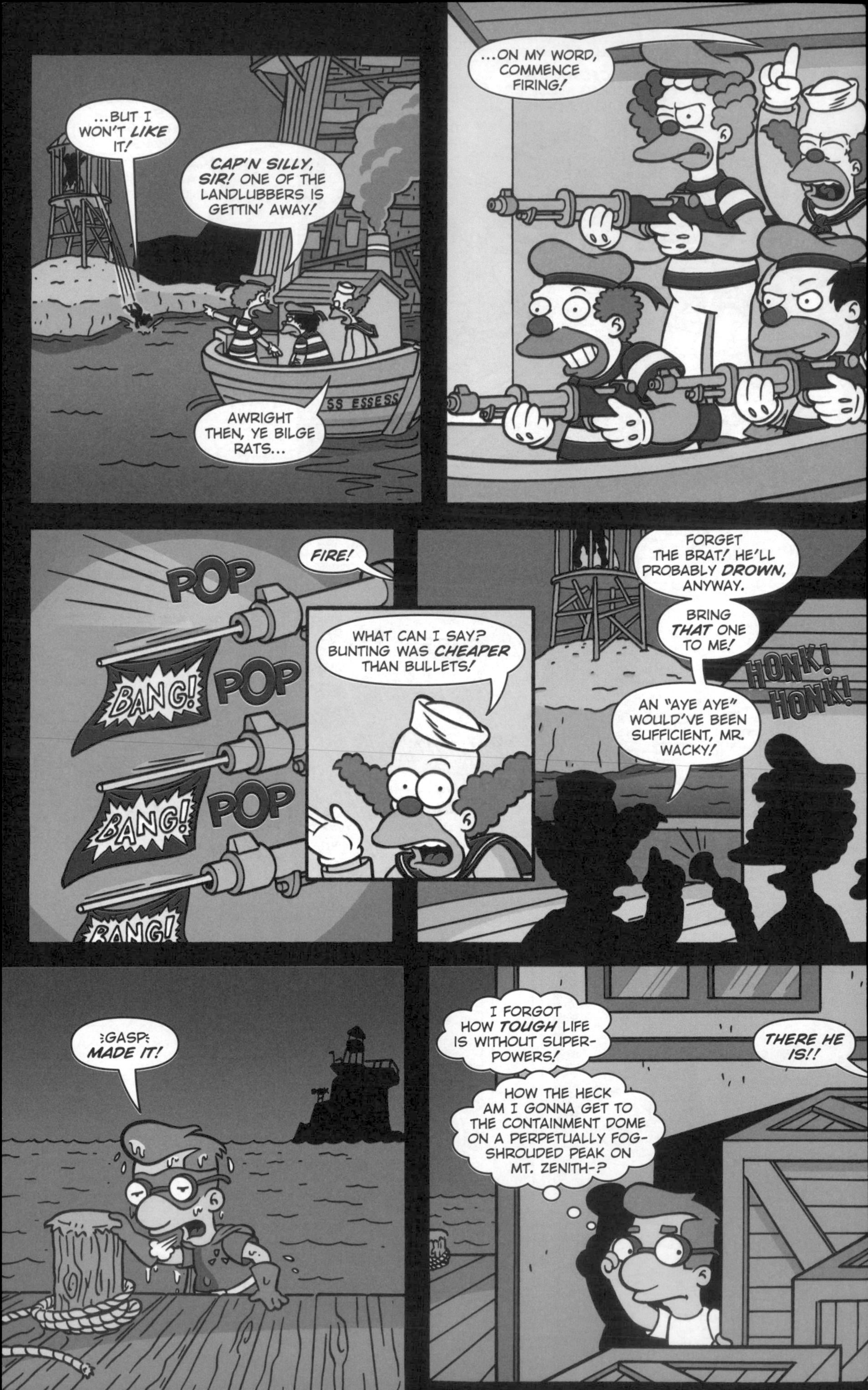

...BUT I WON'T LIKE IT!
CAP'N SILLY, SIR! ONE OF THE LANDLUBBERS IS GETTIN' AWAY!
AWRIGHT THEN, YE BILGE RATS...
SS ESSESS
...ON MY WORD, COMMENCE FIRING!
FIRE!
POP
BANG!
POP
BANG!
POP
BANG!
WHAT CAN I SAY? BUNTING WAS CHEAPER THAN BULLETS!
FORGET THE BRAT! HE'LL PROBABLY DROWN, ANYWAY.
BRING THAT ONE TO ME!
HONK! HONK!
AN "AYE AYE" WOULD'VE BEEN SUFFICIENT, MR. WACKY!
GASP MADE IT!
I FORGOT HOW TOUGH LIFE IS WITHOUT SUPER-POWERS!
HOW THE HECK AM I GONNA GET TO THE CONTAINMENT DOME ON A PERPETUALLY FOG-SHROUDED PEAK ON MT. ZENITH-?
THERE HE IS!!

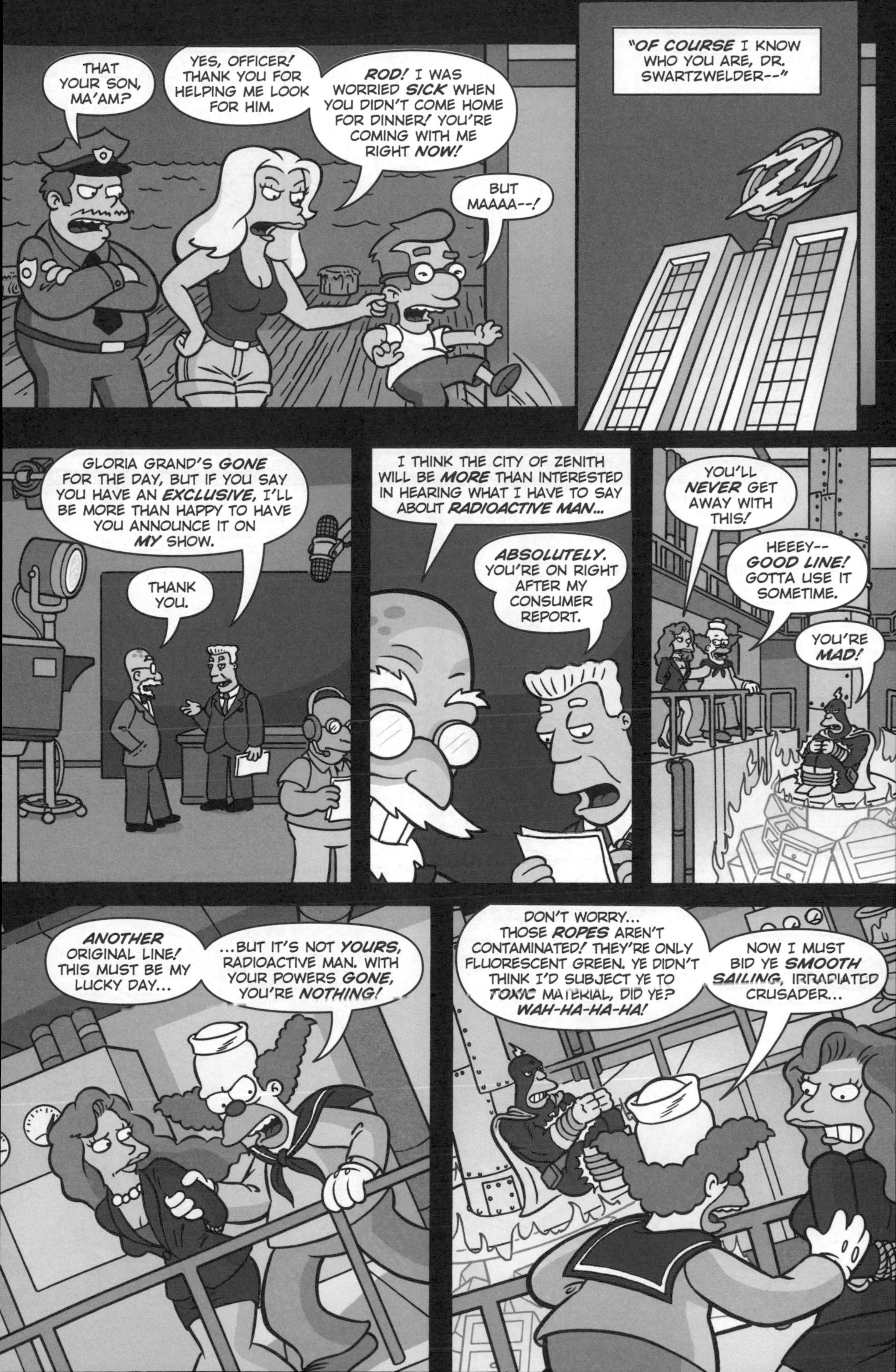
THAT YOUR SON, MA'AM?
YES, OFFICER! THANK YOU FOR HELPING ME LOOK FOR HIM.
ROD! I WAS WORRIED SICK WHEN YOU DIDN'T COME HOME FOR DINNER! YOU'RE COMING WITH ME RIGHT NOW!
BUT MAAAA--!
"OF COURSE I KNOW WHO YOU ARE, DR. SWARTZWELDER--"
GLORIA GRAND'S GONE FOR THE DAY, BUT IF YOU SAY YOU HAVE AN EXCLUSIVE, I'LL BE MORE THAN HAPPY TO HAVE YOU ANNOUNCE IT ON MY SHOW.
THANK YOU.
I THINK THE CITY OF ZENITH WILL BE MORE THAN INTERESTED IN HEARING WHAT I HAVE TO SAY ABOUT RADIOACTIVE MAN...
ABSOLUTELY. YOU'RE ON RIGHT AFTER MY CONSUMER REPORT.
YOU'LL NEVER GET AWAY WITH THIS!
HEEEY-- GOOD LINE! GOTTA USE IT SOMETIME.
YOU'RE MAD!
ANOTHER ORIGINAL LINE! THIS MUST BE MY LUCKY DAY...
...BUT IT'S NOT YOURS, RADIOACTIVE MAN. WITH YOUR POWERS GONE, YOU'RE NOTHING!
DON'T WORRY... THOSE ROPES AREN'T CONTAMINATED! THEY'RE ONLY FLUORESCENT GREEN. YE DIDN'T THINK I'D SUBJECT YE TO TOXIC MATERIAL, DID YE? WAH-HA-HA-HA!
NOW I MUST BID YE SMOOTH SAILING, IRRADIATED CRUSADER...

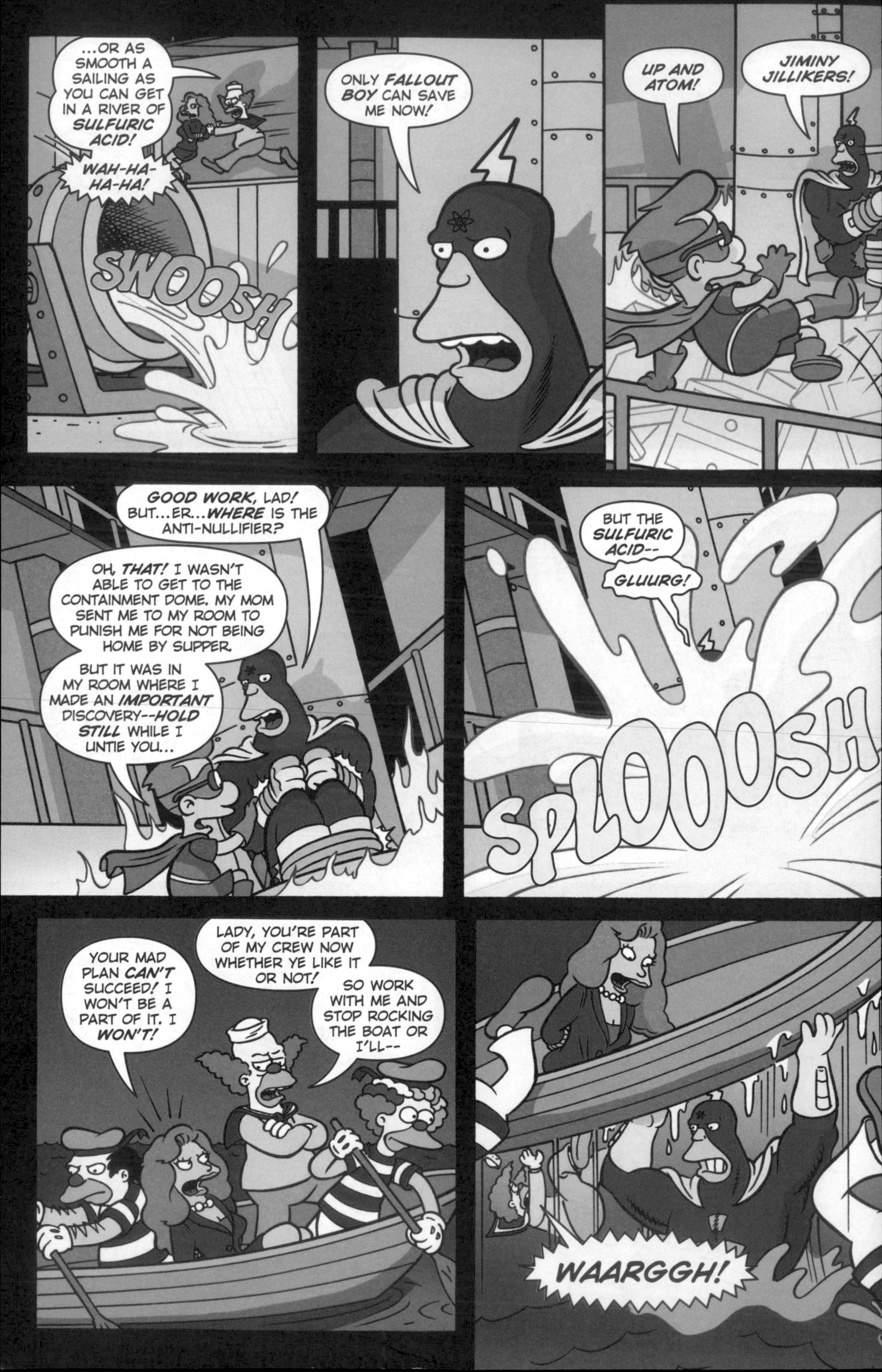
...OR AS SMOOTH A SAILING AS YOU CAN GET IN A RIVER OF SULFURIC ACID!
WAH-HA-HA-HA!
SWOOSH
ONLY FALLOUT BOY CAN SAVE ME NOW!
UP AND ATOM!
JIMINY JILLIKERS!
GOOD WORK, LAD! BUT...ER...WHERE IS THE ANTI-NULLIFIER?
OH, THAT! I WASN'T ABLE TO GET TO THE CONTAINMENT DOME. MY MOM SENT ME TO MY ROOM TO PUNISH ME FOR NOT BEING HOME BY SUPPER.
BUT IT WAS IN MY ROOM WHERE I MADE AN IMPORTANT DISCOVERY--HOLD STILL WHILE I UNTIE YOU...
BUT THE SULFURIC ACID--
GLUURG!
SPLOOOSH
YOUR MAD PLAN CAN'T SUCCEED! I WON'T BE A PART OF IT. I WON'T!
LADY, YOU'RE PART OF MY CREW NOW WHETHER YE LIKE IT OR NOT!
SO WORK WITH ME AND STOP ROCKING THE BOAT OR I'LL--
WAARGGH!

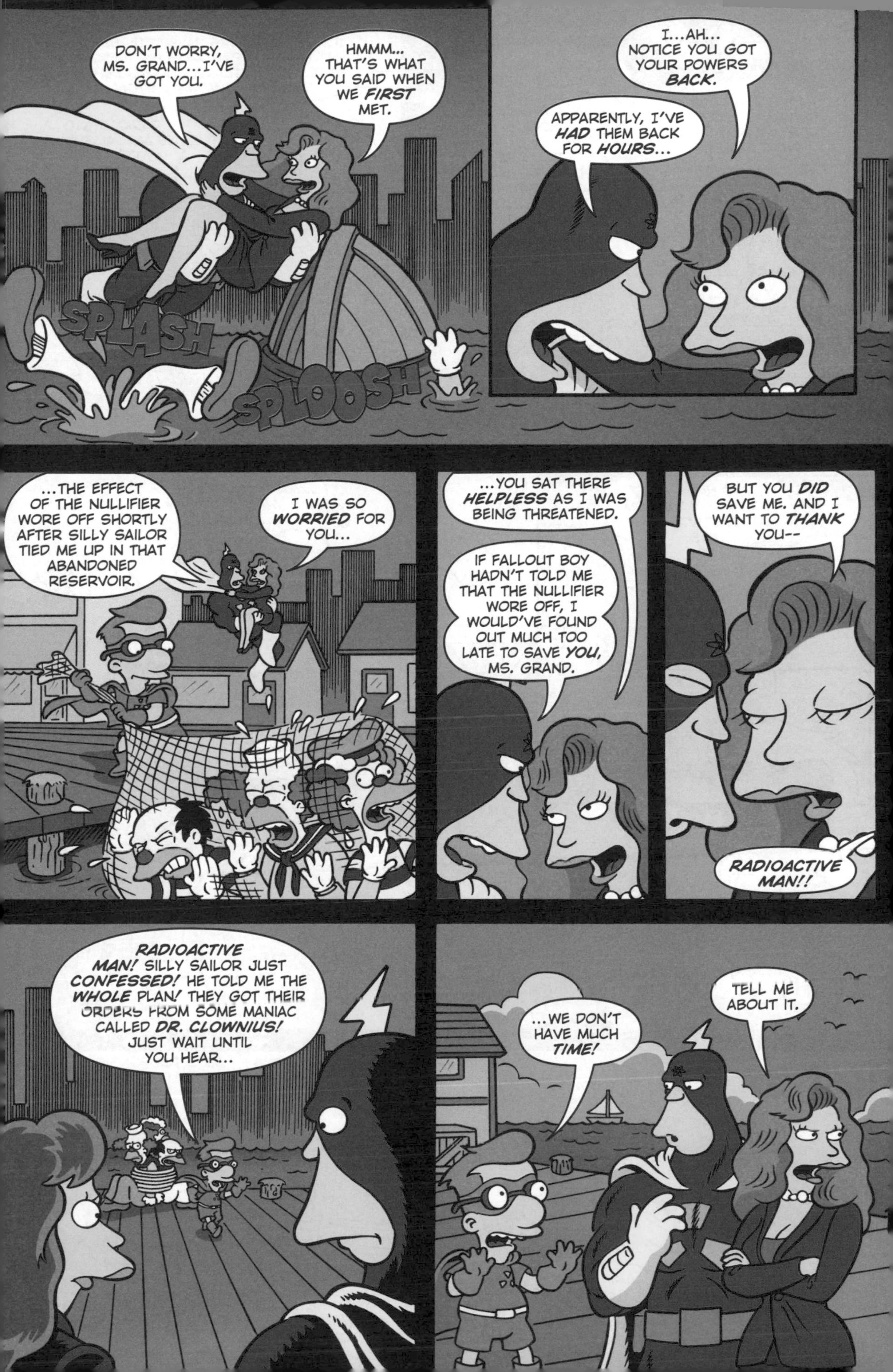
DON'T WORRY, MS. GRAND...I'VE GOT YOU.
HMMM... THAT'S WHAT YOU SAID WHEN WE FIRST MET.
SPLASH
SPLOOSH
I...AH... NOTICE YOU GOT YOUR POWERS BACK.
APPARENTLY, I'VE HAD THEM BACK FOR HOURS...
...THE EFFECT OF THE NULLIFIER WORE OFF SHORTLY AFTER SILLY SAILOR TIED ME UP IN THAT ABANDONED RESERVOIR.
I WAS SO WORRIED FOR YOU...
...YOU SAT THERE HELPLESS AS I WAS BEING THREATENED.
IF FALLOUT BOY HADN'T TOLD ME THAT THE NULLIFIER WORE OFF, I WOULD'VE FOUND OUT MUCH TOO LATE TO SAVE YOU, MS. GRAND.
BUT YOU DID SAVE ME. AND I WANT TO THANK YOU--
RADIOACTIVE MAN!!
RADIOACTIVE MAN! SILLY SAILOR JUST CONFESSED! HE TOLD ME THE WHOLE PLAN! THEY GOT THEIR ORDERS FROM SOME MANIAC CALLED DR. CLOWNIUS! JUST WAIT UNTIL YOU HEAR...
...WE DON'T HAVE MUCH TIME!
TELL ME ABOUT IT.

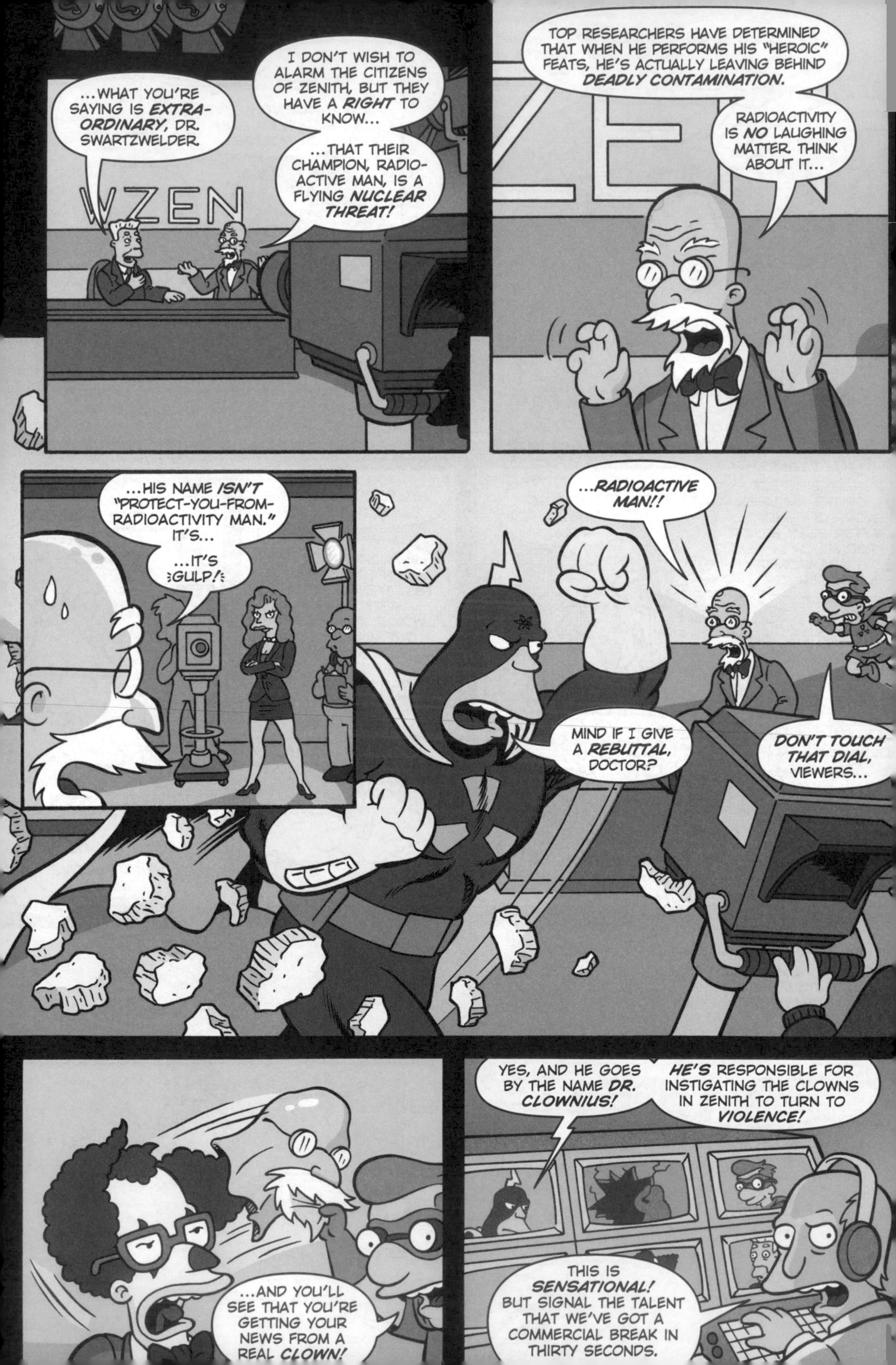

...WHAT YOU'RE SAYING IS EXTRA-ORDINARY, DR. SWARTZWELDER.
I DON'T WISH TO ALARM THE CITIZENS OF ZENITH, BUT THEY HAVE A RIGHT TO KNOW...
...THAT THEIR CHAMPION, RADIO-ACTIVE MAN, IS A FLYING NUCLEAR THREAT!
WZEN
TOP RESEARCHERS HAVE DETERMINED THAT WHEN HE PERFORMS HIS "HEROIC" FEATS, HE'S ACTUALLY LEAVING BEHIND DEADLY CONTAMINATION.
RADIOACTIVITY IS NO LAUGHING MATTER. THINK ABOUT IT...
...HIS NAME ISN'T "PROTECT-YOU-FROM-RADIOACTIVITY MAN." IT'S...
...IT'S GULP!
...RADIOACTIVE MAN!!
MIND IF I GIVE A REBUTTAL, DOCTOR?
DON'T TOUCH THAT DIAL, VIEWERS...
...AND YOU'LL SEE THAT YOU'RE GETTING YOUR NEWS FROM A REAL CLOWN!
YES, AND HE GOES BY THE NAME DR. CLOWNIUS!
HE'S RESPONSIBLE FOR INSTIGATING THE CLOWNS IN ZENITH TO TURN TO VIOLENCE!
THIS IS SENSATIONAL! BUT SIGNAL THE TALENT THAT WE'VE GOT A COMMERCIAL BREAK IN THIRTY SECONDS.

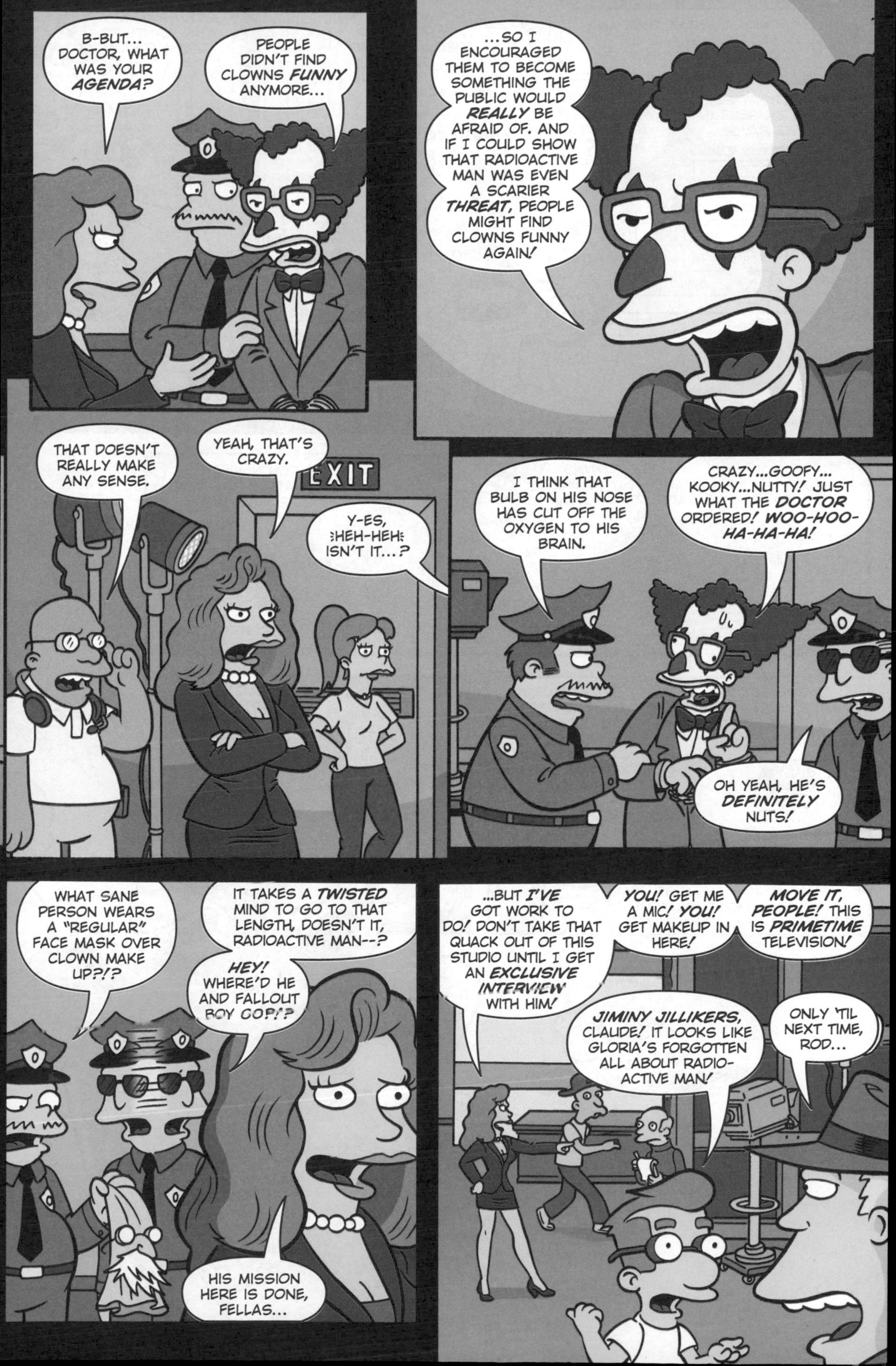
B-BUT... DOCTOR, WHAT WAS YOUR *AGENDA*?
PEOPLE DIDN'T FIND CLOWNS *FUNNY* ANYMORE...
...SO I ENCOURAGED THEM TO BECOME SOMETHING THE PUBLIC WOULD *REALLY* BE AFRAID OF. AND IF I COULD SHOW THAT RADIOACTIVE MAN WAS EVEN A SCARIER *THREAT*, PEOPLE MIGHT FIND CLOWNS FUNNY AGAIN!
THAT DOESN'T REALLY MAKE ANY SENSE.
YEAH, THAT'S CRAZY.
EXIT
Y-ES, HEH-HEH ISN'T IT...?
I THINK THAT BULB ON HIS NOSE HAS CUT OFF THE OXYGEN TO HIS BRAIN.
CRAZY...GOOFY... KOOKY...NUTTY! JUST WHAT THE *DOCTOR* ORDERED! *WOO-HOO-HA-HA-HA!*
OH YEAH, HE'S *DEFINITELY* NUTS!
WHAT SANE PERSON WEARS A "REGULAR" FACE MASK OVER CLOWN MAKE UP?!?
IT TAKES A *TWISTED* MIND TO GO TO THAT LENGTH, DOESN'T IT, RADIOACTIVE MAN--?
HEY! WHERE'D HE AND FALLOUT BOY GO?!?
HIS MISSION HERE IS DONE, FELLAS...
...BUT *I'VE* GOT WORK TO DO! DON'T TAKE THAT QUACK OUT OF THIS STUDIO UNTIL I GET AN *EXCLUSIVE INTERVIEW* WITH HIM!
YOU! GET ME A MIC! *YOU!* GET MAKEUP IN HERE!
MOVE IT, PEOPLE! THIS IS *PRIMETIME* TELEVISION!
JIMINY JILLIKERS, CLAUDE! IT LOOKS LIKE GLORIA'S FORGOTTEN ALL ABOUT RADIO-ACTIVE MAN!
ONLY 'TIL NEXT TIME, ROD...

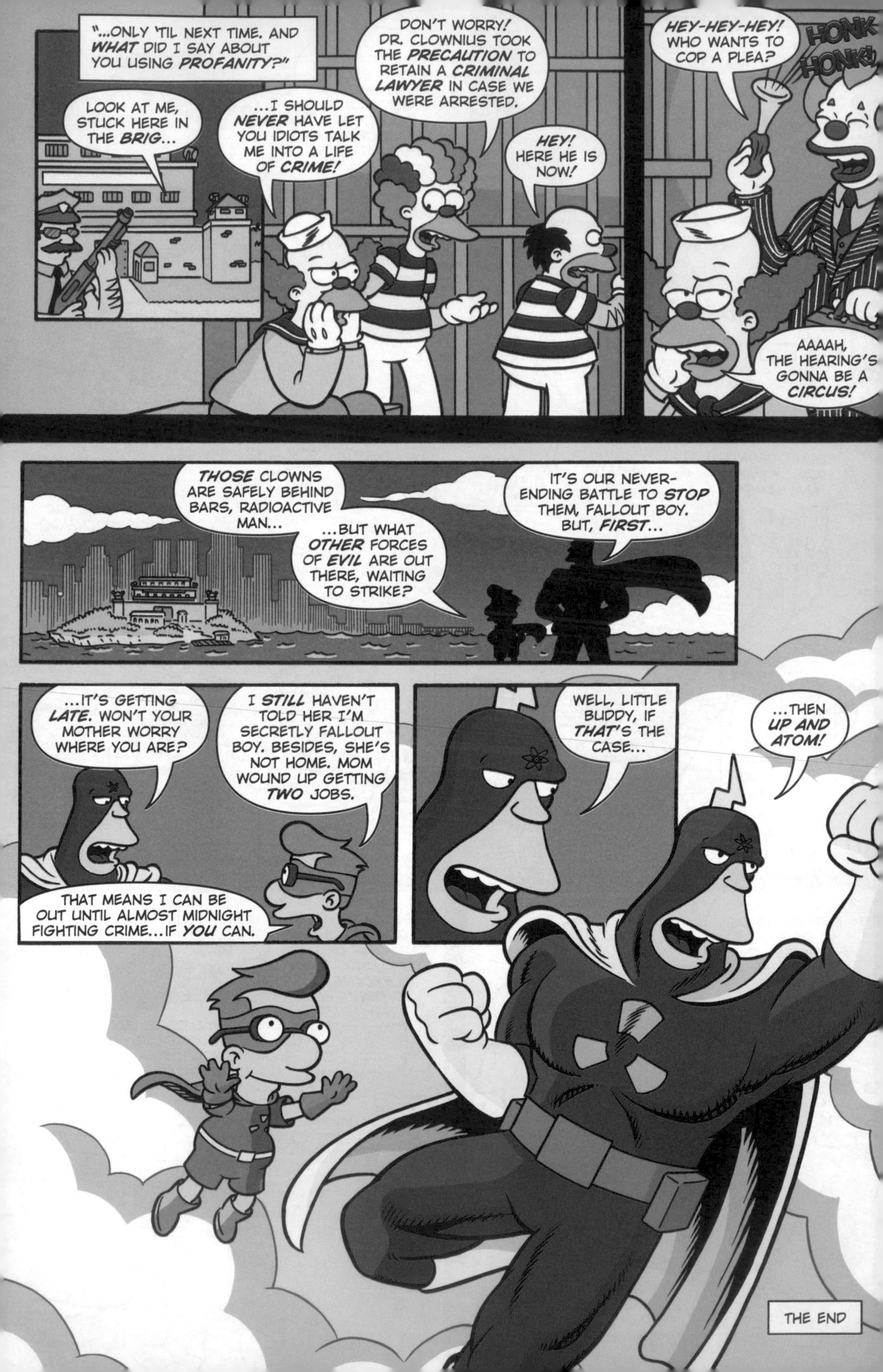

"...ONLY 'TIL NEXT TIME. AND WHAT DID I SAY ABOUT YOU USING PROFANITY?"
LOOK AT ME, STUCK HERE IN THE BRIG...
...I SHOULD NEVER HAVE LET YOU IDIOTS TALK ME INTO A LIFE OF CRIME!
DON'T WORRY! DR. CLOWNIUS TOOK THE PRECAUTION TO RETAIN A CRIMINAL LAWYER IN CASE WE WERE ARRESTED.
HEY! HERE HE IS NOW!
HEY-HEY-HEY! WHO WANTS TO COP A PLEA?
HONK HONK!
AAAAH, THE HEARING'S GONNA BE A CIRCUS!
THOSE CLOWNS ARE SAFELY BEHIND BARS, RADIOACTIVE MAN...
...BUT WHAT OTHER FORCES OF EVIL ARE OUT THERE, WAITING TO STRIKE?
IT'S OUR NEVER-ENDING BATTLE TO STOP THEM, FALLOUT BOY. BUT, FIRST...
...IT'S GETTING LATE. WON'T YOUR MOTHER WORRY WHERE YOU ARE?
I STILL HAVEN'T TOLD HER I'M SECRETLY FALLOUT BOY. BESIDES, SHE'S NOT HOME. MOM WOUND UP GETTING TWO JOBS.
THAT MEANS I CAN BE OUT UNTIL ALMOST MIDNIGHT FIGHTING CRIME...IF YOU CAN.
WELL, LITTLE BUDDY, IF THAT'S THE CASE...
...THEN UP AND ATOM!
THE END

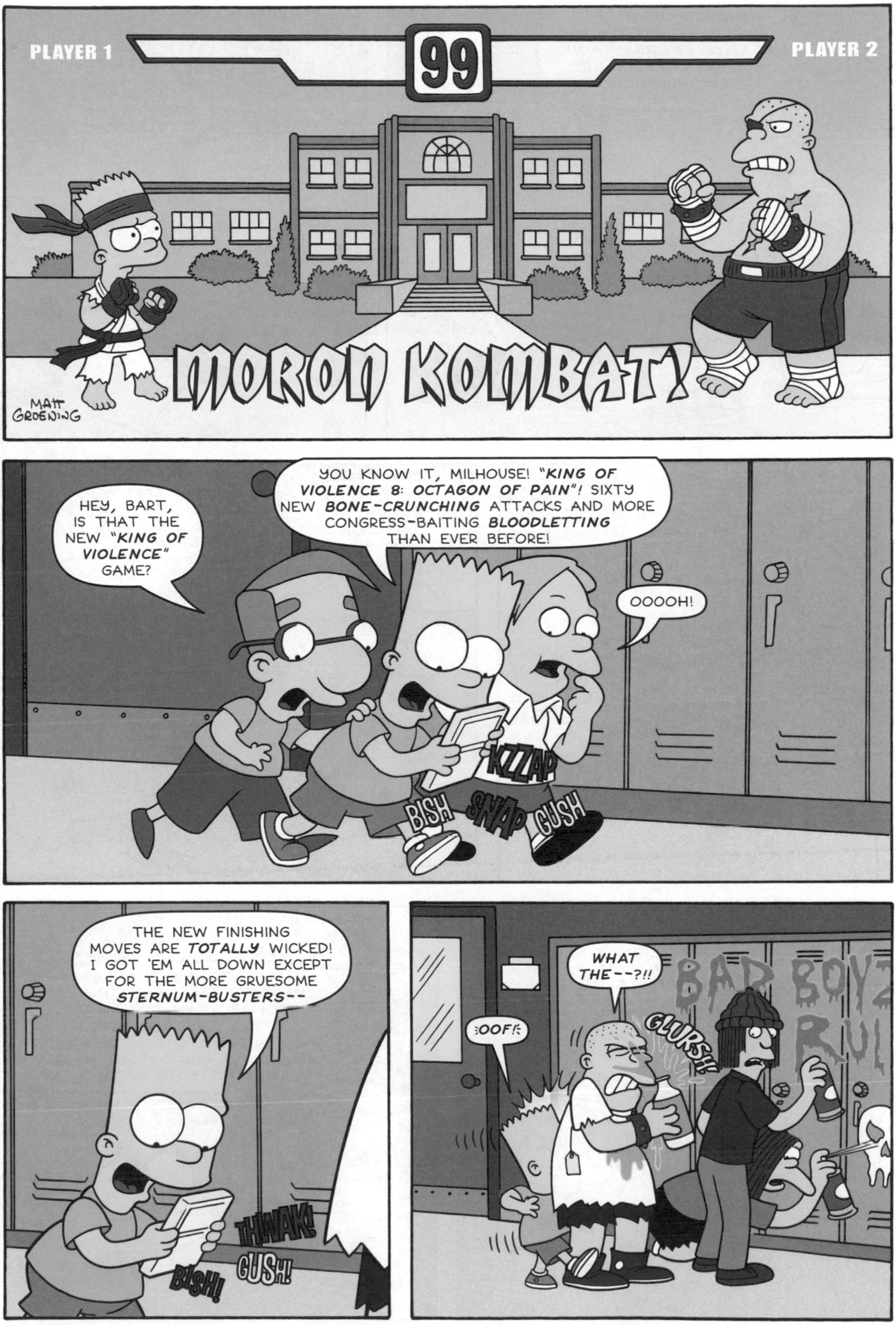
PLAYER 1
99
PLAYER 2
MORON KOMBAT!
MATT GROENING
HEY, BART, IS THAT THE NEW "KING OF VIOLENCE" GAME?
YOU KNOW IT, MILHOUSE! "KING OF VIOLENCE 8: OCTAGON OF PAIN"! SIXTY NEW BONE-CRUNCHING ATTACKS AND MORE CONGRESS-BAITING BLOODLETTING THAN EVER BEFORE!
OOOOH!
KZZAP
BISH
SNAP
GUSH
THE NEW FINISHING MOVES ARE TOTALLY WICKED! I GOT 'EM ALL DOWN EXCEPT FOR THE MORE GRUESOME STERNUM-BUSTERS--
THWAK!
GUSH!
BISH!
WHAT THE--?!!
OOF!
GLURSH!

EVAN DORKIN SCRIPT — **PHIL ORTIZ** PENCILS — **SHANE GLINES** INKS — **RICK REESE** COLORS — **KAREN BATES** LETTERS — **BILL MORRISON** EDITOR

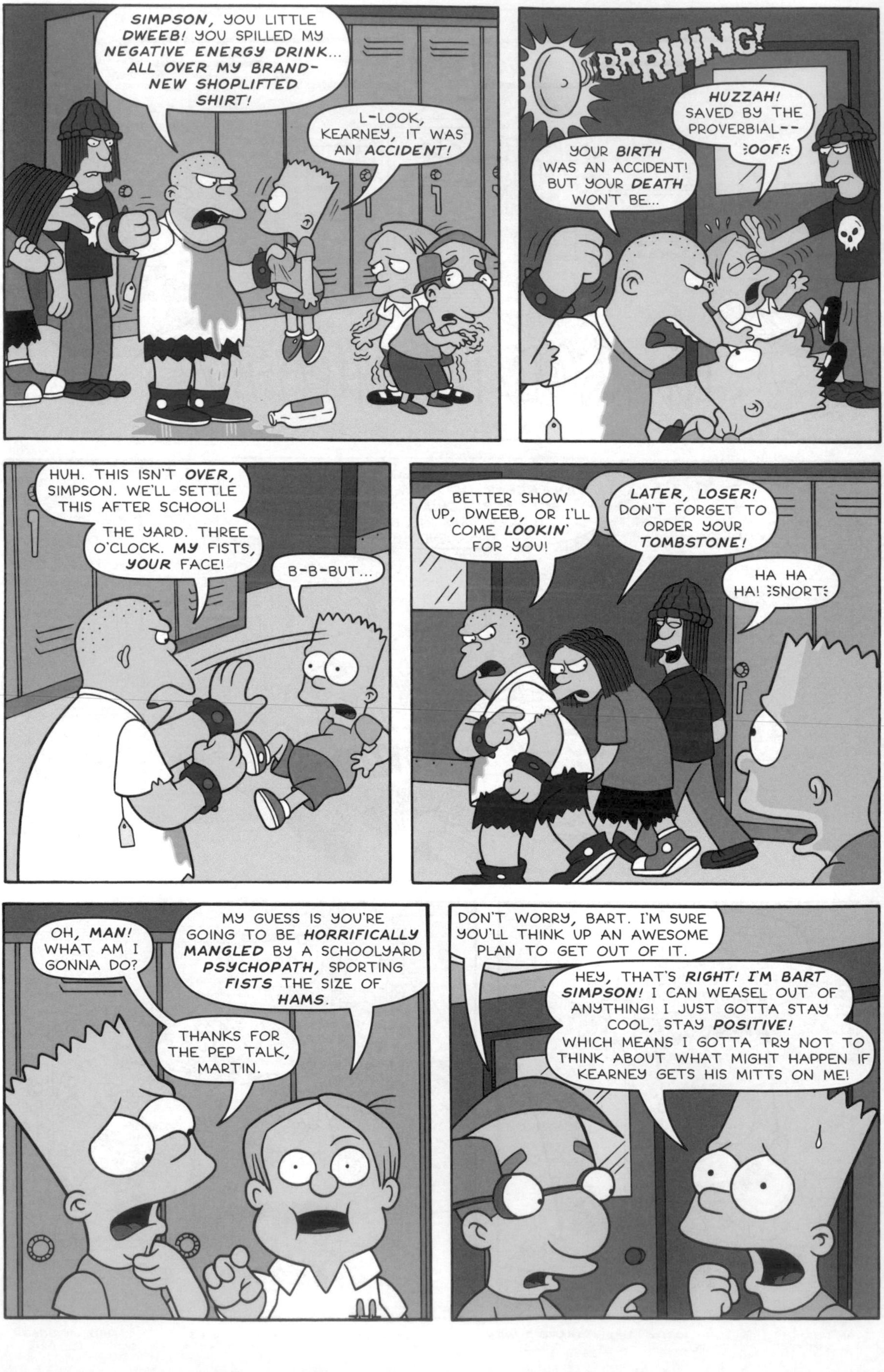
SIMPSON, YOU LITTLE DWEEB! YOU SPILLED MY NEGATIVE ENERGY DRINK... ALL OVER MY BRAND-NEW SHOPLIFTED SHIRT!
L-LOOK, KEARNEY, IT WAS AN ACCIDENT!
BRRIIIING!
YOUR BIRTH WAS AN ACCIDENT! BUT YOUR DEATH WON'T BE...
HUZZAH! SAVED BY THE PROVERBIAL--
OOF!
HUH. THIS ISN'T OVER, SIMPSON. WE'LL SETTLE THIS AFTER SCHOOL!
THE YARD. THREE O'CLOCK. MY FISTS, YOUR FACE!
B-B-BUT...
BETTER SHOW UP, DWEEB, OR I'LL COME LOOKIN' FOR YOU!
LATER, LOSER! DON'T FORGET TO ORDER YOUR TOMBSTONE!
HA HA HA! SNORT
OH, MAN! WHAT AM I GONNA DO?
MY GUESS IS YOU'RE GOING TO BE HORRIFICALLY MANGLED BY A SCHOOLYARD PSYCHOPATH, SPORTING FISTS THE SIZE OF HAMS.
THANKS FOR THE PEP TALK, MARTIN.
DON'T WORRY, BART. I'M SURE YOU'LL THINK UP AN AWESOME PLAN TO GET OUT OF IT.
HEY, THAT'S RIGHT! I'M BART SIMPSON! I CAN WEASEL OUT OF ANYTHING! I JUST GOTTA STAY COOL, STAY POSITIVE!
WHICH MEANS I GOTTA TRY NOT TO THINK ABOUT WHAT MIGHT HAPPEN IF KEARNEY GETS HIS MITTS ON ME!

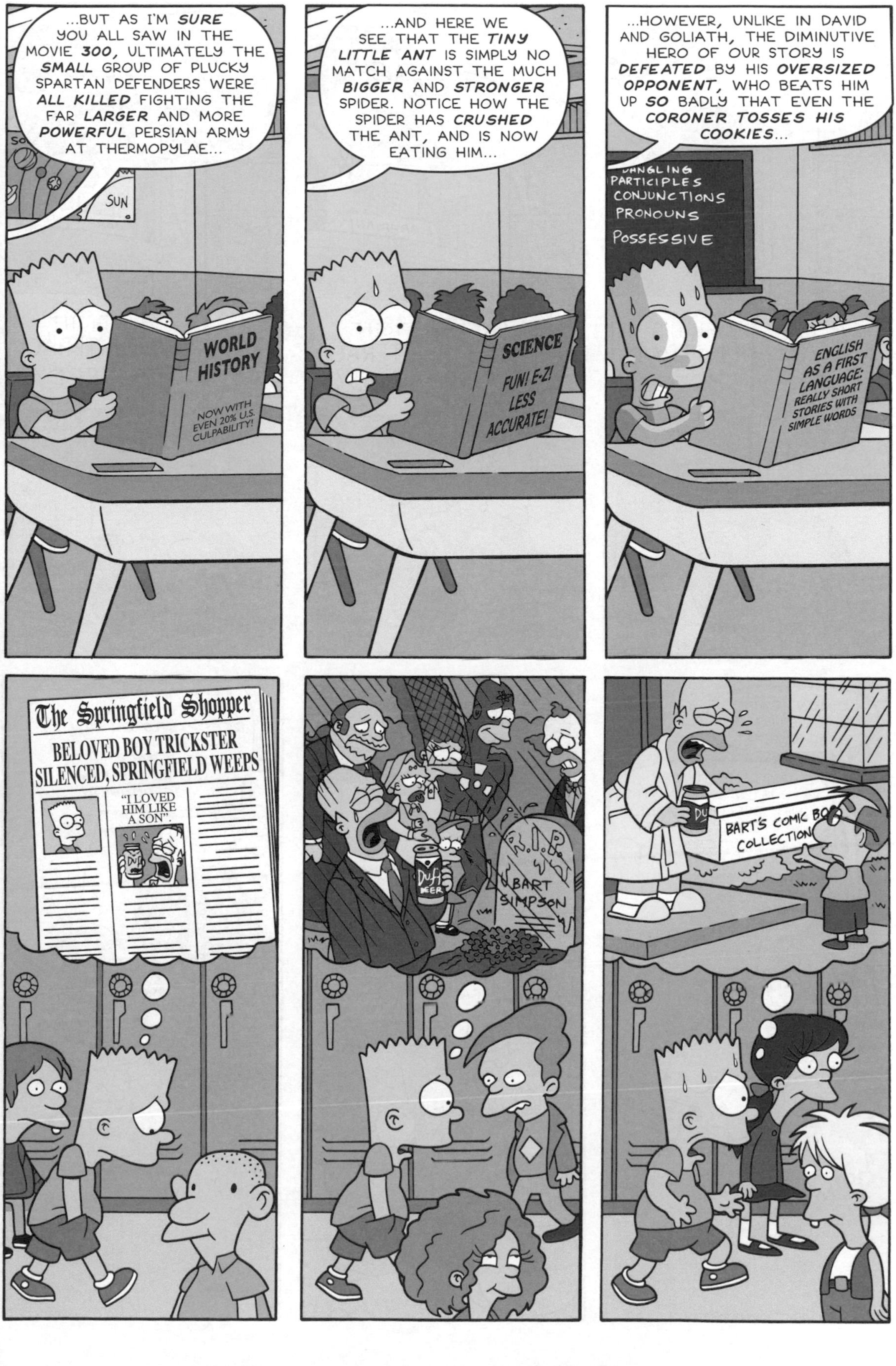
...BUT AS I'M SURE YOU ALL SAW IN THE MOVIE 300, ULTIMATELY THE SMALL GROUP OF PLUCKY SPARTAN DEFENDERS WERE ALL KILLED FIGHTING THE FAR LARGER AND MORE POWERFUL PERSIAN ARMY AT THERMOPYLAE...
SUN
WORLD HISTORY
NOW WITH EVEN 20% U.S. CULPABILITY!
...AND HERE WE SEE THAT THE TINY LITTLE ANT IS SIMPLY NO MATCH AGAINST THE MUCH BIGGER AND STRONGER SPIDER. NOTICE HOW THE SPIDER HAS CRUSHED THE ANT, AND IS NOW EATING HIM...
SCIENCE
FUN! E-Z! LESS ACCURATE!
...HOWEVER, UNLIKE IN DAVID AND GOLIATH, THE DIMINUTIVE HERO OF OUR STORY IS DEFEATED BY HIS OVERSIZED OPPONENT, WHO BEATS HIM UP SO BADLY THAT EVEN THE CORONER TOSSES HIS COOKIES...
DANGLING PARTICIPLES
CONJUNCTIONS
PRONOUNS
POSSESSIVE
ENGLISH AS A FIRST LANGUAGE: REALLY SHORT STORIES WITH SIMPLE WORDS
The Springfield Shopper
BELOVED BOY TRICKSTER SILENCED, SPRINGFIELD WEEPS
"I LOVED HIM LIKE A SON".
R.I.P.
BART SIMPSON
BART'S COMIC BO
COLLECTION

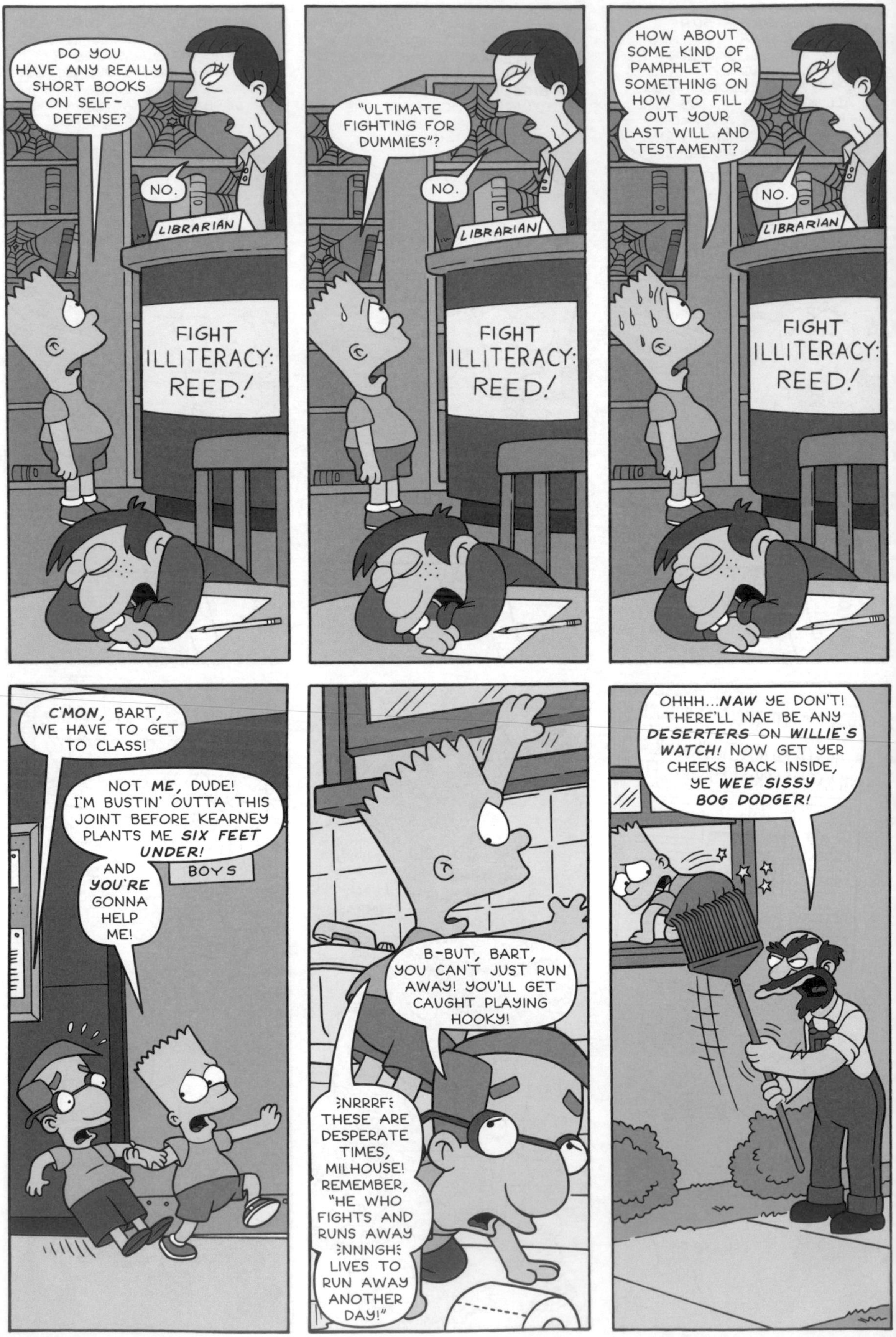
DO YOU HAVE ANY REALLY SHORT BOOKS ON SELF-DEFENSE?
NO.
LIBRARIAN
FIGHT ILLITERACY: REED!
"ULTIMATE FIGHTING FOR DUMMIES"?
NO.
LIBRARIAN
FIGHT ILLITERACY: REED!
HOW ABOUT SOME KIND OF PAMPHLET OR SOMETHING ON HOW TO FILL OUT YOUR LAST WILL AND TESTAMENT?
NO.
LIBRARIAN
FIGHT ILLITERACY: REED!
C'MON, BART, WE HAVE TO GET TO CLASS!
NOT ME, DUDE! I'M BUSTIN' OUTTA THIS JOINT BEFORE KEARNEY PLANTS ME SIX FEET UNDER!
AND YOU'RE GONNA HELP ME!
BOYS
B-BUT, BART, YOU CAN'T JUST RUN AWAY! YOU'LL GET CAUGHT PLAYING HOOKY!
NRRRF THESE ARE DESPERATE TIMES, MILHOUSE! REMEMBER, "HE WHO FIGHTS AND RUNS AWAY NNNGH LIVES TO RUN AWAY ANOTHER DAY!"
OHHH...NAW YE DON'T! THERE'LL NAE BE ANY DESERTERS ON WILLIE'S WATCH! NOW GET YER CHEEKS BACK INSIDE, YE WEE SISSY BOG DODGER!

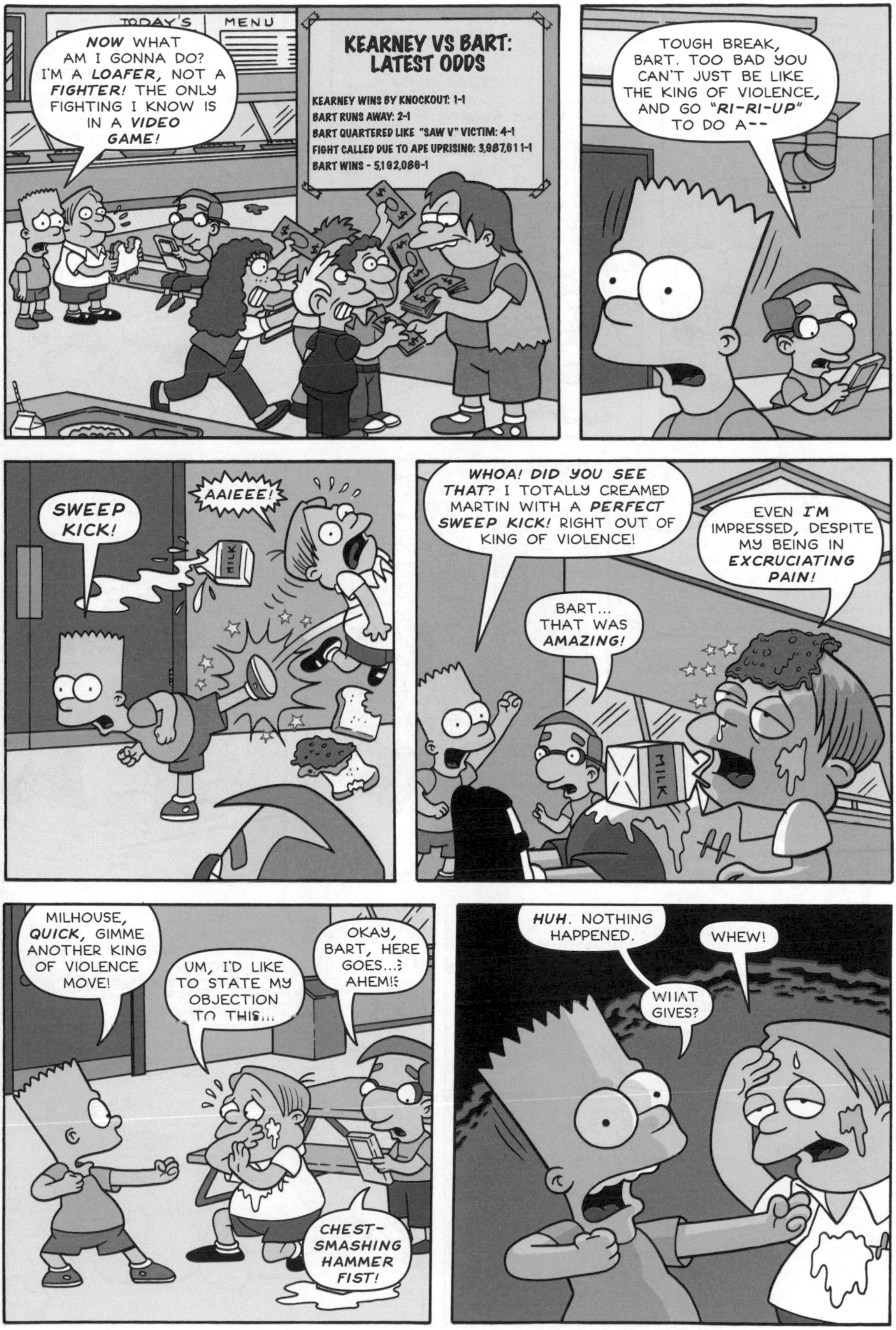
TODAY'S MENU
NOW WHAT AM I GONNA DO? I'M A LOAFER, NOT A FIGHTER! THE ONLY FIGHTING I KNOW IS IN A VIDEO GAME!
KEARNEY VS BART: LATEST ODDS
KEARNEY WINS BY KNOCKOUT: 1-1
BART RUNS AWAY: 2-1
BART QUARTERED LIKE "SAW V" VICTIM: 4-1
FIGHT CALLED DUE TO APE UPRISING: 3,987,611-1
BART WINS - 5,192,086-1
TOUGH BREAK, BART. TOO BAD YOU CAN'T JUST BE LIKE THE KING OF VIOLENCE, AND GO "RI-RI-UP" TO DO A--
SWEEP KICK!
AAIEEE!
MILK
WHOA! DID YOU SEE THAT? I TOTALLY CREAMED MARTIN WITH A PERFECT SWEEP KICK! RIGHT OUT OF KING OF VIOLENCE!
EVEN I'M IMPRESSED, DESPITE MY BEING IN EXCRUCIATING PAIN!
BART... THAT WAS AMAZING!
MILK
MILHOUSE, QUICK, GIMME ANOTHER KING OF VIOLENCE MOVE!
UM, I'D LIKE TO STATE MY OBJECTION TO THIS...
OKAY, BART, HERE GOES... AHEM!
CHEST-SMASHING HAMMER FIST!
HUH. NOTHING HAPPENED.
WHEW!
WHAT GIVES?

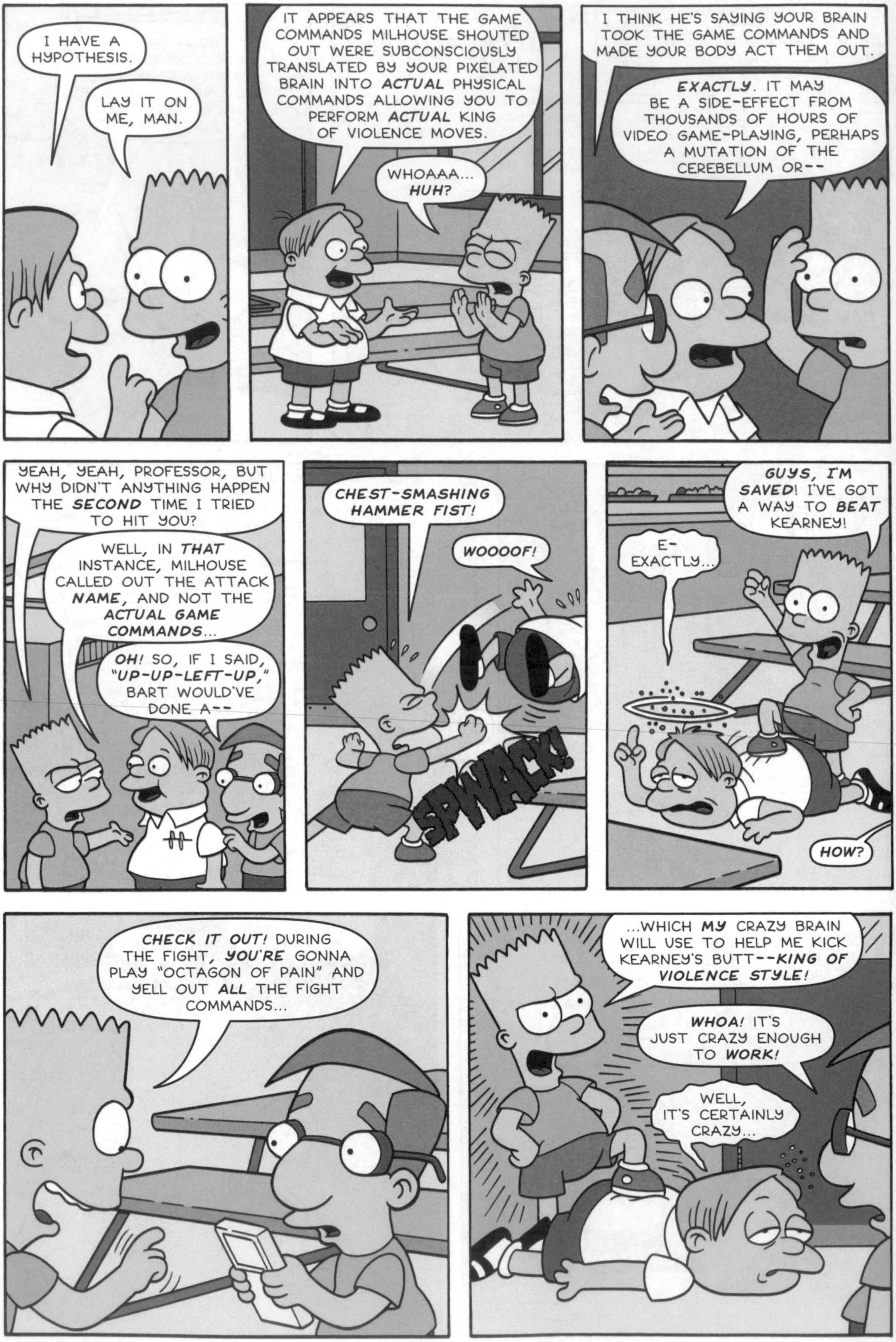
I HAVE A HYPOTHESIS.
LAY IT ON ME, MAN.
IT APPEARS THAT THE GAME COMMANDS MILHOUSE SHOUTED OUT WERE SUBCONSCIOUSLY TRANSLATED BY YOUR PIXELATED BRAIN INTO ACTUAL PHYSICAL COMMANDS ALLOWING YOU TO PERFORM ACTUAL KING OF VIOLENCE MOVES.
WHOAAA... HUH?
I THINK HE'S SAYING YOUR BRAIN TOOK THE GAME COMMANDS AND MADE YOUR BODY ACT THEM OUT.
EXACTLY. IT MAY BE A SIDE-EFFECT FROM THOUSANDS OF HOURS OF VIDEO GAME-PLAYING, PERHAPS A MUTATION OF THE CEREBELLUM OR--
YEAH, YEAH, PROFESSOR, BUT WHY DIDN'T ANYTHING HAPPEN THE SECOND TIME I TRIED TO HIT YOU?
WELL, IN THAT INSTANCE, MILHOUSE CALLED OUT THE ATTACK NAME, AND NOT THE ACTUAL GAME COMMANDS...
OH! SO, IF I SAID, "UP-UP-LEFT-UP," BART WOULD'VE DONE A--
CHEST-SMASHING HAMMER FIST!
WOOOOF!
SPWACK!
GUYS, I'M SAVED! I'VE GOT A WAY TO BEAT KEARNEY!
E-EXACTLY...
HOW?
CHECK IT OUT! DURING THE FIGHT, YOU'RE GONNA PLAY "OCTAGON OF PAIN" AND YELL OUT ALL THE FIGHT COMMANDS...
...WHICH MY CRAZY BRAIN WILL USE TO HELP ME KICK KEARNEY'S BUTT--KING OF VIOLENCE STYLE!
WHOA! IT'S JUST CRAZY ENOUGH TO WORK!
WELL, IT'S CERTAINLY CRAZY...

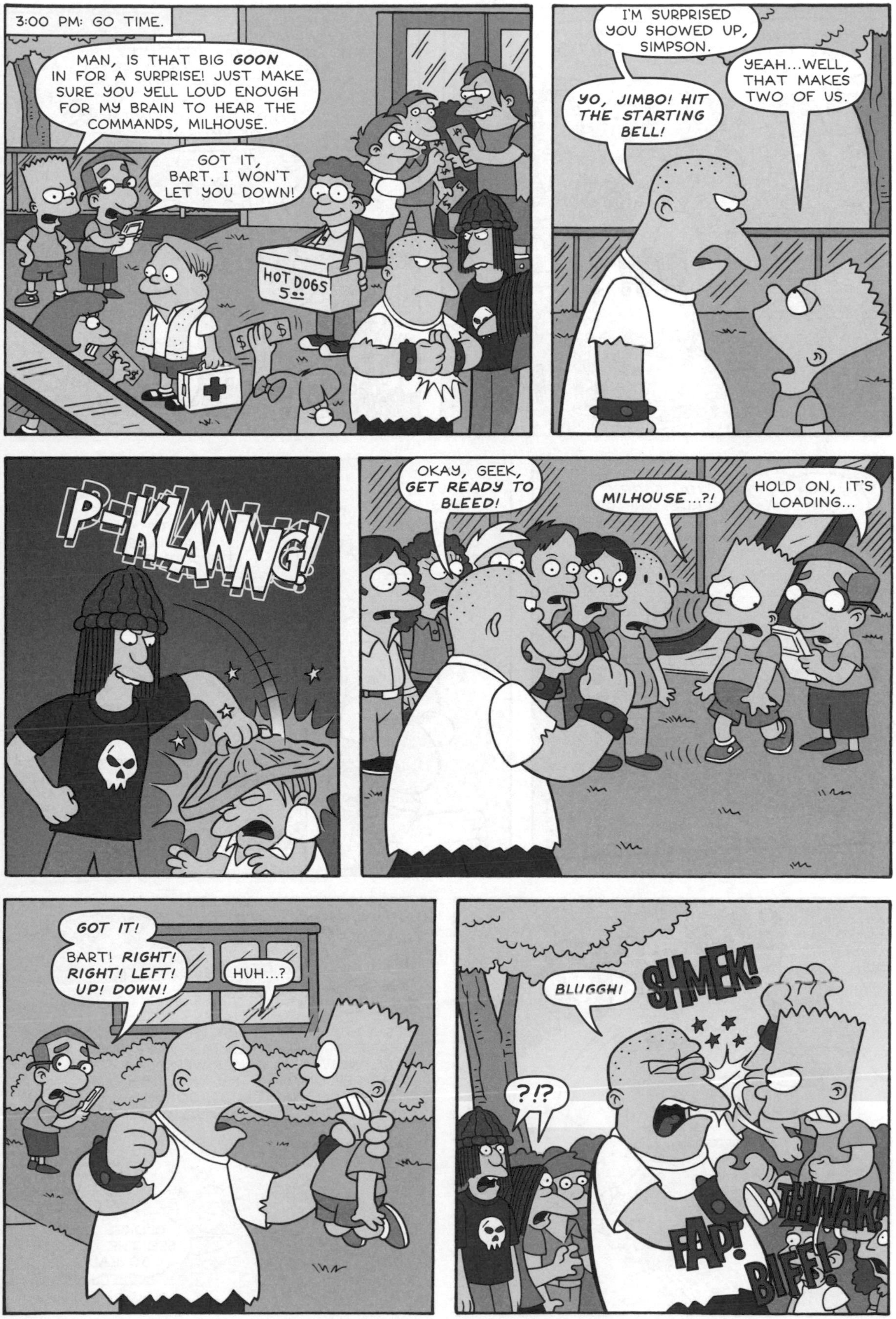
3:00 PM: GO TIME.
MAN, IS THAT BIG GOON IN FOR A SURPRISE! JUST MAKE SURE YOU YELL LOUD ENOUGH FOR MY BRAIN TO HEAR THE COMMANDS, MILHOUSE.
GOT IT, BART. I WON'T LET YOU DOWN!
HOT DOGS 5¢
I'M SURPRISED YOU SHOWED UP, SIMPSON.
YO, JIMBO! HIT THE STARTING BELL!
YEAH...WELL, THAT MAKES TWO OF US.
P-KLANNG!
OKAY, GEEK, GET READY TO BLEED!
MILHOUSE...?!
HOLD ON, IT'S LOADING...
GOT IT!
BART! RIGHT! RIGHT! LEFT! UP! DOWN!
HUH...?
BLUGGH!
SHMEK!
?!?
THWAK!
FAP!
BIFF!

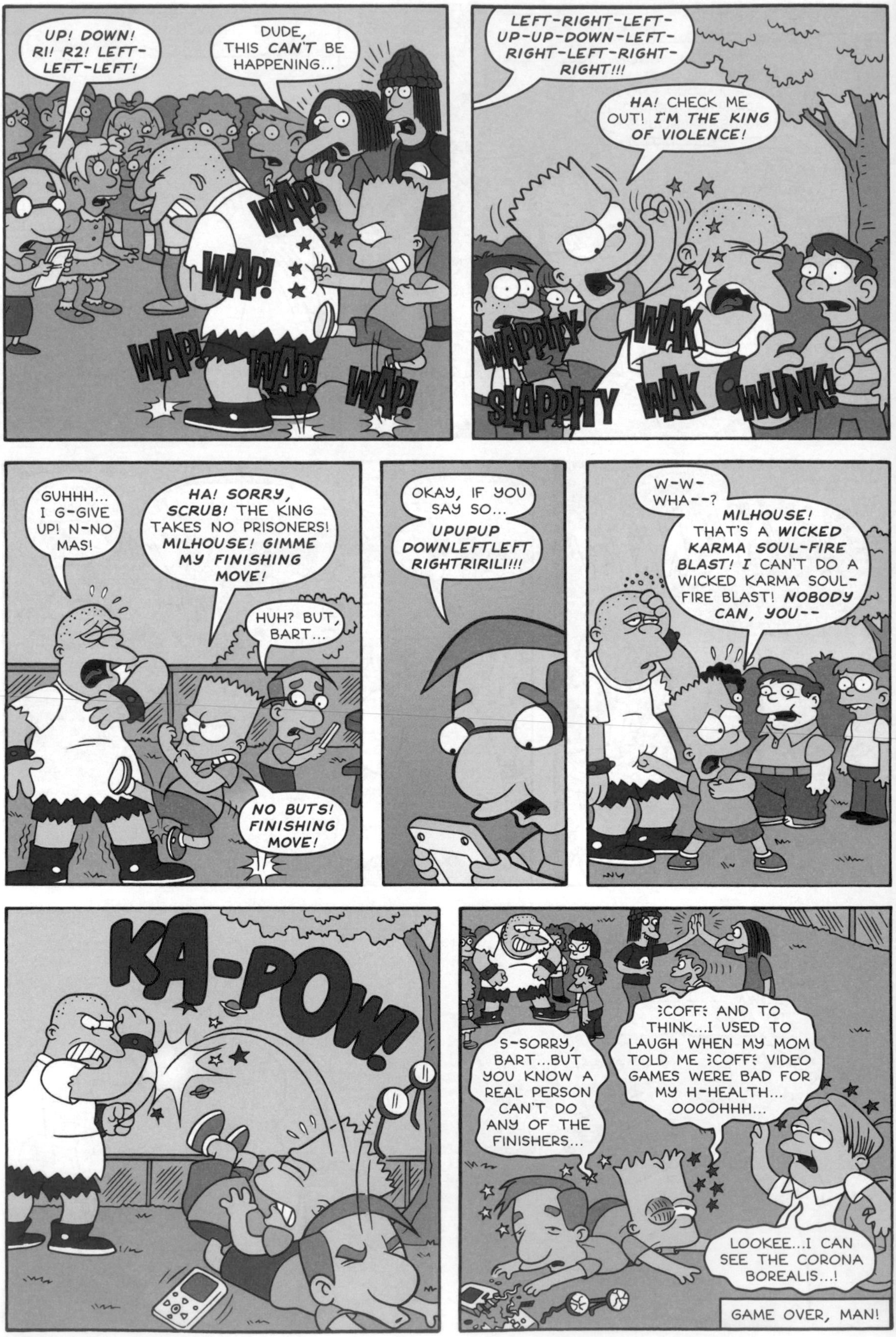

UP! DOWN! R1! R2! LEFT-LEFT-LEFT!
DUDE, THIS CAN'T BE HAPPENING...
WAP!
WAP!
WAP!
WAP!
WAP!
LEFT-RIGHT-LEFT-UP-UP-DOWN-LEFT-RIGHT-LEFT-RIGHT-RIGHT!!!
HA! CHECK ME OUT! I'M THE KING OF VIOLENCE!
WAPPITY
WAK
SLAPPITY
WAK
WUNK!
GUHHH... I G-GIVE UP! N-NO MAS!
HA! SORRY, SCRUB! THE KING TAKES NO PRISONERS! MILHOUSE! GIMME MY FINISHING MOVE!
HUH? BUT, BART...
NO BUTS! FINISHING MOVE!
OKAY, IF YOU SAY SO... UPUPUP DOWNLEFTLEFT RIGHTR1R1L1!!!
W-W-WHA--?
MILHOUSE! THAT'S A WICKED KARMA SOUL-FIRE BLAST! I CAN'T DO A WICKED KARMA SOUL-FIRE BLAST! NOBODY CAN, YOU--
KA-POW!
S-SORRY, BART...BUT YOU KNOW A REAL PERSON CAN'T DO ANY OF THE FINISHERS...
COFF AND TO THINK...I USED TO LAUGH WHEN MY MOM TOLD ME *COFF* VIDEO GAMES WERE BAD FOR MY H-HEALTH... OOOOHHH...
LOOKEE...I CAN SEE THE CORONA BOREALIS...!
GAME OVER, MAN!

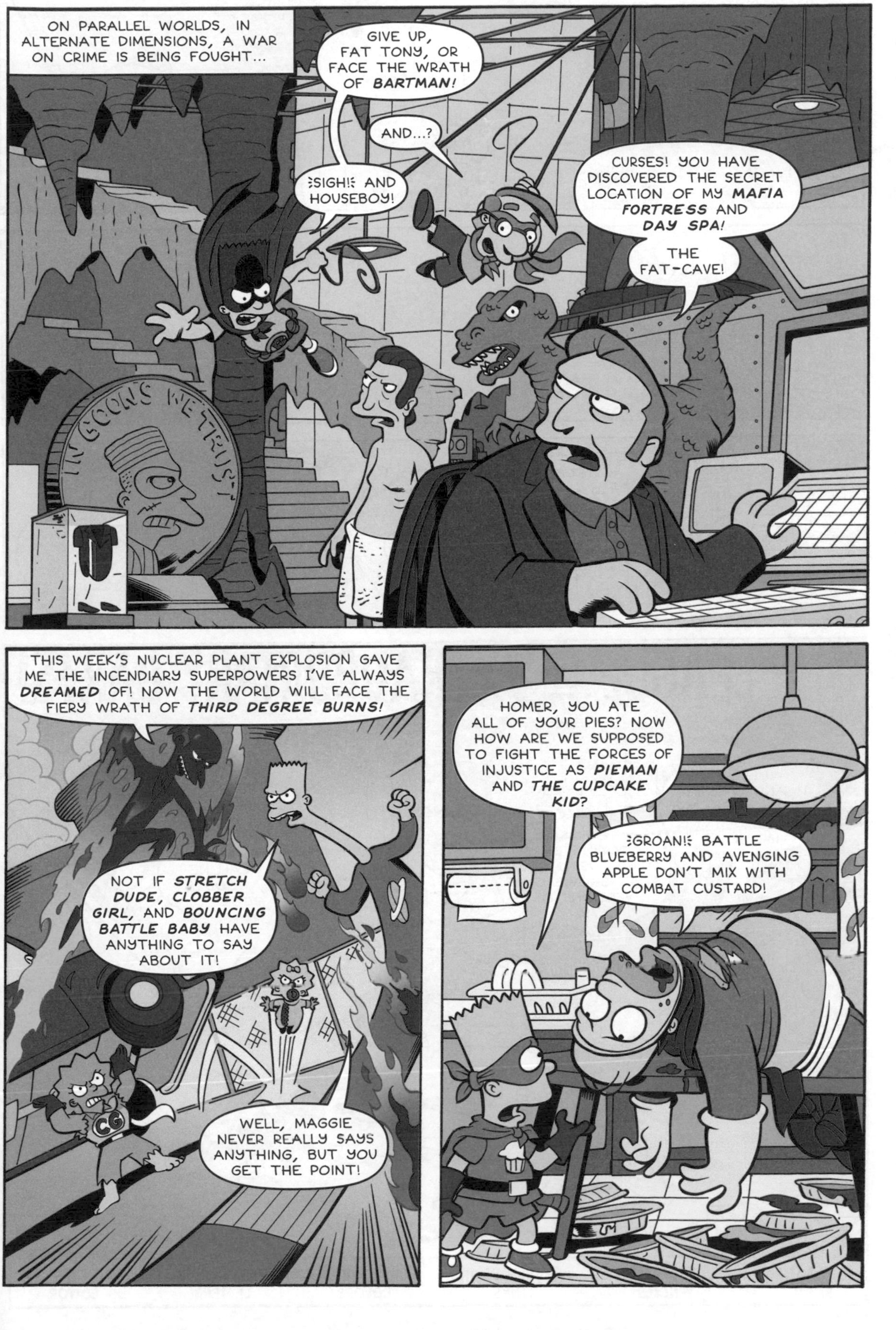

ON PARALLEL WORLDS, IN ALTERNATE DIMENSIONS, A WAR ON CRIME IS BEING FOUGHT...
GIVE UP, FAT TONY, OR FACE THE WRATH OF BARTMAN!
AND...?
SIGH! AND HOUSEBOY!
CURSES! YOU HAVE DISCOVERED THE SECRET LOCATION OF MY MAFIA FORTRESS AND DAY SPA!
THE FAT-CAVE!
IN GOONS WE TRUST
THIS WEEK'S NUCLEAR PLANT EXPLOSION GAVE ME THE INCENDIARY SUPERPOWERS I'VE ALWAYS DREAMED OF! NOW THE WORLD WILL FACE THE FIERY WRATH OF THIRD DEGREE BURNS!
NOT IF STRETCH DUDE, CLOBBER GIRL, AND BOUNCING BATTLE BABY HAVE ANYTHING TO SAY ABOUT IT!
WELL, MAGGIE NEVER REALLY SAYS ANYTHING, BUT YOU GET THE POINT!
CG
HOMER, YOU ATE ALL OF YOUR PIES? NOW HOW ARE WE SUPPOSED TO FIGHT THE FORCES OF INJUSTICE AS PIEMAN AND THE CUPCAKE KID?
GROAN! BATTLE BLUEBERRY AND AVENGING APPLE DON'T MIX WITH COMBAT CUSTARD!

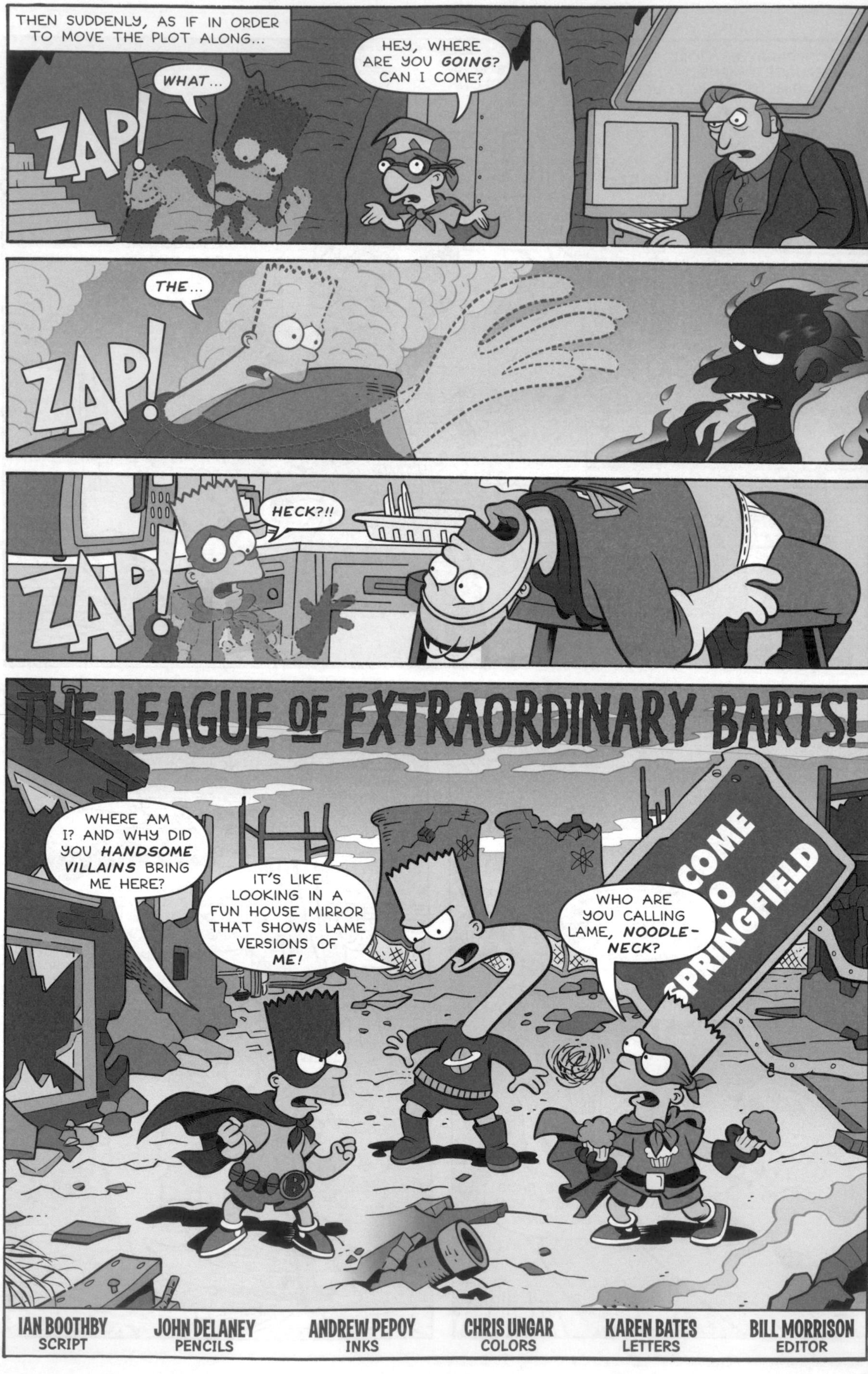
THEN SUDDENLY, AS IF IN ORDER TO MOVE THE PLOT ALONG...
WHAT...
ZAP!
HEY, WHERE ARE YOU *GOING*? CAN I COME?
THE...
ZAP!
ZAP!
HECK?!!
THE LEAGUE OF EXTRAORDINARY BARTS!
WHERE AM I? AND WHY DID YOU *HANDSOME VILLAINS* BRING ME HERE?
IT'S LIKE LOOKING IN A FUN HOUSE MIRROR THAT SHOWS LAME VERSIONS OF *ME!*
WHO ARE YOU CALLING LAME, *NOODLE-NECK?*
IAN BOOTHBY SCRIPT
JOHN DELANEY PENCILS
ANDREW PEPOY INKS
CHRIS UNGAR COLORS
KAREN BATES LETTERS
BILL MORRISON EDITOR

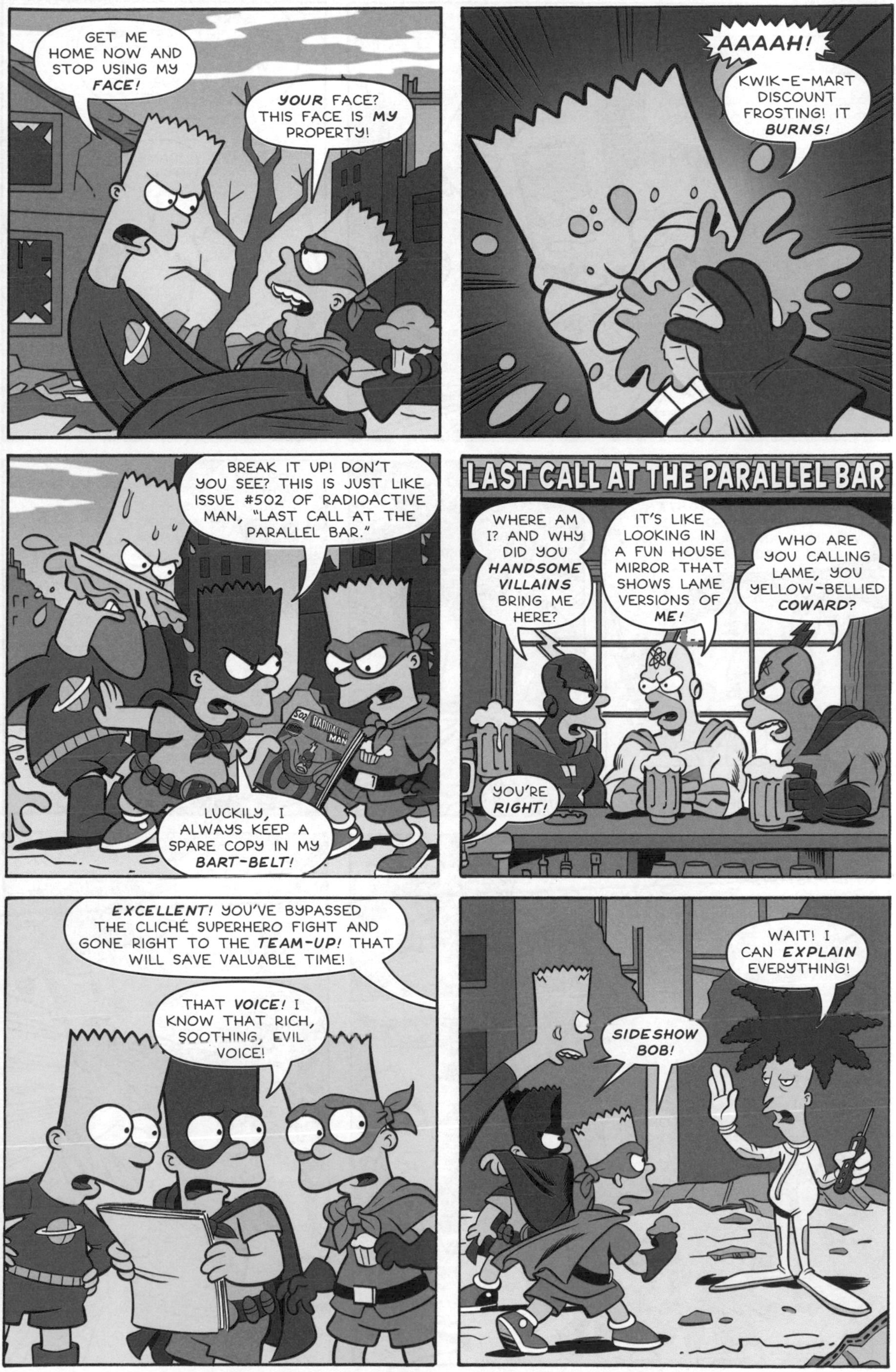
GET ME HOME NOW AND STOP USING MY FACE!
YOUR FACE? THIS FACE IS MY PROPERTY!
AAAAH!
KWIK-E-MART DISCOUNT FROSTING! IT BURNS!
BREAK IT UP! DON'T YOU SEE? THIS IS JUST LIKE ISSUE #502 OF RADIOACTIVE MAN, "LAST CALL AT THE PARALLEL BAR."
502
RADIOACTIVE MAN
LUCKILY, I ALWAYS KEEP A SPARE COPY IN MY BART-BELT!
LAST CALL AT THE PARALLEL BAR
WHERE AM I? AND WHY DID YOU HANDSOME VILLAINS BRING ME HERE?
IT'S LIKE LOOKING IN A FUN HOUSE MIRROR THAT SHOWS LAME VERSIONS OF ME!
WHO ARE YOU CALLING LAME, YOU YELLOW-BELLIED COWARD?
YOU'RE RIGHT!
EXCELLENT! YOU'VE BYPASSED THE CLICHÉ SUPERHERO FIGHT AND GONE RIGHT TO THE TEAM-UP! THAT WILL SAVE VALUABLE TIME!
THAT VOICE! I KNOW THAT RICH, SOOTHING, EVIL VOICE!
WAIT! I CAN EXPLAIN EVERYTHING!
SIDESHOW BOB!

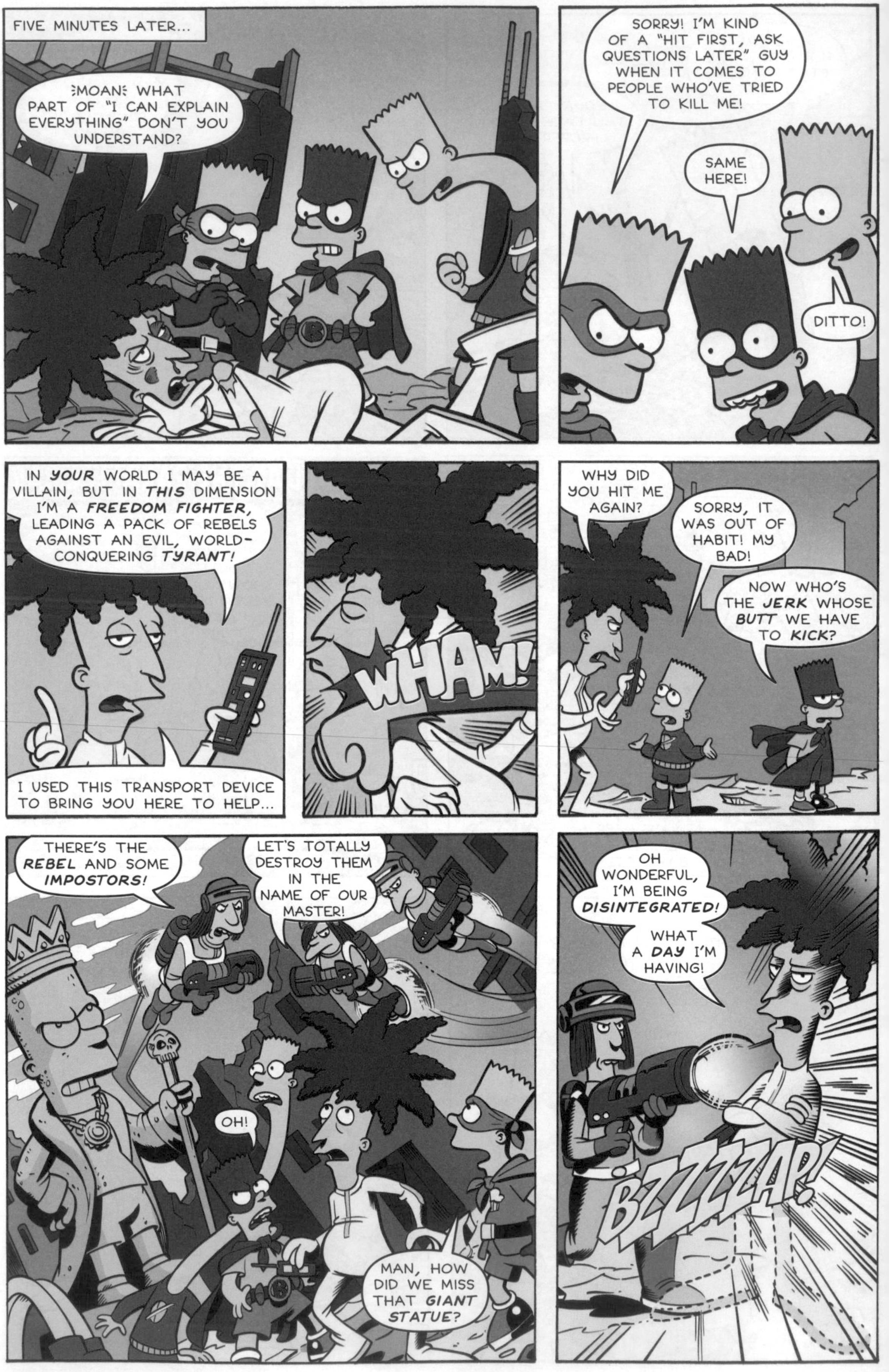
FIVE MINUTES LATER...
MOAN WHAT PART OF "I CAN EXPLAIN EVERYTHING" DON'T YOU UNDERSTAND?
SORRY! I'M KIND OF A "HIT FIRST, ASK QUESTIONS LATER" GUY WHEN IT COMES TO PEOPLE WHO'VE TRIED TO KILL ME!
SAME HERE!
DITTO!
IN YOUR WORLD I MAY BE A VILLAIN, BUT IN THIS DIMENSION I'M A FREEDOM FIGHTER, LEADING A PACK OF REBELS AGAINST AN EVIL, WORLD-CONQUERING TYRANT!
I USED THIS TRANSPORT DEVICE TO BRING YOU HERE TO HELP...
WHAM!
WHY DID YOU HIT ME AGAIN?
SORRY, IT WAS OUT OF HABIT! MY BAD!
NOW WHO'S THE JERK WHOSE BUTT WE HAVE TO KICK?
THERE'S THE REBEL AND SOME IMPOSTORS!
LET'S TOTALLY DESTROY THEM IN THE NAME OF OUR MASTER!
OH!
MAN, HOW DID WE MISS THAT GIANT STATUE?
OH WONDERFUL, I'M BEING DISINTEGRATED!
WHAT A DAY I'M HAVING!
BZZZZAP!

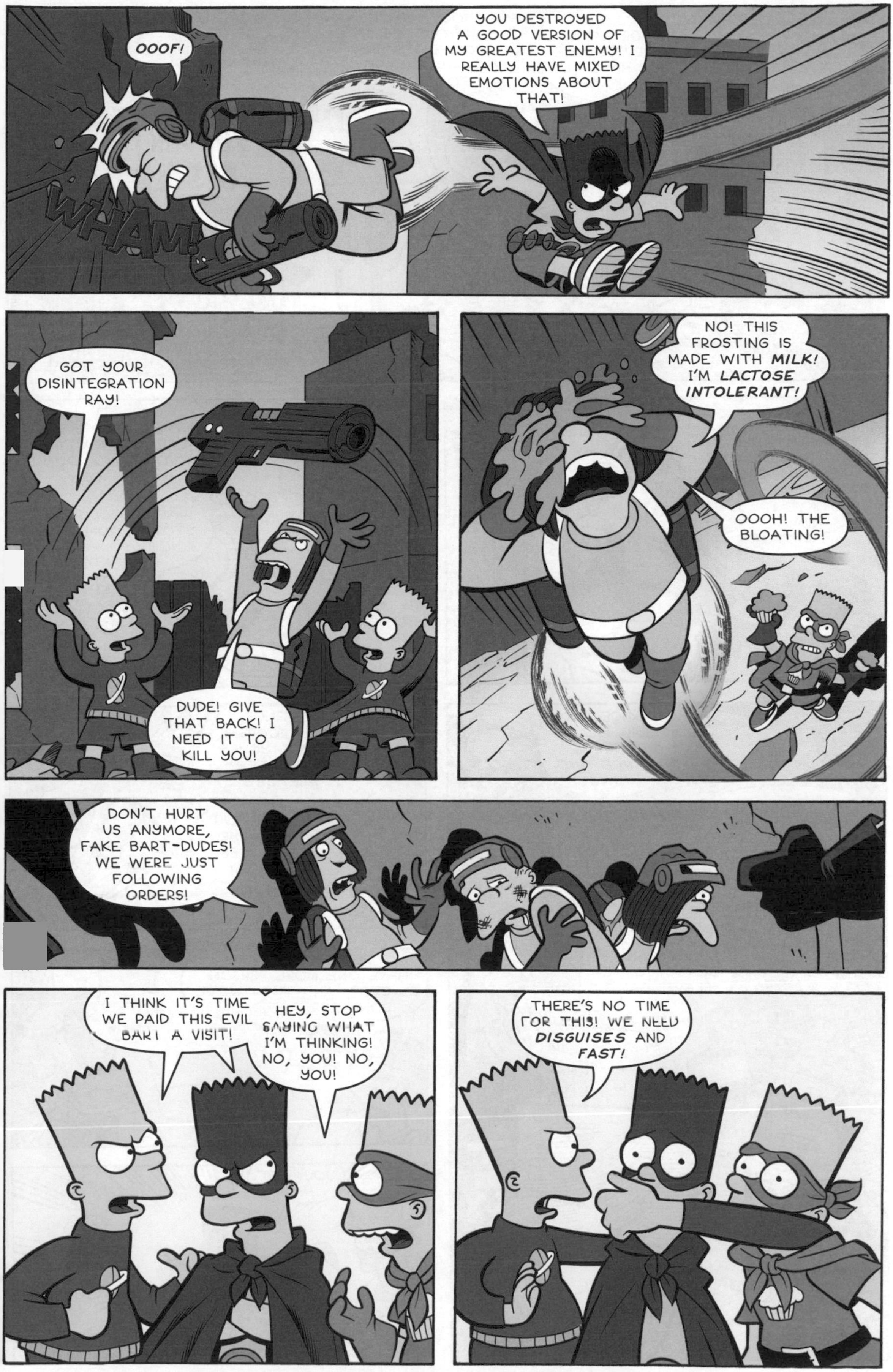
OOOF!
WHAM!
YOU DESTROYED A GOOD VERSION OF MY GREATEST ENEMY! I REALLY HAVE MIXED EMOTIONS ABOUT THAT!
GOT YOUR DISINTEGRATION RAY!
DUDE! GIVE THAT BACK! I NEED IT TO KILL YOU!
NO! THIS FROSTING IS MADE WITH MILK! I'M LACTOSE INTOLERANT!
OOOH! THE BLOATING!
DON'T HURT US ANYMORE, FAKE BART-DUDES! WE WERE JUST FOLLOWING ORDERS!
I THINK IT'S TIME WE PAID THIS EVIL BART A VISIT!
HEY, STOP SAYING WHAT I'M THINKING! NO, YOU! NO, YOU!
THERE'S NO TIME FOR THIS! WE NEED DISGUISES AND FAST!

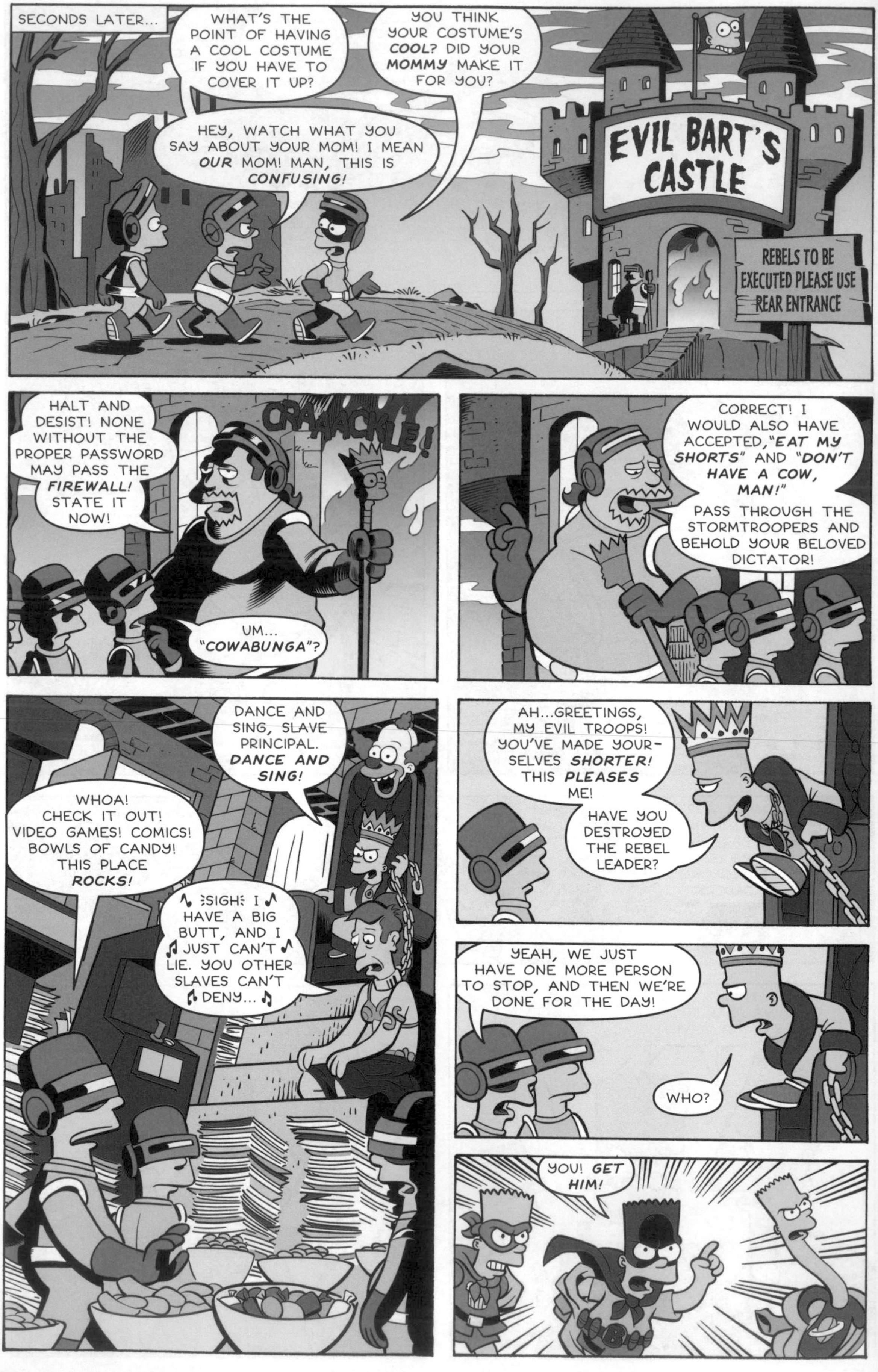
SECONDS LATER...
WHAT'S THE POINT OF HAVING A COOL COSTUME IF YOU HAVE TO COVER IT UP?
YOU THINK YOUR COSTUME'S COOL? DID YOUR MOMMY MAKE IT FOR YOU?
HEY, WATCH WHAT YOU SAY ABOUT YOUR MOM! I MEAN OUR MOM! MAN, THIS IS CONFUSING!
EVIL BART'S CASTLE
REBELS TO BE EXECUTED PLEASE USE REAR ENTRANCE
HALT AND DESIST! NONE WITHOUT THE PROPER PASSWORD MAY PASS THE FIREWALL! STATE IT NOW!
CRAAACKLE!
UM... "COWABUNGA"?
CORRECT! I WOULD ALSO HAVE ACCEPTED, "EAT MY SHORTS" AND "DON'T HAVE A COW, MAN!"
PASS THROUGH THE STORMTROOPERS AND BEHOLD YOUR BELOVED DICTATOR!
WHOA! CHECK IT OUT! VIDEO GAMES! COMICS! BOWLS OF CANDY! THIS PLACE ROCKS!
DANCE AND SING, SLAVE PRINCIPAL. DANCE AND SING!
♪ :SIGH: I ♪ HAVE A BIG BUTT, AND I ♪ JUST CAN'T ♪ LIE. YOU OTHER SLAVES CAN'T ♪ DENY... ♪
AH...GREETINGS, MY EVIL TROOPS! YOU'VE MADE YOURSELVES SHORTER! THIS PLEASES ME!
HAVE YOU DESTROYED THE REBEL LEADER?
YEAH, WE JUST HAVE ONE MORE PERSON TO STOP, AND THEN WE'RE DONE FOR THE DAY!
WHO?
YOU! GET HIM!

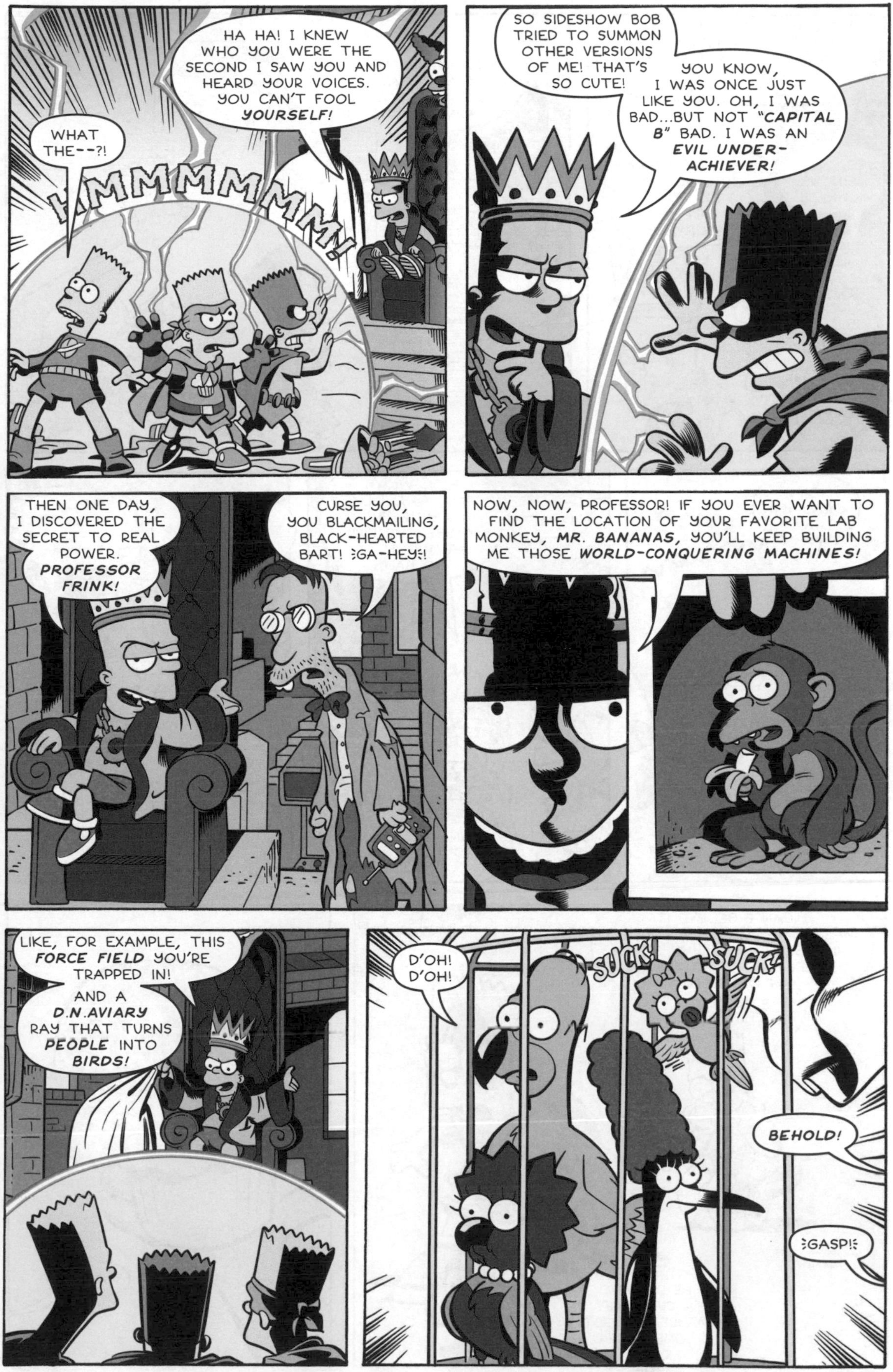
HA HA! I KNEW WHO YOU WERE THE SECOND I SAW YOU AND HEARD YOUR VOICES. YOU CAN'T FOOL YOURSELF!
WHAT THE--?!
SO SIDESHOW BOB TRIED TO SUMMON OTHER VERSIONS OF ME! THAT'S SO CUTE!
YOU KNOW, I WAS ONCE JUST LIKE YOU. OH, I WAS BAD...BUT NOT "CAPITAL B" BAD. I WAS AN EVIL UNDER-ACHIEVER!
THEN ONE DAY, I DISCOVERED THE SECRET TO REAL POWER. PROFESSOR FRINK!
CURSE YOU, YOU BLACKMAILING, BLACK-HEARTED BART! ꞉GA-HEY꞉!
NOW, NOW, PROFESSOR! IF YOU EVER WANT TO FIND THE LOCATION OF YOUR FAVORITE LAB MONKEY, MR. BANANAS, YOU'LL KEEP BUILDING ME THOSE WORLD-CONQUERING MACHINES!
LIKE, FOR EXAMPLE, THIS FORCE FIELD YOU'RE TRAPPED IN!
AND A D.N.AVIARY RAY THAT TURNS PEOPLE INTO BIRDS!
D'OH! D'OH!
SUCK!
SUCK!
BEHOLD!
꞉GASP!꞉

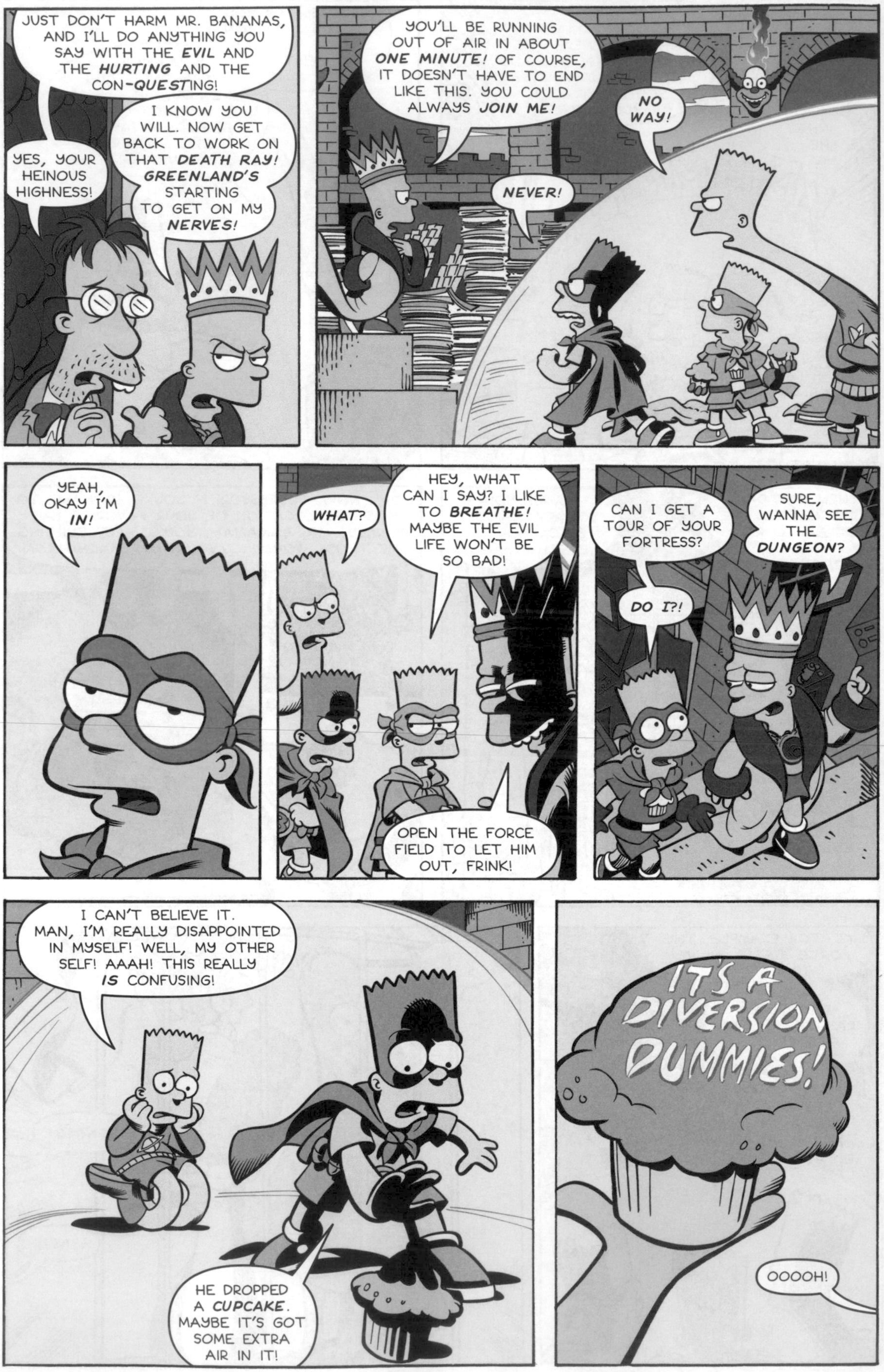
JUST DON'T HARM MR. BANANAS, AND I'LL DO ANYTHING YOU SAY WITH THE EVIL AND THE HURTING AND THE CON-QUESTING!
YES, YOUR HEINOUS HIGHNESS!
I KNOW YOU WILL. NOW GET BACK TO WORK ON THAT DEATH RAY! GREENLAND'S STARTING TO GET ON MY NERVES!
YOU'LL BE RUNNING OUT OF AIR IN ABOUT ONE MINUTE! OF COURSE, IT DOESN'T HAVE TO END LIKE THIS. YOU COULD ALWAYS JOIN ME!
NO WAY!
NEVER!
YEAH, OKAY I'M IN!
WHAT?
HEY, WHAT CAN I SAY? I LIKE TO BREATHE! MAYBE THE EVIL LIFE WON'T BE SO BAD!
OPEN THE FORCE FIELD TO LET HIM OUT, FRINK!
CAN I GET A TOUR OF YOUR FORTRESS?
SURE, WANNA SEE THE DUNGEON?
DO I?!
I CAN'T BELIEVE IT. MAN, I'M REALLY DISAPPOINTED IN MYSELF! WELL, MY OTHER SELF! AAAH! THIS REALLY IS CONFUSING!
HE DROPPED A CUPCAKE. MAYBE IT'S GOT SOME EXTRA AIR IN IT!
IT'S A DIVERSION DUMMIES!
OOOOH!

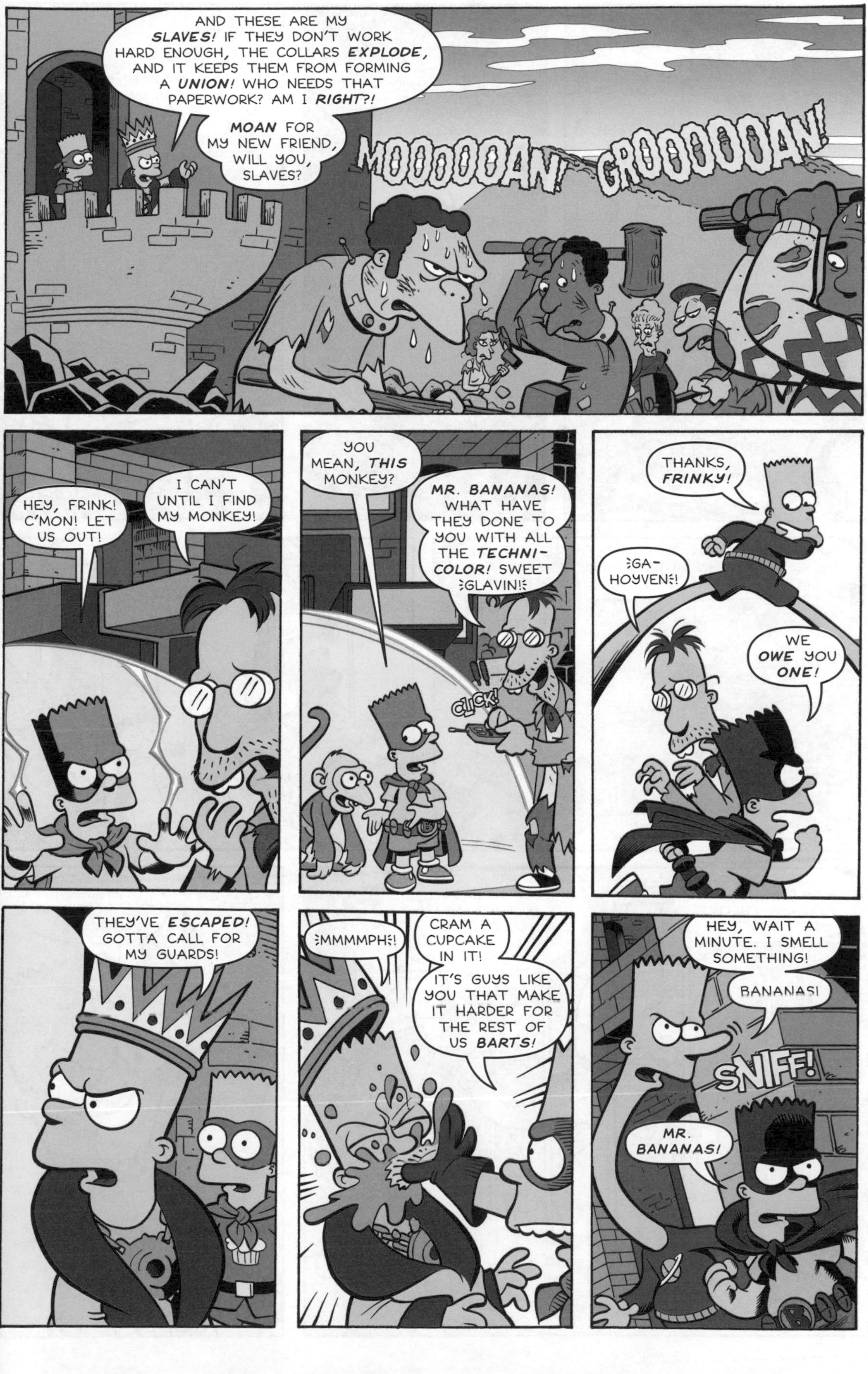
AND THESE ARE MY SLAVES! IF THEY DON'T WORK HARD ENOUGH, THE COLLARS EXPLODE, AND IT KEEPS THEM FROM FORMING A UNION! WHO NEEDS THAT PAPERWORK? AM I RIGHT?!
MOAN FOR MY NEW FRIEND, WILL YOU, SLAVES?
MOOOOOAN!
GROOOOOAN!
HEY, FRINK! C'MON! LET US OUT!
I CAN'T UNTIL I FIND MY MONKEY!
YOU MEAN, THIS MONKEY?
MR. BANANAS! WHAT HAVE THEY DONE TO YOU WITH ALL THE TECHNI-COLOR! SWEET GLAVIN!
CLICK!
THANKS, FRINKY!
GA-HOYVEN!
WE OWE YOU ONE!
THEY'VE ESCAPED! GOTTA CALL FOR MY GUARDS!
MMMMPH!
CRAM A CUPCAKE IN IT!
IT'S GUYS LIKE YOU THAT MAKE IT HARDER FOR THE REST OF US BARTS!
HEY, WAIT A MINUTE. I SMELL SOMETHING!
BANANAS!
SNIFF!
MR. BANANAS!

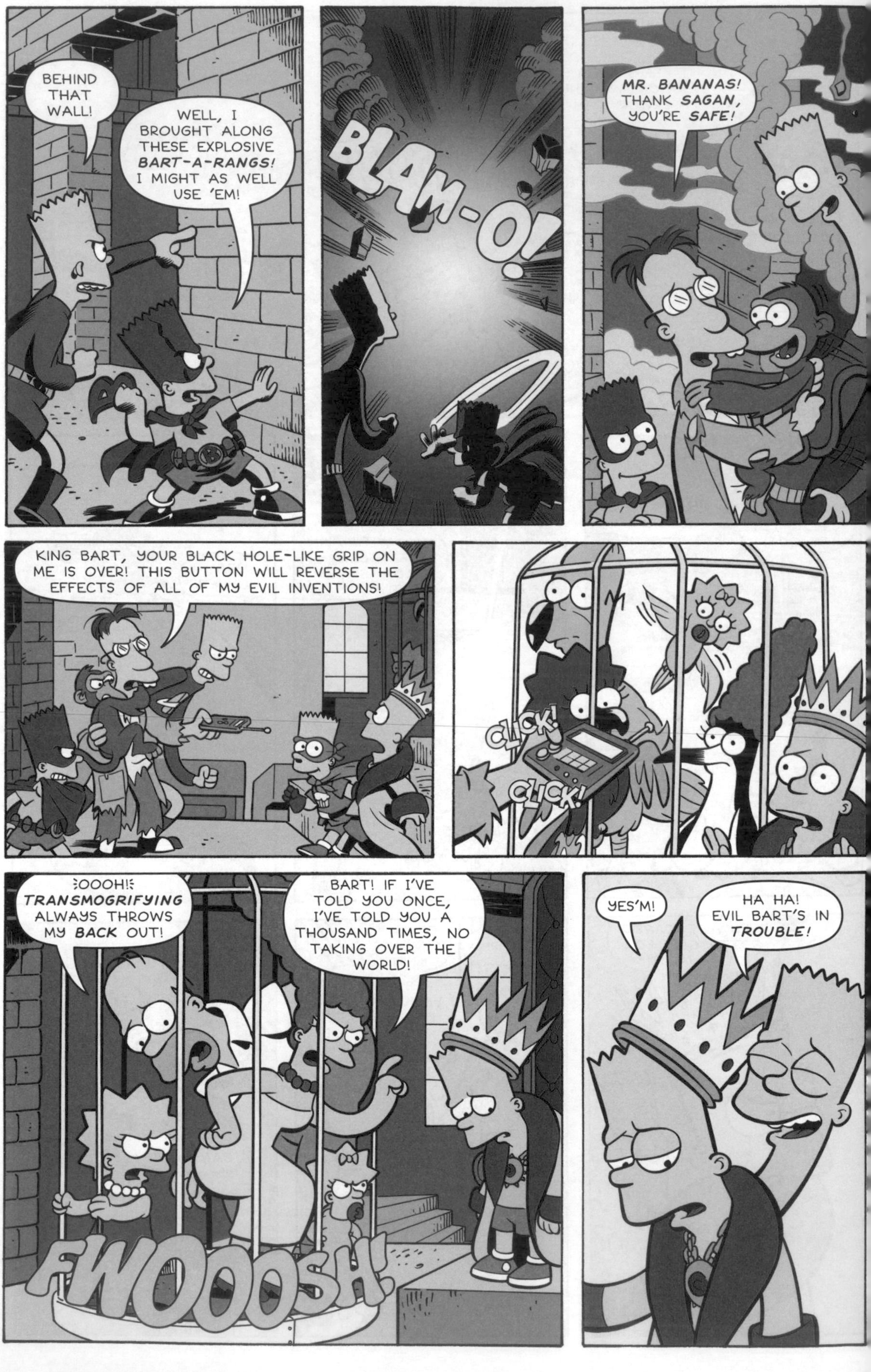
BEHIND THAT WALL!
WELL, I BROUGHT ALONG THESE EXPLOSIVE BART-A-RANGS! I MIGHT AS WELL USE 'EM!
BLAM-O!
MR. BANANAS! THANK SAGAN, YOU'RE SAFE!
KING BART, YOUR BLACK HOLE-LIKE GRIP ON ME IS OVER! THIS BUTTON WILL REVERSE THE EFFECTS OF ALL OF MY EVIL INVENTIONS!
CLICK!
CLICK!
OOOH!! TRANSMOGRIFYING ALWAYS THROWS MY BACK OUT!
BART! IF I'VE TOLD YOU ONCE, I'VE TOLD YOU A THOUSAND TIMES, NO TAKING OVER THE WORLD!
FWOOOSH!
YES'M!
HA HA! EVIL BART'S IN TROUBLE!

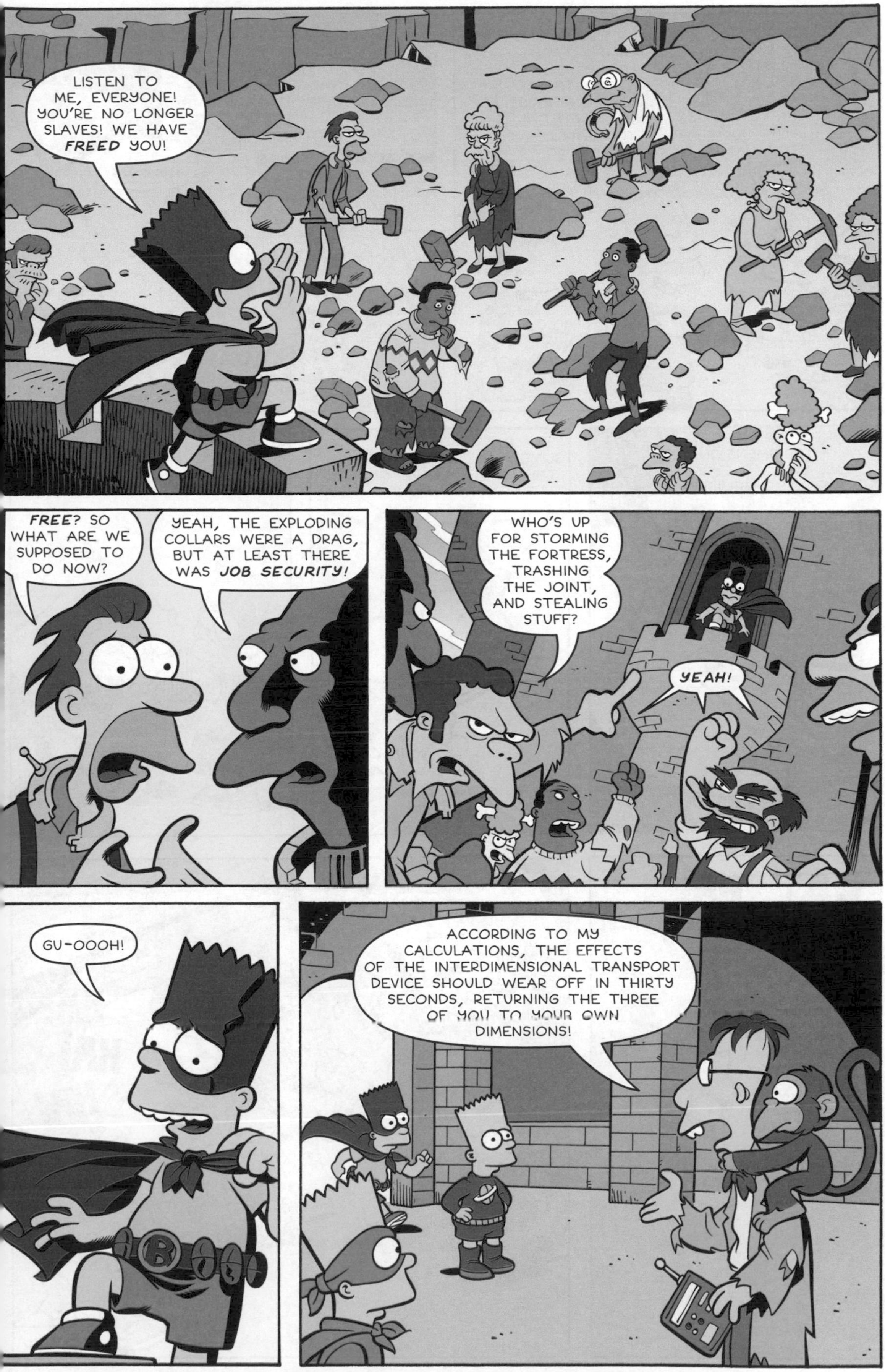

LISTEN TO ME, EVERYONE! YOU'RE NO LONGER SLAVES! WE HAVE FREED YOU!
FREE? SO WHAT ARE WE SUPPOSED TO DO NOW?
YEAH, THE EXPLODING COLLARS WERE A DRAG, BUT AT LEAST THERE WAS JOB SECURITY!
WHO'S UP FOR STORMING THE FORTRESS, TRASHING THE JOINT, AND STEALING STUFF?
YEAH!
GU-OOOH!
ACCORDING TO MY CALCULATIONS, THE EFFECTS OF THE INTERDIMENSIONAL TRANSPORT DEVICE SHOULD WEAR OFF IN THIRTY SECONDS, RETURNING THE THREE OF YOU TO YOUR OWN DIMENSIONS!

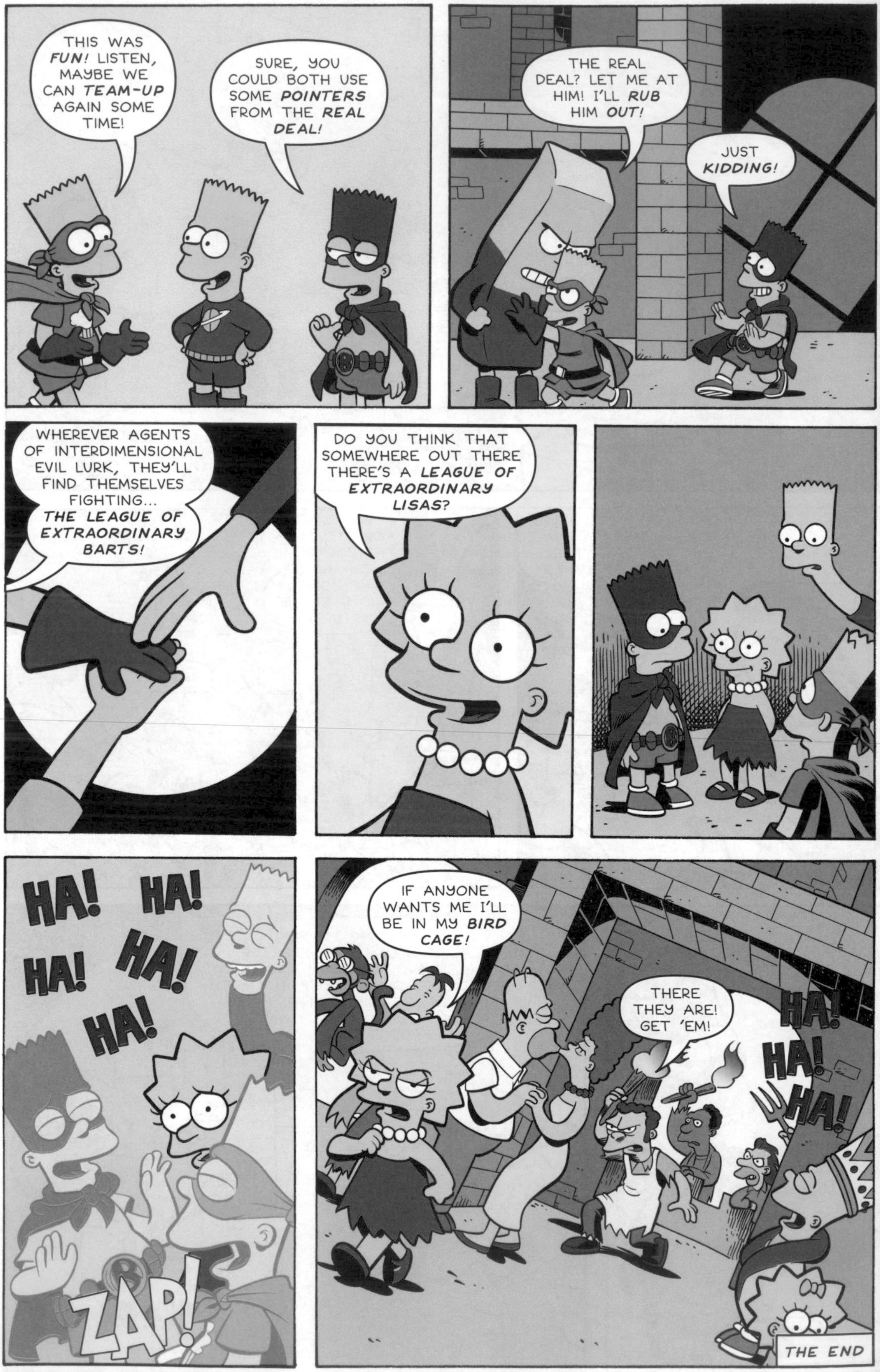
THIS WAS FUN! LISTEN, MAYBE WE CAN TEAM-UP AGAIN SOME TIME!
SURE, YOU COULD BOTH USE SOME POINTERS FROM THE REAL DEAL!
THE REAL DEAL? LET ME AT HIM! I'LL RUB HIM OUT!
JUST KIDDING!
WHEREVER AGENTS OF INTERDIMENSIONAL EVIL LURK, THEY'LL FIND THEMSELVES FIGHTING... THE LEAGUE OF EXTRAORDINARY BARTS!
DO YOU THINK THAT SOMEWHERE OUT THERE THERE'S A LEAGUE OF EXTRAORDINARY LISAS?
HA! HA! HA! HA! HA!
ZAP!
IF ANYONE WANTS ME I'LL BE IN MY BIRD CAGE!
THERE THEY ARE! GET 'EM!
HA! HA! HA!
THE END

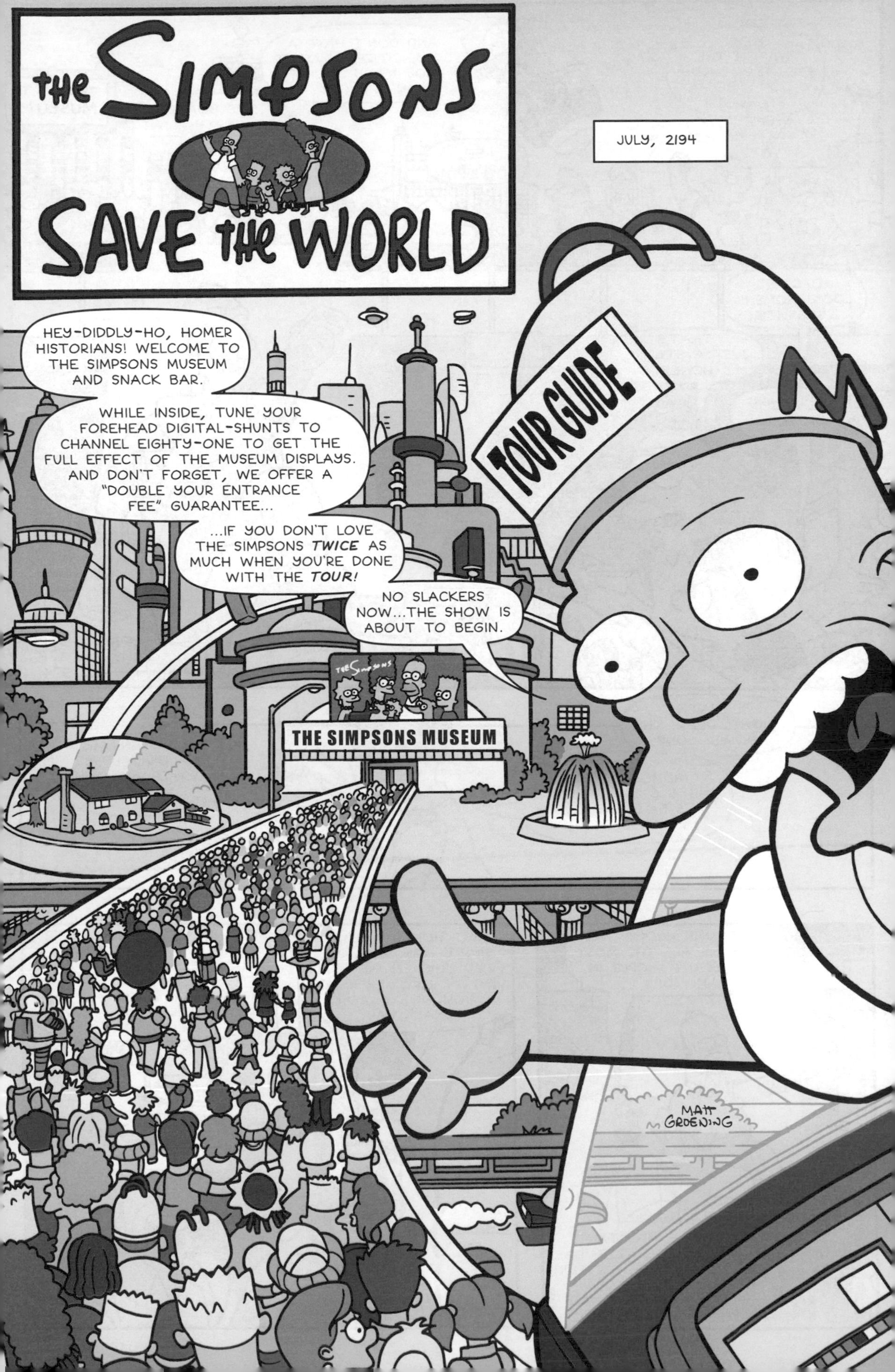
THE SIMPSONS SAVE THE WORLD
JULY, 2194
HEY-DIDDLY-HO, HOMER HISTORIANS! WELCOME TO THE SIMPSONS MUSEUM AND SNACK BAR.
WHILE INSIDE, TUNE YOUR FOREHEAD DIGITAL-SHUNTS TO CHANNEL EIGHTY-ONE TO GET THE FULL EFFECT OF THE MUSEUM DISPLAYS. AND DON'T FORGET, WE OFFER A "DOUBLE YOUR ENTRANCE FEE" GUARANTEE...
...IF YOU DON'T LOVE THE SIMPSONS *TWICE* AS MUCH WHEN YOU'RE DONE WITH THE *TOUR*!
NO SLACKERS NOW...THE SHOW IS ABOUT TO BEGIN.
TOUR GUIDE
THE SIMPSONS MUSEUM
THE SIMPSONS
MATT GROENING

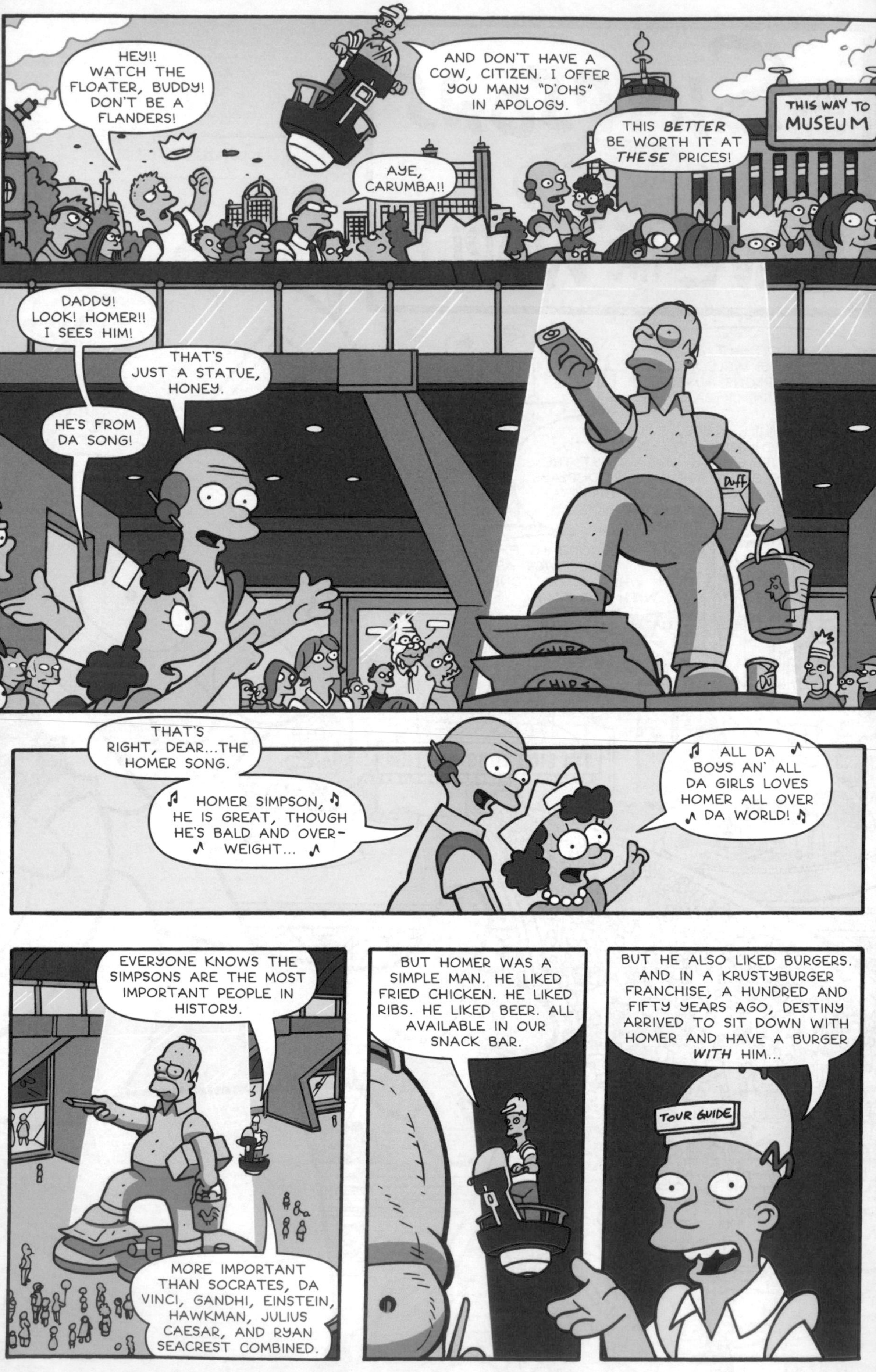
HEY!! WATCH THE FLOATER, BUDDY! DON'T BE A FLANDERS!
AND DON'T HAVE A COW, CITIZEN. I OFFER YOU MANY "D'OHS" IN APOLOGY.
THIS WAY TO MUSEUM
THIS BETTER BE WORTH IT AT THESE PRICES!
AYE, CARUMBA!!
DADDY! LOOK! HOMER!! I SEES HIM!
THAT'S JUST A STATUE, HONEY.
HE'S FROM DA SONG!
THAT'S RIGHT, DEAR...THE HOMER SONG.
♪ HOMER SIMPSON, ♪ HE IS GREAT, THOUGH HE'S BALD AND OVER-WEIGHT... ♪
♪ ALL DA BOYS AN' ALL DA GIRLS LOVES HOMER ALL OVER DA WORLD! ♪
EVERYONE KNOWS THE SIMPSONS ARE THE MOST IMPORTANT PEOPLE IN HISTORY.
MORE IMPORTANT THAN SOCRATES, DA VINCI, GANDHI, EINSTEIN, HAWKMAN, JULIUS CAESAR, AND RYAN SEACREST COMBINED.
BUT HOMER WAS A SIMPLE MAN. HE LIKED FRIED CHICKEN. HE LIKED RIBS. HE LIKED BEER. ALL AVAILABLE IN OUR SNACK BAR.
BUT HE ALSO LIKED BURGERS. AND IN A KRUSTYBURGER FRANCHISE, A HUNDRED AND FIFTY YEARS AGO, DESTINY ARRIVED TO SIT DOWN WITH HOMER AND HAVE A BURGER WITH HIM...
TOUR GUIDE

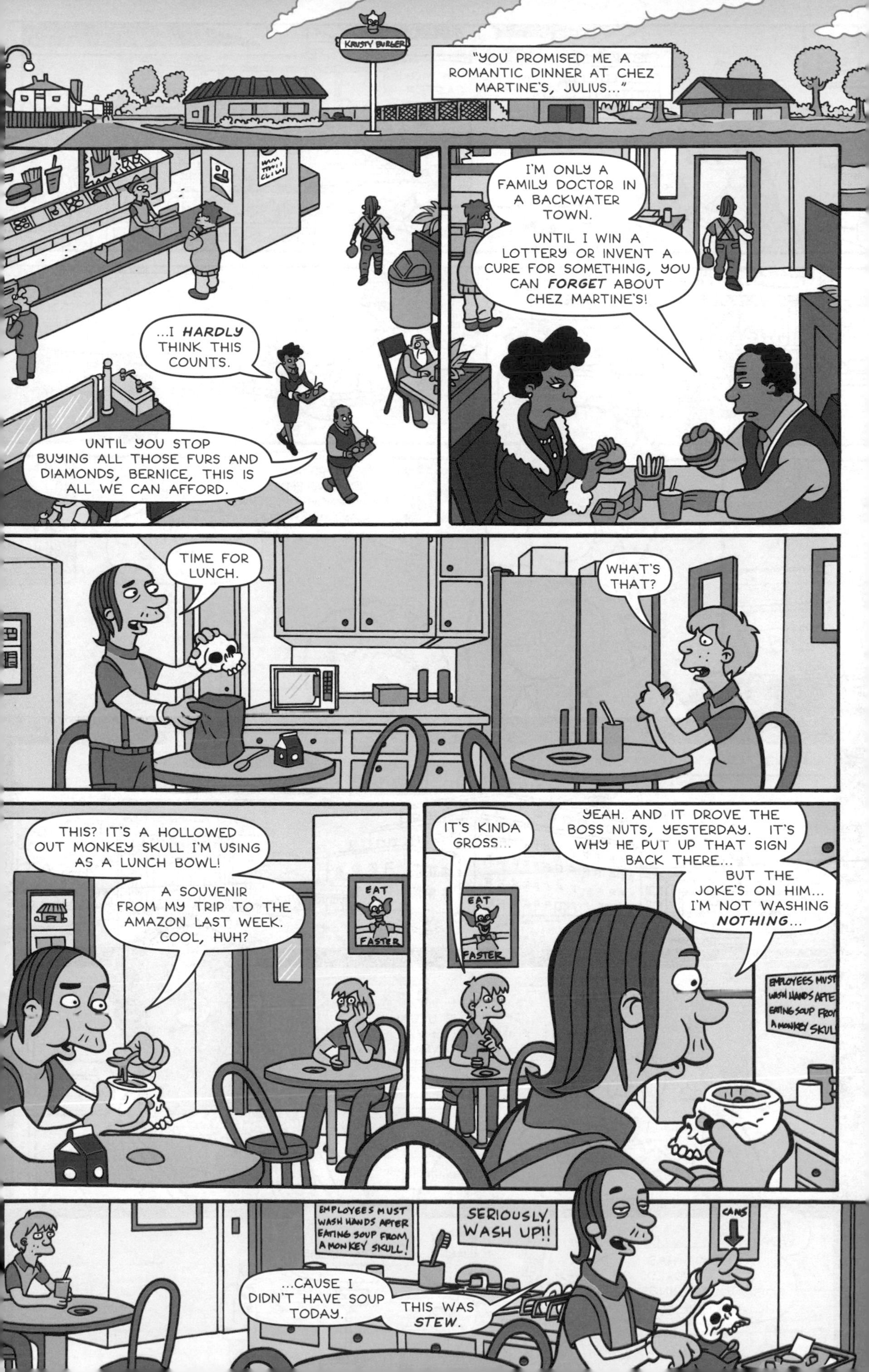
KRUSTY BURGER
"YOU PROMISED ME A ROMANTIC DINNER AT CHEZ MARTINE'S, JULIUS..."
...I HARDLY THINK THIS COUNTS.
UNTIL YOU STOP BUYING ALL THOSE FURS AND DIAMONDS, BERNICE, THIS IS ALL WE CAN AFFORD.
I'M ONLY A FAMILY DOCTOR IN A BACKWATER TOWN.
UNTIL I WIN A LOTTERY OR INVENT A CURE FOR SOMETHING, YOU CAN FORGET ABOUT CHEZ MARTINE'S!
TIME FOR LUNCH.
WHAT'S THAT?
THIS? IT'S A HOLLOWED OUT MONKEY SKULL I'M USING AS A LUNCH BOWL!
A SOUVENIR FROM MY TRIP TO THE AMAZON LAST WEEK. COOL, HUH?
EAT FASTER
IT'S KINDA GROSS...
YEAH. AND IT DROVE THE BOSS NUTS, YESTERDAY. IT'S WHY HE PUT UP THAT SIGN BACK THERE...
BUT THE JOKE'S ON HIM... I'M NOT WASHING NOTHING...
EMPLOYEES MUST WASH HANDS AFTER EATING SOUP FROM A MONKEY SKULL!
SERIOUSLY, WASH UP!!
CANS
...CAUSE I DIDN'T HAVE SOUP TODAY.
THIS WAS STEW.

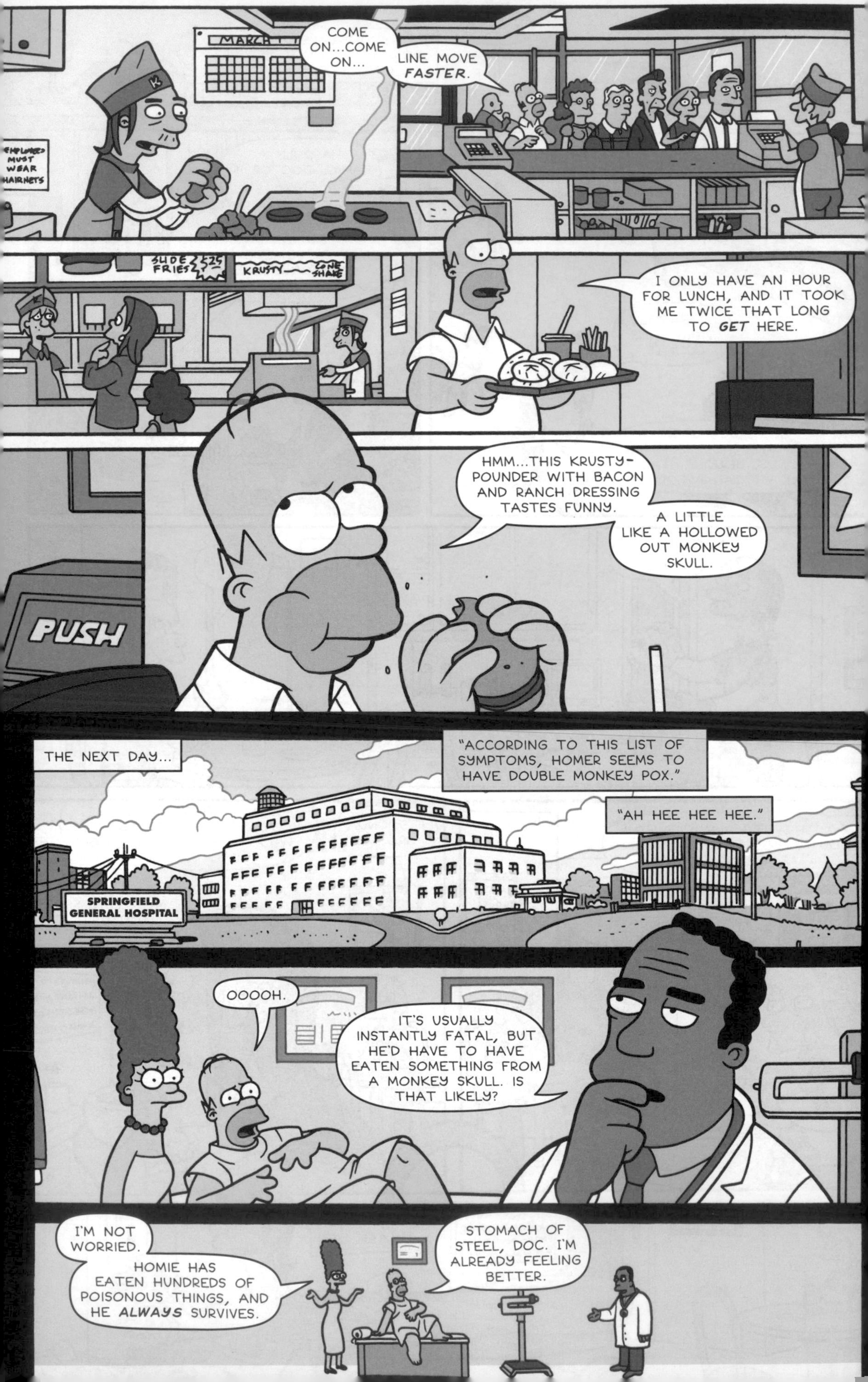
MARCH
COME ON...COME ON...
LINE MOVE FASTER.
MUST WEAR HAIRNETS
I ONLY HAVE AN HOUR FOR LUNCH, AND IT TOOK ME TWICE THAT LONG TO GET HERE.
HMM...THIS KRUSTY-POUNDER WITH BACON AND RANCH DRESSING TASTES FUNNY.
A LITTLE LIKE A HOLLOWED OUT MONKEY SKULL.
PUSH
THE NEXT DAY...
"ACCORDING TO THIS LIST OF SYMPTOMS, HOMER SEEMS TO HAVE DOUBLE MONKEY POX."
"AH HEE HEE HEE."
SPRINGFIELD GENERAL HOSPITAL
OOOOH.
IT'S USUALLY INSTANTLY FATAL, BUT HE'D HAVE TO HAVE EATEN SOMETHING FROM A MONKEY SKULL. IS THAT LIKELY?
I'M NOT WORRIED.
HOMIE HAS EATEN HUNDREDS OF POISONOUS THINGS, AND HE ALWAYS SURVIVES.
STOMACH OF STEEL, DOC. I'M ALREADY FEELING BETTER.

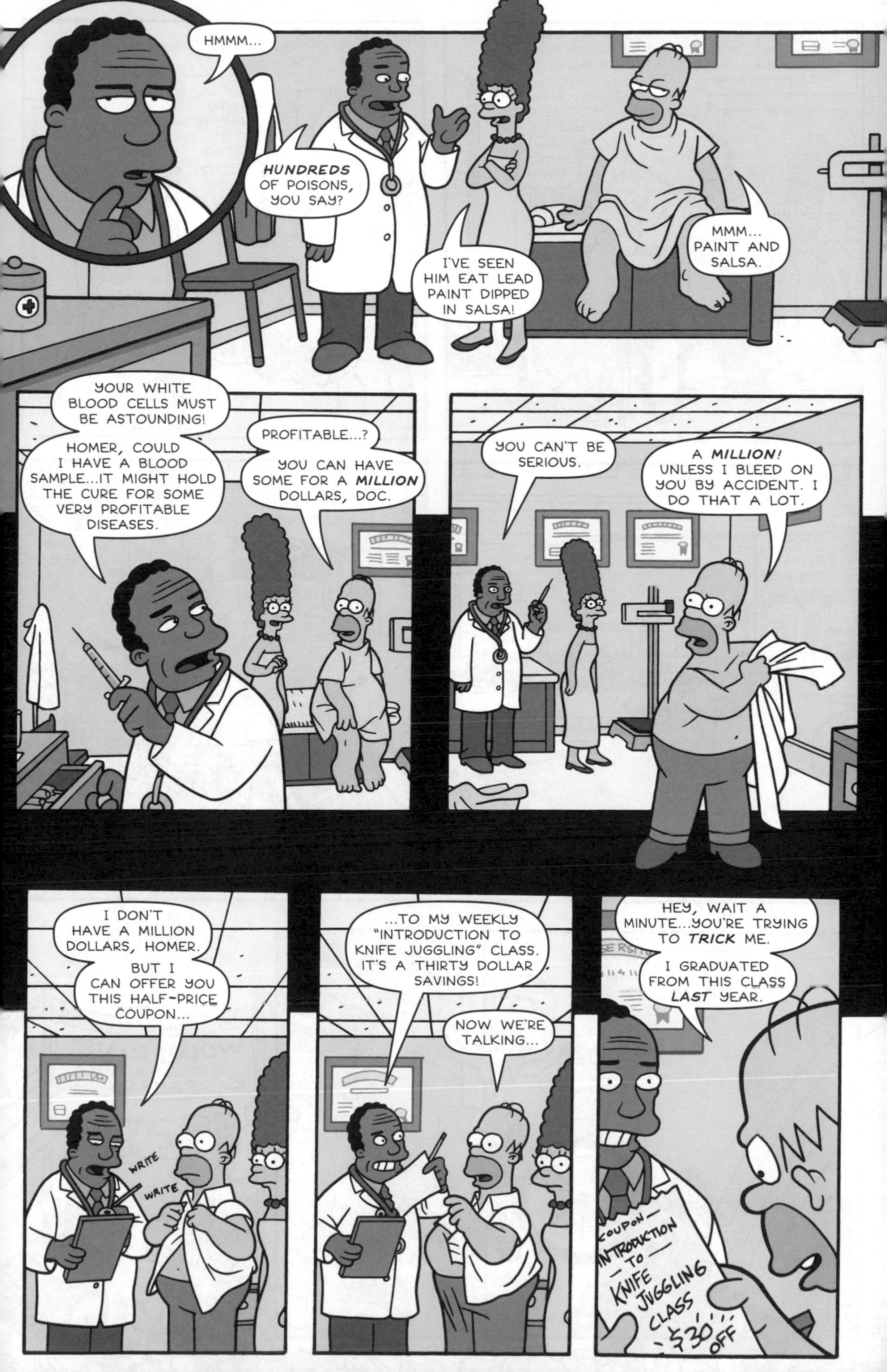
HMMM...
HUNDREDS OF POISONS, YOU SAY?
I'VE SEEN HIM EAT LEAD PAINT DIPPED IN SALSA!
MMM... PAINT AND SALSA.
YOUR WHITE BLOOD CELLS MUST BE ASTOUNDING!
HOMER, COULD I HAVE A BLOOD SAMPLE...IT MIGHT HOLD THE CURE FOR SOME VERY PROFITABLE DISEASES.
PROFITABLE...?
YOU CAN HAVE SOME FOR A MILLION DOLLARS, DOC.
YOU CAN'T BE SERIOUS.
A MILLION! UNLESS I BLEED ON YOU BY ACCIDENT. I DO THAT A LOT.
I DON'T HAVE A MILLION DOLLARS, HOMER.
BUT I CAN OFFER YOU THIS HALF-PRICE COUPON...
WRITE
WRITE
...TO MY WEEKLY "INTRODUCTION TO KNIFE JUGGLING" CLASS. IT'S A THIRTY DOLLAR SAVINGS!
NOW WE'RE TALKING...
HEY, WAIT A MINUTE...YOU'RE TRYING TO TRICK ME.
I GRADUATED FROM THIS CLASS LAST YEAR.
COUPON
INTRODUCTION TO KNIFE JUGGLING CLASS
$30 OFF

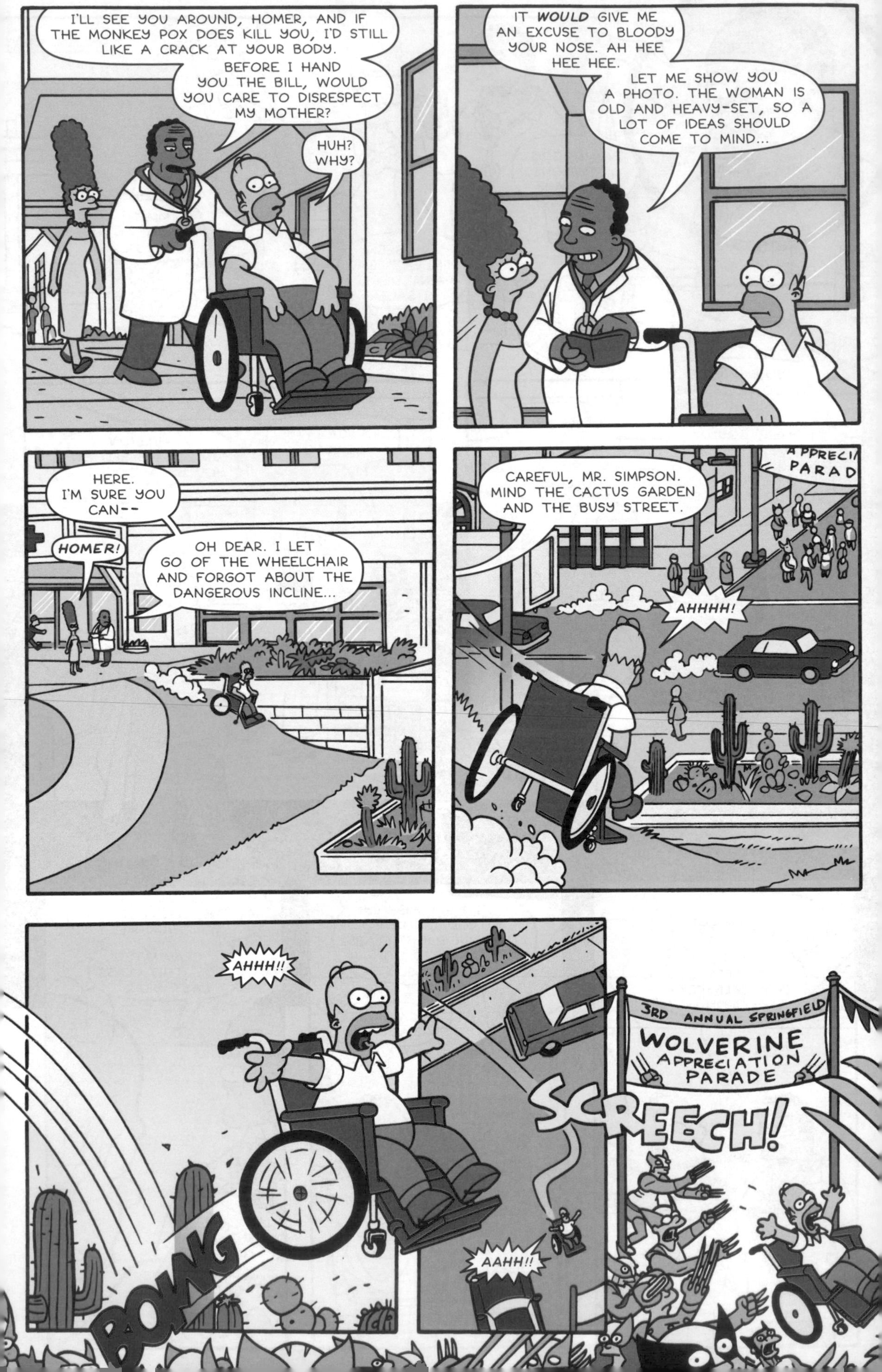
I'LL SEE YOU AROUND, HOMER, AND IF THE MONKEY POX DOES KILL YOU, I'D STILL LIKE A CRACK AT YOUR BODY.
BEFORE I HAND YOU THE BILL, WOULD YOU CARE TO DISRESPECT MY MOTHER?
HUH? WHY?
IT WOULD GIVE ME AN EXCUSE TO BLOODY YOUR NOSE. AH HEE HEE HEE.
LET ME SHOW YOU A PHOTO. THE WOMAN IS OLD AND HEAVY-SET, SO A LOT OF IDEAS SHOULD COME TO MIND...
HERE. I'M SURE YOU CAN--
HOMER!
OH DEAR. I LET GO OF THE WHEELCHAIR AND FORGOT ABOUT THE DANGEROUS INCLINE...
CAREFUL, MR. SIMPSON. MIND THE CACTUS GARDEN AND THE BUSY STREET.
AHHHH!
AHHH!!
BOING
3RD ANNUAL SPRINGFIELD
WOLVERINE
APPRECIATION
PARADE
SCREECH!
AAHH!!

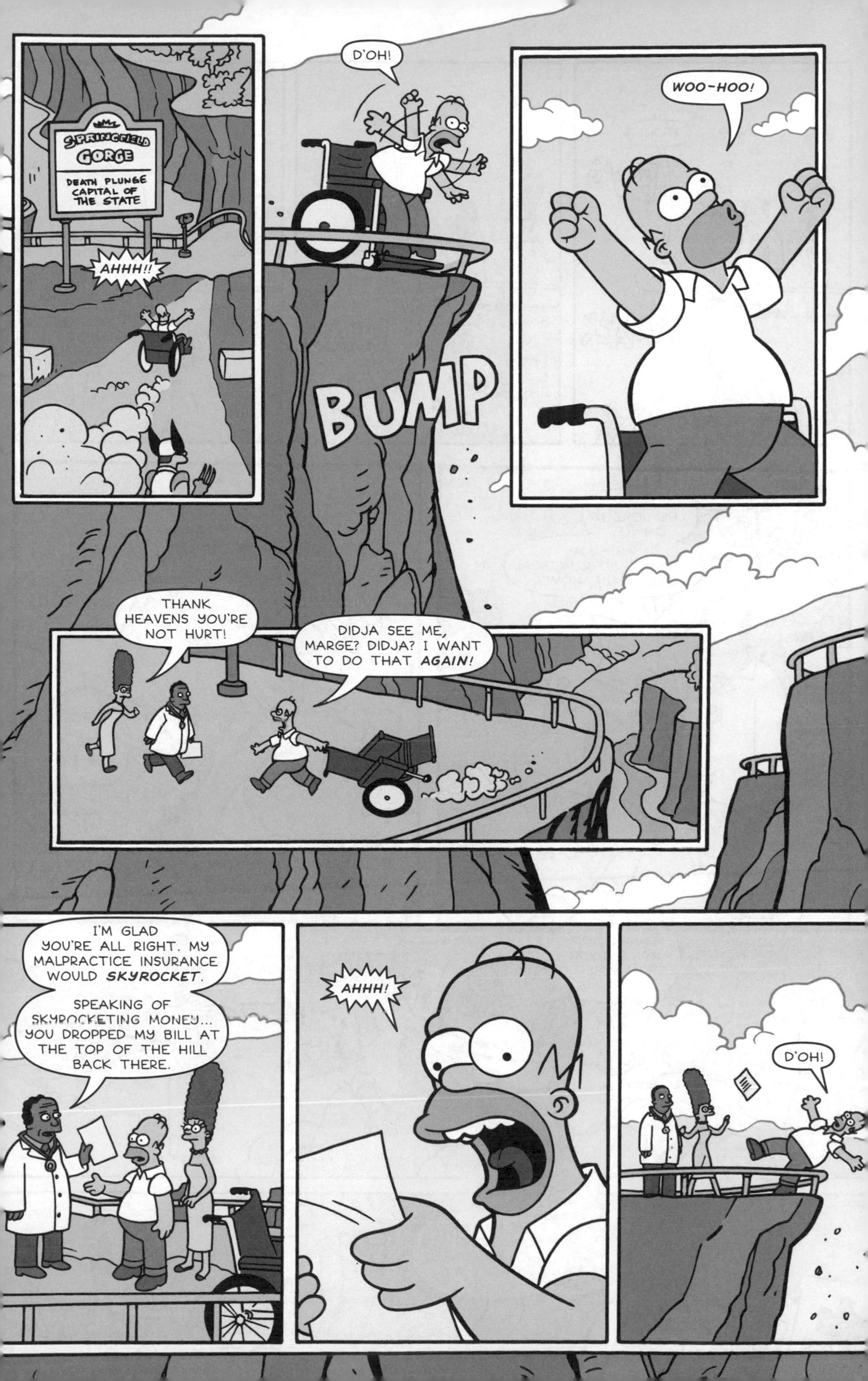
SPRINGFIELD GORGE
DEATH PLUNGE CAPITAL OF THE STATE
AHHH!!
D'OH!
BUMP
WOO-HOO!
THANK HEAVENS YOU'RE NOT HURT!
DIDJA SEE ME, MARGE? DIDJA? I WANT TO DO THAT AGAIN!
I'M GLAD YOU'RE ALL RIGHT. MY MALPRACTICE INSURANCE WOULD SKYROCKET.
SPEAKING OF SKYROCKETING MONEY... YOU DROPPED MY BILL AT THE TOP OF THE HILL BACK THERE.
AHHH!
D'OH!

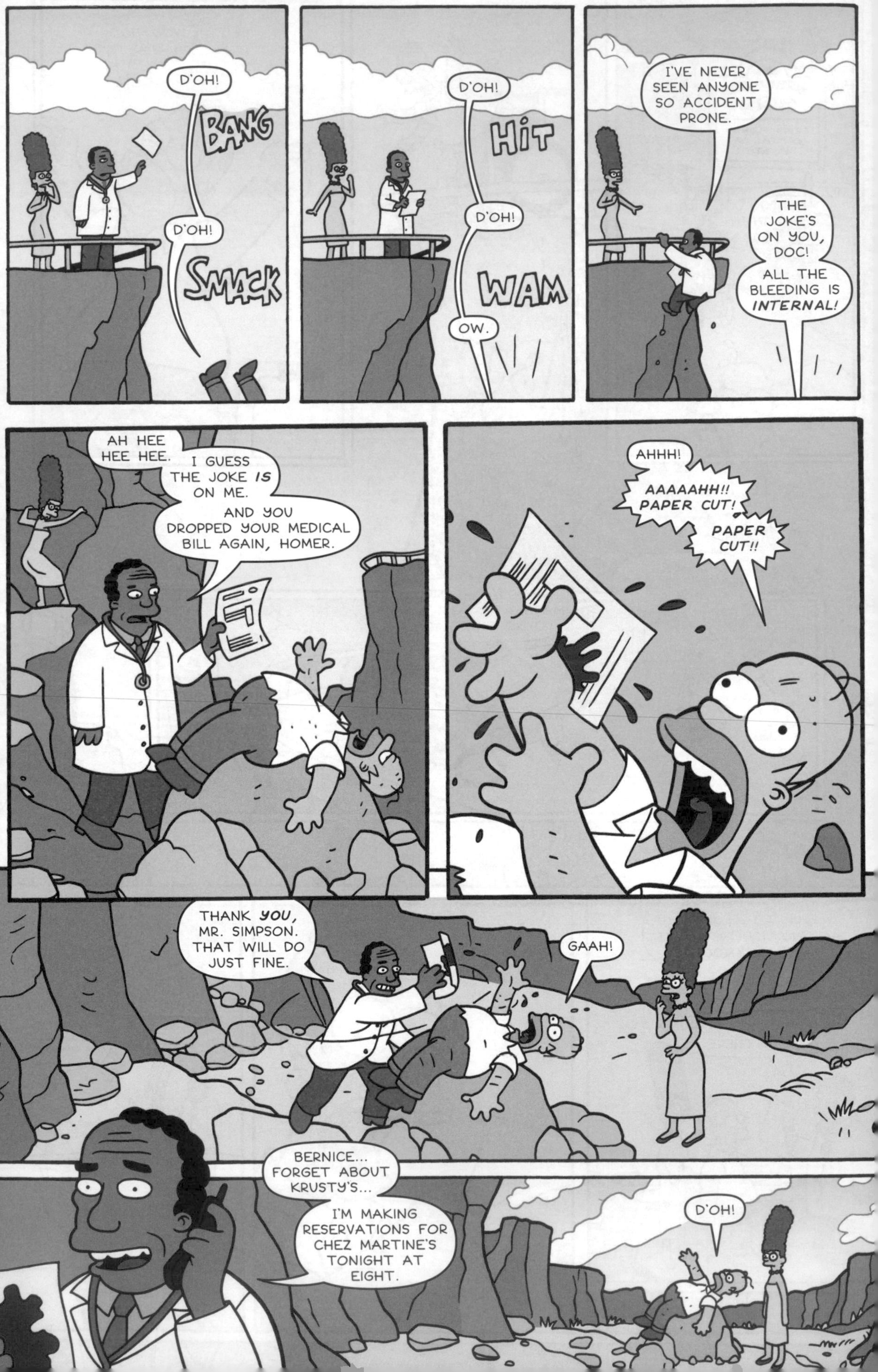
D'OH!
BANG
D'OH!
SMACK
D'OH!
HIT
D'OH!
WAM
OW.
I'VE NEVER SEEN ANYONE SO ACCIDENT PRONE.
THE JOKE'S ON YOU, DOC!
ALL THE BLEEDING IS *INTERNAL!*
AH HEE HEE HEE.
I GUESS THE JOKE *IS* ON ME.
AND YOU DROPPED YOUR MEDICAL BILL AGAIN, HOMER.
AHHH!
AAAAAHH!! PAPER CUT!
PAPER CUT!!
THANK *YOU*, MR. SIMPSON. THAT WILL DO JUST FINE.
GAAH!
BERNICE... FORGET ABOUT KRUSTY'S...
I'M MAKING RESERVATIONS FOR CHEZ MARTINE'S TONIGHT AT EIGHT.
D'OH!

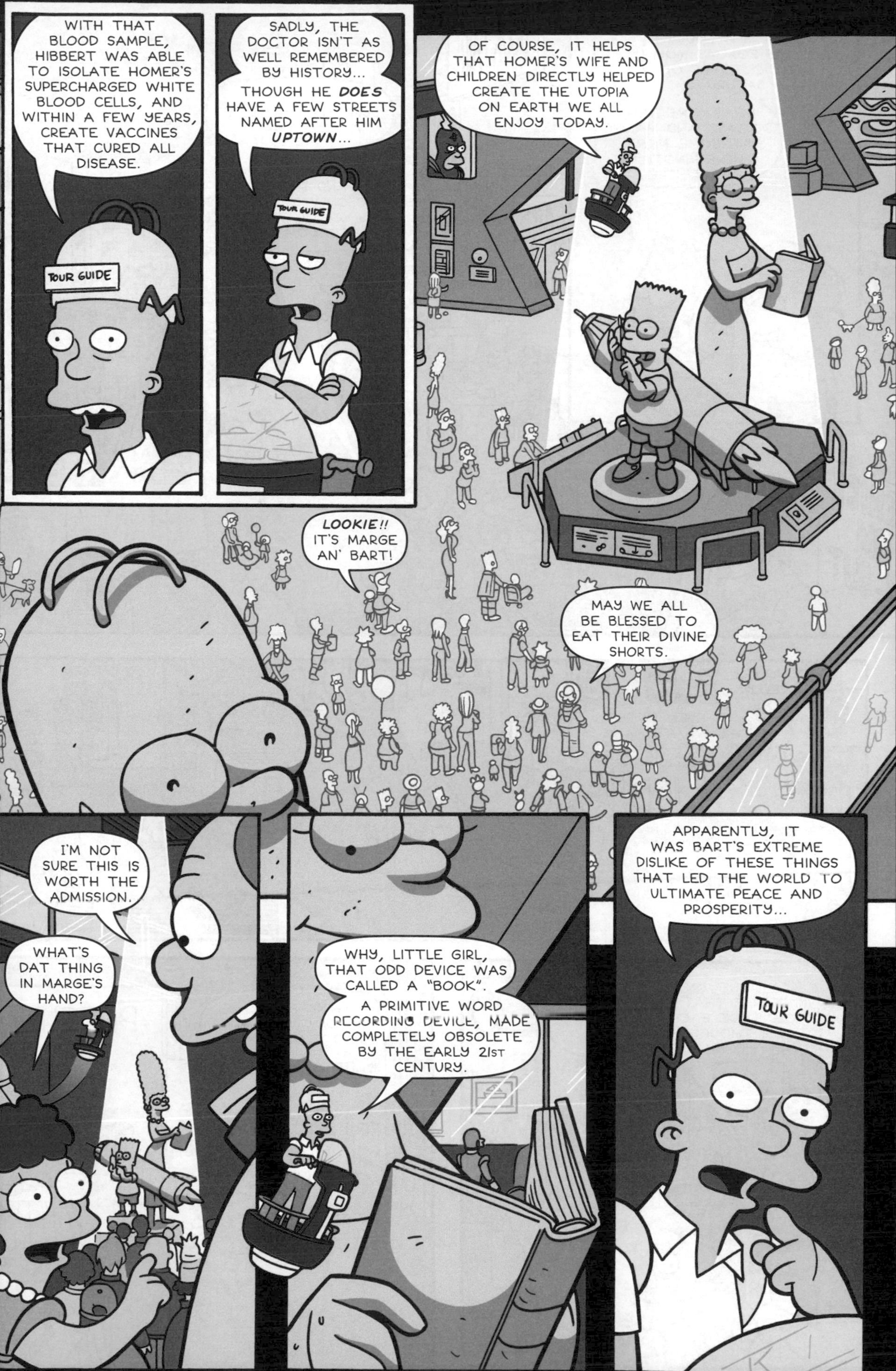
WITH THAT BLOOD SAMPLE, HIBBERT WAS ABLE TO ISOLATE HOMER'S SUPERCHARGED WHITE BLOOD CELLS, AND WITHIN A FEW YEARS, CREATE VACCINES THAT CURED ALL DISEASE.
TOUR GUIDE
SADLY, THE DOCTOR ISN'T AS WELL REMEMBERED BY HISTORY...
THOUGH HE *DOES* HAVE A FEW STREETS NAMED AFTER HIM *UPTOWN*...
TOUR GUIDE
OF COURSE, IT HELPS THAT HOMER'S WIFE AND CHILDREN DIRECTLY HELPED CREATE THE UTOPIA ON EARTH WE ALL ENJOY TODAY.
LOOKIE!! IT'S MARGE AN' BART!
MAY WE ALL BE BLESSED TO EAT THEIR DIVINE SHORTS.
I'M NOT SURE THIS IS WORTH THE ADMISSION.
WHAT'S DAT THING IN MARGE'S HAND?
WHY, LITTLE GIRL, THAT ODD DEVICE WAS CALLED A "BOOK".
A PRIMITIVE WORD RECORDING DEVICE, MADE COMPLETELY OBSOLETE BY THE EARLY 21ST CENTURY.
APPARENTLY, IT WAS BART'S EXTREME DISLIKE OF THESE THINGS THAT LED THE WORLD TO ULTIMATE PEACE AND PROSPERITY...
TOUR GUIDE

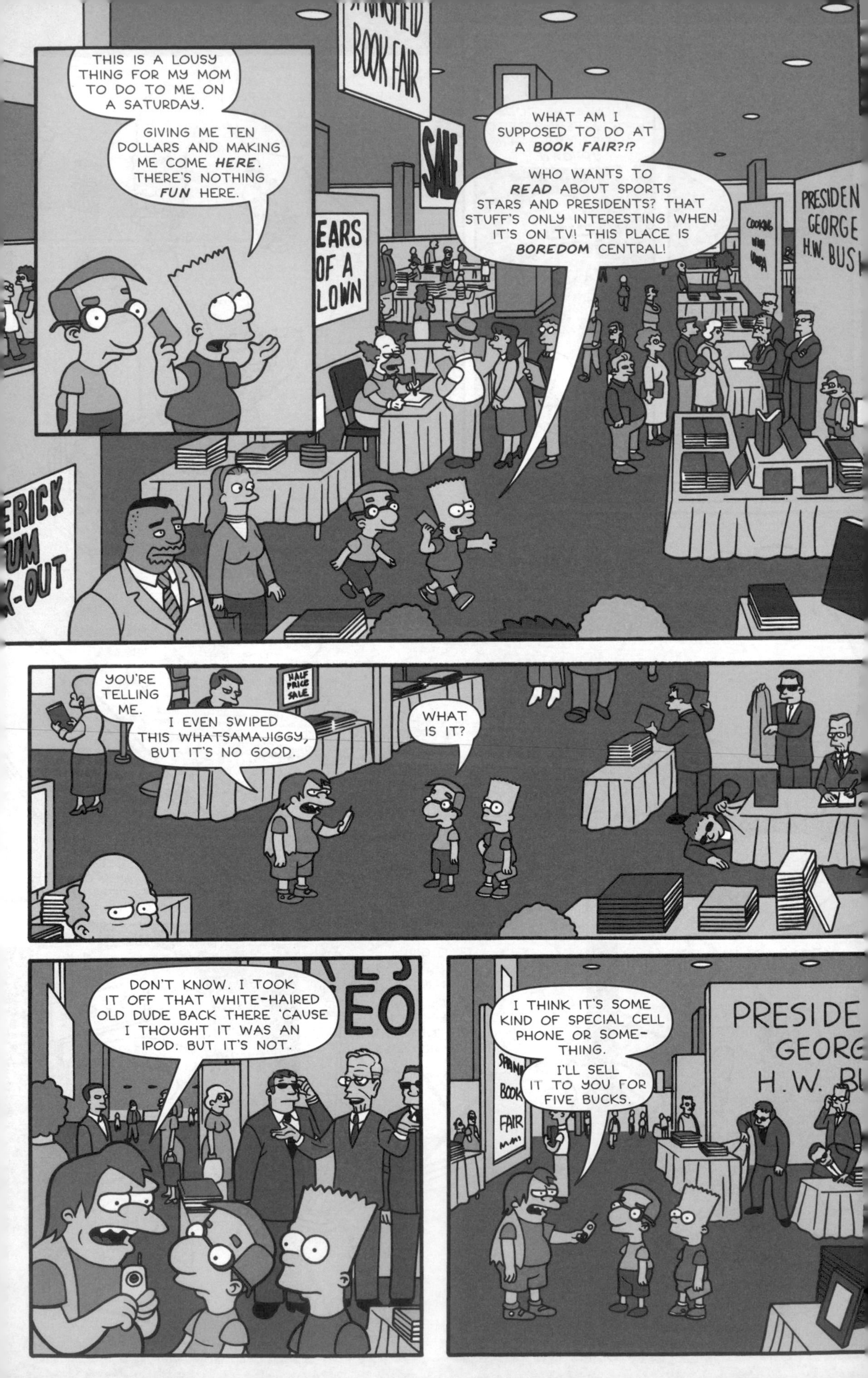
BOOK FAIR
SALE
THIS IS A LOUSY THING FOR MY MOM TO DO TO ME ON A SATURDAY.
GIVING ME TEN DOLLARS AND MAKING ME COME *HERE*. THERE'S NOTHING *FUN* HERE.
WHAT AM I SUPPOSED TO DO AT A *BOOK FAIR*?!?
WHO WANTS TO *READ* ABOUT SPORTS STARS AND PRESIDENTS? THAT STUFF'S ONLY INTERESTING WHEN IT'S ON TV! THIS PLACE IS *BOREDOM* CENTRAL!
HALF PRICE SALE
YOU'RE TELLING ME.
I EVEN SWIPED THIS WHATSAMAJIGGY, BUT IT'S NO GOOD.
WHAT IS IT?
DON'T KNOW. I TOOK IT OFF THAT WHITE-HAIRED OLD DUDE BACK THERE 'CAUSE I THOUGHT IT WAS AN IPOD. BUT IT'S NOT.
I THINK IT'S SOME KIND OF SPECIAL CELL PHONE OR SOME-THING.
I'LL SELL IT TO YOU FOR FIVE BUCKS.

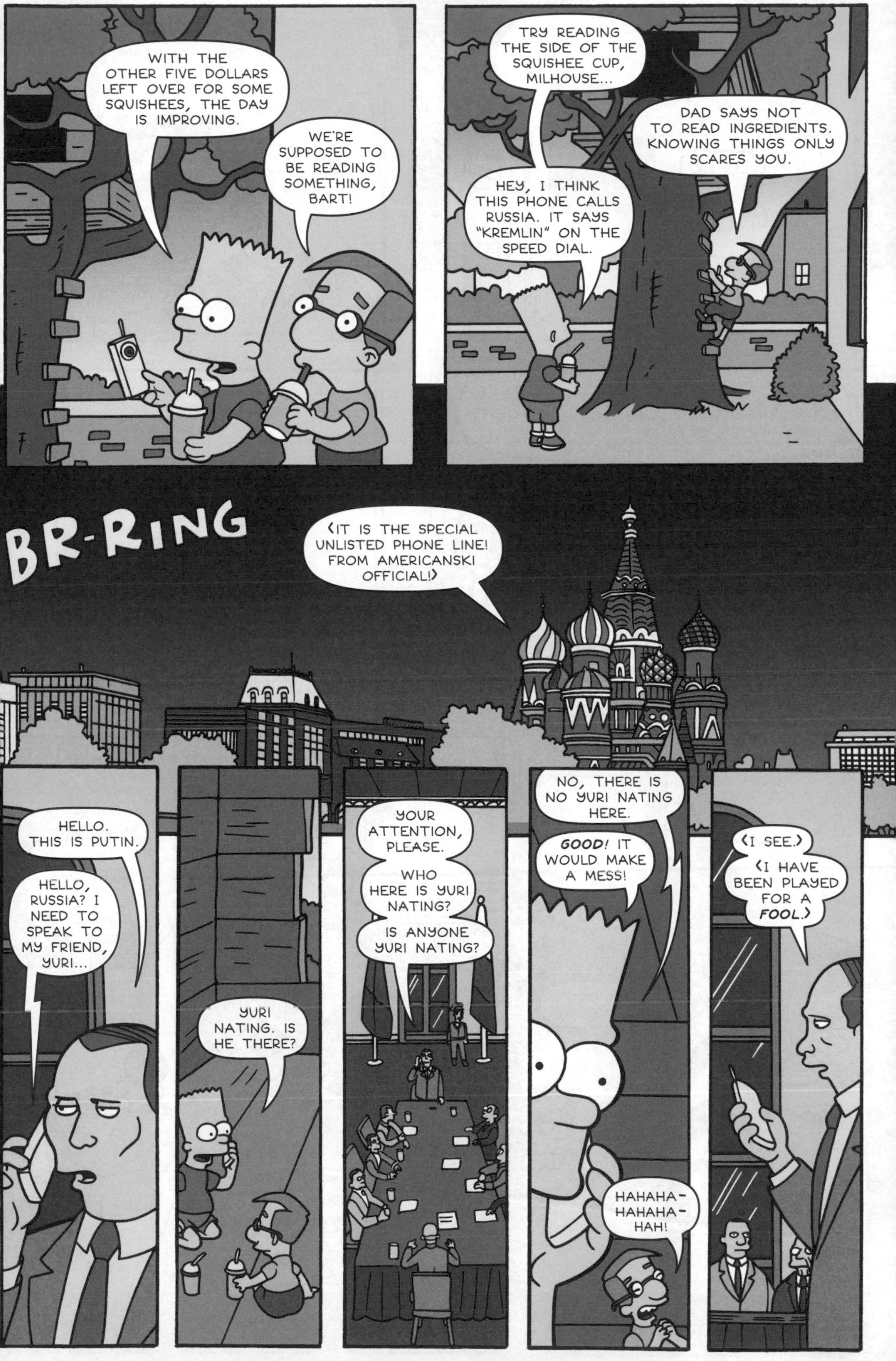
WITH THE OTHER FIVE DOLLARS LEFT OVER FOR SOME SQUISHEES, THE DAY IS IMPROVING.
WE'RE SUPPOSED TO BE READING SOMETHING, BART!
TRY READING THE SIDE OF THE SQUISHEE CUP, MILHOUSE...
DAD SAYS NOT TO READ INGREDIENTS. KNOWING THINGS ONLY SCARES YOU.
HEY, I THINK THIS PHONE CALLS RUSSIA. IT SAYS "KREMLIN" ON THE SPEED DIAL.
BR-RING
‹IT IS THE SPECIAL UNLISTED PHONE LINE! FROM AMERICANSKI OFFICIAL!›
HELLO. THIS IS PUTIN.
HELLO, RUSSIA? I NEED TO SPEAK TO MY FRIEND, YURI...
YURI NATING. IS HE THERE?
YOUR ATTENTION, PLEASE.
WHO HERE IS YURI NATING?
IS ANYONE YURI NATING?
NO, THERE IS NO YURI NATING HERE.
GOOD! IT WOULD MAKE A MESS!
HAHAHA-HAHAHA-HAH!
‹I SEE.›
‹I HAVE BEEN PLAYED FOR A *FOOL.*›

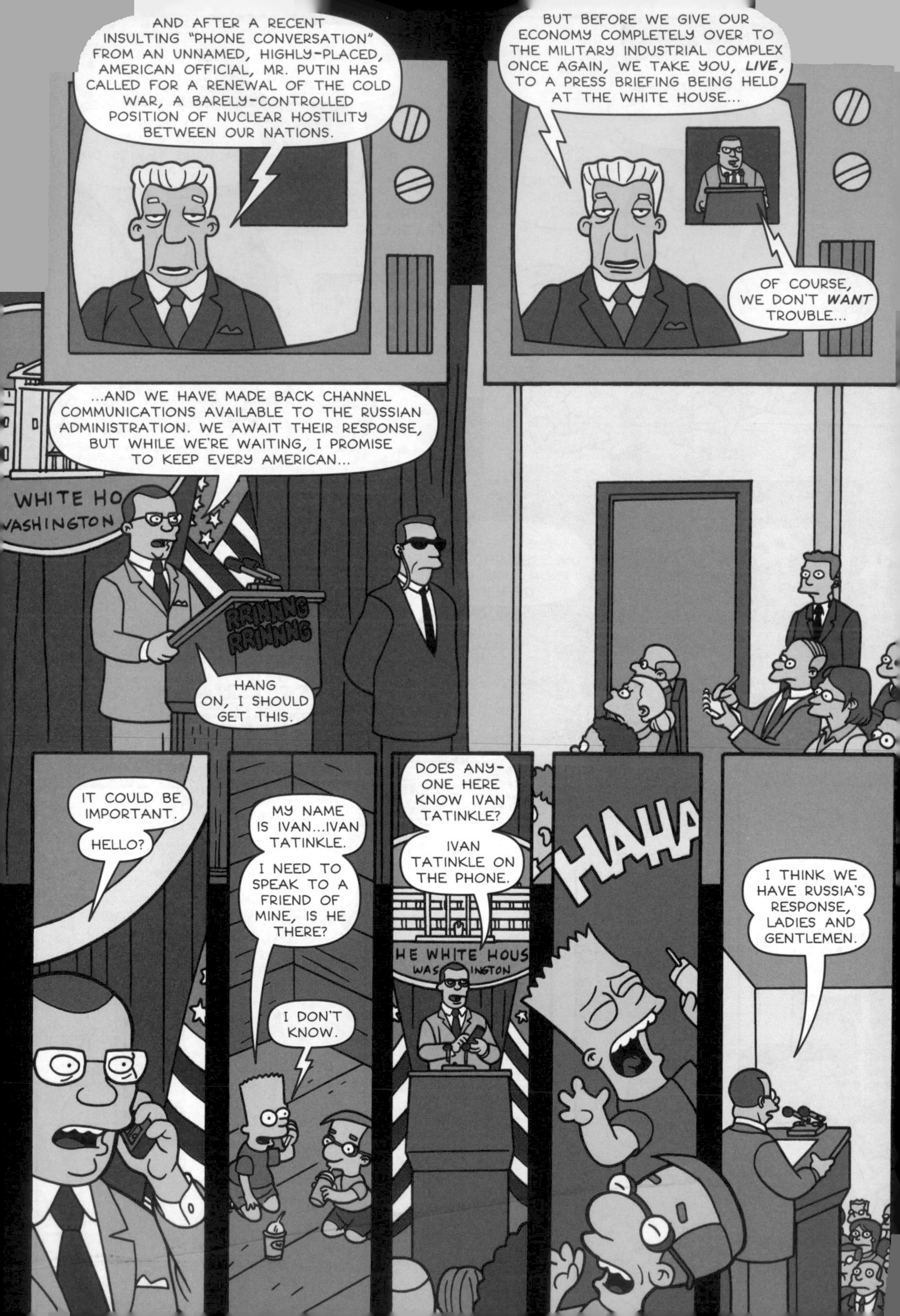
AND AFTER A RECENT INSULTING "PHONE CONVERSATION" FROM AN UNNAMED, HIGHLY-PLACED, AMERICAN OFFICIAL, MR. PUTIN HAS CALLED FOR A RENEWAL OF THE COLD WAR, A BARELY-CONTROLLED POSITION OF NUCLEAR HOSTILITY BETWEEN OUR NATIONS.
BUT BEFORE WE GIVE OUR ECONOMY COMPLETELY OVER TO THE MILITARY INDUSTRIAL COMPLEX ONCE AGAIN, WE TAKE YOU, *LIVE,* TO A PRESS BRIEFING BEING HELD AT THE WHITE HOUSE...
OF COURSE, WE DON'T *WANT* TROUBLE...
...AND WE HAVE MADE BACK CHANNEL COMMUNICATIONS AVAILABLE TO THE RUSSIAN ADMINISTRATION. WE AWAIT THEIR RESPONSE, BUT WHILE WE'RE WAITING, I PROMISE TO KEEP EVERY AMERICAN...
WHITE HO
WASHINGTON
RRINNNG RRINNNG
HANG ON, I SHOULD GET THIS.
IT COULD BE IMPORTANT.
HELLO?
MY NAME IS IVAN...IVAN TATINKLE.
I NEED TO SPEAK TO A FRIEND OF MINE, IS HE THERE?
I DON'T KNOW.
DOES ANY-ONE HERE KNOW IVAN TATINKLE?
IVAN TATINKLE ON THE PHONE.
HE WHITE HOUS
HAHA
I THINK WE HAVE RUSSIA'S RESPONSE, LADIES AND GENTLEMEN.

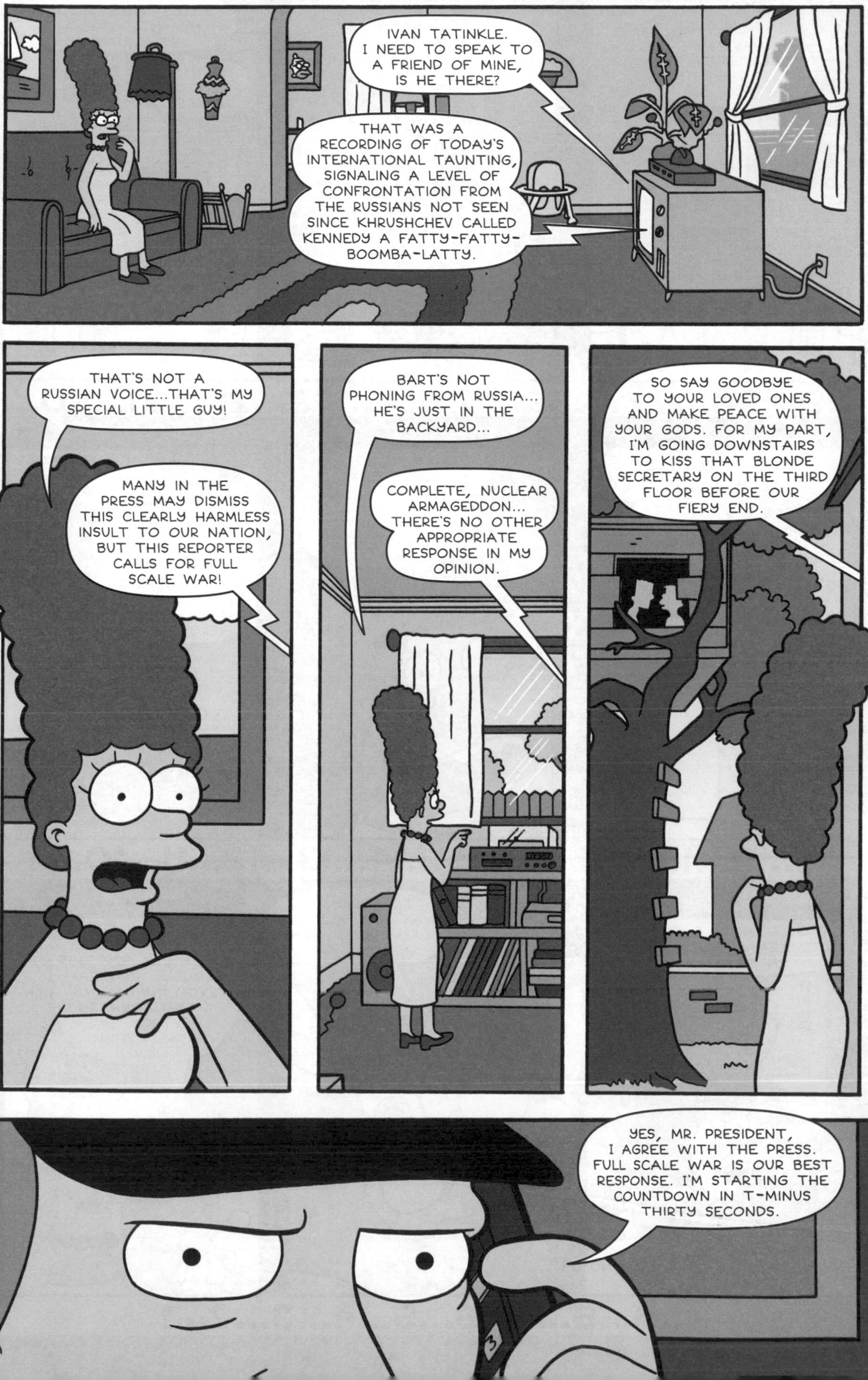
IVAN TATINKLE. I NEED TO SPEAK TO A FRIEND OF MINE, IS HE THERE?
THAT WAS A RECORDING OF TODAY'S INTERNATIONAL TAUNTING, SIGNALING A LEVEL OF CONFRONTATION FROM THE RUSSIANS NOT SEEN SINCE KHRUSHCHEV CALLED KENNEDY A FATTY-FATTY-BOOMBA-LATTY.
THAT'S NOT A RUSSIAN VOICE...THAT'S MY SPECIAL LITTLE GUY!
MANY IN THE PRESS MAY DISMISS THIS CLEARLY HARMLESS INSULT TO OUR NATION, BUT THIS REPORTER CALLS FOR FULL SCALE WAR!
BART'S NOT PHONING FROM RUSSIA... HE'S JUST IN THE BACKYARD...
COMPLETE, NUCLEAR ARMAGEDDON... THERE'S NO OTHER APPROPRIATE RESPONSE IN MY OPINION.
SO SAY GOODBYE TO YOUR LOVED ONES AND MAKE PEACE WITH YOUR GODS. FOR MY PART, I'M GOING DOWNSTAIRS TO KISS THAT BLONDE SECRETARY ON THE THIRD FLOOR BEFORE OUR FIERY END.
YES, MR. PRESIDENT, I AGREE WITH THE PRESS. FULL SCALE WAR IS OUR BEST RESPONSE. I'M STARTING THE COUNTDOWN IN T-MINUS THIRTY SECONDS.

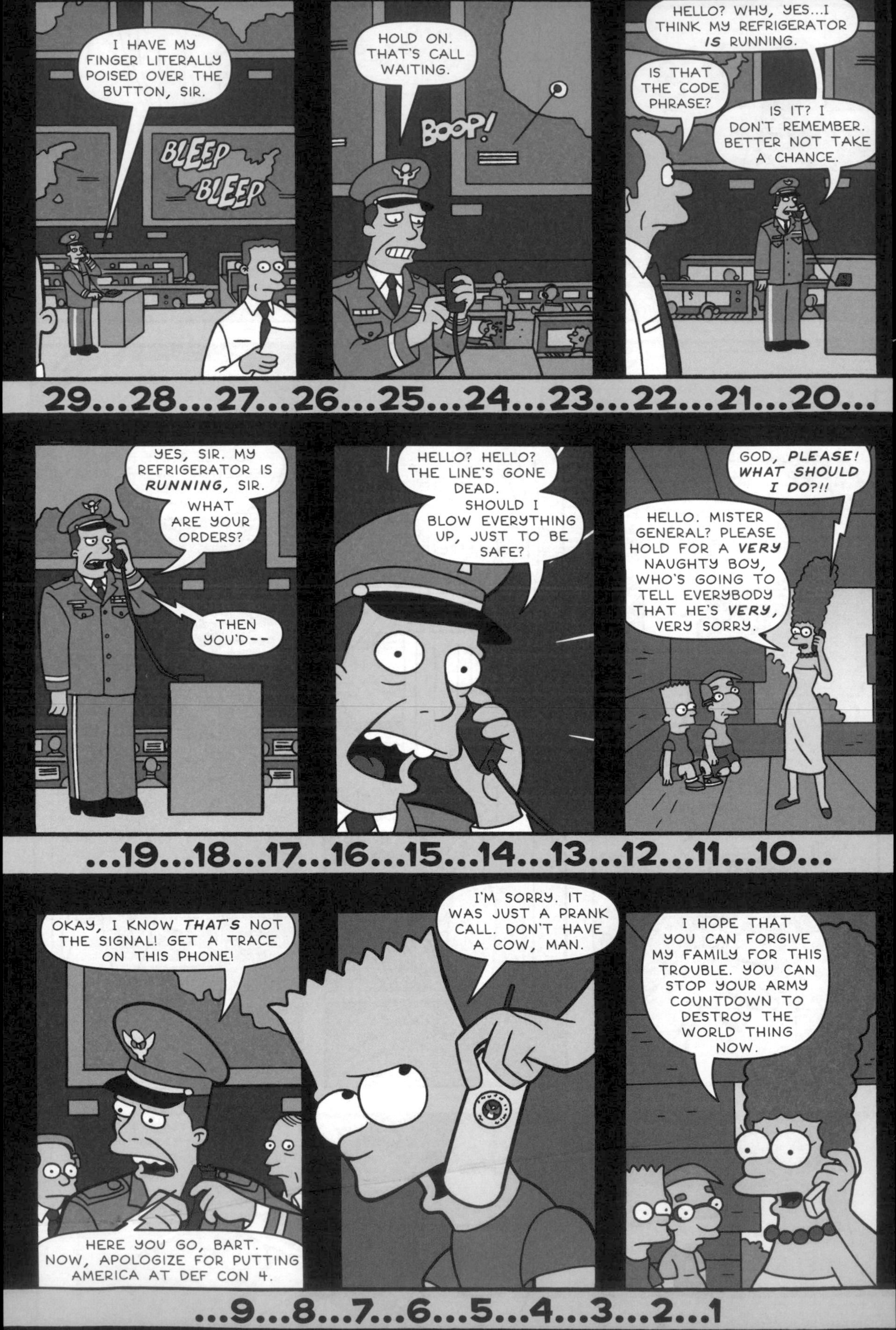
I HAVE MY FINGER LITERALLY POISED OVER THE BUTTON, SIR.
BLEEP BLEEP
HOLD ON. THAT'S CALL WAITING.
BOOP!
HELLO? WHY, YES...I THINK MY REFRIGERATOR IS RUNNING.
IS THAT THE CODE PHRASE?
IS IT? I DON'T REMEMBER. BETTER NOT TAKE A CHANCE.
29...28...27...26...25...24...23...22...21...20...
YES, SIR. MY REFRIGERATOR IS RUNNING, SIR.
WHAT ARE YOUR ORDERS?
THEN YOU'D--
HELLO? HELLO? THE LINE'S GONE DEAD.
SHOULD I BLOW EVERYTHING UP, JUST TO BE SAFE?
GOD, PLEASE! WHAT SHOULD I DO?!!
HELLO. MISTER GENERAL? PLEASE HOLD FOR A VERY NAUGHTY BOY, WHO'S GOING TO TELL EVERYBODY THAT HE'S VERY, VERY SORRY.
...19...18...17...16...15...14...13...12...11...10...
OKAY, I KNOW THAT'S NOT THE SIGNAL! GET A TRACE ON THIS PHONE!
HERE YOU GO, BART. NOW, APOLOGIZE FOR PUTTING AMERICA AT DEF CON 4.
I'M SORRY. IT WAS JUST A PRANK CALL. DON'T HAVE A COW, MAN.
I HOPE THAT YOU CAN FORGIVE MY FAMILY FOR THIS TROUBLE. YOU CAN STOP YOUR ARMY COUNTDOWN TO DESTROY THE WORLD THING NOW.
...9...8...7...6...5...4...3...2...1

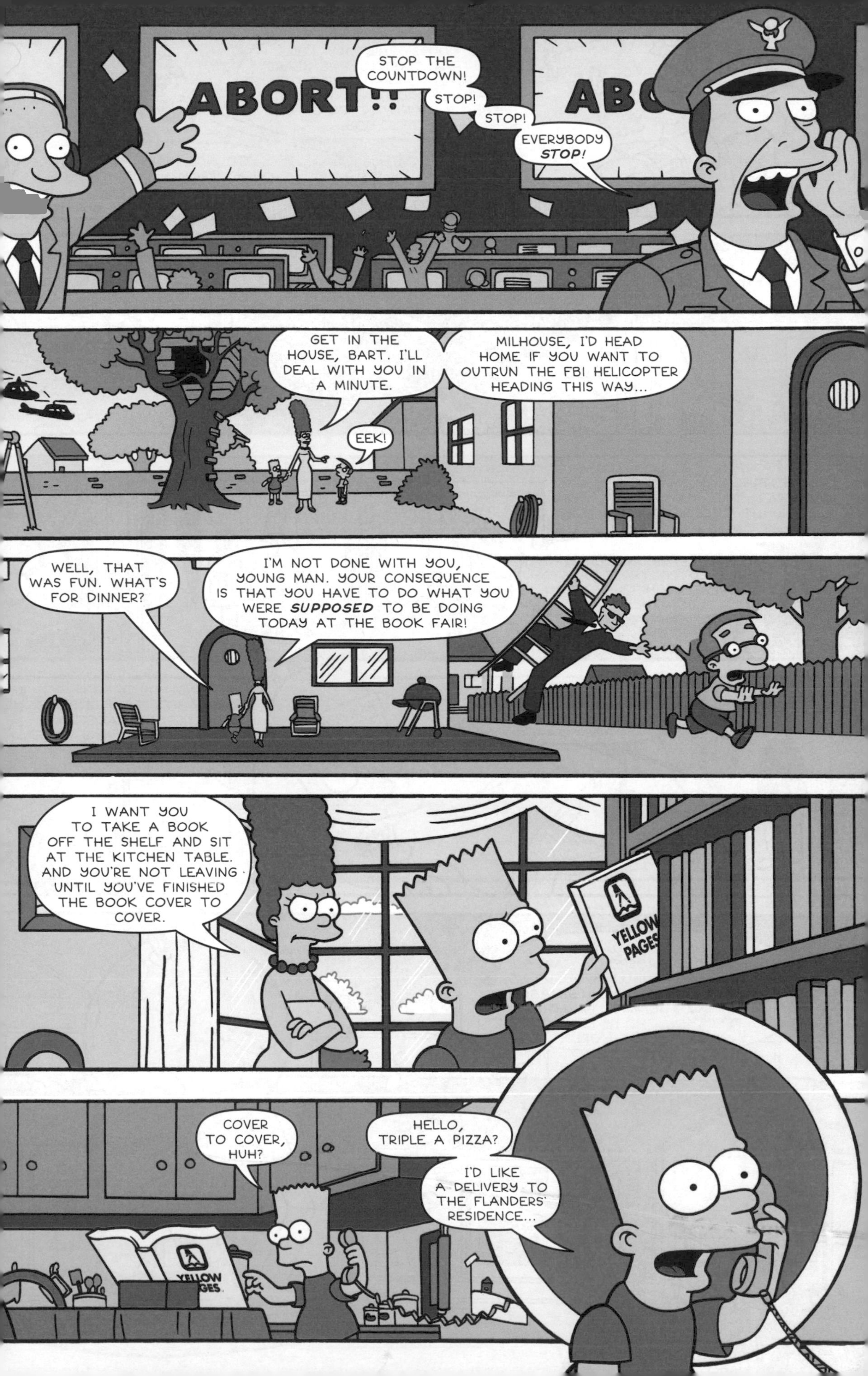
ABORT!!
STOP THE COUNTDOWN!
STOP!
STOP!
EVERYBODY STOP!
ABO
GET IN THE HOUSE, BART. I'LL DEAL WITH YOU IN A MINUTE.
MILHOUSE, I'D HEAD HOME IF YOU WANT TO OUTRUN THE FBI HELICOPTER HEADING THIS WAY...
EEK!
WELL, THAT WAS FUN. WHAT'S FOR DINNER?
I'M NOT DONE WITH YOU, YOUNG MAN. YOUR CONSEQUENCE IS THAT YOU HAVE TO DO WHAT YOU WERE SUPPOSED TO BE DOING TODAY AT THE BOOK FAIR!
I WANT YOU TO TAKE A BOOK OFF THE SHELF AND SIT AT THE KITCHEN TABLE. AND YOU'RE NOT LEAVING UNTIL YOU'VE FINISHED THE BOOK COVER TO COVER.
YELLOW PAGES
COVER TO COVER, HUH?
HELLO, TRIPLE A PIZZA?
I'D LIKE A DELIVERY TO THE FLANDERS' RESIDENCE...
YELLOW PAGES

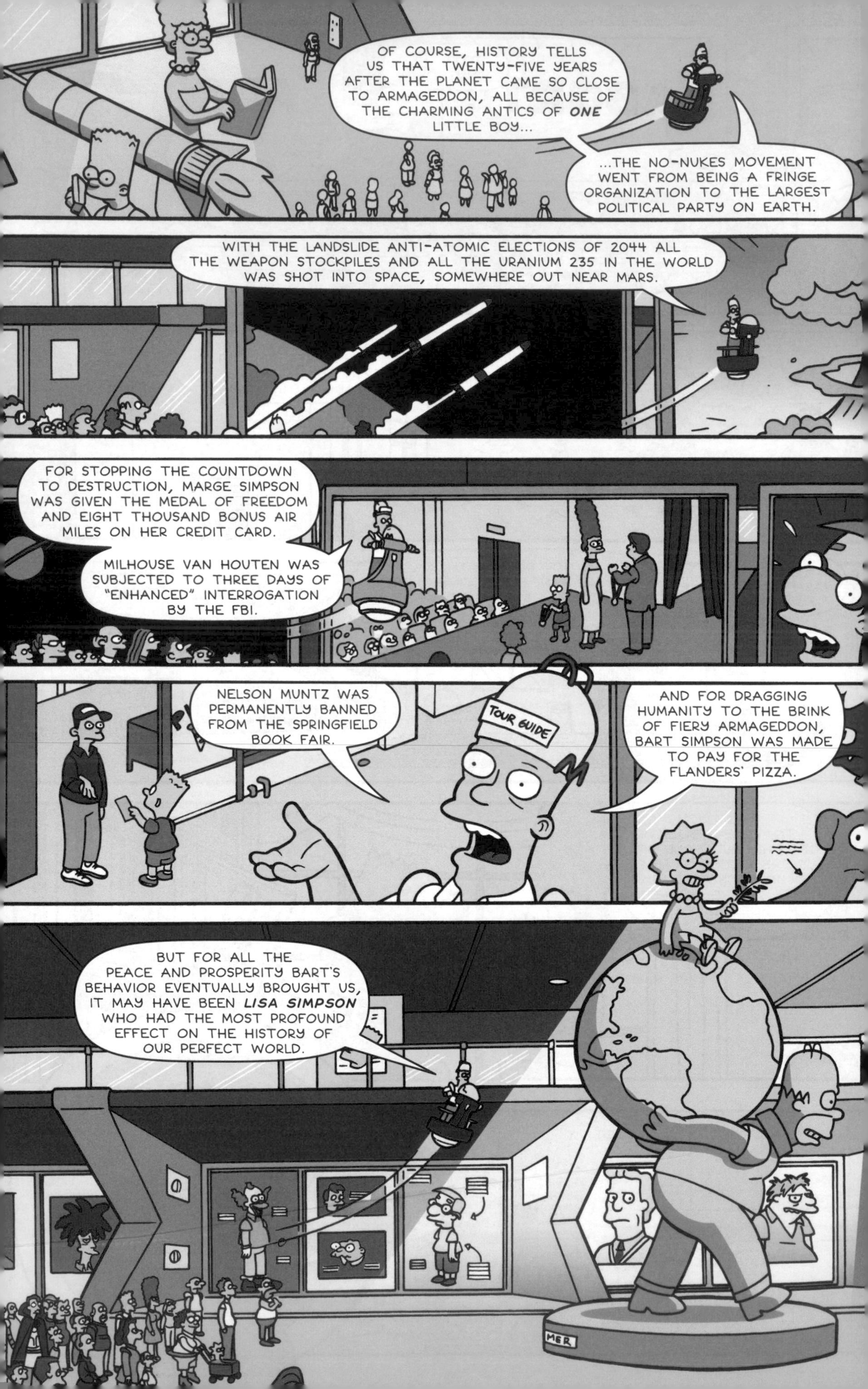
OF COURSE, HISTORY TELLS US THAT TWENTY-FIVE YEARS AFTER THE PLANET CAME SO CLOSE TO ARMAGEDDON, ALL BECAUSE OF THE CHARMING ANTICS OF ONE LITTLE BOY...
...THE NO-NUKES MOVEMENT WENT FROM BEING A FRINGE ORGANIZATION TO THE LARGEST POLITICAL PARTY ON EARTH.
WITH THE LANDSLIDE ANTI-ATOMIC ELECTIONS OF 2044 ALL THE WEAPON STOCKPILES AND ALL THE URANIUM 235 IN THE WORLD WAS SHOT INTO SPACE, SOMEWHERE OUT NEAR MARS.
FOR STOPPING THE COUNTDOWN TO DESTRUCTION, MARGE SIMPSON WAS GIVEN THE MEDAL OF FREEDOM AND EIGHT THOUSAND BONUS AIR MILES ON HER CREDIT CARD.
MILHOUSE VAN HOUTEN WAS SUBJECTED TO THREE DAYS OF "ENHANCED" INTERROGATION BY THE FBI.
NELSON MUNTZ WAS PERMANENTLY BANNED FROM THE SPRINGFIELD BOOK FAIR.
TOUR GUIDE
AND FOR DRAGGING HUMANITY TO THE BRINK OF FIERY ARMAGEDDON, BART SIMPSON WAS MADE TO PAY FOR THE FLANDERS' PIZZA.
BUT FOR ALL THE PEACE AND PROSPERITY BART'S BEHAVIOR EVENTUALLY BROUGHT US, IT MAY HAVE BEEN LISA SIMPSON WHO HAD THE MOST PROFOUND EFFECT ON THE HISTORY OF OUR PERFECT WORLD.
MER

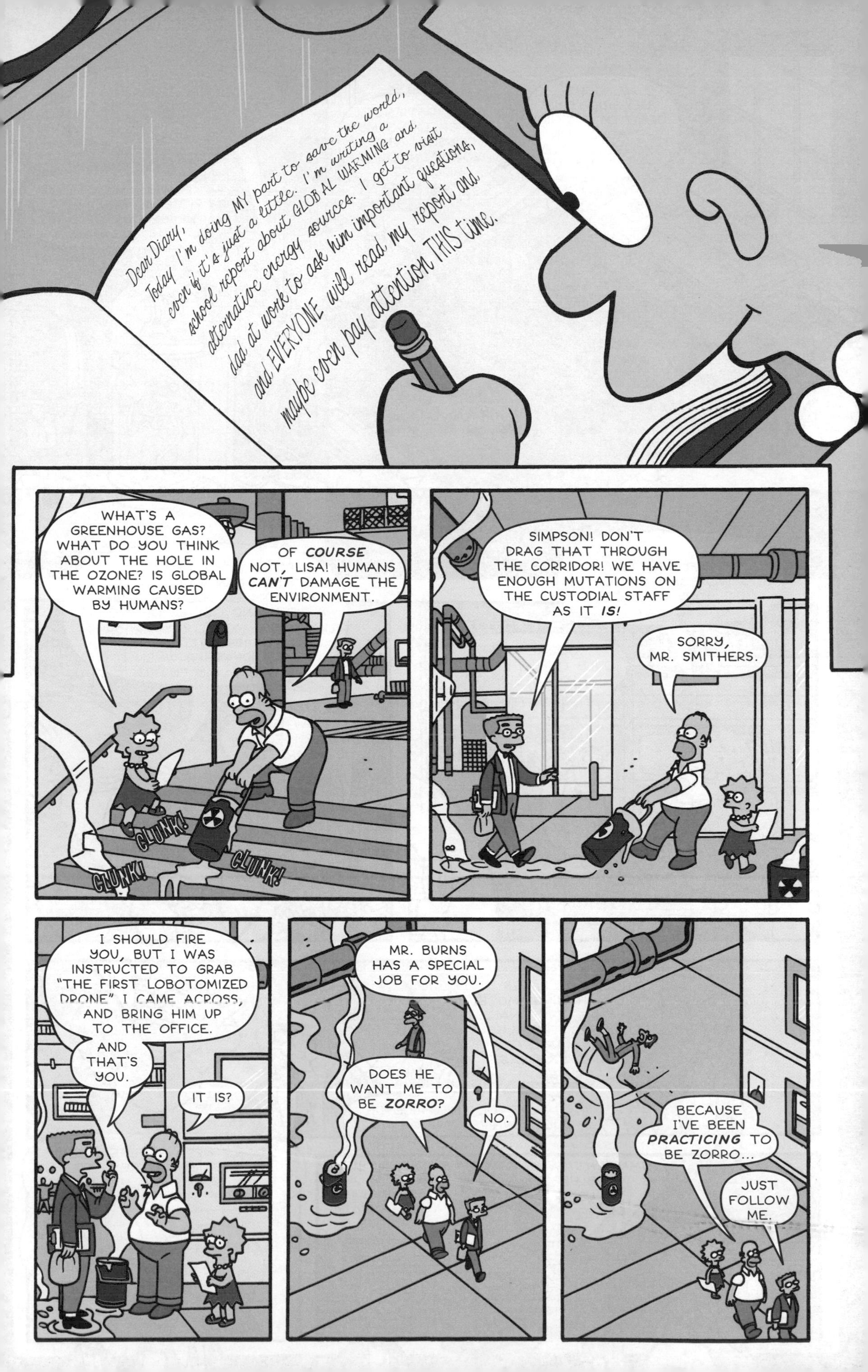
Dear Diary,
Today I'm doing MY part to save the world, even if it's just a little. I'm writing a school report about GLOBAL WARMING and alternative energy sources. I get to visit dad at work to ask him important questions, and EVERYONE will read my report and maybe even pay attention THIS time.
WHAT'S A GREENHOUSE GAS? WHAT DO YOU THINK ABOUT THE HOLE IN THE OZONE? IS GLOBAL WARMING CAUSED BY HUMANS?
OF COURSE NOT, LISA! HUMANS CAN'T DAMAGE THE ENVIRONMENT.
CLUNK!
CLUNK!
CLUNK!
SIMPSON! DON'T DRAG THAT THROUGH THE CORRIDOR! WE HAVE ENOUGH MUTATIONS ON THE CUSTODIAL STAFF AS IT IS!
SORRY, MR. SMITHERS.
I SHOULD FIRE YOU, BUT I WAS INSTRUCTED TO GRAB "THE FIRST LOBOTOMIZED DRONE" I CAME ACROSS, AND BRING HIM UP TO THE OFFICE.
AND THAT'S YOU.
IT IS?
MR. BURNS HAS A SPECIAL JOB FOR YOU.
DOES HE WANT ME TO BE ZORRO?
NO.
BECAUSE I'VE BEEN PRACTICING TO BE ZORRO...
JUST FOLLOW ME.

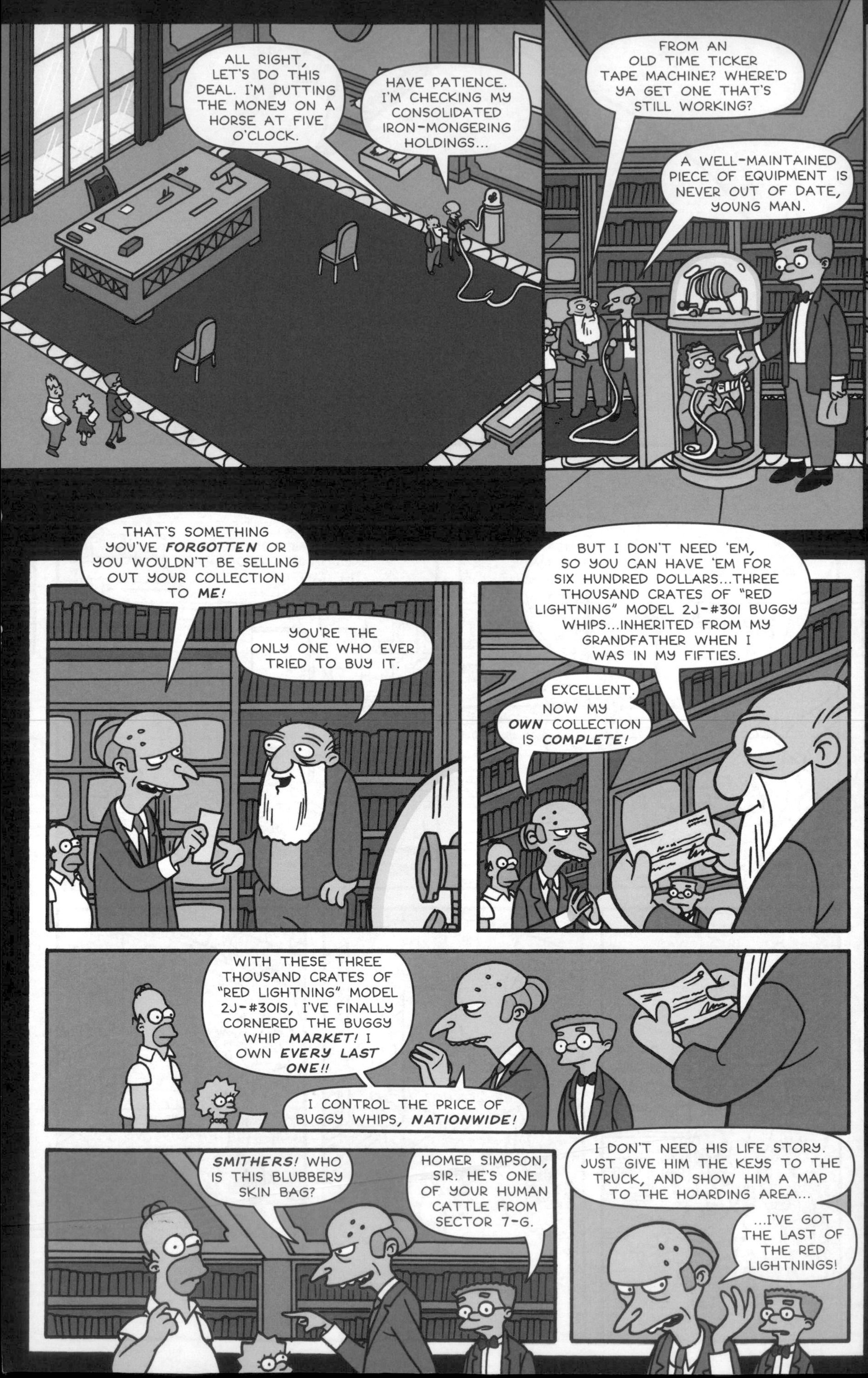
ALL RIGHT, LET'S DO THIS DEAL. I'M PUTTING THE MONEY ON A HORSE AT FIVE O'CLOCK.
HAVE PATIENCE. I'M CHECKING MY CONSOLIDATED IRON-MONGERING HOLDINGS...
FROM AN OLD TIME TICKER TAPE MACHINE? WHERE'D YA GET ONE THAT'S STILL WORKING?
A WELL-MAINTAINED PIECE OF EQUIPMENT IS NEVER OUT OF DATE, YOUNG MAN.
THAT'S SOMETHING YOU'VE ***FORGOTTEN*** OR YOU WOULDN'T BE SELLING OUT YOUR COLLECTION TO ***ME!***
YOU'RE THE ONLY ONE WHO EVER TRIED TO BUY IT.
BUT I DON'T NEED 'EM, SO YOU CAN HAVE 'EM FOR SIX HUNDRED DOLLARS...THREE THOUSAND CRATES OF "RED LIGHTNING" MODEL 2J-#301 BUGGY WHIPS...INHERITED FROM MY GRANDFATHER WHEN I WAS IN MY FIFTIES.
EXCELLENT. NOW MY ***OWN*** COLLECTION IS ***COMPLETE!***
WITH THESE THREE THOUSAND CRATES OF "RED LIGHTNING" MODEL 2J-#301S, I'VE FINALLY CORNERED THE BUGGY WHIP ***MARKET!*** I OWN ***EVERY LAST ONE!!***
I CONTROL THE PRICE OF BUGGY WHIPS, ***NATIONWIDE!***
SMITHERS! WHO IS THIS BLUBBERY SKIN BAG?
HOMER SIMPSON, SIR. HE'S ONE OF YOUR HUMAN CATTLE FROM SECTOR 7-G.
I DON'T NEED HIS LIFE STORY. JUST GIVE HIM THE KEYS TO THE TRUCK, AND SHOW HIM A MAP TO THE HOARDING AREA...
...I'VE GOT THE LAST OF THE RED LIGHTNINGS!

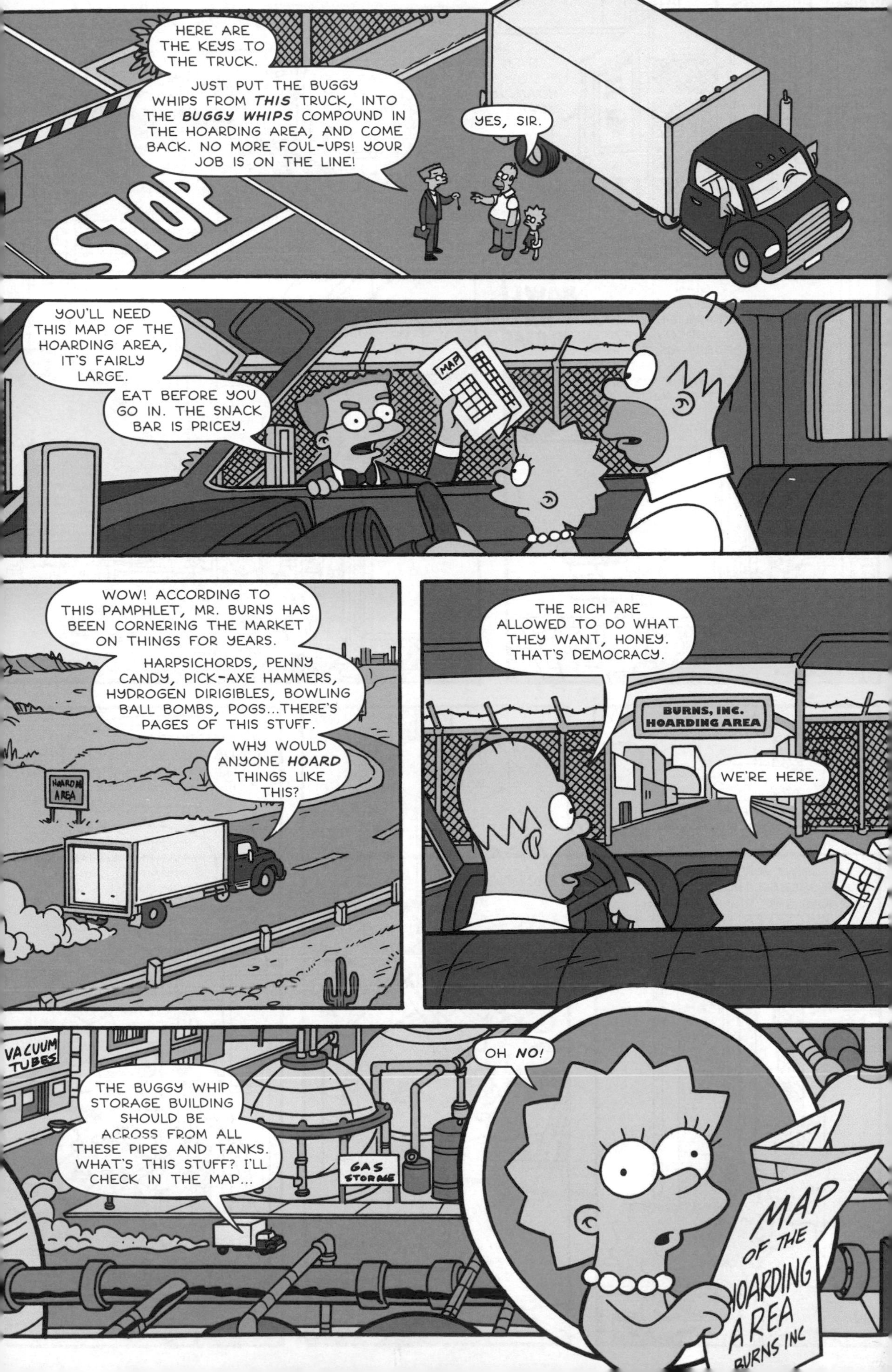
HERE ARE THE KEYS TO THE TRUCK.
JUST PUT THE BUGGY WHIPS FROM **THIS** TRUCK, INTO THE **BUGGY WHIPS** COMPOUND IN THE HOARDING AREA, AND COME BACK. NO MORE FOUL-UPS! YOUR JOB IS ON THE LINE!
YES, SIR.
STOP
YOU'LL NEED THIS MAP OF THE HOARDING AREA, IT'S FAIRLY LARGE.
EAT BEFORE YOU GO IN. THE SNACK BAR IS PRICEY.
MAP
WOW! ACCORDING TO THIS PAMPHLET, MR. BURNS HAS BEEN CORNERING THE MARKET ON THINGS FOR YEARS.
HARPSICHORDS, PENNY CANDY, PICK-AXE HAMMERS, HYDROGEN DIRIGIBLES, BOWLING BALL BOMBS, POGS...THERE'S PAGES OF THIS STUFF.
WHY WOULD ANYONE **HOARD** THINGS LIKE THIS?
HOARDING AREA
THE RICH ARE ALLOWED TO DO WHAT THEY WANT, HONEY. THAT'S DEMOCRACY.
BURNS, INC. HOARDING AREA
WE'RE HERE.
VACUUM TUBES
THE BUGGY WHIP STORAGE BUILDING SHOULD BE ACROSS FROM ALL THESE PIPES AND TANKS. WHAT'S THIS STUFF? I'LL CHECK IN THE MAP...
GAS STORAGE
OH **NO**!
MAP OF THE OARDING AREA URNS INC

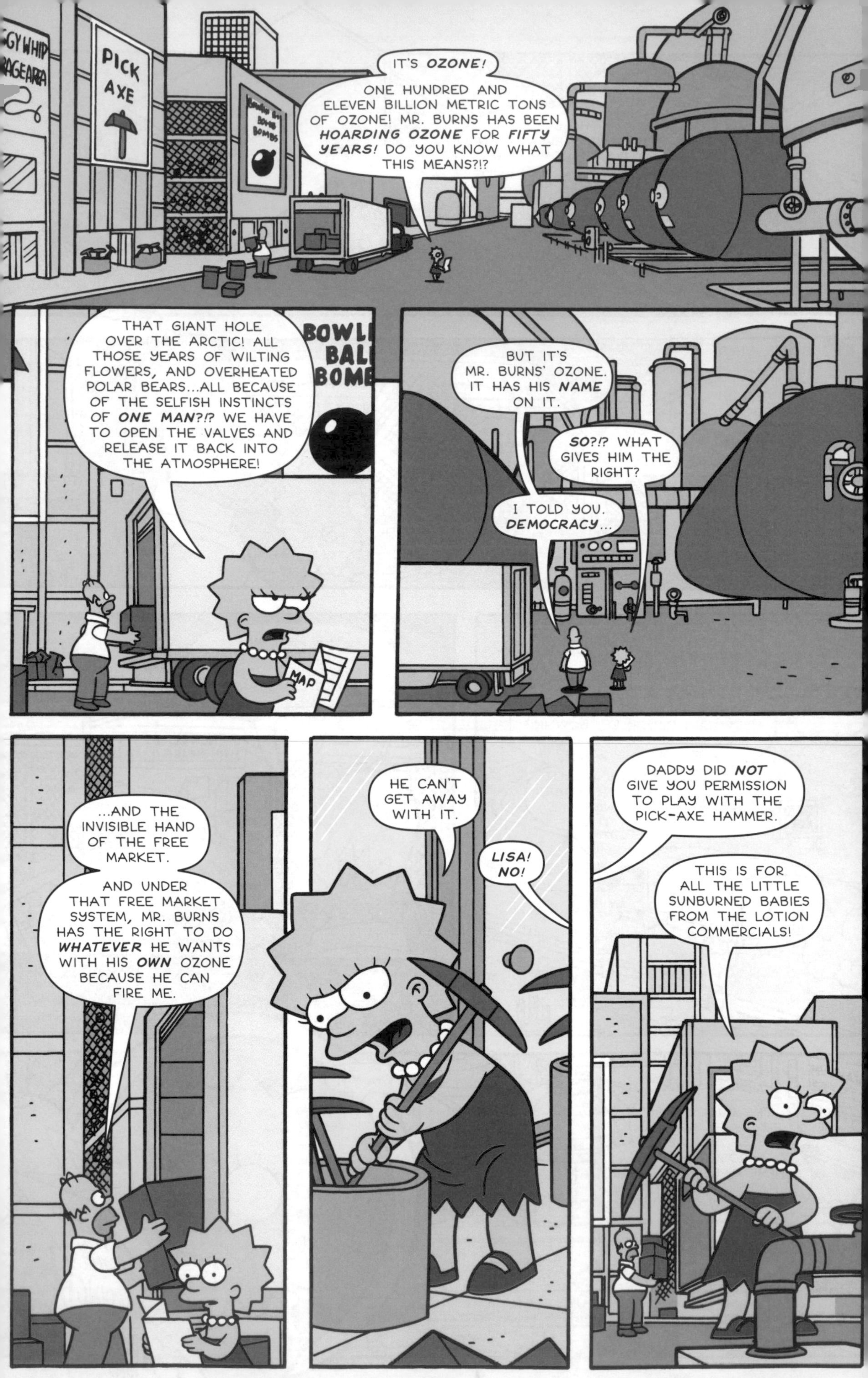
GGY WHIP
RAGEARRA
PICK AXE
BOWLING BALL BOMBS
IT'S OZONE!
ONE HUNDRED AND ELEVEN BILLION METRIC TONS OF OZONE! MR. BURNS HAS BEEN HOARDING OZONE FOR FIFTY YEARS! DO YOU KNOW WHAT THIS MEANS?!?
THAT GIANT HOLE OVER THE ARCTIC! ALL THOSE YEARS OF WILTING FLOWERS, AND OVERHEATED POLAR BEARS...ALL BECAUSE OF THE SELFISH INSTINCTS OF ONE MAN?!? WE HAVE TO OPEN THE VALVES AND RELEASE IT BACK INTO THE ATMOSPHERE!
MAP
BUT IT'S MR. BURNS' OZONE. IT HAS HIS NAME ON IT.
SO?!? WHAT GIVES HIM THE RIGHT?
I TOLD YOU. DEMOCRACY...
...AND THE INVISIBLE HAND OF THE FREE MARKET.
AND UNDER THAT FREE MARKET SYSTEM, MR. BURNS HAS THE RIGHT TO DO WHATEVER HE WANTS WITH HIS OWN OZONE BECAUSE HE CAN FIRE ME.
HE CAN'T GET AWAY WITH IT.
LISA! NO!
DADDY DID NOT GIVE YOU PERMISSION TO PLAY WITH THE PICK-AXE HAMMER.
THIS IS FOR ALL THE LITTLE SUNBURNED BABIES FROM THE LOTION COMMERCIALS!

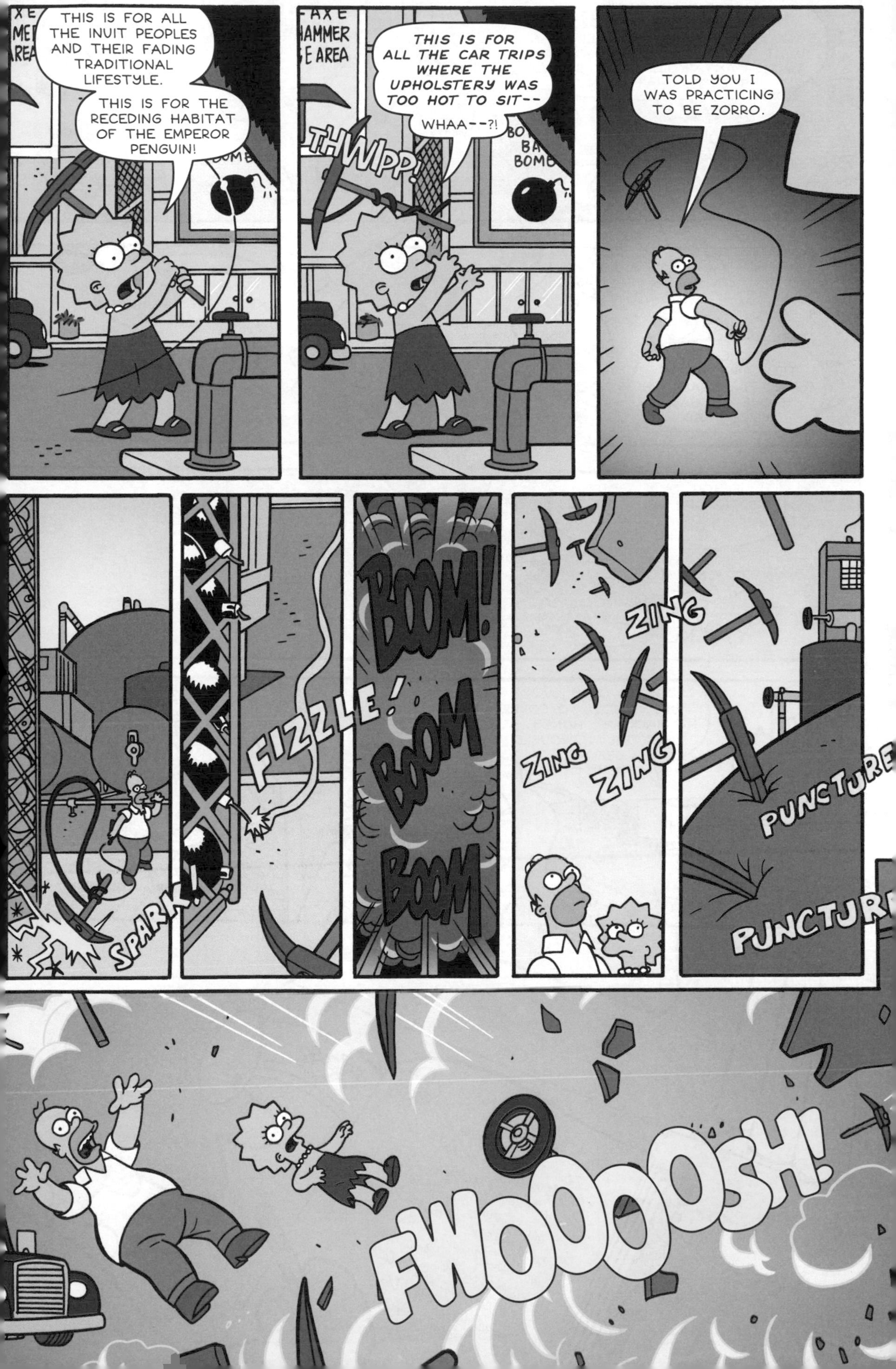
THIS IS FOR ALL THE INUIT PEOPLES AND THEIR FADING TRADITIONAL LIFESTYLE.
THIS IS FOR THE RECEDING HABITAT OF THE EMPEROR PENGUIN!
THIS IS FOR ALL THE CAR TRIPS WHERE THE UPHOLSTERY WAS TOO HOT TO SIT--
WHAA--?!
THWIPP!
TOLD YOU I WAS PRACTICING TO BE ZORRO.
SPARK!
FIZZLE!
BOOM!
BOOM
BOOM
ZING
ZING
ZING
PUNCTURE
FWOOOOOSH!

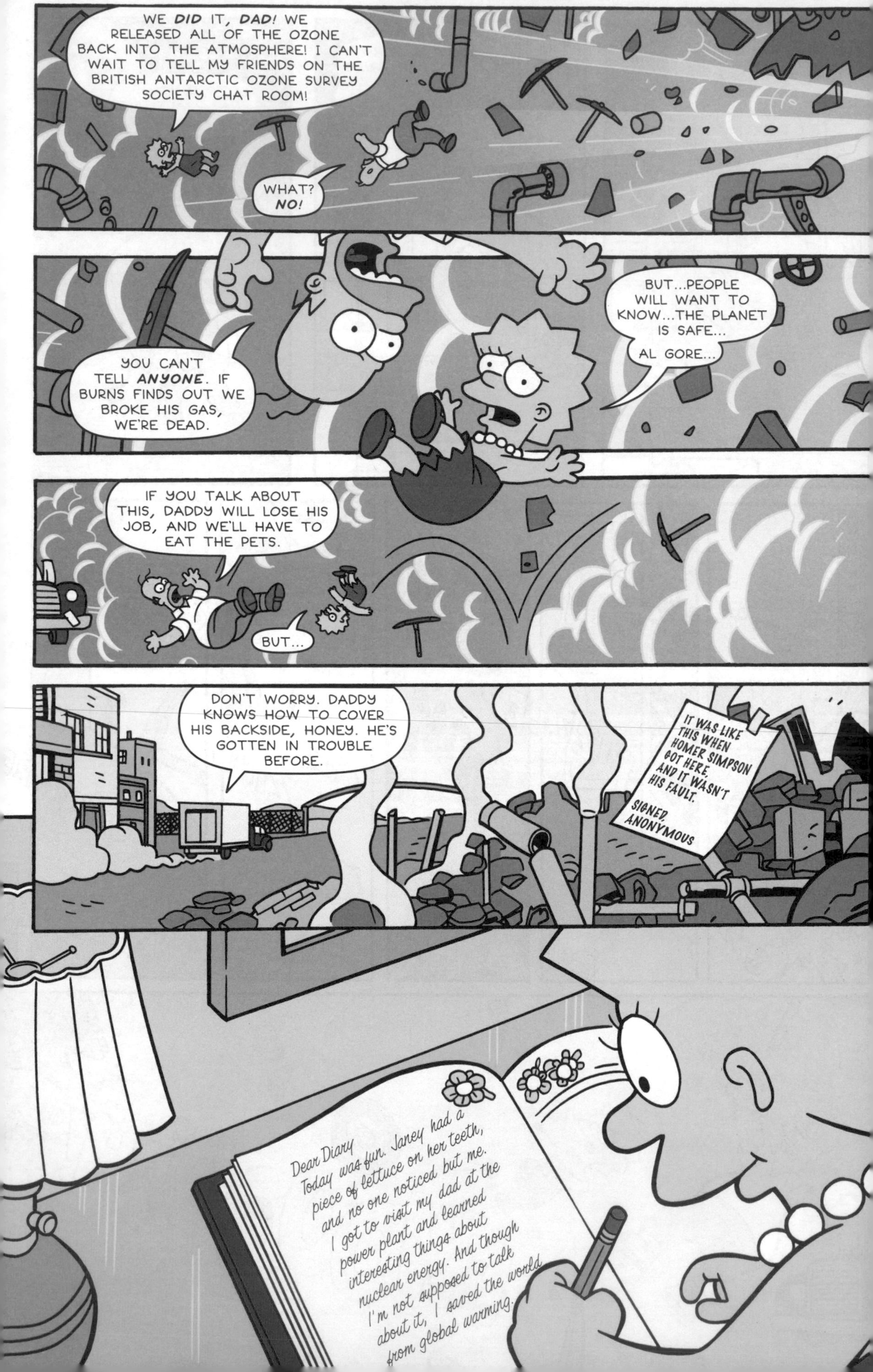
WE DID IT, DAD! WE RELEASED ALL OF THE OZONE BACK INTO THE ATMOSPHERE! I CAN'T WAIT TO TELL MY FRIENDS ON THE BRITISH ANTARCTIC OZONE SURVEY SOCIETY CHAT ROOM!
WHAT? NO!
YOU CAN'T TELL ANYONE. IF BURNS FINDS OUT WE BROKE HIS GAS, WE'RE DEAD.
BUT...PEOPLE WILL WANT TO KNOW...THE PLANET IS SAFE...
AL GORE...
IF YOU TALK ABOUT THIS, DADDY WILL LOSE HIS JOB, AND WE'LL HAVE TO EAT THE PETS.
BUT...
DON'T WORRY. DADDY KNOWS HOW TO COVER HIS BACKSIDE, HONEY. HE'S GOTTEN IN TROUBLE BEFORE.
IT WAS LIKE THIS WHEN HOMER SIMPSON GOT HERE, AND IT WASN'T HIS FAULT.
SIGNED, ANONYMOUS
Dear Diary
Today was fun. Janey had a piece of lettuce on her teeth, and no one noticed but me. I got to visit my dad at the power plant and learned interesting things about nuclear energy. And though I'm not supposed to talk about it, I saved the world from global warming.

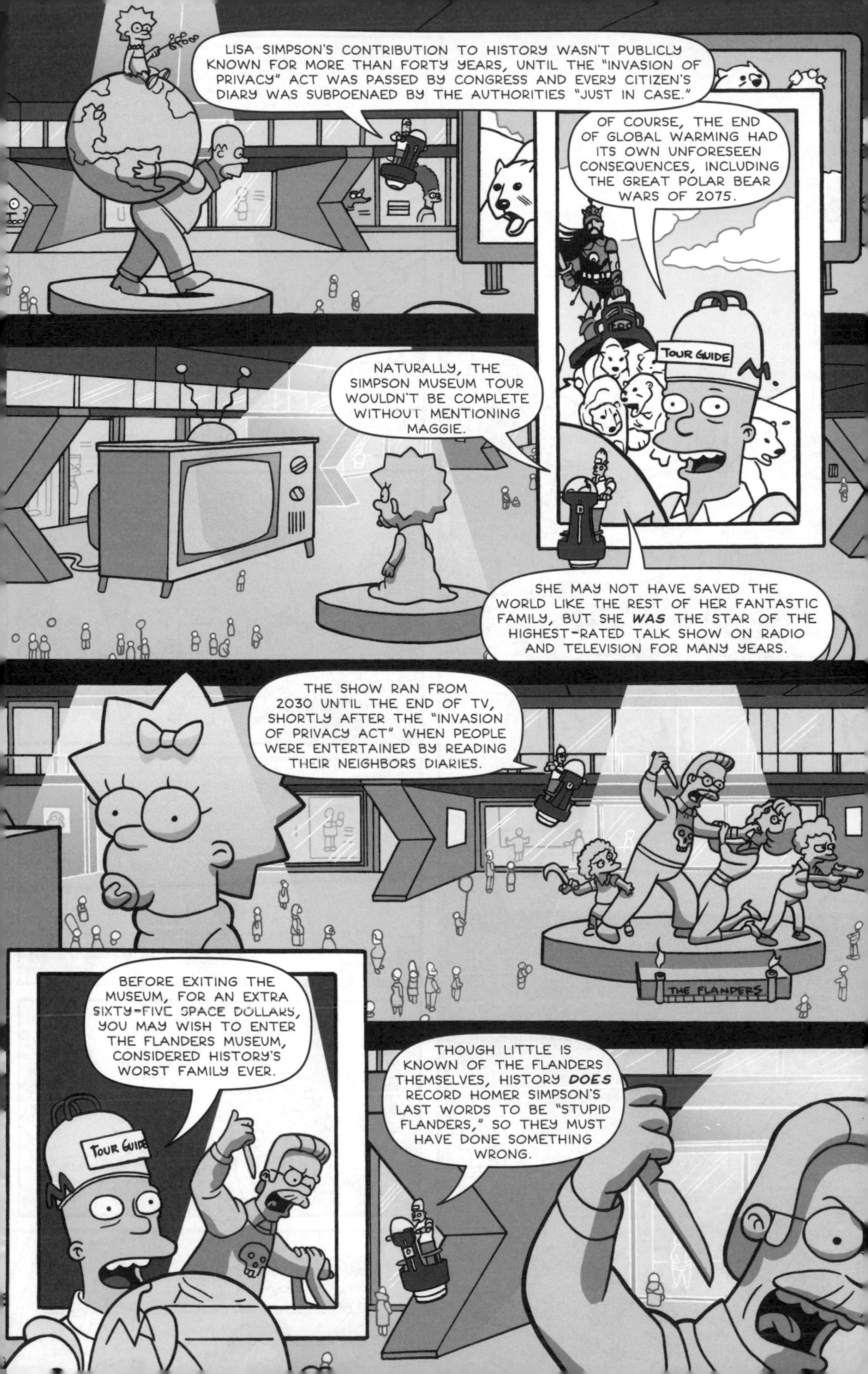
LISA SIMPSON'S CONTRIBUTION TO HISTORY WASN'T PUBLICLY KNOWN FOR MORE THAN FORTY YEARS, UNTIL THE "INVASION OF PRIVACY" ACT WAS PASSED BY CONGRESS AND EVERY CITIZEN'S DIARY WAS SUBPOENAED BY THE AUTHORITIES "JUST IN CASE."
OF COURSE, THE END OF GLOBAL WARMING HAD ITS OWN UNFORESEEN CONSEQUENCES, INCLUDING THE GREAT POLAR BEAR WARS OF 2075.
TOUR GUIDE
NATURALLY, THE SIMPSON MUSEUM TOUR WOULDN'T BE COMPLETE WITHOUT MENTIONING MAGGIE.
SHE MAY NOT HAVE SAVED THE WORLD LIKE THE REST OF HER FANTASTIC FAMILY, BUT SHE ***WAS*** THE STAR OF THE HIGHEST-RATED TALK SHOW ON RADIO AND TELEVISION FOR MANY YEARS.
THE SHOW RAN FROM 2030 UNTIL THE END OF TV, SHORTLY AFTER THE "INVASION OF PRIVACY ACT" WHEN PEOPLE WERE ENTERTAINED BY READING THEIR NEIGHBORS DIARIES.
THE FLANDERS
BEFORE EXITING THE MUSEUM, FOR AN EXTRA SIXTY-FIVE SPACE DOLLARS, YOU MAY WISH TO ENTER THE FLANDERS MUSEUM, CONSIDERED HISTORY'S WORST FAMILY EVER.
TOUR GUIDE
THOUGH LITTLE IS KNOWN OF THE FLANDERS THEMSELVES, HISTORY ***DOES*** RECORD HOMER SIMPSON'S LAST WORDS TO BE "STUPID FLANDERS," SO THEY MUST HAVE DONE SOMETHING WRONG.

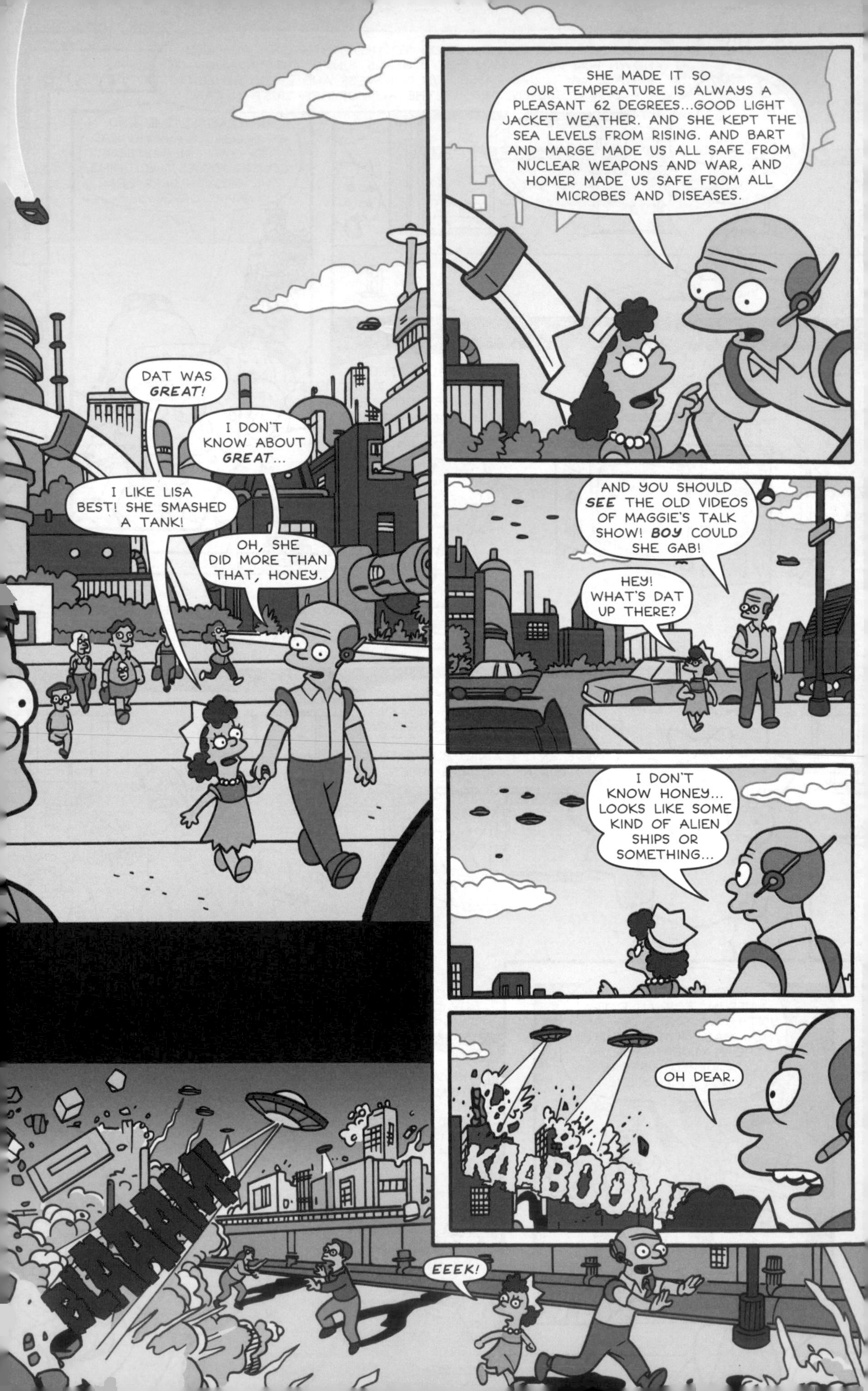
DAT WAS GREAT!
I DON'T KNOW ABOUT GREAT...
I LIKE LISA BEST! SHE SMASHED A TANK!
OH, SHE DID MORE THAN THAT, HONEY.
SHE MADE IT SO OUR TEMPERATURE IS ALWAYS A PLEASANT 62 DEGREES...GOOD LIGHT JACKET WEATHER. AND SHE KEPT THE SEA LEVELS FROM RISING. AND BART AND MARGE MADE US ALL SAFE FROM NUCLEAR WEAPONS AND WAR, AND HOMER MADE US SAFE FROM ALL MICROBES AND DISEASES.
AND YOU SHOULD SEE THE OLD VIDEOS OF MAGGIE'S TALK SHOW! BOY COULD SHE GAB!
HEY! WHAT'S DAT UP THERE?
I DON'T KNOW HONEY... LOOKS LIKE SOME KIND OF ALIEN SHIPS OR SOMETHING...
OH DEAR.
KAABOOM!
BLAAAM!
EEEK!

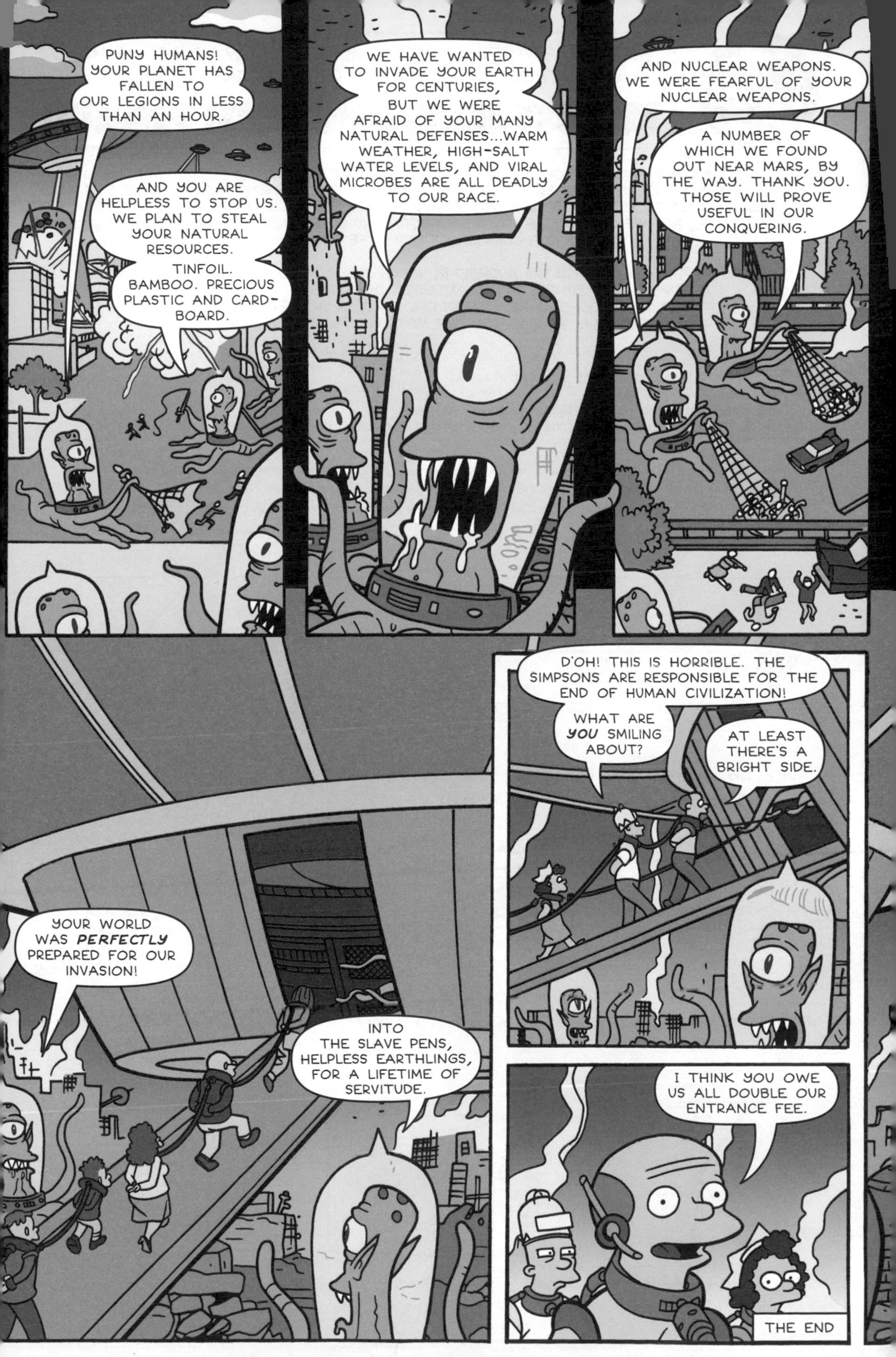
PUNY HUMANS! YOUR PLANET HAS FALLEN TO OUR LEGIONS IN LESS THAN AN HOUR.
AND YOU ARE HELPLESS TO STOP US. WE PLAN TO STEAL YOUR NATURAL RESOURCES.
TINFOIL. BAMBOO. PRECIOUS PLASTIC AND CARD-BOARD.
WE HAVE WANTED TO INVADE YOUR EARTH FOR CENTURIES,
BUT WE WERE AFRAID OF YOUR MANY NATURAL DEFENSES...WARM WEATHER, HIGH-SALT WATER LEVELS, AND VIRAL MICROBES ARE ALL DEADLY TO OUR RACE.
AND NUCLEAR WEAPONS. WE WERE FEARFUL OF YOUR NUCLEAR WEAPONS.
A NUMBER OF WHICH WE FOUND OUT NEAR MARS, BY THE WAY. THANK YOU. THOSE WILL PROVE USEFUL IN OUR CONQUERING.
YOUR WORLD WAS *PERFECTLY* PREPARED FOR OUR INVASION!
INTO THE SLAVE PENS, HELPLESS EARTHLINGS, FOR A LIFETIME OF SERVITUDE.
D'OH! THIS IS HORRIBLE. THE SIMPSONS ARE RESPONSIBLE FOR THE END OF HUMAN CIVILIZATION!
WHAT ARE *YOU* SMILING ABOUT?
AT LEAST THERE'S A BRIGHT SIDE.
I THINK YOU OWE US ALL DOUBLE OUR ENTRANCE FEE.
THE END

WHAT HO, FAITHFUL COMIC READER! IT IS MY DUBIOUS HONOR TO INTRODUCE BONGO'S VERY FIRST INSTALLMENT OF

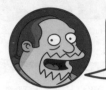

THE BUSY HANDS PAPERCRAFT PROJECT!

EACH VOLUME OF THE COLOSSAL COMPENDIUM SERIES WILL INCLUDE A BUILDABLE REPLICA OF ONE OF SPRINGFIELD'S FINEST LANDMARKS. WITH A LITTLE PLUCK (AND COPIOUS AMOUNTS OF TAPE) YOU WILL BE ABLE TO BUILD YOUR VERY OWN SPRINGFIELD IN NO TIME AT ALL. (ACTUALLY IT WILL TAKE SEVERAL YEARS; BUT WE COLLECTORS ARE A STUBBORN AND DETERMINED LOT, WHO WOULD RATHER DIE THAN SEE OUR COMPLETIST THIRST BE LEFT UN-SLAKED.)

I, THUSLY, PRESENT TO YOU THE ANDROID DUNGEON AND COMIC BOOK STORE IN MINUSCULE. COMICS AND POP CULTURE EPHEMERA NOT INCLUDED, OF COURSE. FOR THOSE, YOU WILL HAVE TO VISIT MY LAVISH 600-SQUARE FOOT RETAIL SPACE IN THE HEART OF SPRINGFIELD'S MERCHANT DISTRICT, WHERE OUR MOTTO IS, "NO PERSONAL CHECKS!"

WHAT YOU WILL NEED:

- Scissors, adhesive tape, and a straight edge (such as a ruler).
- An ability to fold along straight lines.
- An additional "mint condition" copy of this book secured elsewhere!
  (Be forewarned... cutting up this collection will reduce the grade from "mint" to "poor plus" at best!)

1. Before cutting out the building and awning shapes, use a ruler and a slightly rounded metal tool (like the edge of a key) to rst score, and then fold lightly along all the interior lines (this will make nal folds much easier).
2. Cut along the exterior shape. Make sure to cut all the way to where the walls, the roof, and the aps lines meet (Fig 1).

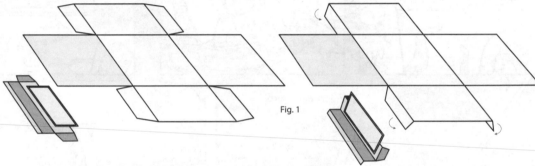

Fig. 1

3. Fold awning as shown (Fig. 2) and attach it to the front of the building by folding the aps around the front wall and securing them with tape (Fig. 3).

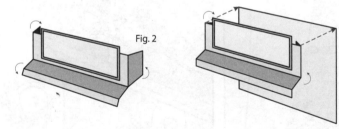

Fig. 2

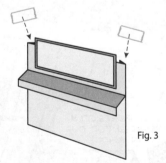

Fig. 3

4. Form building by folding walls into place (Fig. 4) and secure all tabs to the interior of the building with tape (Fig. 5).

Fig. 4

Fig. 5

5. Cut out gures and bases.
6. Cut along the dotted line at the base of each gure and also the center of each curved base. (Be careful not to cut too far!)
7. Connect base to gure as shown.

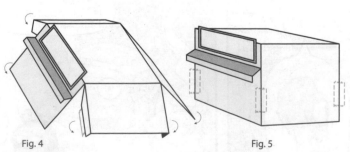

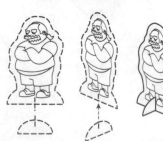

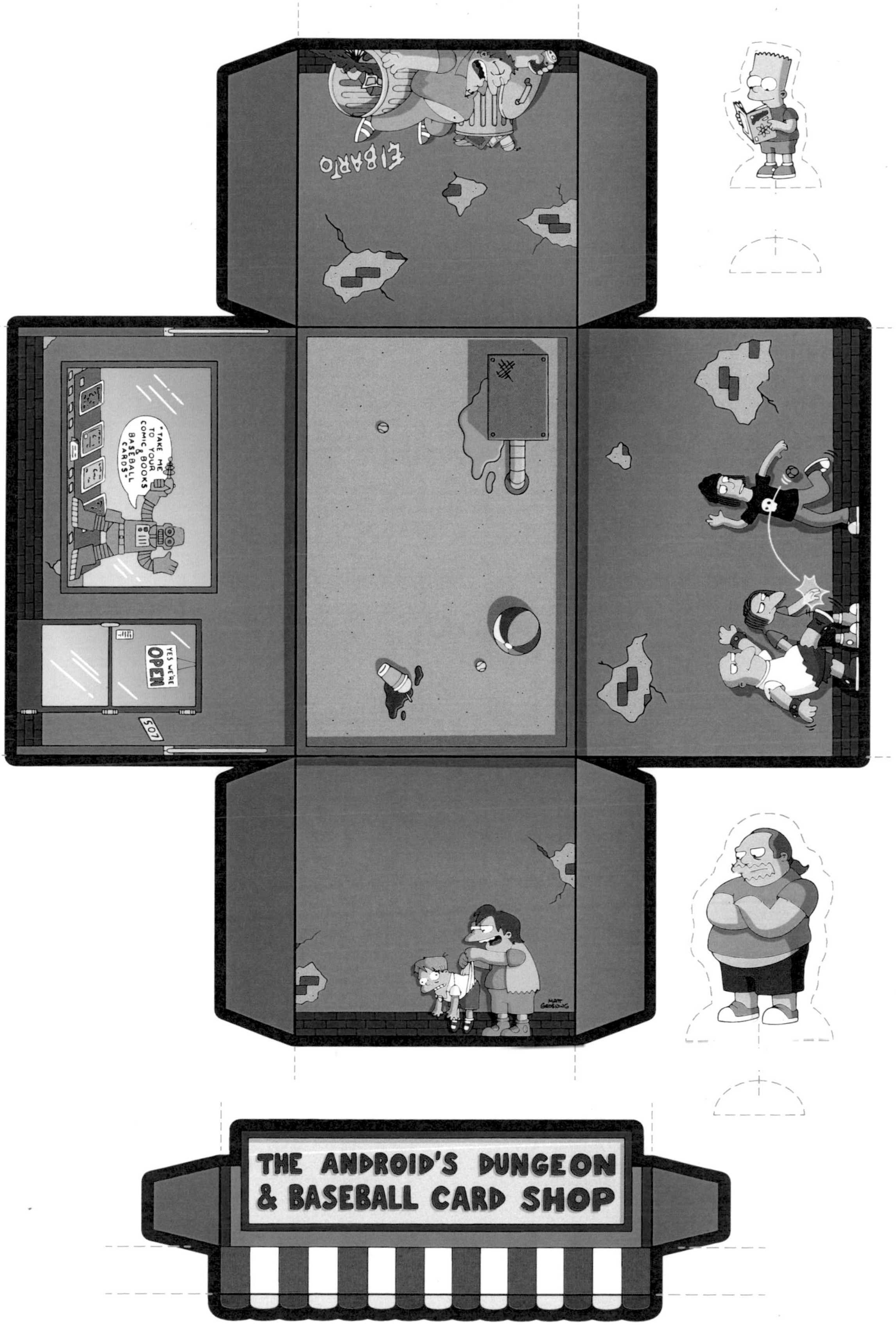
El BARTO
"TAKE ME TO YOUR COMIC BOOKS & BASEBALL CARDS"
YES WE'RE OPEN
507
MATT GROENING
THE ANDROID'S DUNGEON & BASEBALL CARD SHOP